Combatting Digital Arrest Fraud and Identity Theft With AI and Decision Support Systems

Brij B. Gupta
https://orcid.org/0000-0003-4929-4698

Asia University, Taichung, Taiwan & VIZJA University, Warsaw, Poland

Chun Ho Wu
https://orcid.org/0000-0003-1259-4048

Hang Seng University of Hong Kong, Hong Kong

Andrew W.H. Ip
https://orcid.org/0000-0001-6609-0713

University of Saskatchewan, Canada

IGI Global
Scientific Publishing
Publishing Tomorrow's Research Today

Vice President of Editorial Melissa Wagner
Director of Acquisitions Mikaela Felty
Director of Book Development Jocelynn Hessler
Production Manager Mike Brehm
Cover Design Jose Rosado

Published in the United States of America by
IGI Global Scientific Publishing
701 East Chocolate Avenue
Hershey, PA, 17033, USA
Tel: 717-533-8845 | Fax: 717-533-7115
Website: https://www.igi-global.com E-mail: cust@igi-global.com

Library of Congress Cataloging-in-Publication Data

Names: Gupta, Brij B., 1982- editor | Wu, C. H., (Ph.D. in Systems Engineering) editor | Ip, Andrew W. H. editor
Title: Combatting digital arrest fraud and identity theft with AI and decision support systems / edited by Brij B. Gupta, Chun Ho Wu, Andrew W.H. Ip.
Description: Hershey, PA : IGI Global Scientific Publishing, 2026. | Includes bibliographical references and index. | Summary: "This book explores cutting-edge strategies for detecting and preventing digital arrest fraud and identity theft using AI and intelligent decision support systems. It provides a comprehensive understanding of how machine learning, behavioral analytics, and real-time data fusion can empower law enforcement, financial institutions, and cybersecurity professionals"-- Provided by publisher.
Identifiers: LCCN 2025035571 (print) | LCCN 2025035572 (ebook) | ISBN 9798337341491 hardcover | ISBN 9798337341507 paperback | ISBN 9798337341514 ebook
Subjects: LCSH: Computer crimes--Prevention | Decision support systems | Artificial intelligence--Criminal justice applications
Classification: LCC HV6773 .C6494 2025 (print) | LCC HV6773 (ebook)
LC record available at https://lccn.loc.gov/2025035571
LC ebook record available at https://lccn.loc.gov/202503557

British Cataloguing in Publication Data
A Cataloguing in Publication record for this book is available from the British Library.

This book is dedicated with profound appreciation and affection to our families, whose unwavering support and encouragement have been a constant source of strength throughout this journey.

Table of Contents

Detailed Table of Contents

to evolving threats while minimising false positives and negatives. ML-powered solutions integrate biometric authentication, behavioural analytics, and risk scoring to deliver real-time decision support that balances security, user experience, and regulatory compliance. This strengthens digital security across banking, e-commerce, government, and healthcare sectors where identity breaches are costly. With predictive capabilities enabling proactive fraud prevention, ML stands as a cornerstone of adaptive cybersecurity. This chapter explores core frameworks, applications, case studies, and emerging trends, showing how ML-driven identity verification mitigates risks while enhancing trust, efficiency, and scalability in safeguarding digital ecosystems.

The cyber world is becoming increasingly complex due to the diverse nature of cybercrimes. Although crimes like fraud, harassment, and identity theft exist in both the cyber and physical worlds, their magnitude is unpredictably high in the cyber world. However, digital arrest fraud is unique to cyberspace. Digital arrest fraud and identity theft are the top-listed cybercrimes, causing unimaginable monetary loss, anxiety, depression, fear, and isolation among the victims. The current cybersecurity measures and tools, as well as the legal and ethical framework, fail to address the evolving nature of cybercrimes. Such a scenario demands more collaborative efforts and a renewed approach to ensure global cybersecurity. From this perspective, this chapter critically examines the evolving nature of cybercrimes and the available legal and ethical framework to underline the importance of leveraging cybersecurity through some required changes in the ethico-legal landscape. It argues for a globally accepted regulatory system and international cooperation to ensure cybersecurity.

Fraud communication detection is a must due to complex web interactions and AI-driven fraud. Heuristic systems struggle with advanced fraud, including multilingual behavior, deepfakes, and LLM phishing. This study compares NLP for fraud communication detection, focusing on transformer-based models (BERT, RoBERTa, FinChain-BERT), hybrid AI-rule systems, graph data, multilingual detection, and adversarial robustness. Research indicates that an 85–95% accurate NLP model can

Preface

The accelerating digital transformation of financial systems, public services, communication platforms, and everyday transactions has profoundly reshaped how identities are created, verified, and exploited. While digital technologies have improved efficiency, accessibility, and global connectivity, they have also enabled increasingly sophisticated forms of cybercrime. Among these, *digital arrest fraud*—a coercive scam exploiting fear, authority, and legal ambiguity—and large-scale *identity theft* have emerged as particularly damaging threats, often amplified through artificial intelligence (AI), automation, and cross-border anonymity.

Combatting Digital Arrest Fraud and Identity Theft With AI and Decision Support Systems is conceived as a timely and comprehensive response to this evolving threat landscape. This edited reference book brings together contributions from scholars and practitioners across computer science, cybersecurity, law, ethics, public policy, and data science to examine how AI, decision support systems (DSS), machine learning, and advanced analytics can be leveraged responsibly to prevent, detect, and respond to identity-related cybercrime. At the same time, the volume recognizes that technological innovation must be accompanied by ethical safeguards, legal clarity, and effective governance to ensure trust, accountability, and protection of fundamental rights.

The chapters collectively highlight that digital arrest fraud and identity theft are not merely technical problems, but socio-technical challenges. They intersect with human behavior, regulatory frameworks, institutional capacities, and international cooperation. By integrating technical solutions with ethical analysis, legal perspectives, and policy insights, this book aims to support researchers, policymakers, cybersecurity professionals, financial institutions, and law enforcement agencies in building resilient and trustworthy digital ecosystems.

What follows is a chapter-by-chapter overview of the contributions contained in this volume.

CHAPTER OVERVIEWS

Chapter 1: Introduction to Digital Fraud and Identity Theft

Serving as a conceptual foundation, this chapter introduces key definitions, patterns, and forms of digital fraud and identity theft. It explains how advances in information and communication technologies have enabled cybercriminals to conduct malware attacks, data breaches, and internet-based fraud at scale. The chapter also discusses the financial, reputational, psychological, and privacy-related impacts of identity theft, emphasizing the importance of understanding crime typologies as a basis for effective cybersecurity strategies.

Chapter 2: Decision Support Systems for Real-Time Fraud Response

This chapter lays the technological foundation of the book by examining AI-enabled Decision Support Systems for real-time fraud detection and response. It explores system architectures that integrate data ingestion, machine learning, behavioral analytics, anomaly detection, and automated decision-making. Emphasis is placed on digital arrest fraud and identity-based attacks, illustrating how DSS can support rapid, evidence-based responses while maintaining explainability and regulatory compliance. Case studies from finance and government demonstrate how adaptive risk strategies and feedback mechanisms enhance organizational resilience and digital trust.

Chapter 3: Role of Machine Learning in Identity Verification

The final chapter focuses on machine learning as a cornerstone of modern identity verification systems. It examines supervised, unsupervised, and deep learning approaches used to detect anomalies, authenticate users, and prevent identity theft and digital arrest fraud. By integrating biometrics, behavioral analytics, and real-time risk scoring, ML-driven systems enhance accuracy, scalability, and user experience across sectors such as banking, e-commerce, healthcare, and government. The chapter concludes by identifying emerging trends and future research directions in adaptive identity verification.

Together, these chapters provide a comprehensive, interdisciplinary perspective on combatting digital arrest fraud and identity theft. By uniting AI-driven technologies with ethical reflection, legal analysis, and policy insight, this volume aims to advance both scholarly understanding and practical solutions for securing identities and building trust in the digital age.

Chapter 4: Leveraging Cybersecurity in the Context of Digital Arrest Fraud and Identity Theft: An Ethico-Legal Perspective

This chapter examines digital arrest fraud as a crime unique to cyberspace, highlighting its severe emotional, social, and economic consequences for victims. It critiques existing cybersecurity tools and legal frameworks for their inability to keep pace with evolving cybercrime tactics. From an ethico-legal standpoint, the chapter argues for renewed global collaboration, stronger regulatory alignment, and reforms in cybersecurity governance to effectively combat digital arrest fraud and identity theft while safeguarding victims' rights.

Chapter 5: Natural Language Processing for Fraudulent Communication Detection

Addressing communication-centric fraud, this chapter evaluates the role of Natural Language Processing in detecting fraudulent messages across platforms and languages. It compares heuristic approaches with advanced transformer-based models, hybrid AI-rule systems, and graph-based techniques. Challenges such as model degradation, low-resource languages, deepfakes, and adversarial attacks are discussed. The chapter emphasizes continuous learning, human oversight, explainable AI, and multimodal detection as critical for scalable and resilient fraud communication systems.

Chapter 6: Ethical Implications of AI in Identity Management

Focusing on the ethical challenges of AI-driven identity systems, this chapter critically analyzes issues of transparency, fairness, privacy, accountability, and governance. It addresses concerns such as algorithmic opacity, biometric surveillance, real-time identity verification trade-offs, and cross-border regulatory inconsistencies. Drawing on theory, case studies, and stakeholder perspectives, the chapter underscores the importance of explainable AI, inclusive governance, and interdisciplinary design approaches to ensure that identity technologies align with human rights and societal values.

Chapter 7: Policy Implications of AI in Combatting Cyber Fraud and Identity Theft

This chapter explores the governance and policy challenges associated with deploying AI for cyber fraud prevention. It presents a taxonomy of AI techniques used in fraud detection and prediction while addressing risks related to algorithmic bias, transparency, and privacy. The chapter advocates for balanced, evidence-based regulatory frameworks that enable innovation while protecting civil liberties, and highlights the need for cross-sector and international policy coordination.

Chapter 8: Hermeneutics and Anti-Money Laundering (AML) Policies in the Digital Age: A Comparative Study of Indonesia and Latvia

This chapter applies a hermeneutic approach to interpret and compare AML policies in Indonesia and Latvia within the context of digital finance. While both countries adhere to FATF standards, the analysis reveals persistent vulnerabilities related to informal financial sectors, financial scandals, and emerging digital assets. The chapter highlights regulatory "grey areas" associated with cryptocurrency and decentralized finance, recommending greater harmonization, technology evaluation metrics, and adaptive international collaboration to strengthen AML effectiveness.

Acknowledgement

We would like to express our sincere gratitude to everyone who has contributed to the completion of this book, Combatting Digital Arrest Fraud and Identity Theft With AI and Decision Support Systems. This endeavor would not have been possible without the invaluable support, guidance, and dedication of many individuals.

First and foremost, we extend our heartfelt appreciation to the authors and reviewers of each chapter. Their expertise, insightful feedback, and unwavering commitment have played a crucial role in shaping the depth and quality of this book. Their contributions have been instrumental in ensuring that this volume serves as a comprehensive resource in the field.

We are also profoundly grateful to the team at IGI Global Publishing for their continuous support, technical expertise, and encouragement throughout this journey. Their professional guidance and commitment have been invaluable in bringing this project to fruition.

A special note of thanks goes to our families, whose unwavering love, patience, and encouragement have been a constant source of strength. Their support has sustained us through the challenges of this endeavor and has been instrumental in its successful completion.

Lastly, we are deeply thankful to the Almighty for granting us the strength, resilience, and determination to navigate this journey and see this work through to completion.

To all those who have contributed in various ways, we extend our deepest gratitude. Your support and efforts are truly appreciated.

Brij B. Gupta
Asia University, Taichung, Taiwan & VIZJA University, Warsaw, Poland

Chun Ho Wu
Hang Seng University of Hong Kong, Hong Kong

Andrew W. H. Ip
University of Saskatchewan, Canada

Chapter 1
Introduction to Digital Fraud and Identity Theft

Qori Halimatul Hidayah
https://orcid.org/0009-0008-7567-4102
Esa Unggul University, Indonesia

Jusung Moon
https://orcid.org/0009-0004-2513-9364
Asia University, Taiwan

Sourasis Chattopadhyay
https://orcid.org/0009-0000-7435-6550
Kalinga Institute of Industrial Technology, India

Agung M. Mulyo Widodo
https://orcid.org/0000-0002-9792-7114
Esa Unggul University, Indonesia

Dewi Setiowati
https://orcid.org/0009-0005-5747-1094
Esa Unggul University, Indonesia

ABSTRACT

Identity theft has grown harder. Because information and communication technology is being used more rapidly, it has made it easier for criminals to operate digitally. This type of crime covers breaking security systems, spreading harmful software, internet-based fraud and attacks meant to illegally access information, damage technology or make money. A person commits identity theft when they get and use someone else's private data without their permission, with the goal of carrying out fraud or other crimes. Among the sorts of information they access may be names,

DOI: 10.4018/979-8-3373-4149-1.ch001

addresses, credit card numbers, identification codes or login passwords. Both cybercrime and identity theft, when coupled, may bring about serious consequences for all involved, including money loss, damage to reputation and the violation of individuals' privacy. As a result, knowing the different patterns of these crimes is essential to help create solutions and increase the level of cyber security.

□1. GENERAL OVERVIEW

1.1 Definition of Digital Fraud

Digital fraud refers to deceitful actions carried out through digital platforms and devices, such as email phishing, fake social media accounts, identity theft, and the use of fraudulent websites or applications. These tactics are commonly used to achieve financial advantage, spread misinformation, or serve political purposes, thereby undermining public trust and compromising cybersecurity (Verma, I., 2024).

Digital fraud comes in a wide range of forms when seen in action. Phishing is a familiar way thieves use email to trick people by pretending to be real institutions and persuading them to divulge important info such as their passwords or credit cards. Offenders may use made-up social media handles to make people trust an account they have set up to steal money, where the perpetrator pretends to be a certain individual or institution in order to deceive the victim (Kadashevich et al., 2014). Through identity theft, someone else uses your personal information to create problems or make purchases on your behalf. There are also imposter websites or programs that pretend to be official, hoping to steal user information or carry out untrue transactions.

People behind digital fraud usually use social engineering to persuade others into actions that eventually damage them. For the most part, these acts are performed for money, although some cases involve sharing fake news, destroying someone's reputation or influencing politics. Such risks can harm us individually and can also increase the chance of bigger cybersecurity attacks on financial markets, government institutions and public organizations (Zhou et al., 2025).

Greater use of technology and the internet means that digital fraud is becoming more common. Therefore, people and organizations need to raise awareness and quickly implement strong information security plans. Firms should formally educate their staff on cyber security, use powerful authentication everywhere and regularly keep an eye on their network activity to deter digital fraud (Apsimet et al., 2024).

In practice, digital fraud can appear in various forms. In addition, fraud can also occur through fake accounts on social media. Identity theft is also a serious mode of digital fraud, where a person's personal data is used to carry out illegal transactions or activities in the name of the victim. Other forms include fake websites or applications designed to resemble official services with the aim of stealing user data or carrying out fictitious transactions (Li et al., 2023).

Through the use of digital media and technology, digital fraud takes place, usually to achieve illegal payouts. This involves different approaches that accept the modern capabilities of connected devices and use the mistakes people often make in keeping their personal and important data secure (Alieyan et al., 2021).

It is a kind of cybercrime in which someone uses digital methods and tools to deceive others to get unlawful money or something else. A range of techniques and methods are used in this activity, together exploiting digital devices, internet connections and personal information.

1.2 Definition of Identity Theft

The rise of online transactions and the widespread use of online platforms have rendered identity theft increasingly prevalent, placing it at the forefront of problems in the realm of cybercrime.

In the computer era, identity theft is generally aided by activities such as hacking, phishing, and physical theft of documents in order to obtain personal data. These activities allow the perpetrators to access pre-existing accounts or create new fake ones. Manipulative emotions or social engineering are also widely utilized to deceive victims into divulging confidential information. Payment technology advances have also made the number of identity thefts rise, with nearly 1 in 10 adults being targeted annually (Reynolds, D., 2023).

The various types of identity theft reveal that threats to personal information are highly diverse and may occur in many areas of life. Hence, people and organizations must study these types of identity theft to create awareness and secure personal data. Identity theft can leave the victim vulnerable and cause serious complications in other aspects of their life—especially during the current era, as nearly everyone utilizes social media as a tool for communication and social interaction. Identity theft has become a new trend in cybercrime (Mishra & Gupta, 2018).

Identity theft for internet loan fraud is becoming more and more common in Indonesia. The victim does not take the loan, but it appears as if they are the ones who took it and then get threatened to repay with extremely high interest rates.

Identity theft is not only normally carried out for monetary purposes but for other personal and private purposes as well. The more the number of users of social media, the greater the risk of identity theft and other cybercrimes. Whereas digital identity theft and fraud are usually tightly interconnected as well as practically overlapping, the two terms also have essential differences in essence, scope, and primary objectives (Upadhyay et al., 2024).

Digital fraud is a blanket term to refer to various forms of fraudulent activities executed by leveraging digital means and information technology. These activities typically encompass manipulative, deceptive, or exploitative actions executed online with the intention of obtaining illegal gains. Common examples of cyber fraud are phishing, fake online stores, spoofed websites, and investment scams disseminated through electronic media. Cyber fraud in the majority of cases does not always imply the abuse of personal data; rather, scammers usually exploit users' unawareness, carelessness, or bad digital literacy to reach their objective ("AI IN FRAUD PREVENTION AND FINANCIAL SECURITY," 2024).

On the other hand, identity theft is a specific form of cybercrime which involves the unauthorized purchase or misuse of another individual's personal information—his complete name, identification number, address, or money details—to do stuff that is detrimental to the victim. Identity theft usually forms components of bigger plots of online deceit, but not all incidents of online deceit involve the misappropriation of identity. The general objective of identity theft is to act as someone else in order to get to a service, a resource, or an illicit benefit, such as opening bank accounts, applying for loans, or performing transactions in the victim's name.

Hence, it can be said that identity theft is a form of cyber fraud, but cyber fraud is more extensive in its range, including other forms of deceitful behavior that need not always rely on the misuse of personal identity information.

2. TYPES OF DIGITAL FRAUD

With the more advanced digital era of the present, various forms of digital fraud are increasingly becoming prevalent with the progress of the era with increasing dependence of society on technology and the internet (Suela, 2024). Online fraud exists in various forms and modes of operation, albeit they all have the same goal, which is to deceive victims with the aim of gaining advantages either in terms of finance, information, or access to systems (Apsimet et al., 2024).

One of the most common and widespread forms of online fraud experienced by the general public is phishing, which is a deceptive act to pose as an official entity via email, website, or other electronic communication in order to get victims' personal information such as passwords or credit card information (Yunoose et al., 2022). The other similar forms are smishing, whereby it is carried out through SMS messages, and vishing, whereby it is performed through voice calls as a form of fraud. The three types are founded upon psychological manipulation in a way that the victims will trust and reveal confidential information (Redi & Ernasari, 2023). Although today not many people use SMS messages, a number of people are still deceived and lose funds through smishing offenses.

Spear phishing is a highly targeted type of internet fraud, in which the perpetrator impersonates a trusted source or person to trick a specific victim into divulging secret information, such as passwords, financial data, or other sensitive data (Shukla, 2023). Spear phishing differs from regular phishing, in which messages are sent to many people at once, in that spear phishing targets a specific individual or group and the message is made to be very customized and credible. The perpetrator often does some preliminary research on the victim, for instance, their position, work relationships, habits, or use of social media, so that the message sent seems more legitimate and relevant.

A very dangerous and prevalent type of fraud is identity theft, in which the fraudster utilizes someone else's personal information to carry out transactions or criminal activities in the victim's name. In some cases, the fraudster even creates a fake account using this personal information to apply for an online loan or to deceive others. Social media fraud is also being increasingly experienced.

The perpetrator creates a spoofed account resembling a specific individual or entity to build trust and deceive the victim, for example, by asking for a money transfer or spreading disinformation. That is not all, online shopping scams are also common, especially when the perpetrator offers non-existent products, receives payment, but fails to deliver the promised products. There are scammers who impersonate buyers in order to trick sellers into buying goods in bulk but never pay and send fake proof of payment in order to deceive the seller. Perpetrators often target new users who do not yet understand the platform's security system. To avoid fraud, users are advised to continue transacting in official systems, be wary of prices that are too cheap, and not share personal information carelessly. Improving education and security systems from e-commerce platforms is also very important to prevent this crime (Malik, 2024).

In cybercrime, skimming and carding are two methods widely used by criminals to steal credit or debit card details and use it illegitimately. They are both spreading fast with the increased use of non-cash transactions by citizens (Nembo et al., 2024). Skimming is the act of stealing someone else's credit or debit card information using an instrument called a skimmer (Wibowo et al., 2021). The instrument is usually secretly installed in the card reader of a restaurant or store paying machine or ATM. When a victim swipes the card, the instrument will read and clone information from the magnetic stripe on the card. The offender in certain cases also places a hidden camera so that it can record the victim entering his PIN, so that both the card details and the use of it are under the offender's control. The information stolen in such a manner is further used to create replica cards that are just like the victim's. With such a forged card, the criminal can make payments or cash out with no awareness of the owner of the card (Stojković-Numanović et al., 2023).

Carding, however, pertains to the unauthorized usage of someone else's credit or debit card details, typically to shop online. Offenders who use carding employ several methods of getting access to card details, which may involve skimming, phishing, data violations, or purchasing stolen data on the dark net. After the offender has complete details such as card number, validity period, and CVV number, the offender uses it in purchasing goods, online digital commodities, vouchers, or even online bill payments for certain. Carding is normally done sequentially and on a large scale. Offenders even use programmed bots to try thousands of potential card number combinations quickly, until they have gotten authentic information that can be used (Rahaman, Chappu, et al., 2025). Even though skimming and carding differ in method, both end up costing card owners as well as banks which bear the costs of illegal transactions. Therefore, the public must be even more vigilant, for example by ensuring at all times the genuineness of the ATM or EDC machines prior to inserting the card, and avoiding disclosing card information through non-secure communication channels (Arifin et al., 2020).

Additionally, there are even existing investment scams such as Ponzi schemes or fake investments that promise immediate huge returns with no risk involved (Daud et al., 2024). Such scams typically involve people who do not know the digital financial system and have trust in promises.

Another form of digital fraud also considered dangerous is the employment of fake applications or sites. The websites or applications are designed very similar to the original ones, with the aim to steal login credentials or perpetrate unauthorized transactions without the knowledge of the victim. In business, BEC fraud also often occurs, whereby fraudsters get into the company's email system and impersonate powerful officials demanding illegal transfers of funds (Almutairi et al., 2025).

One form of cybercrime that is now increasingly experienced by regular users of social media is doxing. Doxing refers to the act of making an individual's personal details public without their consent, for instance, personally identifiable details such as telephone numbers or home addresses. While it may appear to be identity theft, doxing is not primarily done for financial motives but rather to humiliate, harass, or intimidate the victim (Rahaman, Putra, et al., 2025).

Doxing is increasingly being used as a tool of political activism, reflecting societal tensions around race, gender, power, and inequality. The chief objective of doxing is to intimidate, shame, or harm the victim, either psychologically or physically (Doxing, 2022). No less serious is doxing which refers to the act of propagating someone's personal information without permission for the aim of threatening, humiliating, or intimidating. Although not necessarily to do with money, doxing falls under digital fraud owing to its ill psychological and social impacts. It is likely to happen to frequent social media users who easily disseminate information when sharing daily activities on social media status, unaware the information disseminated can easily be confidential information easily accessed and can easily constitute a personal threat (Rahaman et al., 2022). Majority of individuals who are not familiar with social media do not know the information that has to be shared and the information that cannot be shared.

3. METHODS OF IDENTITY THEFT

Identity theft may happen both in the cyber and offline worlds, through various channels including data breaches and relationship-based identity theft. Identity theft is facilitated by the anonymity of the internet, whereby criminals are able to do business without ease of traceability, thus having global impacts on victims as well as being a very huge headache for government agencies and institutions (Szakonyi et al., 2021). Criminals use various methods to obtain a person's personal data illegally, using it for fraud, breaking into accounts, or unauthorized operations. Each example suggests that identity theft does not only exist on the Internet, but may also occur in real life (Merdović & Jovanović, 2024). Therefore, it is necessary for every individual to protect their own personal details, online as well as offline, so as to be free from victimization of identity crime.

3.1 Malware and Keyloggers

One of the most dangerous methods of identity theft is through malware, which is malicious software designed to infect the system of a user (Kadari et al., 2024). One of the malware types is keyloggers, and they are software that records all keystrokes on the victim's keyboard, even when typing usernames, passwords, or credit card information. Malware is usually spread through malicious links, phishing emails, or downloads from unofficial sites. Unbeknownst to them, the victim's information is recorded and sent to the perpetrator covertly.

This research paper talks about malware as an offending program that invades a system's confidentiality, integrity, and performance. The main focus lies on the importance of implementing a deep learning-based Malware Detection System (MDS) as a counter attack against advanced malware attacks, which are tasked with maintaining national security and economic stability (Girija, 2022).

3.2 Data Breaches

Data breach is an instance when the security firewall of a company or an online organization is compromised and private information of its users leaks into the public domain or is exchanged in the darknet (Patil et al., 2023). Data breach is when an unauthorized third party gains access to confidential or sensitive data that eventually leads to the leakage, theft, or misappropriation of the information.

The implications can be very damaging, ranging from identity theft and financial fraud to individuals' and institutions' reputational loss (Spanca & Salihu, 2024). The leaked data may include full names, addresses, phone numbers, ID cards, and financial information. Once the data is in the possession of the attackers, they have the ability to use it to create fraudulent accounts, borrow money online, or participate in other types of illegal activity using the victim's name. Data breaches typically involve large corporations and expose millions of users at the same time.

Government data breaches frequently occur, especially in third-world countries lacking strong cyber security in the era of digitalization, resulting in dozens of government department data breach cases. The ways to handle instances of data leak cybersecurity experts highlight are increasing levels of digital literacy, regular security checks, and transparency in handling data leak cases so that public trust can be achieved (Rahaman, Cajes, et al., 2025).

3.3 Impersonation (Digital Falsification)

Impersonation, or cyber disguise, is a tactic where a criminal poses as someone else—an individual or an institution—to take advantage of the victim's trust (Vilardo, 2004). For example, a criminal may pretend to be a bank representative who calls the victim and asks for confidential information for the purpose of verification. This spoofing is also achievable via social media or email, where the attacker creates a fake profile that closely resembles the real person so that the victim does not get to know and provides the wanted information. This approach relies a lot on psychological manipulation (social engineering).

Impersonation-type of fraud, such as CEO fraud or business email compromise (BEC), is when the fraudster has manipulated a virtual identity to obtain credibility and trigger monetary loss. These techniques can range from presenting counterfeit signatures or mimicking a government representative or agency, highlighting the importance of embracing robust protection strategies and detection techniques (Bruno, 2019).

4. IMPACTS OF DIGITAL FRAUD AND IDENTITY THEFT

Digital fraud and identity theft are two forms of cyber threats that continue to grow along with the increasing digitalization in various sectors. Both not only impact individuals as direct victims, considering this has serious consequences for corporate entities and the stability of the country as a whole (Tripathi & Tripathi, 2024).

4.1 On Individuals

In addition, identity theft and cyber fraud result in enormous monetary losses. Victims' identities are typically employed to commit illegal transactions, apply for online loans, and open false accounts, which cause them to lose their own money (Smith, 2009). Victims also stand to suffer from reputational damage if they are used for criminal activities. The psychological aspect cannot be eliminated since the majority of the victims experience anxiety, stress, and even trauma upon losing control of their personal data. This shows that the impact of computer crime on individuals is multidimensional, ranging from economic, social, to emotional aspects.

4.2 On Companies

Data theft incidents are disastrous for large corporations in terms of reputation threats and disruption in business processes. Such a violation can have long-term effects, and it might be difficult to restore consumer trust at a deep and timely level, as seen in the case studies of Target and Equifax (Sharma, 2024).

For the private sector, digital fraud and data theft are major issues for maintaining customers' trust and business development in the future. It can cause untrusted reputational losses in the short run by breaching customer data, financial information, or company internal plans. Apart from that, organizations could face economic losses in the form of regulatory fines, lawsuits, and post-incident mitigation cash flow (Prabu & Nurhaliza, 2023). In some cases, cyber attacks such as ransomware have even paralyzed a firm's information system, thus disrupting customer service, and reducing productivity. Violations of data protection statutes, such as the Personal Data Protection Act (PDP Act), also expose the institution and the ecosystem to legal threats that can impact them.

5. PREVENTION AND PROTECTION

The rapid development of information technology, besides its huge benefits, also brings onerous challenges, especially how to protect personal information and avert digital frauds (Ilmih & Wulandari, 2024). Therefore, an integrative solution is needed in risk avoidance measures, which include reliance on high-tech security technology, strengthening the digital literacy of the community, and imposing strict and systemic legal rules.

With the merge of deployment of adequate security technology, increasing digital literacy, and strong legal regulation support behind it, one hopes that digital fraud and data leaks prevention and protection activities can effectively be carried out so as to provide a secure and trusted digital environment for all.

5.1 Personal Data Security

Data protection is one of the most important aspects in preventing online fraud. People and organizations have to embrace safe handling of data, from data collection to storage, to disposal (Salsabila, 2024). Safe handling of passwords, limiting access to levels of need, and encrypting data are major steps to prevent leakage and theft of sensitive information. Effective internal security guidelines and continuous surveillance for potential breaches make effective data security governance.

5.2 Use of Security Technologies (2FA, VPN, Antivirus)

Technologies such as two-factor authentication (2FA), Virtual Private Network (VPN), and antivirus software are integral components of digital protection. Two-factor authentication increases account access security by adding a second authentication factor beyond the password, reducing the likelihood of unauthorized access (Vaithyasubramanian et al., 2015). VPN allows users to encrypt internet traffic, especially when accessing the internet through public networks, reducing the risk of data interception. Meanwhile, antivirus supports the detection and removal of malware or malicious code that could steal data or hurt the system (Mehra, 2025).

5.3 Digital Literacy and Public Education

Encouraging digital literacy among people is a strategic action to prevent digital fraud. Proper education can make users more sensitive to fraud trends, cyber attack patterns, and safeguarding personal data independently. Training programs, bulk campaigns, and convenient access to information are sound means of instituting a strong digital security culture. Literate citizens in the digital space would be critical and vigilant while conducting transactions online, thus fewer fraud victims and data breaches.

5.4 Legal Actions and Applicable Regulations

Legislative and regulatory efforts make significant contributions by providing the legal canopy and penalties for digital crime perpetrators (Lopes et al., 2024). In Indonesia, ratification of the Personal Data Protection Law (UU PDP) is a significant milestone in the regulation of personal data governance and consumer protection. The law regulates data owners' and data management organizations' rights and obligations, including data collection permit provisions, transparency, and violation reporting mechanisms (Kurdi & Cahyono, 2024). In addition, resorting to criminal and administrative sanctions is an effective law enforcement mechanism to deter data breaches and fraud. Coordination between the regulators, law enforcement, and the private sector must be such that rules function optimally and act as a deterrent.

6. Conclusion

Digital fraud and identity theft are two forms of cybercrime that are growing with the evolution of information technology. Online fraud encompasses a broad spectrum of deceptive activities through online media with the objective to gain unauthorized benefits, while identity theft is one specific category involving misuse of personal information for impersonation or criminal activity purposes. While both have a considerable impact on people and companies, digital fraud is an overarching term and does not necessarily involve personal information, while identity theft is a focused attack on the person's personal data. It is important to have a clear understanding of the nature and differences of these two offenses while designing prevention strategies and awareness about online security.

REFERENCES

AI IN FRAUD PREVENTION AND FINANCIAL SECURITY. (2024, September 24). *Insights2Techinfo.* https://insights2techinfo.com/ai-in-fraud-prevention-and-financial-security/

Alieyan, K., Almomani, A., Anbar, M., Alauthman, M., Abdullah, R., & Gupta, B. B. (2021). DNS rule-based schema to botnet detection. *Enterprise Information Systems, 15*(4), 545–564. DOI: 10.1080/17517575.2019.1644673

Almutairi, A. M., Kang, B., & AL Hashimy, N. (2025). *Business Email Compromise: A Comprehensive Taxonomy for Detection and Prevention.* DOI: 10.1145/3700706.3700714

Apsimet, N., Smanova, A., & Utegenova, G. (2024). The role of the Internet in the evolution of fraud: A historical aspect. *Л.Н. Гумилев Атында ы Еуразия лтты Университетiнi Хабаршысы, 146*(1), 247–257. DOI: 10.32523/2616-6844-2024-1-247-257

Arifin, R., Atikasari, H., & Waspiah, W. (2020). The Intersection of Criminal Law. *Technology and Business Commercial Law on Carding as Cyber Fraud., 11*(2), 235–246. DOI: 10.26555/novelty.v11i2.a15700

Bruno, M. (2019). *Impersonation Fraud Scenarios: How to Protect.* Detect and Respond., DOI: 10.69554/NHAM3165

Daud, M., Armia, Y., Hakim, L., & Aziz, D. (2024). Edukasi dan Literasi Keuangan Kepada Kelompok Masyarakat tentang Investasi Ilegal di Era Digital. *Jurnal Pengabdian Masyarakat, 3*(2), 207–217. DOI: 10.70340/japamas.v3i2.158

Doxing. (2022). (pp. 1–3). The Wiley-Blackwell Encyclopedia of Social and Political Movements., DOI: 10.1002/9780470674871.wbespm554

Girija, A. (2022). Malware detection using machine learning techniques. *Indian Scientific Journal Of Research In Engineering And Management, 06*(08). Advance online publication. DOI: 10.55041/IJSREM16162

Ilmih, A. A., & Wulandari, F. P. (2024). *Perlindungan Data Pribadi Dalam Kejahatan Transnasional Lintas-Negara.* DOI: 10.59246/aladalah.v2i4.925

Kadari, S. R., Radhika, G., Shekar, M., Shankar, R., & Madhu, Ch. (2024). A Study on the Key Applications of Malware. *International Journal of Advanced Research in Science. Tongxin Jishu, 481–485.* Advance online publication. DOI: 10.48175/IJARSCT-19359

Kadashevich, A. J., Marcus, J. B., Piziak, J. L., & Trivedi, P. K. (2014). *Identifying an imposter account in a social network*. https://www.iprdb.com/content/US9648030B2

Kurdi, K., & Cahyono, J. (2024). Perlindungan Data Pribadi di Era Digital Berdasarkan Undang-Undang Nomor 27 Tahun 2022. *JUNCTO*, *6*(2), 330–339. DOI: 10.31289/juncto.v6i2.5443

Li, S., Gao, L., Han, C., Gupta, B., Alhalabi, W., & Almakdi, S. (2023). Exploring the effect of digital transformation on Firms' innovation performance. *Journal of Innovation & Knowledge*, *8*(1), 100317. DOI: 10.1016/j.jik.2023.100317

Lopes, L. D. R., Oliveira, D., Da Silva, I. T., Dutra, Y. F., & Lima, O. D. S. F. C. (2024). Crimes Cibernéticos E Direito Penal: A Regulação E A Resposta Jurídica Ao Crime No Ambiente Digital. *IOSR Journal of Business and Management, 26*(11), 01–11. DOI: 10.9790/487X-2611080111

Malik, A. A. (2024). Online shopping, Cyber frauds and Fraud prevention Strategies. *International Journal for Electronic Crime Investigation*. DOI: 10.54692/ijeci.2024.0801186

Mehra, T. (2025). The Critical Role of Two-Factor Authentication (2FA) in Mitigating Ransomware and Securing Backup, Recovery, and Storage Systems. *International Journal of Science and Research Archive*, *14*(1), 274–277. DOI: 10.30574/ijsra.2025.14.1.0019

Merdović, B., & Jovanović, B. (2024). Understanding identity theft and fraud. *Kultura Polisa. Casopis Za Negovanje Demokratske Političke Kulture*, *21*(2). Advance online publication. DOI: 10.51738/Kpolisa2024.21.2r.17mj

Mishra, A., & Gupta, B. (2018). Intelligent phishing detection system using similarity matching algorithms. *International Journal of Information and Communication Technology*, *12*(1–2), 51–73. DOI: 10.1504/IJICT.2018.089022

Nembo, L. G., Wilhelmus, B. V., & Fallo, D. F.Ludgardis Goo NemboBhisa Vitus WilhelmusDebi F.Ng. Fallo. (2024). Pertanggungjawaban Pidana Bagi Pelaku Tindak Pidana Pencurian Data Nasabah Perbankan dengan Mode Skimming Ditinjau dari Undang-Undang Nomor 1 Tahun 2024 Tentang Informasi dan Transaksi Elektronik. *Mandub*, *2*(4), 189–197. DOI: 10.59059/mandub.v2i4.1760

Patil, R., Pise, G., & Bhosale, Y. (2023). Root causes, ongoing difficulties, proactive prevention techniques, and emerging trends of enterprise data breaches. *arXiv.Org, abs/2311.16303*. https://doi.org//arxiv.2311.16303DOI: 10.48550

Prabu, A. V., & Nurhaliza, S. (2023). Digital Transformation in the Financial Sector. *Implications for Consumer Trust and Security.*, *1*(1), 10–14. DOI: 10.62951/ijecm.v1i1.303

Rahaman, M., Cajes, N., Gupta, B. B., Chui, K. T., & Nedjah, N. (2025). Defending against smishing attacks: State-of-the-art techniques, challenges, limitations, and future directions. *Computer Networks*, *273*, 111758. DOI: 10.1016/j.comnet.2025.111758

Rahaman, M., Chappu, B., Jana, S., Haque, A., Firmansyah, G., & Chattopadhyay, S. (2025). Security Benefits in Small Medium Business Enterprise Through Cloud Adoption. In N. Nedjah, G. Martinez Perez, & B. B. Gupta (Eds.), *International Conference on Smart Systems and Advanced Computing (SysCom 2022)* (pp. 168–180). Springer Nature Switzerland. DOI: 10.1007/978-3-031-40905-9_18

Rahaman, M., Putra, K. T., Irawan, B., & Biyanto, T. R. (2025). Industrial Evolution: The Integration of AI in Robotics and Drone Systems. In *AI Developments for Industrial Robotics and Intelligent Drones* (pp. 85–114). IGI Global Scientific Publishing. DOI: 10.4018/979-8-3693-2707-4.ch005

Rahaman, M., Wisnujati, A., Widodo, A. M., Haque, A., Sakar, R., & Chen, H. C. (2022). *Privacy Preservation Agri-Food SCM Operation Based on Online/Offline RFID Using Block Chain.* 413–426. DOI: 10.2991/978-94-6463-084-8_34

Redi, A., & Ernasari, N. (2023). *Efforts to Overcome Web-Based Phishing Crimes in the World of Cyber Crime.* DOI: 10.4108/eai.28-10-2023.2341807

Reynolds, D. (2023). *Identity Theft.* Oxford Research Encyclopedia of Criminology and Criminal Justice., DOI: 10.1093/acrefore/9780190264079.013.797

Salsabila, F. A. (2024). *IImih, A. A.* Penyalahgunaan Data Pribadi Sebagai Bentuk Kejahatan Sempurna Dalam Perspektlf Hukum Siber., DOI: 10.59246/aladalah.v2i4.968

Sharma, A. (2024). The impact of cybersecurity breaches on big businesses. *International Journal of Advanced Research*, *12*(10), 10–25. DOI: 10.21474/IJAR01/19614

Shukla, A. (2023). *Spear Watch: A Thorough Examination to Identify Spear Phishing Attacks.* DOI: 10.35940/ijitee.H9680.0712823

Smith, R. G. (2009). *Identity theft and fraud.* Routledge Handbooks Online., DOI: 10.4324/9781843929338.ch14

Spanca, F., & Salihu, A. (2024). *Unveiling the Consequences of Data Breaches: Risks, Impacts, and Mitigation in the Digital Age.* 1–8. DOI: 10.1109/ICECCE63537.2024.10823432

Stojković-Numanović, K., Merdovic, B., & Živaljević, D. (2023). *Forging payment cards and cybercrime.* Pravo., DOI: 10.5937/ptp2304138S

Suela, L. C. (2024). *Online Fraud Exposed: Tactics and Strategies of Cyber Scammers.* Indian Scientific Journal Of Research In Engineering And Management., DOI: 10.55041/IJSREM31604

Szakonyi, A., Leonard, B. M., & Dawson, M. (2021). *Dark Web: A Breeding Ground for ID Thefts and Financial Crimes.* IGI Global., DOI: 10.4018/978-1-7998-5567-5.ch025

Tripathi, R., & Tripathi, S. (2024). *Frauds and Cyber Security Issues in the Finance Sector.* IGI Global., DOI: 10.4018/979-8-3693-1503-3.ch008

Upadhyay, U., Kumar, A., Sharma, G., Saini, A. K., Arya, V., Gaurav, A., & Chui, K. T. (2024). Mitigating Risks in the Cloud-Based Metaverse Access Control Strategies and Techniques. [IJCAC]. *International Journal of Cloud Applications and Computing*, *14*(1), 1–30. DOI: 10.4018/IJCAC.334364

Vaithyasubramanian, S., Christy, A., & Saravanan, D. (2015). *Two factor authentications for secured login in support of effective information preservation and network security.*

Verma, I., Khan, S. Z., Diwakar, R., Garg, M., & Muabshshir, M. (2024). Social Media Fraud: Students Participating in Social Media Fraud. *International Journal of Research Publication and Reviews*, *5*(5), 8014–8016. DOI: 10.55248/gengpi.5.0524.1328

Vilardo, M. F. (2004). *Online impersonation in securities scams.* *2*(3), 82–85. DOI: 10.1109/MSP.2004.19

Wibowo, S. A., Syahrin, A., & Mulyadi, M. (2021). *Pertanggungjawaban Pidana Bagi Pelaku Tindak Pidana Pencurian Data Nasabah Perbankan Dengan Metode Skimming Di Tinjau Menurut Undang-Undang Informasi Dan Transaksi Elektronik.* DOI: 10.55357/is.v2i2.100

Yunoose, A., & Varghese, A. R. (2022). Phishing. *International Journal of Engineering Technology and Management Sciences*, *6*(5), 574–579. DOI: 10.46647/ijetms.2022.v06i05.092

Zhou, F., Zhang, N., Li, X., Han, C., & Gupta, B. B. (2025). Managing inter-organizational dependencies operation for discovering digital business model innovation in corporate innovation ecosystem. *Operations Management Research : Advancing Practice Through Research*, *18*(2), 574–590. DOI: 10.1007/s12063-024-00501-4

Chapter 2
Decision Support Systems for Real-Time Fraud Response

Muhammad Faisal
https://orcid.org/0000-0003-1469-9468
Muhammadiyah University of Makassar, Indonesia

Nizirwan Anwar
https://orcid.org/0000-0003-1189-9093
Universitas Esa Unggul, Indonesia

Tomy Ronaldi
https://orcid.org/0000-0002-0517-7505
Indonesia Defense University, Indonesia

Imam Asrowardi
Politeknik Negeri Lampung, Indonesia

Hani Dewi Ariessanti
Universitas Esa Unggul, Indonesia

Rudi Kurniawan
STMIK IKMI Cirebon, Indonesia

Tuti Hartati
Universitas Wanita Internasional, Indonesia

Varsha Arya
Hong Kong Metropolitan University, Hong Kong

Bayu Pamungkas
Universitas Esa Unggul, Indonesia

ABSTRACT

As digital transactions become integral to modern life, identity theft and advanced fraud schemes demand agile, intelligent countermeasures. This chapter explores the design of Decision Support Systems (DSS) for real-time fraud response, with emphasis on digital arrest fraud and identity-based attacks. AI-driven DSS leverage machine learning, behavioural analytics, and anomaly detection to enable rapid detection and response. The chapter discusses architectural elements such as data integration, real-time analytics, and decision automation, along with explainability and compliance. Case studies from finance and government show how adaptive

DOI: 10.4018/979-8-3373-4149-1.ch002

risk strategies and feedback loops enhance resilience. Predictive models aid in identity theft prevention, while DSS support teams with evidence-based responses. The chapter offers a framework for embedding AI-powered fraud detection in DSS, uniting innovation, policy, and human-centred design to boost digital trust.

1 INTRODUCTION

The digital economy has revolutionized commerce, communication, and financial transactions, leading to an unprecedented reliance on electronic methods for conducting business. Consumers increasingly rely on online platforms for shopping, banking, and other activities, which has heightened the incidence of fraud targeting these channels (Angela et al., 2024). Recent reports indicate a surge in various forms of fraud, including identity theft and credit card fraud, posing significant threats to individuals and organizations (Verma & Tyagi, 2022; Baesens, 2023).

Real-time fraud detection has emerged as a crucial component in counteracting identity theft and fraud. As cybercriminals develop sophisticated techniques, traditional reactive measures are insufficient to protect against their evolving strategies (Baesens, 2023). Organizations have responded by adopting advanced technologies that enable continuous monitoring and evaluation of transactions to detect anomalies indicative of fraud (Angela et al., 2024).

At the intersection of these challenges and technological advancements lies the concept of Decision Support Systems (DSS). DSS utilize artificial intelligence (AI) and machine learning (ML) to facilitate real-time fraud detection and prevention through analytics and predictive modeling (Carminati et al., 2015). By integrating vast amounts of transaction data, behavioural analytics, and user interactions, DSS provides actionable insights that enable organizations to make informed decisions and significantly reduce their exposure to risk (Amasiatu & Shah, 2018). As these systems evolve, their ability to enhance fraud management strategies will be paramount in maintaining consumer trust and safeguarding financial assets in an increasingly digital world (Baesens, 2023).

2 THE EVOLUTION OF AI IN FRAUD DETECTION

Fraud detection has undergone a remarkable transformation, evolving from traditional manual methods to sophisticated AI-driven approaches. Initially, rule-based systems, based on predefined criteria, were the primary method of fraud detection. However, these rigid systems struggled to adapt to the ever-changing nature of fraudulent tactics, requiring manual updates and oversight. As the complexity of fraudulent schemes increased, their limitations became evident, prompting the exploration of more resilient and automated solutions (Jain & Gupta, 2019).

The transition from traditional rule-based systems to artificial intelligence (AI) methodologies represents a significant advancement in fraud detection capabilities. AI introduces adaptive algorithms that can learn from new data inputs, enabling them to identify complex patterns and anomalies that were previously undetectable. Machine learning (ML) further enhances this adaptability, allowing systems to revise their parameters autonomously and respond to emerging fraud strategies in real-time (Vajrobol et al., 2024).

For instance, a study by Bhatia and Kaur (2021) demonstrated how AI models maintain robust detection rates, significantly outperforming their rule-based predecessors. These AI models achieved nearly 90% accuracy in fraud detection tasks, showcasing their effectiveness in identifying fraudulent activities.

Advanced techniques, particularly deep learning and neural networks, have revolutionized fraud detection systems. These methodologies, with their multi-layered architectures, process vast datasets, enabling the identification of intricate and subtle fraudulent behaviors concealed within transactional data (N. Jain & Patil, 2024). Neural networks' ability to extract features and abstract data provides a comprehensive understanding of transaction dynamics, significantly enhancing the effectiveness of fraud detection frameworks (Lei & Ghorbani, 2012). (Lai, 2023). Moreover, advanced AI models not only improve efficiency but also handle complex data types, giving organizations an edge in identifying fraud across various sectors, including finance and e-commerce (Cirqueira et al., 2021; Villegas-Ortega et al., 2021). The shift towards AI-enhanced fraud detection goes beyond automation; it represents a paradigm shift in how organizations perceive fraud prevention. By leveraging real-time data analysis powered by machine learning, companies can proactively mitigate risks before they escalate into substantial financial losses. This strategy bolsters financial institutions' resilience against the evolving landscape of sophisticated fraudulent tactics, positioning AI as an indispensable tool in safeguarding digital transactions (Negi, 2021; Ismaeil, 2024). The evolution of fraud detection from rule-based systems to AI-driven methodologies emphasizes the need for adaptable, data-driven solutions in an era of technological advancements and increasingly sophisticated fraudulent activities. As organizations refine their fraud detection strategies, incorporating AI promises not only enhanced operational efficiency but also a proactive approach to preserving the integrity of critical financial systems (Olubusola Odeyemi et al., 2024; Ismaeil, 2024).

3 ARCHITECTURAL FOUNDATIONS OF DECISION SUPPORT Systems

Decision Support Systems (DSS) play a crucial role in fraud detection by harnessing advanced technologies like artificial intelligence (AI) and machine learning to enhance real-time response capabilities. These systems are meticulously designed with several key components: data integration pipelines that consolidate and preprocess data from various sources; real-time analytics engines that identify anomalies and patterns indicative of fraud; decision automation modules that promptly trigger alerts or take actions based on analytic outcomes; and a strong emphasis on explainability to ensure transparency and regulatory compliance. By combining these elements, organizations can swiftly identify and respond to fraudulent activities while upholding ethical and legal standards (Xu, Cao, & Zhang, 2020).

3.1. Data Integration Pipelines for Comprehensive Data Handling

Data integration pipelines are crucial for the successful deployment of data science systems (DSS) in fraud detection. These pipelines streamline the seamless aggregation and processing of data from various sources, such as transactional data, customer profiles, and external databases. By consolidating this information, organizations can generate comprehensive datasets that offer a holistic view of user behavior, which is essential for identifying suspicious activities that may indicate fraud. The efficacy of these pipelines directly impacts the quality of insights derived from integrated data, leading to more accurate detection of fraud patterns (Mohan et al., 2024). In practice, robust data integration enables the continuous updating of datasets, which is vital as fraud tactics evolve and change rapidly (Majumder, 2024).

3.2. Real-Time Analytics Engines to Process Transaction Data

Real-time transaction data processing is a fundamental aspect of effective fraud detection. Real-time analytics engines enable DSS to analyze incoming transaction data as it flows into the system, facilitating immediate identification of suspicious activities (Henriques et al., 2022). Research by (Adelakun et al., 2024) underscores the significance of real-time processing capabilities in detecting anomalies and preventing fraudulent transactions before they occur. This is crucial for maintaining trust in financial systems. Moreover, the incorporation of machine learning algorithms in these engines allows for dynamic adjustments based on transaction characteristics, enhancing detection rates and response times (Chopra & Binwal, 2024). This adaptability is particularly vital in modern high-volume transaction environments where delays can result in substantial financial losses.

3.3. Decision Automation Modules for Rapid Response to Fraud Alerts

Decision automation modules, integral to data integration and analytical capabilities, enable rapid responses to fraud alerts. These modules, utilizing predefined criteria and learning algorithms, assess and respond to alerts without human intervention (Cirqueira et al., 2021). Research underscores the significant reduction in response time to potential fraud when decision-making processes are automated, thereby mitigating losses and enhancing overall system efficacy (Adelakun et al., 2024). Beyond operational efficiency, these automated systems minimize human error in critical decision-making contexts where speed is paramount (Gupta et al., 2025).

3.4. Importance of Explainability and Regulatory Compliance (Explainable AI)

The integration of Explainable AI (XAI) in Decision Support Systems (DSS) frameworks is crucial, especially in light of regulatory compliance demands (Rahmati, 2025). As regulators seek greater transparency in AI decision-making processes, the ability to explain how algorithms arrive at specific outcomes becomes paramount. Explainability fosters user trust and ensures that organizations can demonstrate compliance with legal requirements (Chopra & Binwal, 2024). Furthermore, as outlined by Rahmati (2025), incorporating explainability into DSS mitigates the "black-box" problem commonly associated with AI systems. This allows stakeholders to comprehend the rationale behind fraud detection outcomes, which is not only essential for compliance but also for refining fraud detection strategies based on observed patterns and behaviors (Venigandla & Vemuri, 2022). In essence, the architectural foundation of DSS in fraud detection comprises essential components that empower organizations to swiftly and effectively respond to fraudulent activities. By integrating comprehensive data handling, real-time analytics, decision automation, and the imperative for explainability, DSS emerges as a pivotal pillar in the ongoing battle against fraud in digital transactions (Gaurav et al., 2025).

4 AI METHODOLOGIES IN FRAUD DETECTION

Artificial Intelligence (AI) and Machine Learning (ML) have revolutionized fraud detection by introducing advanced analytical capabilities that surpass traditional rule-based systems. These methodologies enable the identification of intricate fraud patterns, adaptability to emerging tactics, and improvement in detection accuracy through continuous learning from new data.

a) Machine Learning Techniques

In fraud detection contexts, various Machine Learning techniques are employed. Supervised learning models, such as logistic regression, decision trees, random forests, and gradient boosting machines, are widely used to classify transactions as fraudulent or legitimate based on labeled historical data. These models learn discriminative patterns by training on extensive datasets containing examples of both fraudulent and non-fraudulent cases. Unsupervised learning methods, including clustering and anomaly detection algorithms like k-means and isolation forests, are crucial for detecting novel fraud types by identifying outliers that deviate from established normal behavior without prior labelling (Jain et al., 2022).

Another important category encompasses semi-supervised methods that leverage a limited amount of labeled data alongside large unlabeled datasets. These methods are particularly useful when fraud labels are scarce or costly to obtain. Reinforcement learning is emerging as a promising approach where systems iteratively improve decision-making policies to optimize fraud detection outcomes over time.

b) Advanced Analytical Methods

Beyond classical machine learning, advanced analytical methods like deep learning and natural language processing (NLP) have gained prominence. Deep learning architectures, including convolutional neural networks (CNNs), recurrent neural networks (RNNs), and their variants, excel at capturing intricate, non-linear relationships and temporal dependencies in large-scale data, such as transaction sequences, user behavior logs, or multimedia evidence. For instance, RNNs and long short-term memory networks (LSTMs) are particularly effective in modeling sequential transaction data to detect subtle temporal fraud patterns.

NLP techniques enable the automated analysis of unstructured text data, such as customer communications, claims descriptions, or social media content, to identify indicators of fraudulent intent or supporting evidence. Techniques like sentiment analysis, named entity recognition, and topic modeling enhance fraud investigations by extracting actionable insights from textual information.

Evaluating AI-driven fraud detection systems requires a nuanced approach, given the imbalanced and high-stakes nature of fraud data. Common performance metrics include precision, recall, F1-score, area under the Receiver Operating Characteristic curve (AUC-ROC), and area under the Precision-Recall curve (AUC-PR). Precision measures the proportion of detected fraud cases that are true positives, emphasizing the minimization of false positives that can disrupt legitimate customers. Recall quantifies the ability to identify actual fraud cases, which is critical for minimizing financial losses. The F1-score balances precision and recall, providing a single measure of effectiveness.

In real-world applications, cost-sensitive metrics that consider the financial and reputational impact of misclassifications are increasingly adopted. Moreover, model interpretability and explainability have become essential to ensure regulatory compliance and maintain stakeholder trust. This requires guiding the choice of algorithms and performance evaluation frameworks, as discussed in Bolton & Hand (2002), Phua et al. (2010), and Xu et al. (2020).

4.1 Overview of Machine Learning Techniques

Machine learning techniques in fraud detection can be broadly categorized into supervised and unsupervised learning methods. Supervised learning involves training algorithms on labeled datasets to predict outcomes and accurately classify new data. Common algorithms used in this domain include Support Vector Machines, Random Forests, and Neural Networks (Cho, 2023). These methods have demonstrated significant success in detecting fraudulent transactions by learning from historical data to identify patterns indicative of fraud (Olubusola Odeyemi et al., 2024). For instance, supervised methods enable systems to learn the characteristics of fraudulent and legitimate transactions, facilitating efficient classification and anomaly detection (Faraji, 2022).

Conversely, unsupervised learning is employed when labeled data is scarce or unavailable. It utilizes algorithms to discover inherent structures within the data, detecting anomalies or outliers that could signal fraudulent activity (Cho, 2023). Techniques such as clustering algorithms (e.g., K-means, DBSCAN) are commonly used to identify unusual patterns in transaction data, enabling organizations to uncover potentially fraudulent behaviors hidden within vast datasets (Faraji, 2022).

With the increasing complexity of fraud schemes, blending both supervised and unsupervised methodologies into hybrid models can enhance the robustness and reliability of fraud detection systems (Shoetan & Familoni, 2024).

4.2 Advanced Techniques

In recent years, the adoption of advanced AI techniques, particularly deep learning and natural language processing (NLP), has significantly enhanced the capabilities of fraud detection systems. Deep learning algorithms, particularly those utilizing neural networks, excel at analyzing vast datasets and identifying intricate patterns that conventional machine learning models might overlook. For instance, recurrent neural networks (RNNs), including Long Short-Term Memory (LSTM) networks, have demonstrated remarkable promise in sequential data modeling, particularly in credit card transactions (Esenogho et al., 2022). These deep learning architectures enable continuous learning from evolving transaction behaviors, enabling them to adapt more effectively to emerging fraud types compared to conventional methods (Omair & Alturki, 2020). Natural Language Processing (NLP) also plays a vital role in fraud detection, especially when dealing with unstructured data such as transaction descriptions, customer feedback, and security logs. NLP techniques empower systems to extract valuable insights from textual data, facilitating the identification of fraudulent communication patterns or phishing attempts that could compromise user security (Mazumder et al., 2024). By leveraging NLP, organizations can automate the triage of alerts generated by suspicious activities, thereby improving response times and operational efficiency (Olubusola Odeyemi et al., 2024).

4.3 Discussion of AI Performance Metrics

Evaluation metrics are crucial for assessing the performance of AI-driven fraud detection systems. Common metrics include accuracy, precision, recall, F1-score, and ROC-AUC (Receiver Operating Characteristic Area Under Curve). These metrics collectively provide a comprehensive understanding of model performance (Huda et al., 2020). For instance, accuracy measures the proportion of true results among the total number of cases examined. Precision evaluates the ratio of correctly predicted positive instances to the total predicted positives. Recall, on the other hand, assesses the model's ability to identify all relevant instances within a dataset (Snorovikhina & Zaytsev, 2021). Utilizing these metrics is essential for refining models and ensuring that fraud detection systems minimize false positives while maximizing true positive detection rates. As the fraud landscape evolves, continuous monitoring and adjustment of these performance metrics are necessary to maintain effective fraud prevention strategies (Muhamed, 2022). The advancement of AI methodologies in fraud detection underscores the pivotal role of machine learning, deep learning, and NLP technologies in enhancing the accuracy and efficiency of detecting fraudulent activities. By employing a diverse range of algorithms and meticulously evaluating their performance, organizations can proactively combat fraud in an increasingly intricate digital environment.

5 ADAPTIVE RISK MANAGEMENT STRATEGIES

In the face of increasingly sophisticated fraud threats, adaptive risk management strategies have become crucial for effective fraud mitigation. Predictive analytics, a key component of this approach, utilizes historical data and machine learning algorithms to identify patterns and anomalies indicative of potential fraudulent activity. By forecasting risks before they occur, organizations can proactively bolster their defenses.

Equally important is the integration of continuous learning mechanisms within risk management frameworks. Fraud tactics are constantly evolving, necessitating systems that not only detect known threat signatures but also adapt to emerging methods. Continuous learning enables fraud detection models to update in real time, incorporating new intelligence and feedback to enhance their accuracy and responsiveness.

Together, predictive analytics and continuous learning form a dynamic duo that empowers organizations to stay ahead of fraudsters. This collaborative approach reduces financial losses and safeguards reputation through a resilient and evolving defense posture, as highlighted by Ngai et al. (2011).

5.1 The Role of Predictive Analytics in Identifying Potential Fraud Before It Occurs

Predictive analytics plays a crucial role in adaptive risk management, enabling organizations to anticipate potential fraudulent activities before they happen. By leveraging advanced statistical models and machine learning algorithms, predictive analytics systems can analyze historical data alongside real-time transaction flows to identify patterns that may precede fraudulent events (Vashishth et al., 2025). Integrating these analytical capabilities allows financial institutions to detect unusual behaviors and flag transactions indicative of fraud with greater accuracy (Vashishth et al., 2025). The effectiveness of predictive analytics lies in its ability to learn from past incidents and continuously refine models. For instance, these models can be tailored to prioritize specific risk factors historically associated with fraud, enabling organizations to concentrate their prevention efforts in the most critical areas (Sharma et al., 2024). This approach not only enhances detection capabilities but also improves the overall response strategy to fraud, facilitating quicker mitigation actions when anomalies are identified.

5.2 Implementation of Continuous Learning Mechanisms to Adapt to Evolving Fraud Tactics

Continuous learning mechanisms are crucial for maintaining the effectiveness of fraud detection systems in a rapidly evolving threat landscape. As fraudsters persistently refine their techniques to evade detection, systems must remain equally dynamic. Adaptive AI systems, leveraging machine learning, can evolve by learning from new data, thereby enhancing detection accuracy and reducing false positives (Daiya, 2024).

Incorporating adaptive algorithms enables systems to recognize changes in transactional behavior in real time, allowing for immediate adjustments to detection models. This adaptability is vital as traditional static rule-based systems struggle to keep pace with the innovative strategies employed by fraudsters (Vashishth et al., 2025). Additionally, ensemble methods that combine multiple predictive models can improve resilience against diverse fraud tactics by capturing a broader range of patterns within data (Xia et al., 2024).

Furthermore, integrating feedback loops into these systems enhances continuous learning. When alerts are triggered, and fraud is confirmed or disproven, this feedback can be utilized to retrain and refine the models (Vashishth et al., 2025). Consequently, organizations can develop a more comprehensive understanding of the characteristics typical of fraudulent behaviors, leading to improved predictive accuracy over time. By adopting adaptive risk management strategies supported by predictive analytics and continuous learning mechanisms, organizations can proactively address fraud before it manifests. By leveraging technology that evolves alongside emerging threats, businesses can significantly enhance their fraud detection capabilities and safeguard their assets in an increasingly complex digital landscape.

6 CASE STUDIES: SUCCESSFUL COLLABORATION MODELS

Decision Support Systems (DSS) have proven effective in combating fraud across various industries, particularly in finance and government sectors. This section delves into specific industry applications, presenting empirical evidence to demonstrate how AI-driven approaches enhance fraud detection and prevention. By examining successful collaboration models, we can gain valuable insights for designing future initiatives.

One notable collaboration model in digital forensics involves formal partnerships between educational institutions and law enforcement agencies. These partnerships facilitate technology transfer and knowledge sharing, contributing to improved fraud detection rates and faster response times. Another collaborative approach involves cooperative agreements that promote technology transfer and knowledge sharing.

Real-world case studies offer valuable insights into the benefits and challenges of collaboration in digital forensics. These case studies highlight improved fraud detection rates, faster response times, and reduced financial losses. However, they also reveal the challenges of conflicting priorities, data privacy concerns, and regulatory hurdles. By analyzing these case studies, we can develop strategies to overcome these obstacles and foster successful collaboration in digital forensics.

6.1. Financial Sector Applications

In the financial industry, the integration of AI and machine learning within data science frameworks has revolutionized fraud detection strategies. Research has identified several case studies where advanced analytics have been effectively implemented to mitigate risks associated with fraudulent transactions. For instance, financial institutions have increasingly adopted machine learning algorithms to analyze transaction data in real-time, significantly enhancing their ability to identify suspicious activities before they escalate into serious fraud. This study illustrates how institutions like banks and insurance companies have reduced fraud losses by leveraging sophisticated algorithms that continuously learn from new patterns, thereby improving detection accuracy. Furthermore, empirical analysis shows that financial organizations utilizing machine learning techniques have reported substantial improvements in the effectiveness of their fraud detection systems. By employing supervised learning algorithms, such as logistic regression and decision trees, these banks can effectively analyze vast datasets to identify patterns indicative of fraud. Additionally, case studies demonstrate that through adaptive fraud detection models, some banks have achieved precision rates exceeding 90%, significantly lowering their risk exposure.

6.2. Government Sector Applications

The government's ability to combat fraud has been significantly enhanced by the deployment of AI-driven Data Science Systems (DSS). Agencies responsible for managing public funds or social services have begun implementing advanced analytics to detect and prevent fraudulent claims, as evidenced by the findings of (Pan, 2024). These agencies effectively utilized data-driven frameworks to improve oversight and accountability in financial disbursements. For instance, various government programs employed predictive modeling techniques to flag unusual patterns in claims, enabling them to prevent fraudulent payouts before they occurred. Moreover, success stories from government entities showcase the positive impact of machine learning applications in combating identity fraud and ensuring compliance with regulatory standards. The use of data analytics has led to a decrease in fraudulent transactions detected in public assistance programs, further improving resource allocation efficiency (Yuhertiana & Hadi Amin, 2024). Additionally, automated auditing processes driven by real-time data analysis have facilitated governments in enforcing stricter compliance regulations and enhancing transparency.

6.3 Analysis of Case Studies Highlighting Effectiveness of AI

The effectiveness of AI in real-world fraud detection scenarios is evident from several compelling case studies. For instance (Olubusola Odeyemi et al., 2024) detailed the implementation of a DSS in a major Nigerian bank. This resulted in the detection and prevention of fraudulent transactions worth millions of dollars. The bank employed algorithms that adaptively learned from historical fraud data, enabling it to make informed real-time decisions and enhancing its operational resilience against fraud.

Another case study (Z. Zhao and Bai, 2022), showcased how a healthcare organization implemented a machine-learning solution to process billing data. This solution identified anomalies, leading to the detection of fraudulent billing practices. The data-driven approach not only safeguarded financial resources but also improved patient care by ensuring compliance with healthcare regulations.

These case studies, along with empirical evidence, demonstrate the integral role of data analytics in enhancing the efficiency of fraud detection systems. The combination of industry-specific applications and empirical evidence provides a robust understanding of how AI-driven DSS is reshaping the landscape of fraud detection across sectors. By embracing innovative fraud detection methodologies, organizations can effectively reduce risk, enhance operational integrity, and maintain consumer trust in an increasingly digital world.

6.4 Example 1: Collaborative Research in Healthcare Fraud

Consider a scenario where a university research team collaborates with a healthcare provider and a government agency to develop an AI-powered fraud detection system for medical claims. The university researchers leverage their expertise in machine learning and data analytics, while the healthcare provider provides access to real-world claims data. The government agency offers regulatory guidance and oversight, ensuring the system's accuracy and reliability. This collaborative effort leads to a highly accurate fraud detection system that identifies suspicious claims with minimal false positives. Consequently, it reduces financial losses for the healthcare provider and enhances the integrity of the healthcare system. Qualitative data from law enforcement underscores the significance of national-local collaboration in combating cybercrime, emphasizing the value of collaboration in addressing complex challenges (Wang, 2023).

6.5 Example 2: Public-Private Partnership in Financial Fraud

In another instance, a financial institution collaborates with a cybersecurity firm and a regulatory body to develop a real-time fraud response system for online banking transactions. The financial institution provides access to transaction data and insights into fraud patterns, while the cybersecurity firm contributes its expertise in threat intelligence and incident response. The regulatory body ensures compliance with data protection laws and financial regulations. This collaborative effort leverages machine learning algorithms to detect and prevent fraudulent transactions in real time, safeguarding customers from financial losses and preserving the reputation of the financial institution. Public-private partnerships can also lead to the development of innovative solutions to combat financial crime, such as systems for detecting and preventing money laundering and terrorist financing. Moreover, multi-organizational partnerships between law enforcement agencies and financial institutions demonstrate how collaboration can effectively combat serious and organized crime (Fiorito et al., 2023). However, law enforcement and intelligence agencies in different countries and branches often face challenges due to technical and legal differences that complicate international cybercrime investigations.

The success of such partnerships highlights the significance of collaboration in addressing intricate challenges and developing effective solutions to combat financial fraud (Udeh et al., 2024). International cooperation and close collaboration with global service providers are paramount to securing data, conducting investigations, and tracing illicit funds in cross-border cybercrime cases (Velasco, 2022). Cybercrime necessitates law enforcement officials to enhance their technical knowledge and skills to effectively investigate and prosecute cybercriminals (Koziarski & Lee, 2020). Law enforcement agencies must collaborate with academia and the private sector to stay ahead of cybercriminals' evolving techniques and technologies (Amoo et al., 2024). Given the increasing number of criminal investigations and the borderless nature of the Internet, such collaborations require effective measures (Casino, Pina, et al., 2022). Cybersecurity is an ongoing race between attackers and defenders, necessitating law enforcement and other relevant organizations to continually adapt to the evolving threat landscape (Jahankhani et al., 2014). Law enforcement agencies and security practitioners must adapt to this ever-changing reality to prevent and combat crime (Demestichas et al., 2021). Understanding these technologies and their development is crucial for security and law enforcement professionals to perform their job roles effectively (Horan & Saiedian, 2021). Mutual legal assistance among nations can significantly contribute to combating cybercrime, resulting in a mutually beneficial situation (Rana & Awwal, 2020).

6.6 Example 3: Industry-Regulatory Partnership in Financial Fraud

Another impactful model involves an industry-regulatory partnership, particularly in addressing financial fraud. In this scenario, a financial institution collaborates with a regulatory body to proactively combat emerging fraud schemes and trends (Coelho et al., 2019). The financial institution shares its expertise in fraud detection and prevention, along with insights into the latest tactics employed by fraudsters. In return, the regulatory body provides guidance on compliance requirements and regulatory expectations. This collaboration leads to the development of industry-wide best practices for fraud prevention and the implementation of new regulatory measures to address emerging fraud risks (Casino, Pina, et al., 2022; Kierkegaard, 2015). Such collaboration ensures that regulatory frameworks remain relevant and effective in the face of evolving fraud schemes.

These examples demonstrate the potential of collaborative efforts in developing effective decision support systems for real-time fraud response. By leveraging the unique expertise and resources of researchers, industry, and regulatory bodies, it is possible to create more robust and adaptive systems that can effectively combat digital fraud and protect individuals and organizations from financial losses. To effectively combat financial cybercrime, new methods must be developed and deployed across organizations to prevent further losses to their business, customer data, and reputation (Nicholls et al., 2021). The integration of technological components significantly enhances the capacity to recognize and address cyber threats (Hafez et al., 2025). Technology firms, regulators, and law enforcement officials can use these solutions to identify and remove content in near real-time to proactively protect the public (Mackey, 2018).

7 ETHICAL CONSIDERATIONS AND GOVERNANCE

As organizations increasingly rely on AI-powered solutions for fraud detection and prevention, addressing ethical considerations and establishing robust governance frameworks becomes paramount to ensure responsible practices. Ethical policies prioritize protecting individual privacy, mitigating biases in AI algorithms, and safeguarding against the misuse of sensitive data, particularly in combating identity theft and fraud. These policies contribute to maintaining trust and transparency between organizations and their stakeholders.

Corporate governance strategies play a pivotal role in overseeing the deployment and operation of AI technologies. This includes implementing clear accountability structures, continuous monitoring for fairness and compliance, and fostering a culture of ethical awareness across all organizational levels. By integrating ethical principles with governance frameworks, organizations can maximize the benefits of AI-driven fraud prevention while minimizing risks associated with discrimination, privacy violations, and other unintended consequences (Jobin et al., 2019).

7.1 Examination of Ethical Policies in Combating Identity Theft and Fraud

The pervasive challenge of identity theft demands well-defined ethical policies that address the rights and responsibilities of stakeholders involved in preventing and responding to such crimes. Advocate for comprehensive ethical frameworks that guide organizations in managing identity theft risks, as emphasized by Payne and Kennett-Hensel (2017). These frameworks emphasize the dual necessity of legal compliance and moral responsibility, ensuring businesses adopt best practices to mitigate threats while protecting consumer rights and privacy.

Key components of these policies include ensuring transparency in personal data collection, use, and sharing, as well as establishing robust mechanisms for accountability and redress when identity theft occurs. Organizations are encouraged to foster a culture of ethics within their operations, where employees are trained to recognize identity theft risks and engage in practices that uphold consumer trust. Implementing measures such as identity theft protection services and informing customers about preventive actions further enhances ethical policies.

Furthermore, ethical frameworks must account for the psychological impacts of identity theft on victims. Studies show that emotional distress often follows instances of fraud, particularly among vulnerable populations (DeLiema et al., 2021). Addressing these human aspects through empathetic communication and support services is essential for a holistic approach to combating identity fraud.

7.2 Corporate Governance Strategies Supporting Responsible AI Use

Corporate governance plays a crucial role in ensuring that AI technologies are deployed responsibly in fraud detection contexts. Research emphasizes the importance of implementing effective governance strategies to support responsible AI use while maintaining stakeholder trust in fraud detection systems (Betz-Hamilton, 2023).

These strategies involve creating policies that outline the ethical implications of AI implementations, establishing oversight committees, and promoting transparency in algorithmic decisions.

A significant aspect of governance in AI fraud detection is the establishment of an ethical code that guides technological applications. This code ensures that systems do not inadvertently perpetuate biases or invade consumer privacy. For instance, involving diverse stakeholders in the development and implementation of AI systems can help identify and mitigate ethical concerns. Organizations are encouraged to adopt guidelines that support the continuous monitoring of AI systems, allowing for real-time adjustments to address any emergent ethical issues.

Furthermore, corporate governance strategies should integrate training programs aimed at promoting awareness of ethical AI practices across the organization. These programs ensure that employees understand the implications of the technology they use and how it may impact customers and other stakeholders. Such proactive measures contribute to building trust between companies and their customers, reinforcing the integrity of both the organization and its deployed technologies.

8 COLLABORATION BETWEEN RESEARCHERS, INDUSTRY, AND REGULATORY BODIES

Combating digital arrest fraud and identity theft in today's digital age demands a multifaceted strategy. Collaboration between researchers, industry practitioners, and regulatory bodies is crucial to advance decision support systems for real-time fraud response (Chang et al., 2024). The complexity of digital fraud necessitates a concerted effort to integrate diverse expertise and resources to develop more effective and adaptive solutions.

Financial fraud, a pervasive issue with far-reaching consequences, erodes confidence in the financial industry, destabilizes economies, and diminishes individuals' financial well-being (West et al., 2015). The rapid evolution of digital technologies has led to an unprecedented surge in digital financial fraud, creating an urgent need for innovative strategies to protect financial systems and consumers (Udeh et al., 2024).

However, the current landscape is characterized by inconsistencies in investigative approaches and practical challenges in tackling digital fraud, underscoring the need for a more standardized and effective response (Donegan, 2019). The volume of data generated by daily business operations poses a significant hurdle in combating fraud. The amount of data captured in investigations grows exponentially (Hipgrave, 2013). Integrating data from various sources, departments, and formats is further complicated by the transnational nature of fraud (Torres et al., 2024). The need for forensic accounting is constantly evolving with emerging technologies (Hossain, 2023).

8.1 The Need for Collaboration

The convergence of expertise from academia, industry, and regulatory agencies is crucial in developing decision support systems that excel at real-time fraud detection and prevention. Academic researchers contribute theoretical frameworks, advanced algorithms, and cutting-edge techniques for data analysis and pattern recognition (Haddad et al., 2024). Industry practitioners provide practical insights into the operational realities of fraud detection, highlighting the specific challenges and constraints faced by financial institutions and other organizations. Regulatory bodies offer essential oversight and guidance, ensuring that fraud detection systems comply with legal and ethical standards while also fostering innovation and collaboration. This collaborative approach ensures that decision support systems are grounded in rigorous research, tailored to real-world needs, and aligned with regulatory requirements, thereby enhancing their effectiveness and promoting widespread adoption. Forensic accountants must stay informed about the latest developments in data analytics to avoid relying solely on traditional methods for detecting fraud in the digital age (Akinbowale et al., 2023). The increasing prevalence of corporate malfeasance underscores the indispensable role of forensic accounting, a discipline that integrates accounting expertise, auditing protocols, and investigative prowess to identify and thwart fraud, corruption, and other financial improprieties (Haddad et al., 2024). The digital transformation of financial transactions has heightened the complexity and scale of fraud, necessitating continuous innovation in forensic accounting techniques. Financial frauds and scams have far-reaching consequences, impacting organizations regardless of their size or industry (Singleton & Singleton, 2010).

8.2 Digital Arrest Fraud and Identity Theft Landscape

In today's digital age, digital arrest fraud and identity theft pose significant threats due to their sophisticated techniques and rapidly evolving tactics (Odeyemi et al., 2024). Perpetrators of digital arrest fraud often employ social engineering tactics to deceive individuals into providing sensitive information or transferring funds under false pretenses. Identity theft, on the other hand, involves the unauthorized acquisition and use of personal information for fraudulent purposes, such as opening fraudulent accounts, making unauthorized purchases, or obtaining government benefits. The impact of these crimes can be devastating, leading to financial losses, reputational damage, and emotional distress for victims.

To effectively combat these threats, fraud risk management programs incorporate preventive and detective controls to mitigate the risk of fraud. However, fraud risk identification requires evaluating motivations, pressures, and possibilities for committing fraud. The dynamic nature of these threats necessitates constant vigilance and proactive measures to protect individuals and organizations from falling victim to these scams. The sophistication and volume of fraudulent activities have increased exponentially with the proliferation of emerging technologies and the expansion of digital financial ecosystems, posing unprecedented challenges for detection and prevention.

8.3 Collaboration Imperative for Enhanced Fraud Detection

Collaboration between researchers, industry practitioners, and regulatory bodies is crucial for advancing the development and deployment of effective decision support systems for real-time fraud response (Shen & Kurshan, 2020). Researchers can contribute their expertise in data analytics, machine learning, and cybersecurity to develop innovative algorithms and techniques for fraud detection. Industry practitioners can provide real-world data and insights into emerging fraud trends and vulnerabilities, informing the design and implementation of practical solutions (Mutemi & Bação, 2024). Regulatory bodies can establish standards and guidelines for data privacy, security, and transparency, ensuring that decision support systems are deployed responsibly and ethically. Financial institutions, regulatory organizations, and politicians must understand the effects and limitations of AI, as it offers promising solutions to reduce the risks associated with financial fraud (Adhikari et al., 2024). This collaborative approach fosters knowledge sharing, accelerates innovation, and promotes the adoption of best practices in fraud prevention and detection (Pan, 2024). Collaboration in combating scams involves a multifaceted approach, involving coordinated efforts between government agencies, financial institutions, telecommunications companies, and technology providers (Pappachan et al., 2025).

Financial crime detection requires an ongoing effort to identify aberrant transactions, including fraudulent transactions, unusual payments, and money laundering (Zhang et al., 2023). The need for collaboration across the financial services sector is highlighted in order to combat the GenAI-induced crime waves (Kurshan et al., 2024). Law enforcement organizations, financial institutions, and cybersecurity firms must work together to share threat information, coordinate investigations, and bring criminals to justice (Patil, 2025). By combining their resources and expertise, stakeholders can enhance their ability to detect, prevent, and respond to digital arrest fraud and identity theft effectively (V. Jain et al., 2024).

8.4 Current Challenges in Real-Time Fraud Response

Several challenges hinder the effectiveness of real-time fraud response, including data quality issues, model interpretability concerns, and integration complexities with existing systems (Pan, 2024). Fraud detection systems often face data imbalances, where legitimate transactions significantly outnumber fraudulent ones, potentially skewing the algorithm's ability to accurately identify fraudulent behavior (Yazıcı, 2020). Addressing these challenges necessitates a multifaceted approach involving data preprocessing techniques, explainable AI methods, and standardized integration protocols. Additionally, privacy regulations and ethical considerations restrict the collection, use, and sharing of sensitive data, limiting the development of comprehensive fraud detection models.

Interagency cooperation is crucial in tracking down and prosecuting fraudsters, especially when fraud crosses international borders. Overcoming these hurdles requires a concerted effort to promote data sharing initiatives, develop privacy-preserving technologies, and establish ethical guidelines for the use of AI in fraud detection.

A comprehensive fraud detection system should include continuous transaction monitoring, which involves applying predefined business rules, anomaly detection, and machine learning algorithms to identify unusual patterns indicative of fraud. To safeguard sensitive financial data, it is imperative to address privacy issues in fraud detection systems through the implementation of robust data encryption, anonymization methods, and adherence to relevant data privacy regulations.

The surge in digital activity, accelerated by events like the COVID-19 pandemic, has led to a corresponding increase in financial crime and fraud, underscoring the urgent need for enhanced fraud detection mechanisms (Rouhollahi, 2021). Real-time fraud detection would be highly beneficial, as it could prevent fraudsters from making subsequent transactions (West et al., 2015). The recent rise in mobile payment services has highlighted the growing need for automated detection systems that enable immediate detection and prevention of fraudulent transactions (Hajek et al., 2023).

8.5 Lack of Collaboration

The lack of collaboration between researchers and industry hinders the translation of academic findings into practical solutions. For instance, the effective implementation of AI and ML in financial fraud detection requires a thorough understanding of the algorithms, techniques, and tools used (Sowmya & Sathisha, 2023). However, the lack of standardized data formats and integration protocols impedes the seamless exchange of information between different systems and organizations (Mytnyk et al., 2023). Furthermore, the absence of clear regulatory frameworks and guidelines creates uncertainty and confusion, discouraging investment in innovative fraud detection technologies (Adhikari et al., 2024). Additionally, the limited availability of labeled training data and benchmark datasets restricts the development and evaluation of machine learning models for fraud detection.

To effectively implement AI and ML in financial fraud detection, researchers must understand the algorithms, techniques, and tools involved, as well as the challenges and limitations associated with their application (Sowmya & Sathisha, 2023). By employing sophisticated algorithms powered by ML, often in conjunction with rules, manual investigations can be significantly reduced. This combination offers considerable advantages over fraud detection based solely on rules (Uchhana et al., 2021).

The lack of collaboration poses a significant impediment to progress in combating digital arrest fraud and identity theft. To address this challenge, concerted efforts are required to foster partnerships, promote open communication, and establish shared goals among stakeholders.

8.6 Need for Collaboration: A Multifaceted Approach

Collaborative platforms and consortia can facilitate the exchange of best practices, threat intelligence, and data analytics expertise among researchers, industry practitioners, and regulatory bodies. This exchange can lead to the development of more comprehensive fraud detection models by streamlining data sharing and integration through the establishment of industry standards and protocols. However, these obstacles can be overcome by federated learning strategies, which enable collaborative model training without directly exchanging sensitive data (Awosika et al., 2024).

Regulatory sandboxes and innovation hubs provide a safe environment for testing and validating new fraud detection technologies. Additionally, data analytics and machine learning techniques can improve the detection of early-stage fraud by identifying subtle patterns and anomalies that may indicate fraudulent activity (Luo et al., 2023).

Furthermore, promoting educational initiatives and training programs can enhance the skills and knowledge of fraud detection professionals, enabling them to stay ahead of emerging threats. However, confirming suspected fraud in a timely manner can be challenging due to legal restrictions and delays in investigations, which may lead to inaccurate or unknown labels (Vanini et al., 2023).

Fraudsters continuously adapt their strategies, so models need to be updated frequently to remain effective (Binsawad, 2025). Establishing open communication channels and knowledge-sharing networks can promote collaboration and coordination among stakeholders, leading to a more unified and effective response to fraud.

To proactively combat the evolving landscape of digital fraud, decision support systems must incorporate real-time data feeds, advanced analytics, and machine learning algorithms (Rudman et al., 2009).

Collaboration between researchers, industry, and regulatory bodies is crucial in shaping the future direction of decision support systems for real-time fraud response (Correia et al., 2017; Spann, 2012; Tax et al., 2021; L. Zhao et al., 2021). Establishing trust and transparency in AI systems is vital for their adoption and acceptance by stakeholders (Wang, 2023). Additionally, the creation of interpretability tools and explainable AI techniques can enhance understanding of model behavior and decision-making processes (Patil, 2025).

8.7 Benefits of Collaboration

Collaboration between researchers, industry, and regulatory bodies offers several key benefits in combating digital arrest fraud and identity theft. By sharing expertise and resources, they can accelerate innovation and the development of advanced fraud detection technologies. Artificial intelligence fraud detection systems are becoming increasingly common, but it's crucial to carefully assess their effectiveness across various industries to avoid exacerbating existing issues (Adhikari et al., 2024). Continuous benchmarking of payment card fraud detection methods in the industry is essential to ensure the successful implementation of artificial intelligence and machine learning (Ryman-Tubb et al., 2018). This collaboration also helps align research efforts with industry needs, ensuring that new technologies are practical and effective in real-world scenarios.

Regulatory bodies play a vital role in providing guidance and oversight to ensure that fraud detection systems comply with ethical standards and legal requirements. The ultimate goal of this cooperation is to transform regulatory compliance into a proactive and predictive model, ultimately leading to a more reliable and secure financial system (V. Jain et al., 2024). This collaboration fosters a level playing field, preventing unfair competition and promoting consumer protection. The strategy utilizes machine learning, natural language processing, and predictive analytics to process vast amounts of data and identify trends indicative of fraud. Additionally, it addresses ethical concerns associated with AI, such as data privacy and the need for transparency in AI decision-making (Pappachan et al., 2024).

8.8 Framework for Collaboration

To foster effective collaboration, it's crucial to establish a well-defined framework that outlines the roles, responsibilities, and communication channels for all stakeholders. This framework should promote transparency, trust, and mutual understanding, enabling participants to work together towards common goals. Clear guidelines and protocols for data sharing, privacy protection, and intellectual property rights are essential components of such a framework. Regular meetings, workshops, and conferences provide opportunities for researchers, industry experts, and regulators to exchange ideas, share experiences, and build relationships. These platforms also serve as forums for discussing challenges, identifying opportunities, and developing joint initiatives.

Hybrid digital forensic task forces, which involve formal partnerships between educational institutions and law enforcement agencies, exemplify effective collaboration by enhancing education, research, and investigative capacity in the digital forensic field (Dolliver et al., 2017). To drive harmonization and knowledge management, investigative advisors with operational experience and forensic advisors with scientific backgrounds are essential (Casey, 2019). Sharing systems that facilitate the sharing of training materials and actionable intelligence for ongoing cases should be developed at the regional or national level (Woods et al., 2023). A clear framework for collaboration promotes trust, transparency, and mutual understanding, enabling participants to work effectively toward common goals.

The establishment of consortia or partnerships involving academic institutions, industry players, and regulatory agencies can facilitate collaborative research and development projects. These collaborations can also help ensure that decision support systems are aligned with legal and ethical standards (Casino, Dasaklis, et al., 2022).

8.9 Joint Research Initiatives

Collaborative research projects that involve researchers, industry experts, and regulators can yield valuable insights and accelerate innovation in fraud detection and response. These initiatives focus on developing new algorithms, testing emerging technologies, and evaluating the effectiveness of different intervention strategies. These collaborative studies are driven by individual efforts and government support, leading to the development of several models of cooperation that hold promise for continued partnership (Silver et al., 2021). These projects also provide opportunities for interdisciplinary learning and knowledge transfer, fostering a more holistic understanding of the challenges and opportunities in this field. According to Edmond Lockard's exchange principle, digital forensics would benefit from closer collaborations and cross-topic research, as researchers and practitioners often attempt to find solutions to the same problems simultaneously (Casino, Pina, et al., 2022).

Establishing digital forensics as a field requires a substantial number of researchers, academics, and educators to address research agendas and teaching concerns (Cooper et al., 2010). Through joint research, relevant agencies can expand their scope of services, promptly investigate national case requests, open more cases for international investigations, and better meet the needs of their citizens (James & Jang, 2014). Joint research projects between universities and industry facilitate the exchange of knowledge and the development of practical solutions to real-world problems (Nikkel, 2020). Digital forensic investigators face challenges related to systems availability, usability, and computer-supported collaborative work, underscoring the need for user-centric workflows and tools (Nouh et al., 2019).

9 FUTURE DIRECTIONS: EMERGING TRENDS IN AI AND MACHINE LEARNING FOR IMPROVING FRAUD DETECTION

The landscape of fraud detection is undergoing rapid transformation due to advancements in artificial intelligence (AI) and machine learning (ML). Financial institutions and organizations must adapt to these changes by identifying emerging trends and collaborating among stakeholders to ensure the ethical deployment of these technologies (Rahaman et al., 2025).

The ongoing integration of AI and ML technologies is reshaping fraud detection methodologies. Research has highlighted the transformative potential of advanced AI models, such as deep learning, generative models, and reinforcement learning, in enhancing fraud prevention (N. Jain & Patil, 2024). These models offer improved accuracy and the ability to automate decision-making processes, particularly beneficial in detecting sophisticated fraudulent schemes that traditional methods might overlook.

Future directions in AI-driven fraud detection include exploring novel algorithms like federated learning. This approach allows multiple institutions to collaborate on fraud detection efforts without compromising sensitive customer data (N. Jain & Patil, 2024; Ramachandran et al., 2024). Federated learning facilitates shared learning from diverse data sets while maintaining privacy, representing a significant step forward in enhancing the robustness of fraud detection systems.

The integration of explainable AI is also gaining importance in fraud detection. As organizations strive to understand and trust AI algorithms, ensuring that decision-making processes are transparent and interpretable is crucial (Ramachandran et al., 2024). This aligns with the overall trend toward improving accountability and ethical considerations in technology deployments.

10 CONCLUSION

In conclusion, the deployment of AI-driven Decision Support Systems (DSS) plays a crucial role in enhancing digital security, particularly in the realm of fraud detection and prevention. These advanced technologies have the remarkable ability to analyze vast amounts of transactional data in real-time, enabling organizations to identify and mitigate fraudulent activities before they escalate. This proactive approach significantly reduces financial losses and enhances consumer trust (Sontan & Samuel, 2024).

Throughout this discussion, it has been evident that AI's capacity to learn from historical patterns, adapt to emerging fraud tactics, and facilitate automated decision-making makes it a transformative force in combating fraud and identity theft (Shahana et al., 2024). However, as we embrace these technological advancements, it is imperative to prioritize ethical considerations and governance. Organizations must manage the complexities of deploying AI responsibly, ensuring that their use of technology aligns with ethical standards and regulatory compliance (Pasha et al., 2022).

Establishing guidelines that address the implications of AI on privacy, accountability, and potential biases inherent in algorithmic decision-making is crucial. By doing so, stakeholders can foster public trust and confidence in AI-driven fraud detection systems.

Looking forward, collaboration across researchers, industry leaders, and regulatory bodies is essential to establish a framework for ethical AI practices in fraud detection (Samtani et al., 2020). This partnership will enhance the development of responsible technology and create an environment where innovations in AI can be applied confidently and ethically.

In summary, the journey ahead must be characterized by a commitment to continuous innovation and ethical responsibility. By fostering collaborative efforts and adhering to principles that prioritize societal well-being, we can harness the full potential of AI-driven DSS to create a secure digital landscape for all stakeholders (Baird & Clare, 2017).

REFERENCES

Adelakun, B. O., Onwubuariri, E. R., Adeniran, G. A., & Ntiakoh, A. (2024). Enhancing fraud detection in accounting through AI: Techniques and case studies. *Finance & Accounting Research Journal*, *6*(6), 978–999. DOI: 10.51594/farj.v6i6.1232

Adhikari, P., Hamal, P., & Baidoo, F. (2024). Artificial Intelligence in fraud detection: Revolutionizing financial security. *International Journal of Science and Research Archive*, *13*(1), 1457–1472. DOI: 10.30574/ijsra.2024.13.1.1860

Akinbowale, O. E., Mashigo, P., & Zerihun, M. F. (2023). The integration of forensic accounting and big data technology frameworks for internal fraud mitigation in the banking industry. *Cogent Business & Management*, *10*(1), 2163560. Advance online publication. DOI: 10.1080/23311975.2022.2163560

Amasiatu, C. V., & Shah, M. H. (2018). First party fraud management: Framework for the retail industry. *International Journal of Retail & Distribution Management*, *46*(4), 350–363. DOI: 10.1108/IJRDM-10-2016-0185

Amoo, O. O., Atadoga, A., Abrahams, T. O., Farayola, O. A., Osasona, F., & Ayinla, B. S. (2024). The legal landscape of cybercrime: A review of contemporary issues in the criminal justice system. In World Journal of Advanced Research and Reviews (Vol. 21, Issue 2, pp. 205–217). GSC Online Press. DOI: 10.30574/wjarr.2024.21.2.0438

Angela, O., Atoyebi, I., Soyele, A., & Ogunwobi, E. (2024). *Enhancing Fraud Detection and Prevention in Fintech: Big Data and Machine Learning Approaches*. World Journal of Advanced Research and Reviews., DOI: 10.30574/wjarr.2024.24.2.3617

Awosika, T., Shukla, R. M., & Pranggono, B. (2024). Transparency and Privacy: The Role of Explainable AI and Federated Learning in Financial Fraud Detection. *IEEE Access : Practical Innovations, Open Solutions*, *12*, 64551–64560. DOI: 10.1109/ACCESS.2024.3394528

Baesens, B. (2023). Fraud analytics: A research. *Journal of Chinese Economic and Business Studies*, *21*(1), 137–141. DOI: 10.1080/14765284.2022.2162246

Baird, M., & Clare, J. (2017). Removing the opportunity for contract cheating in business capstones: A crime prevention case study. *International Journal for Educational Integrity*, *13*(1), 6. Advance online publication. DOI: 10.1007/s40979-017-0018-1

Betz-Hamilton, A. (2023). Reporting behaviours of familiar identity theft victims: An empirical test of Black's theory of law. *Journal of Financial Crime*, *30*(4), 1055–1065. DOI: 10.1108/JFC-04-2022-0085

Binsawad, M. (2025). Enhanced Financial Fraud Detection Using an Adaptive Voted Perceptron Model with Optimized Learning and Error Reduction. *Electronics (Basel), 14*(9), 1875. DOI: 10.3390/electronics14091875

Bolton, R. J., & Hand, D. J. (2002). Statistical fraud detection: A review. *Statistical Science, 17*(3), 235–255. DOI: 10.1214/ss/1042727940

Carminati, M., Caron, R., Maggi, F., Epifani, I., & Zanero, S. (2015). BankSealer: A decision support system for online banking fraud analysis and investigation. *Computers & Security, 53*, 175–186. DOI: 10.1016/j.cose.2015.04.002

Casey, E. (2019). The chequered past and risky future of digital forensics. *The Australian Journal of Forensic Sciences, 51*(6), 649–664. DOI: 10.1080/00450618.2018.1554090

Casino, F., Dasaklis, T. K., Spathoulas, G. P., Anagnostopoulos, M., Ghosal, A., Borocz, I., Solanas, A., Conti, M., & Patsakis, C. (2022). Research Trends, Challenges, and Emerging Topics in Digital Forensics: A Review of Reviews. In Access, I. E. E. E. (Ed.), Vol. 10, pp. 25464–25493). Cornell University., DOI: 10.1109/ACCESS.2022.3154059

Casino, F., Pina, C., López-Aguilar, P., Batista, E., Solanas, A., & Patsakis, C. (2022). SoK: Cross-border criminal investigations and digital evidence. *Journal of Cybersecurity, 8*(1), tyac014. Advance online publication. DOI: 10.1093/cybsec/tyac014

Cho, S. T. (2023). Fraud Detection in Malaysian Financial Institutions using Data Mining and Machine Learning. *Journal of Information Technology, 7*(1), 13–21. DOI: 10.53819/81018102t4152

Chopra, P. K., & Binwal, A. (2024). *The Role of AI/ML in Enhancing Security and Fraud Detection in Digital Payments*. International Journal for Multidisciplinary Research., DOI: 10.36948/ijfmr.2024.v06i06.30337

Cirqueira, D., Helfert, M., & Bezbradica, M. (2021). Towards Design Principles for User-Centric Explainable AI in Fraud Detection. Lecture Notes in Computer Science (Including Subseries Lecture Notes in Artificial Intelligence and Lecture Notes in Bioinformatics), 12797 LNAI, 21–40. DOI: 10.1007/978-3-030-77772-2_2

Coelho, R., De Simoni, M., & Prenio, J. (2019). Suptech applications for anti-money laundering. FSI Insights on Policy Implementationon Policy Implementation, 18. https://www.bis.org/fsi/publ/insights18.htm

Cooper, P., Finley, G. T., & Kaskenpalo, P. (2010). Towards standards in digital forensics education. Proceedings of the Conference on Integrating Technology into Computer Science Education, ITiCSE, 87–95. DOI: 10.1145/1971681.1971688

Correia, I., Artikis, A., Katzouris, N., Baber, C., Morar, N., Skarbovsky, I., Fournier, F., & Paliouras, G. (2017). Demo: Demonstration of a prototype for credit card fraud management. DEBS 2017 - Proceedings of the 11th ACM International Conference on Distributed Event-Based Systems, 335–338. DOI: 10.1145/3093742.3095096

Daiya, H. (2024). AI-Driven Risk Management Strategies in Financial Technology. Journal of Artificial Intelligence General Science (JAIGS) ISSN:3006-4023, 5(1), 194–216. DOI: 10.60087/jaigs.v5i1.194

DeLiema, M., Burnes, D., & Langton, L. (2021). The Financial and Psychological Impact of Identity Theft Among Older Adults. *Innovation in Aging*, *5*(4), igab043. Advance online publication. DOI: 10.1093/geroni/igab043 PMID: 34988295

Demestichas, K., Peppes, N., Alexakis, T., & Adamopoulou, E. (2021). An advanced abnormal behaviour detection engine embedding autoencoders for the investigation of financial transactions. *Information (Basel)*, *12*(1), 1–18. DOI: 10.3390/info12010034

Dolliver, D. S., Collins, C., & Sams, B. (2017). Hybrid approaches to digital forensic investigations: A comparative analysis in an institutional context. *Digital Investigation*, *23*, 124–137. DOI: 10.1016/j.diin.2017.10.005

Donegan, M. (2019). Crime script for mandate fraud. *Journal of Money Laundering Control*, *22*(4), 770–781. DOI: 10.1108/JMLC-03-2019-0025

Esenogho, E., Mienye, I. D., Swart, T. G., Aruleba, K., & Obaido, G. (2022). A Neural Network Ensemble with Feature Engineering for Improved Credit Card Fraud Detection. *IEEE Access : Practical Innovations, Open Solutions*, *10*, 16400–16407. DOI: 10.1109/ACCESS.2022.3148298

Faraji, Z. (2022). A Review of Machine Learning Applications for Credit Card Fraud Detection with A Case study. *SEISENSE Journal of Management*, *5*(1), 49–59. DOI: 10.33215/sjom.v5i1.770

Fiorito, T. L., Nagel, C., Veenswijk, M. B., & Drori, I. (2023). Navigating Paradoxical Tensions in the Context of Coopetition: Emotional Transcendence in a Dutch Public–Private Partnership. *Journal of Change Management*, *23*(2), 177–199. DOI: 10.1080/14697017.2023.2197908

Gaurav, A., Pan, V. S.-H., Arya, V., Attar, R. W., Alhazmi, A. H., Alhomoud, A., Gupta, B. B., & Chui, K. T. (2025). Defense-optimized BERT architecture against digital arrest attacks in intelligent systems. *Telecommunication Systems: Modelling, Analysis. Design and Management*, *88*(3), 1–9.

Gupta, B. B., Gaurav, A., Attar, R. W., Arya, V., Bansal, S., Alhomoud, A., & Chui, K. T. (2025). A hybrid Ant Lion Optimization algorithm based lightweight deep learning framework for cyber attack detection in IoT environment. *Computers & Electrical Engineering*, *122*, 109944. DOI: 10.1016/j.compeleceng.2024.109944

Haddad, H., Alharasis, E. E., Fraij, J., & Al-Ramahi, N. M. (2024). How Do Innovative Improvements in Forensic Accounting and Its Related Technologies Sweeten Fraud Investigation and Prevention? *WSEAS Transactions on Business and Economics*, *21*, 1115–1141. DOI: 10.37394/23207.2024.21.93

Hafez, I. Y., Hafez, A. Y., Saleh, A., Abd El-Mageed, A. A., & Abohany, A. A. (2025). A systematic review of AI-enhanced techniques in credit card fraud detection. In Journal of Big Data (Vol. 12, Issue 1). Springer Science+Business Media. DOI: 10.1186/s40537-024-01048-8

Hajek, P., Abedin, M. Z., & Sivarajah, U. (2023). Fraud Detection in Mobile Payment Systems using an XGBoost-based Framework. *Information Systems Frontiers*, *25*(5), 1985–2003. DOI: 10.1007/s10796-022-10346-6 PMID: 36258679

Henriques, J., Caldeira, F., Cruz, T., & Simões, P. (2022). An automated closed-loop framework to enforce security policies from anomaly detection. *Computers & Security*, *123*, 102949. Advance online publication. DOI: 10.1016/j.cose.2022.102949

Hipgrave, S. (2013). Smarter fraud investigations with big data analytics. *Network Security*, *2013*(12), 7–9. DOI: 10.1016/S1353-4858(13)70135-1

Horan, C., & Saiedian, H. (2021). Cyber Crime Investigation: Landscape, Challenges, and Future Research Directions. *Journal of Cybersecurity and Privacy*, *1*(4), 580–596. DOI: 10.3390/jcp1040029

Hossain, M. Z. (2023). Emerging Trends in Forensic Accounting: Data Analytics, Cyber Forensic Accounting, Cryptocurrencies, and Blockchain Technology for Fraud Investigation and Prevention. SSRN Electronic Journal. DOI: 10.2139/ssrn.4450488

Huda, S. Aripin, Naufal, M. F., Martianova Yudianingtias, V., & Anisti. (2020). Fraud Patterns Classification: A study of Fraud in business Process of Indonesian Online Sales Transaction. MECnIT 2020 - International Conference on Mechanical, Electronics, Computer, and Industrial Technology, 212–217. DOI: 10.1109/MECnIT48290.2020.9166644

Ismaeil, M. K. A. (2024). Harnessing AI for Next-Generation Financial Fraud Detection: A Data-Driven Revolution. *Journal of Ecohumanism*, *3*(7), 811–821. DOI: 10.62754/joe.v3i7.4248

Jahankhani, H., Al-Nemrat, A., & Hosseinian-Far, A. (2014). Cybercrime classification and characteristics. In *Cyber Crime and Cyber Terrorism Investigator's Handbook* (pp. 149–164). Elsevier BV., DOI: 10.1016/B978-0-12-800743-3.00012-8

Jain, A. K., & Gupta, B. B. (2019). A machine learning based approach for phishing detection using hyperlinks information. *Journal of Ambient Intelligence and Humanized Computing*, *10*(5), 2015–2028. DOI: 10.1007/s12652-018-0798-z

Jain, A. K., Gupta, B. B., Kaur, K., Bhutani, P., Alhalabi, W., & Almomani, A. (2022). A content and URL analysis-based efficient approach to detect smishing SMS in intelligent systems. *International Journal of Intelligent Systems*, *37*(12), 11117–11141. DOI: 10.1002/int.23035

Jain, N., & Patil, S. (2024). *Artificial Intelligence Models for Fraud Detection: Advancements*. Challenges, and Future Prospects., DOI: 10.21428/e90189c8.6d8ab5f6

Jain, V., Balakrishnan, A., Beeram, D., Najana, M., & Chintale, P. (2024). Leveraging Artificial Intelligence for Enhancing Regulatory Compliance in the Financial Sector. *International Journal of Computer Trends and Technology*, *72*(5), 124–140. DOI: 10.14445/22312803/IJCTT-V72I5P116

James, J. I., & Jang, Y. J. (2014). Measuring digital crime investigation capacity to guide international crime prevention strategies. In Lecture Notes in Electrical Engineering: Vol. 276 LNEE (pp. 361–366). Springer Science+Business Media. DOI: 10.1007/978-3-642-40861-8_51

Jobin, A., Ienca, M., & Vayena, E. (2019). The global landscape of AI ethics guidelines. *Nature Machine Intelligence*, *1*(9), 389–399. DOI: 10.1038/s42256-019-0088-2

Kierkegaard, S. M. (2015). Cracking Down On Cybercrime Global Response: The Cybercrime Convention. *Communications of the IIMA*, *5*(1). Advance online publication. DOI: 10.58729/1941-6687.1255

Koziarski, J., & Lee, J. R. (2020). Connecting evidence-based policing and cybercrime. *Policing*, *43*(1), 198–211. DOI: 10.1108/PIJPSM-07-2019-0107

Kurshan, E., Mehta, D., Bruss, B., & Balch, T. (2024). AI versus AI in Financial Crimes and Detection: GenAI Crime Waves to Co-Evolutionary AI. ArXiv (Cornell University). /arxiv.2410.09066DOI: 10.1145/3677052.3698655

Lai, K. K. (2023). *Machine Learning in Financial Fraud Detection: Real-Time Approaches and Challenges*. Financial Technology Press.

Lei, J. Z., & Ghorbani, A. A. (2012). Improved competitive learning neural networks for network intrusion and fraud detection. *Neurocomputing*, *75*(1), 135–145. DOI: 10.1016/j.neucom.2011.02.021

Luo, B., Zhen, Z., Wang, Q., Ke, A., Lu, S., & He, B. (2023). AI-powered Fraud Detection in Decentralized Finance: A Project Life Cycle Perspective. ArXiv (Cornell University). https://doi.org//arxiv.2308.15992DOI: 10.48550

Mackey, T. K. (2018). Opioids and the Internet: Convergence of Technology and Policy to Address the Illicit Online Sales of Opioids. *Health Services Insights*, *11*, 1178632918800995. Advance online publication. DOI: 10.1177/1178632918800995 PMID: 30245569

Majumder, T. (2024). The Evaluating Impact of Artificial Intelligence on Risk Management and Fraud Detection in the Commercial Bank in Bangladesh. *International Journal of Applied and Natural Sciences*, *1*(1), 67–76. DOI: 10.61424/ijans.v1i1.75

Mazumder, M. S. A., Rahman, M. A., & Chakraborty, D. (2024). Patient Care and Financial Integrity in Healthcare Billing Through Advanced Fraud Detection Systems. Academic Journal on Business Administration. *Innovation & Sustainability*, *4*(2), 82–93. DOI: 10.69593/ajbais.v4i2.74

Mohan, R., Boopathi, M., Ranjan, P., Najana, M., Chaudhary, P. K., & Chotrani, A. K. (2024). Ai in Fraud Detection: Evaluating the Efficacy of Artificial Intelligence in Preventing Financial Misconduct. *Journal of Electrical Systems*, *20*(3s), 1332–1338. DOI: 10.52783/jes.1508

Muhamed, S. J. (2022). Detection and Prevention WEB-Service for Fraudulent E-Transaction using APRIORI and SVM. *Al-Mustansiriyah Journal of Science*, *33*(4), 72–79. DOI: 10.23851/mjs.v33i4.1242

Mutemi, A., & Bação, F. (2024). E-Commerce Fraud Detection Based on Machine Learning Techniques: Systematic Literature Review. *Big Data Mining and Analytics*, *7*(2), 419–444. DOI: 10.26599/BDMA.2023.9020023

Mytnyk, B., Tkachyk, O., Shakhovska, N., Федушко, С., & Syerov, Y. (2023). Application of Artificial Intelligence for Fraudulent Banking Operations Recognition. *Big Data and Cognitive Computing*, *7*(2), 93. DOI: 10.3390/bdcc7020093

Negi, D. (2021). Automating Fraud Detection in Financial Services: An AI-based Approach. *Mathematical Statistician and Engineering Applications*, *70*(2), 1315–1325. DOI: 10.17762/msea.v70i2.2323

Ngai, E. W. T., Hu, Y., Wong, Y. H., Chen, Y., & Sun, X. (2011). The application of data mining techniques in financial fraud detection: A classification framework and an academic review of literature. *Decision Support Systems*, *50*(3), 559–569. DOI: 10.1016/j.dss.2010.08.006

Nicholls, J., Kuppa, A., & Le-Khac, N. A. (2021). Financial cybercrime: A comprehensive survey of deep learning approaches to tackle the evolving financial crime landscape. *IEEE Access : Practical Innovations, Open Solutions*, *9*, 163965–163986. DOI: 10.1109/ACCESS.2021.3134076

Nikkel, B. (2020). Fintech forensics: Criminal investigation and digital evidence in financial technologies. *Forensic Science International Digital Investigation*, *33*, 200908. DOI: 10.1016/j.fsidi.2020.200908

Nouh, M., Nurse, J. R. C., Webb, H., & Goldsmith, M. (2019). *Cybercrime Investigators are Users Too!* Understanding the Socio-Technical Challenges Faced by Law Enforcement., DOI: 10.14722/usec.2019.23032

Odeyemi, O., Ibeh, C. V., Mhlongo, N. Z., Asuzu, O. F., Awonuga, K. F., & Olatoye, F. O. (2024). FORENSIC ACCOUNTING AND FRAUD DETECTION: A REVIEW OF TECHNIQUES IN THE DIGITAL AGE. In Finance & Accounting Research Journal (Vol. 6, Issue 2, pp. 202–214). Fair East Publishers. DOI: 10.51594/farj.v6i2.788

Odeyemi, O., Mhlongo, N. Z., Nwankwo, E. E., & Soyombo, O. T. (2024). Reviewing the role of AI in fraud detection and prevention in financial services. *International Journal of Science and Research Archive*, *11*(1), 2101–2110. DOI: 10.30574/ijsra.2024.11.1.0279

Omair, B., & Alturki, A. (2020). A Systematic Literature Review of Fraud Detection Metrics in Business Processes. *IEEE Access : Practical Innovations, Open Solutions*, *8*, 26893–26903. DOI: 10.1109/ACCESS.2020.2971604

Pan, E. (2024). Machine Learning in Financial Transaction Fraud Detection and Prevention. Transactions on Economics. *Business and Management Research*, *5*, 243–249. DOI: 10.62051/16r3aa10

Pappachan, P., Rahaman, M., Cages, N., & Gupta, B. B. (2025). Case Studies of Cyber Incidents in Space Missions. In *Advanced Cyber Defense for Space Missions and Operations: Concepts and Applications* (pp. 383–400). IGI Global Scientific Publishing. DOI: 10.4018/979-8-3693-7939-4.ch016

Pappachan, P., Rahaman, M., Sreerakuvandana, S., Bansal, S., & Arya, V. (2024). Beyond Current Cryptography: Exploring New Frontiers. In *Innovations in Modern Cryptography* (pp. 1–30). IGI Global Scientific Publishing. DOI: 10.4018/979-8-3693-5330-1.ch001

Pasha, S. A., Ali, S., & Jeljeli, R. (2022). *Artificial Intelligence Implementation to Counteract Cybercrimes Against Children in Pakistan*. Human Arenas., DOI: 10.1007/s42087-022-00312-8

Patil, D. (2025). Artificial Intelligence In Financial Risk Assessment And Fraud Detection: Opportunities And Ethical Concerns. SSRN Electronic Journal. DOI: 10.2139/ssrn.5057434

Payne, D., & Kennett-Hensel, P. A. (2017). Combatting Identity Theft: A Proposed Ethical Policy Statement and Best Practices. *Business and Society Review*, *122*(3), 393–420. DOI: 10.1111/basr.12121

Phua, C., Lee, V., Smith, K., & Gayler, R. (2010). A comprehensive survey of data mining-based fraud detection research. arXiv preprint arXiv:1009.6119. https://arxiv.org/abs/1009.6119

Rahaman, M., Cajes, N., Gupta, B. B., Nedjah, N., & Chui, K. T. (2025). Real-Time Machine Learning Techniques in Robotics for Detecting Phishing Attacks. *2025 IEEE International Conference on Real-Time Computing and Robotics (RCAR)*, 1124–1129. DOI: 10.1109/RCAR65431.2025.11139819

Rahmati, M. (2025). Real-Time Financial Fraud Detection Using Adaptive Graph Neural Networks and Federated Learning. DOI: 10.21203/rs.3.rs-6026136/v1

Ramachandran, M. S., Sajithabanu, S., Ponmalar, A., Mohamed Sithik, M., & Jose Anand, A. (2024). Fraud Detection and Risk Management Using AI in Business Intelligence. 117–150. DOI: 10.4018/979-8-3693-5288-5.ch005

Rana, S., & Awwal, M. R. (2020). Reasons behind Money Laundering and Ways to Controlling it in Bangladesh. Canadian Journal of Business and Information Studies, 157–169. DOI: 10.34104/cjbis.020.01570169

Rouhollahi, Z. (2021). Towards Artificial Intelligence Enabled Financial Crime Detection. ArXiv (Cornell University). https://doi.org//arxiv.2105.10866DOI: 10.48550

Rudman, W. J., Eberhardt, J., Pierce, W. S., & Hart-Hester, S. (2009). *Health Care Fraud and Abuse*. Health Care Policy and Politics A to Z., DOI: 10.4135/9781452240121.n149

Samtani, S., Kantarcioglu, M., & Chen, H. (2020). Trailblazing the Artificial Intelligence for Cybersecurity Discipline: A Multi-Disciplinary Research Roadmap. *ACM Transactions on Management Information Systems, 11*(4), 1–19. Advance online publication. DOI: 10.1145/3430360

Shahana, A., Hasan, R., Farabi, S. F., Akter, J., Al Mahmud, M. A., Johora, F. T., & Suzer, G. (2024). AI-Driven Cybersecurity: Balancing Advancements and Safeguards. *Journal of Computer Science and Technology Studies*, *6*(2), 76–85. DOI: 10.32996/jcsts.2024.6.2.9

Sharma, R., Harish, V., & Rana, G. (2024). Navigating Risk. In *The Age Of Artificial Intelligence: Assessing And Identifying Risks With AI Strategies*. Educational Administration Theory and Practices., DOI: 10.53555/kuey.v30i4.1824

Shen, H., & Kurshan, E. (2020). Deep Q-network-based adaptive alert threshold selection policy for payment fraud systems in retail banking. 1–7. DOI: 10.1145/3383455.3422563

Shoetan, P. O., & Familoni, B. T.Philip Olaseni ShoetanBabajide Tolulope Familoni. (2024). Transforming Fintech Fraud Detection With Advanced Artificial Intelligence Algorithms. *Finance & Accounting Research Journal*, *6*(4), 602–625. DOI: 10.51594/farj.v6i4.1036

Silver, J., Craun, S. W., Wyman, J. V., & Simons, A. B. (2021). A coproduction research model between academia and law enforcement responsible for investigating threats. *Journal of Policing Intelligence and Counter Terrorism*, *16*(1), 32–43. DOI: 10.1080/18335330.2021.1880018

Singleton, T., & Singleton, A. J. (2010). Fraud Auditing and Forensic Accounting. DOI: 10.1002/9781118269183

Snorovikhina, V., & Zaytsev, A. (2021). Unsupervised Anomaly Detection for Discrete Sequence Healthcare Data. Lecture Notes in Computer Science (Including Subseries Lecture Notes in Artificial Intelligence and Lecture Notes in Bioinformatics), 12602 LNCS, 391–403. DOI: 10.1007/978-3-030-72610-2_30

Sontan, A. D., & Samuel, S. V.Adewale Daniel SontanSegun Victor Samuel. (2024). The Intersection of Artificial Intelligence and Cybersecurity: Challenges and Opportunities. *World Journal of Advanced Research and Reviews*, *21*(2), 1720–1736. DOI: 10.30574/wjarr.2024.21.2.0607

Sowmya, G. S., & Sathisha, H. K.Sowmya G SSathisha H K. (2023). Detecting Financial Fraud in the Digital Age: The AI and ML Revolution. *International Journal For Multidisciplinary Research*, *5*(5), 6139. Advance online publication. DOI: 10.36948/ijfmr.2023.v05i05.6139

Spann, D. (2012). *The Evolution of Fraud Analytics*., DOI: 10.1002/9781118284049

Tax, N., de Vries, K. J., de Jong, M., Dosoula, N., van den Akker, B., Smith, J., Thuong, O., & Bernardi, L. (2021). Machine Learning for Fraud Detection in E-Commerce: A Research Agenda. In Communications in computer and information science (pp. 30–54). Springer Science+Business Media. DOI: 10.1007/978-3-030-87839-9_2

Torres, J. A. S., da Silva, D. A., de Oliveira Albuquerque, R., Nze, G. D. A., Orozco, A. L. S., & Villalba, L. J. G. (2024). Ontology Development for Asset Concealment Investigation: A Methodological Approach and Case Study in Asset Recovery. *Applied Sciences (Basel, Switzerland)*, *14*(21), 9654. DOI: 10.3390/app14219654

Uchhana, N., Ranjan, R., Sharma, S., Agrawal, D., & Punde, A. (2021). Literature Review of Different Machine Learning Algorithms for Credit Card Fraud Detection. *International Journal of Innovative Technology and Exploring Engineering*, *10*(6), 101–108. DOI: 10.35940/ijitee.C8400.0410621

Udeh, E. O., Amajuoyi, P., Adeusi, K. B., & Scott, A. O. (2024). The role of big data in detecting and preventing financial fraud in digital transactions. *World Journal of Advanced Research and Reviews*, *22*(2), 1746–1760. DOI: 10.30574/wjarr.2024.22.2.1575

Vajrobol, V., Gupta, B. B., & Gaurav, A. (2024). Mutual information based logistic regression for phishing URL detection. *Cyber Security and Applications*, *2*, 100044. DOI: 10.1016/j.csa.2024.100044

Vanini, P., Rossi, S., Zvizdic, E., & Domenig, T. (2023). Online payment fraud: From anomaly detection to risk management. *Financial Innovation*, *9*(1), 66. Advance online publication. DOI: 10.1186/s40854-023-00470-w

Vashishth, T. K., Chaudhary, A., Sharma, V., Chaudhary, S., Sharma, N., Sharma, R., Kaushik, V., & Sharma, S. (2025). Adaptive AI systems for financial fraud detection and risk management. Artificial Intelligence for Financial Risk Management and Analysis, 431–453. DOI: 10.4018/979-8-3373-1200-2.ch021

Velasco, C. (2022). Cybercrime and Artificial Intelligence. An overview of the work of international organizations on criminal justice and the international applicable instruments. ERA Forum, 23(1), 109–126. DOI: 10.1007/s12027-022-00702-z

Venigandla, K., & Vemuri, N. (2022). *RPA and AI-Driven Predictive Analytics in Banking for Fraud Detection*. Tuijin Jishu/Journal of Propulsion Technology., DOI: 10.52783/tjjpt.v43.i4.5531

Verma, P., & Tyagi, P. (2022). Analysis of Supervised Machine Learning Algorithms in the Context of Fraud Detection. Ecs Transactions. https://doi.org/DOI: 10.1149/10701.7189ecst

Villegas-Ortega, J., Bellido-Boza, L., & Mauricio, D. (2021). Fourteen Years of Manifestations and Factors of Health Insurance Fraud, 2006–2020: A Scoping Review. Health \& Justice. DOI: 10.1186/s40352-021-00149-3

Wang, Y. (2023). Application of Machine Learning Models in Detecting Financial Fraud in Publicly Traded Companies. SSRN Electronic Journal. DOI: 10.2139/ssrn.4635606

West, J., Bhattacharya, M., & Islam, R. (2015). Intelligent Financial Fraud Detection Practices: An Investigation. ArXiv (Cornell University). /arxiv.1510.07165DOI: 10.1007/978-3-319-23802-9_16

Woods, D., Hollywood, J. S., Barnum, J. D., Fenimore, D., Vermeer, M., & Jackson, B. A. D., W. A., Bates, J. A., Pamela, A., Ciphertrace, C., Blockchain, A. C., Davidson, M. H., Gupta, R., County, O., Attorney, D., Lemieux, F., Murat, M. T., Orman, E., Jersey, N., … Montgomery, M. H. (2023). Cryptocurrency and Blockchain Needs for Law Enforcement. In RAND Corporation eBooks. DOI: 10.7249/RRA108-17

Xia, P., Zhu, X., Charles, V., Zhao, X., & Peng, M. (2024). A Novel Heuristic-Based Selective Ensemble Prediction Method for Digital Financial Fraud Risk. *IEEE Transactions on Engineering Management*, *71*, 8002–8018. Advance online publication. DOI: 10.1109/TEM.2024.3385298

Xu, X., Cao, L., & Zhang, Z. (2020). Artificial intelligence-enabled decision support systems: A review and future directions. *Decision Support Systems*, *130*, 113239. DOI: 10.1016/j.dss.2019.113239

Xu, X., Cao, L., & Zhang, Z. (2020). Artificial intelligence-enabled decision support systems: A review and future directions. *Decision Support Systems*, *130*, 113239. DOI: 10.1016/j.dss.2019.113239

Yazıcı, Y. (2020). Approaches to Fraud Detection on Credit Card Transactions using Artificial Intelligence Methods. 235–244. DOI: 10.5121/csit.2020.101018

Yuhertiana, I., & Hadi Amin, A. (2024). *Artificial Intelligence Driven Approaches for Financial Fraud Detection: A Systematic Literature Review*. KnE Social Sciences., DOI: 10.18502/kss.v9i20.16551

Zhang, H., Hong, J., Dong, F., Drew, S., Xue, L., & Zhou, J. (2023). A Privacy-Preserving Hybrid Federated Learning Framework for Financial Crime Detection. ArXiv (Cornell University). https://doi.org//arxiv.2302.03654DOI: 10.48550

Zhao, L., Hui, P., Zhang, P., Huang, J., Wang, B., Tian, L., Zhang, J., Gao, J., & Tang, X. (2021). What Happens Behind the Scene? Towards Fraud Community Detection in E-Commerce from Online to Offline. Companion Proceedings of the The Web Conference 2018, 105–113. DOI: 10.1145/3442442.3451147

Zhao, Z., & Bai, T. (2022). Financial Fraud Detection and Prediction in Listed Companies Using SMOTE and Machine Learning Algorithms. *Entropy (Basel, Switzerland)*, *24*(8), 1157. Advance online publication. DOI: 10.3390/e24081157 PMID: 36010821

Chapter 3
Role of Machine Learning in Identity Verification

Nurdiansyah Nurdiansyah
Universitas DIPA Makassar, Indonesia

Nizirwan Anwar
https://orcid.org/0000-0003-1189-9093
Universitas Esa Unggul, Indonesia

Linda Arisanty Razak
Universitas Muhammadiyah Makassar, Indonesia

Nini Apriani Rumata
Universitas Muhammadiyah Makassar, Indonesia

Muhammad Faisal
https://orcid.org/0000-0003-1469-9468
Muhammadiyah University of Makassar, Indonesia

Muhammad Syafaat S. Kuba
Muhammadiyah University of Makassar, Indonesia

Agung Mulyo Widodo
https://orcid.org/0000-0002-9792-7114
Universitas Esa Unggul, Indonesia

Sourasis Chattopadhyay
https://orcid.org/0009-0000-7435-6550
Kalinga Institute of Industrial Technology, India

Abhay Ratnaparkhi
eBuy Inc., USA

ABSTRACT

Machine Learning (ML) is a vital enabler in modern identity verification, combating digital arrest fraud and identity theft through supervised, unsupervised, and deep learning models. These systems analyse complex datasets to detect anomalies, behavioural inconsistencies, and authenticate identities with high accuracy, adapting to evolving threats while minimising false positives and negatives. ML-powered solutions integrate biometric authentication, behavioural analytics, and risk scoring to deliver real-time decision support that balances security, user experience,

DOI: 10.4018/979-8-3373-4149-1.ch003

and regulatory compliance. This strengthens digital security across banking, e-commerce, government, and healthcare sectors where identity breaches are costly. With predictive capabilities enabling proactive fraud prevention, ML stands as a cornerstone of adaptive cybersecurity. This chapter explores core frameworks, applications, case studies, and emerging trends, showing how ML-driven identity verification mitigates risks while enhancing trust, efficiency, and scalability in safeguarding digital ecosystems.

1. INTRODUCTION

In an increasingly connected digital environment, reliable identity verification has become a fundamental requirement across multiple sectors, including public administration, financial services, healthcare, and private organizations. Effective identity verification underpins secure system access, builds institutional trust, and supports operational safety (Ketcham et al., 2025). However, traditional verification practices - such as manual examination of physical credentials or dependence on easily exploitable personal data - are proving inadequate in the face of rapid digitalization and the growing sophistication of fraud techniques (Jain & Gupta, 2018; Yousefi et al., 2019; Gope et al., 2021). These limitations have contributed to a surge in identity theft and online fraud, underscoring the demand for more robust and dependable verification solutions.

Machine learning has consequently emerged as a key enabler in addressing these challenges. By automating verification workflows, machine learning enhances accuracy, operational efficiency, and security in identity validation processes (Jain & Gupta, 2018; Yazıcı, 2019a; Asmar & Tuqan, 2024; Aslam et al., 2022a). Its capacity to analyze large-scale datasets, detect subtle fraud indicators, and adapt to newly emerging attack patterns enables a more proactive and flexible approach to identity verification (Yousefi et al., 2019). The transformative role of machine learning lies in its advanced analytical capabilities - particularly anomaly detection and continuous model adaptation - which allow systems to respond effectively to evolving fraud strategies (Carcillo et al., 2021; Yazıcı, 2019b).

Integrating machine learning into cybersecurity infrastructures further supports automated and timely decision-making, enabling organizations to respond rapidly to dynamic and heterogeneous threat landscapes (Okoli et al., 2024). The ability of machine learning models to extract meaningful patterns from complex, high-volume data renders them indispensable for strengthening cyber defenses (Okoli et al., 2024; Chachra & Sharma, 2019), especially as cyberattacks increase in frequency and sophistication. Moreover, the adaptive nature of machine learning facilitates continuous refinement of security mechanisms, providing dynamic protection against emergent threats. This integration improves threat detection accuracy, shortens incident response times, and substantially reinforces organizational resilience against cyberattacks. Given the limitations of static, rule-based security approaches in confronting diverse and unpredictable attacks, the self-learning capabilities of machine learning have become increasingly critical for modern cybersecurity architectures (Alshaikh et al., 2024).

2. MACHINE LEARNING IS USED TO IMPROVE IDENTITY VERIFICATION

Machine learning algorithms represent a substantive shift in identity verification by enabling systems to process large-scale data, recognize fraud-related patterns, and continuously adapt to emerging attack strategies. Unlike static, rule-based approaches, machine learning supports multi-dimensional analysis that integrates biometric, behavioral, and contextual attributes, thereby allowing verification platforms to assess identity risk in a more holistic manner (Asmar & Tuqan, 2024). Through the analysis of extensive datasets, machine learning techniques are particularly effective at identifying fraudulent behavior and uncovering complex relationships among variables that are difficult to detect through manual or deterministic methods, positioning machine learning as a core component of modern fraud detection systems (Yousefi et al., 2019).

Supervised learning methods, including classification and regression, can be trained using labeled datasets that distinguish legitimate from fraudulent identities, enabling reliable prediction and categorization of new identity claims (Yazıcı, 2019b). In contrast, unsupervised learning techniques - such as clustering and anomaly detection - do not rely on predefined labels and are well suited to identifying atypical or previously unseen patterns that may indicate emerging fraud tactics. These approaches are particularly valuable for detecting novel and evolving fraudulent behaviors (Yousefi et al., 2019; Carcillo et al., 2021). Moreover, machine learning-based systems can learn incrementally as new data become available, improving detection capability over time and adapting to concept drift (Dal Pozzolo et al., 2015; Carcillo et al., 2021). By capturing subtle transactional and behavioral patterns that often escape human analysis, machine learning models can more effectively flag suspicious activities (Yazıcı, 2019a; Aslam et al., 2022).

The advantages of applying machine learning to identity verification also include the capacity to develop task-specific models, such as those designed for phishing detection and related threats (Shahrivari et al., 2020). Beyond enhancing detection accuracy, machine learning accelerates incident response by reinforcing automated and adaptive security workflows. In practice, machine learning-driven verification has been widely deployed in domains such as facial recognition, behavioral biometrics, and automated document authentication (Jain & Gupta, 2018). Facial recognition systems use machine learning to analyze facial images or video streams and match them against reference databases to confirm user identity. Behavioral biometrics provide an additional layer of protection by modeling distinctive user interaction patterns - such as keystroke dynamics and mouse movements - which are inherently more resistant to traditional spoofing techniques than static credentials (Yazıcı, 2019b). Furthermore, machine learning enables automated document verification by validating identity documents, including passports and driver's licenses, against trusted templates and data sources to assess their authenticity (Gope et al., 2021).

2.1 Machine Learning Algorithms in Identity Verification

Within supervised learning paradigms, relatively simple models such as logistic regression are commonly applied to binary classification tasks - for example, distinguishing legitimate identities from fraudulent ones - by modeling relationships between extracted identity features and outcome labels. Logistic regression is particularly effective when predictor variables exhibit approximately linear associations and has been widely utilized in domains such as credit risk assessment and anomaly detection (Manek et al., 2019). Moving beyond linear methods, support vector machines (SVMs) provide more expressive classification capabilities by leveraging kernel functions to map input data into higher-dimensional feature spaces, enabling the construction of optimal separating hyperplanes (Hasan & Rizvi, 2022). Owing to their strong generalization ability and precision, SVMs are especially suitable for high-dimensional biometric data and can effectively accommodate heterogeneous and nonlinear identity attributes (Panigrahi et al., 2024).

Identity analytics is further enhanced through nonlinear, probabilistic, and instance-based models, including decision trees, Naïve Bayes classifiers, neural networks, and k-nearest neighbor (KNN). Decision trees are valued for their transparency and interpretability, while Naïve Bayes enables efficient probabilistic reasoning under conditional independence assumptions (Yazıcı, 2019a). Neural networks are well suited for capturing complex and multimodal relationships, such as those involving facial and vocal features, whereas KNN relies on similarity measures to classify identities based on proximity in feature space. Recent studies increasingly advocate ensemble learning approaches to improve predictive accuracy and robustness, particularly in adversarial contexts. In practice, ensemble models such as random forests - which aggregate multiple decision trees - and gradient boosting techniques have gained widespread adoption, as they iteratively refine weak learners to form more accurate and stable predictors (Ikudabo & Kumar, 2024). By combining complementary model strengths, ensemble strategies enhance generalization performance and system resilience.

The integration of statistical modeling with pattern recognition techniques has significantly advanced machine learning–based identity verification systems. Contemporary models are capable of delivering scalable and near–real-time authentication while maintaining a degree of interpretability, a critical requirement in cybersecurity contexts where accuracy, usability, and privacy must be balanced. Overall, the application of machine learning to fraud detection represents a fundamental transformation in financial analytics and cybersecurity, as adaptive, data-driven models outperform static rule-based systems in capturing subtle behavioral anomalies and evolving fraud patterns (Almomani et al., 2024).

2.2 Machine Learning in Fraud Detection

Supervised learning continues to dominate deployed machine learning–based fraud detection systems because the availability of labeled data enables models to learn discriminative characteristics between legitimate and fraudulent activities (Yousefi et al., 2019; Dal Pozzolo et al., 2015). By leveraging historical transaction data, these models can identify abnormal geographic behavior, irregular spending patterns, and other salient fraud indicators, enabling accurate classification of new and incoming transactions. In practical credit-card fraud detection scenarios, algorithms such as logistic regression, random forests, gradient boosting models, and SVMs are routinely applied to streaming transaction data to automatically flag suspicious behavior (Carcillo et al., 2021). A key strength of these approaches lies in their ability to maintain robust generalization performance under highly imbalanced class distributions - where legitimate transactions vastly outnumber fraudulent ones - thereby preserving recall and minimizing missed fraud cases (Jain & Gupta, 2019).

Model effectiveness is typically evaluated using standard performance metrics, including precision, accuracy, recall, F1-score, area under the ROC curve (AUC–ROC), and confusion matrices. These metrics provide insight into false-positive and false-negative rates across training and validation phases and support the calibration of operational decision thresholds prior to deployment (Aslam & Hussain, 2024). While single-model pipelines remain useful, ensemble learning techniques - such as random forests, AdaBoost, and gradient boosting - frequently achieve superior performance by aggregating multiple weak learners into unified predictive frameworks capable of modeling the complex and nonlinear patterns characteristic of financial data (Carcillo et al., 2021). Ensemble models also reduce overfitting and improve stability in dynamic fraud environments.

To complement supervised approaches, unsupervised anomaly detection methods - including Isolation Forest (IF) and Local Outlier Factor (LOF) - are increasingly employed to identify rare or previously unseen fraud patterns. Isolation Forest isolates anomalies through randomized partitioning, whereas LOF evaluates deviations in local data density relative to neighboring instances. These techniques are particularly valuable when labeled fraud examples are scarce or when fraud strategies evolve rapidly (Arowolo et al., 2023).

More recently, hybrid frameworks integrating supervised and unsupervised learning have emerged as robust solutions for long-term adaptability. By uncovering latent relationships across heterogeneous data sources, such frameworks enhance resilience against emerging fraud tactics. When combined with ensemble-based detection, natural language processing, and behavioral analytics, these systems enable multi-layered defense mechanisms capable of identifying impersonation, social-engineering, and other sophisticated fraud schemes. Collectively, ensemble and anomaly detection strategies represent a significant advancement toward intelligent, adaptive fraud prevention systems capable of countering increasingly complex forms of financial crime (Alauthman et al., 2023).

3. DIGITAL ARREST FRAUD AND IDENTITY THEFT: AN OVERVIEW

As digital transformation continues to accelerate, cyber-enabled crimes such as digital arrest scams and identity theft have evolved into increasingly sophisticated and rapidly adapting threats. These forms of fraud exploit structural weaknesses in social networks, technological vulnerabilities in online verification systems, and psychological manipulation within digital communication channels. Their rapid proliferation has been driven by the global expansion of internet connectivity, the widespread adoption of remote authentication mechanisms, and the growth of instant digital payment infrastructures, all of which create opportunities to exploit individual vulnerabilities at scale (Mallick & Ganguli, 2024).

Digital arrest scams typically involve offenders impersonating law-enforcement officers or government authorities to intimidate victims into transferring funds or disclosing sensitive personal information under the pretense of legal consequences. Such schemes rely heavily on social engineering strategies that invoke fear, urgency, and perceived institutional authority to coerce compliance (Raihan & Kurniawati, 2023). Initial contact is commonly made through phone calls, messaging platforms, or email, with fabricated claims of outstanding warrants or legal violations. Victims are pressured to make immediate payments or provide confidential identifiers to supposedly “resolve” the issue. Increasingly, these scams incorporate advanced deception techniques, including spoofed caller identification, falsified digital documents, and deepfake audio or video, thereby blending traditional social engineering with contemporary forgery technologies (Mallick & Ganguli, 2024).

In contrast, identity theft involves the unauthorized acquisition, replication, and misuse of personal identifiers, such as names, national identification numbers, passwords, and biometric data. Compromised credentials may be exploited to open fraudulent bank accounts, secure illicit credit, submit false tax claims, or access restricted services, including healthcare systems. The scale of identity theft has been amplified by frequent data breaches, pervasive phishing campaigns, and the existence of dark-web marketplaces that trade stolen identity records. Beyond immediate financial harm, victims often suffer prolonged consequences, including damaged credit histories, psychological distress, and complex legal remediation processes.

The rapid expansion of digital platforms - including e-commerce services, mobile banking, and remote identity verification - has significantly enlarged the attack surface available to cybercriminals. Each additional authentication process, online service, or data repository introduces potential entry points for impersonation and system intrusion. Addressing this growing risk requires layered defense strategies that integrate advanced technological safeguards with human-centered interventions. Machine learning–based detection systems play a critical role by identifying anomalous behaviors, suspicious device fingerprints, and irregular transaction patterns that differentiate legitimate users from malicious actors (Gupta & Srivastava, 2023). Both supervised and unsupervised machine learning models can detect unusual login locations, abnormal session durations, or atypical spending behaviors, while techniques such as Random Forests, Isolation Forests, and neural networks enable real-time identification of high-risk activity, thereby reducing financial and identity-related losses (Gupta & Srivastava, 2023).

Nevertheless, technological solutions alone are insufficient to fully mitigate digital arrest scams and identity theft, as human factors remain central to these crimes. Many such attacks succeed by exploiting trust, fear, and authority, making user education and digital literacy essential components of effective prevention strategies. Educating individuals to recognize common warning signs - such as urgent payment demands, threats of legal action, or unsolicited requests for sensitive credentials - can significantly reduce victimization rates (Rahaman et al., 2025). Public awareness initiatives, regulatory advisories, and AI-driven scam alerts further contribute to building a culture of informed skepticism that disrupts manipulative narratives before harm occurs. Ultimately, combating digital arrest fraud and identity theft requires a comprehensive, multi-stakeholder approach that combines intelligent machine learning–driven defenses, regulatory enforcement, and sustained public awareness to prevent, deter, and disrupt attacks, thereby protecting digital identities and reinforcing trust in digital ecosystems (Rahaman et al., 2025).

3.1 The Scope of Digital Arrest Fraud

Digital arrest fraud is characterized by the impersonation of law-enforcement authorities to intimidate victims into transferring money. Perpetrators commonly employ caller-ID spoofing to replicate official telephone numbers and disseminate carefully constructed emails that convey institutional authority, thereby enhancing the credibility of fraudulent demands. The continued escalation of online fraud highlights the critical need for resilient identity verification mechanisms capable of identifying and preventing such abuses. As digital transactions proliferate, artificial intelligence (AI) and machine learning techniques have been increasingly adopted to monitor transactional activity and detect deviations from normal behavioral patterns (Kurshan et al., 2024; Bynagari, 2015).

However, effective law-enforcement intervention is often hindered by investigative complexity, jurisdictional challenges, and limited resources (Donegan, 2019). Empirical evidence further indicates a strong association between the growth of financial transactions and rising levels of financial fraud (Udeh et al., 2024), while the widespread misuse of personal identity data reinforces the urgency of implementing more robust identity verification frameworks. Collectively, these security threats erode consumer trust in online banking platforms and digital financial services.

3.2 Identity Theft Techniques in the Digital Age

Identity theft capitalizes on the high degree of interconnectedness in contemporary information systems and the widespread availability of personal data in online environments. The unauthorized acquisition and misuse of personally identifiable information (PII) - including names, identification numbers, passwords, financial credentials, and biometric identifiers - enables a broad spectrum of criminal activities, such as fraudulent account creation, unauthorized transactions, falsified tax filings, and illicit access to healthcare services. While digital payment systems and cloud-based data storage have increased efficiency and accessibility, they have simultaneously expanded the attack surface, allowing cybercriminals to operate with relative anonymity across national boundaries.

Phishing, social engineering, and psychological manipulation remain among the most prevalent techniques used to perpetrate identity theft. In these attacks, adversaries impersonate trusted institutions - such as banks, government agencies, or online platforms - through emails, text messages, or social media communications to deceive individuals into disclosing credentials or financial information. These communications commonly exploit urgency, fear, and the visual cues of official branding to override rational decision-making. Because phishing primarily targets human vulnerabilities rather than technical system flaws, user education and sustained digital literacy initiatives constitute essential defensive measures (Chaganti et al., 2021).

Malware-based attacks represent another significant vector for identity theft. Malicious software is deployed to infiltrate devices and exfiltrate sensitive credentials, frequently in conjunction with phishing links that redirect users to compromised websites. Advanced malware strains employ encryption, obfuscation, and polymorphic techniques to evade detection and maintain persistence within target systems. Additionally, social engineering strategies such as pretexting, baiting, and voice phishing (vishing) exploit emotional triggers and cognitive biases, underscoring that effective cybersecurity must address human behavior alongside technical safeguards (Chaganti et al., 2021).

Large-scale data breaches further constitute a systemic driver of identity theft. Compromised datasets are routinely traded on underground marketplaces and subsequently leveraged in credential-stuffing attacks to gain unauthorized access to multiple services using reused credentials. The repercussions of identity theft extend well beyond immediate financial damage; victims often endure long-term credit impairment, significant psychological stress, and protracted recovery processes involving legal action and reputational repair.

3.3 Costs and Consequences of Identity Theft

Identity theft has escalated into a global crisis with far-reaching financial, psychological, and social consequences. Victims frequently experience direct monetary losses, impaired credit histories, and significant emotional distress, including anxiety and reduced confidence in digital environments (Farina, 2015). Compromised identities are routinely exploited for illicit activities such as unauthorized purchases, tax fraud, and the creation of fraudulent accounts. Consequently, affected individuals often contend with unresolved debts and inaccurate legal or financial records over prolonged periods.

Empirical evidence underscores the scale and persistence of the problem. Global credit-card fraud losses were estimated at approximately USD 25 billion in 2018, with losses continuing to rise alongside online payment adoption (Tian et al., 2023). In the United States alone, more than 406,000 identity theft cases were reported in 2017. Between 2005 and 2018, over 1.24 billion records were exposed in data breaches worldwide, providing an extensive reservoir for identity-based attacks (Mantha & García de Soto, 2021). At a societal level, identity theft undermines consumer trust, increases cybersecurity expenditures, and imposes significant strain on financial institutions and law-enforcement agencies.

3.4 The Role of Machine Learning in Identity Verification

Machine learning algorithms are capable of analyzing large-scale and heterogeneous datasets to uncover patterns and anomalies that signal fraudulent behavior, thereby strengthening identity verification mechanisms. By training on historical transaction and identity records, machine learning models can recognize fraudulent activities and atypical patterns associated with identity theft (Xu et al., 2023). Unlike static rule-based systems, machine learning approaches are adaptive, enabling continuous learning and rapid response to evolving fraud strategies.

These systems leverage features such as IP addresses, device fingerprints, geolocation data, and transaction histories to assess risk in real time. Machine learning has been extensively applied in credit-card fraud detection, improving accuracy by modeling complex relationships within transactional data (Nguyen et al., 2020). Real-time monitoring and automated anomaly detection enable early intervention before fraudulent transactions are finalized (Ahmadi, 2024). Consequently, organizations that integrate machine learning into identity verification frameworks are better positioned to adopt proactive protection strategies that mitigate both financial losses and reputational harm (Yesare, 2023).

4. THE ROLE OF ARTIFICIAL INTELLIGENCE IN COMBATING FRAUD

AI has fundamentally transformed financial fraud detection by redefining how institutions identify, assess, and mitigate illicit activities. Its deployment across sectors such as banking, insurance, e-commerce, and healthcare has enabled the development of scalable, adaptive, and self-learning security systems. Unlike traditional rule-based approaches - which depend on static thresholds and predefined patterns that are ill-suited to the evolving nature of financial crime AI-driven systems can process massive volumes of data in real time. This capability allows them to uncover latent correlations, anomalies, and behavioral deviations that may remain undetected by conventional analytics or human experts.

A central strength of AI lies in its ability to model complex, nonlinear relationships among transactional attributes and user behaviors. Techniques encompassing machine learning, deep learning, and natural language processing enable continuous learning from historical and streaming data, thereby improving predictive accuracy over time. Supervised algorithms, such as random forests, support vector machines, and gradient boosting models, classify transactions based on learned fraud signatures, while unsupervised techniques - including clustering, autoencoders, and Isolation Forests - identify previously unseen fraud patterns by isolating anomalies (Nguyen et al., 2023). This adaptability is particularly critical as fraudsters increasingly employ personalization, data spoofing, and synthetic identities. AI's capacity for real-time analysis empowers institutions to screen millions of transactions instantaneously and generate alerts within milliseconds, substantially reducing potential financial losses (Wang et al., 2023).

Beyond detection, AI systems integrate diverse signals - such as geolocation data, device fingerprints, and behavioral biometrics - to construct multi-layered risk assessments that reduce false positives and improve decision accuracy. AI also supports higher-level strategic functions, including customer risk profiling, credit scoring, and compliance monitoring, thereby enhancing operational efficiency and regulatory adherence. By automating routine detection tasks, AI reduces manual workloads and enables human analysts to focus on complex investigations, improving cost efficiency, customer satisfaction, and return on investment. Additionally, AI-powered chatbots and virtual assistants contribute to improved customer engagement and service continuity.

Despite these advantages, AI integration introduces significant challenges. Model effectiveness depends heavily on data quality, fairness, transparency, and interpretability. Poorly trained or biased models may generate discriminatory outcomes or false accusations, raising ethical and legal concerns (Adrian & Mancini-Griffoli, 2019). The opacity of black-box models further complicates accountability, necessitating mechanisms to ensure that automated decisions are explainable, auditable, and compliant with privacy regulations such as the General Data Protection Regulation. As fraudsters increasingly adopt AI-driven attack strategies, defensive systems must evolve accordingly. Consequently, the future of fraud mitigation is likely to rely on hybrid intelligence, combining machine-driven precision with human judgment to ensure ethical integrity and strategic resilience. AI thus represents both a powerful opportunity and a significant responsibility in financial fraud prevention.

4.1 Artificial Intelligence in Fraud Detection

AI has become a cornerstone of modern fraud detection and crime prevention, playing a vital role in sustaining trust within digital financial ecosystems. Traditional rule-based systems are insufficient against sophisticated, rapidly evolving fraud schemes, whereas machine learning and deep learning approaches can process vast, heterogeneous datasets and adapt to emerging attack vectors (Buchanan, 2019). By analyzing structured and unstructured data - including transaction records, device identifiers, geolocation signals, and biometric features - AI systems construct comprehensive user behavior profiles and flag deviations that warrant intervention.

Machine learning models are iteratively trained on historical and real-time data to enhance predictive performance, enabling systems to classify transactions as legitimate or suspicious based on indicators such as abnormal transaction frequency, unusual login behavior, or inconsistent spending patterns (Antwi et al., 2024). AI further strengthens preventive capabilities through continuous monitoring and automated decision-making, significantly reducing response latency and improving real-time interception of fraudulent activity (Adesoga et al., 2024). This integration shifts institutional security strategies from retrospective analysis to proactive, predictive defense - an essential transition as fraud increasingly incorporates synthetic identities, deepfakes, and cross-platform laundering techniques.

The adaptive learning capacity of AI, which allows models to update continuously as new data become available, is central to combating emerging cyber threats. This adaptability also enhances transparency by generating actionable insights for auditors and compliance officers. Consequently, AI-driven fraud detection represents a move toward data-driven, accountable governance in financial security.

4.2 Machine Learning Algorithms for Fraud Prevention

Within the financial sector, AI and machine learning have become indispensable tools for fraud detection, cybersecurity, and regulatory compliance. As digital transaction volumes expand, institutions must carefully balance the operational benefits of AI with ethical, legal, and regulatory risks. The automation of cybercrime and the rise of identity-centric deception demand machine learning systems capable not only of detecting existing fraud but also of anticipating emerging threats.

Machine learning models analyze high-dimensional datasets to identify subtle relationships and anomalies that traditional systems often overlook, enabling predictive risk analysis to surface vulnerabilities before they escalate (Bajpai, 2024). Continuous learning mechanisms ensure that these models remain responsive to evolving behaviors and tactics, increasing contextual awareness and detection agility. The proactive integration of machine learning transforms organizational security postures from reactive incident response to predictive intelligence, fostering the development of adaptive architectures that respond dynamically to data flows, threat landscapes, and compliance requirements.

AI also plays a critical role in regulatory technology (RegTech) by automating compliance monitoring, anomaly detection, and adherence to standards such as Basel III, GDPR, and anti-money laundering (AML) and know-your-customer (KYC) frameworks (Truby et al., 2020). While these capabilities deliver substantial cost savings, operational efficiencies, and enhanced customer experiences, rapid AI adoption necessitates robust risk management. Algorithmic bias, excessive reliance on automation, and privacy breaches remain significant concerns. Given that AI systems increasingly emulate human cognitive processes, issues of explainability and accountability demand ongoing ethical audits and rigorous validation (Mhlanga, 2020).

4.3 Natural Language Processing for Identifying Fraudulent Communication

The application of AI and machine learning to fraud detection has significantly improved institutions' ability to identify illicit activities, yet its effectiveness depends on data quality, algorithm robustness, and system flexibility. Key challenges include class imbalance, real-time processing constraints, model interpretability, and privacy protection (Adhikari et al., 2024).

Class imbalance is particularly problematic, as fraudulent transactions often constitute less than 0.5% of total data, causing models to favor the majority class and overlook critical fraud cases. Techniques such as synthetic minority oversampling (SMOTE), cost-sensitive learning, and ensemble methods are commonly employed to enhance sensitivity to minority classes without sacrificing precision (Adhikari et al., 2024). Real-time fraud detection further requires low-latency decision-making in streaming environments, achieved through online learning, incremental model updates, and distributed computing architectures capable of millisecond-level inference.

A thorough understanding of algorithmic capabilities is essential for effective deployment. Supervised models - including logistic regression, decision trees, SVMs, random forests, and gradient boosting - are widely used for classification tasks, while unsupervised approaches such as k-means clustering, autoencoders, and Isolation Forests support anomaly detection when labeled data are limited. Advanced deep learning architectures, including long short-term memory (LSTM) networks and graph neural networks (GNNs), enable modeling of sequential behaviors and relational transaction networks (Adhikari et al., 2024). Collectively, these tools underpin adaptive fraud detection systems that evolve in response to new attack strategies, strengthening online banking security and reinforcing customer trust.

4.4 The Future of AI in Fraud Detection

AI adoption within financial institutions is accelerating, fundamentally reshaping security, fraud detection, and risk assessment practices. As digital finance expands through mobile banking, digital payments, and blockchain-based services, transaction volumes and velocities continue to rise, intensifying fraud complexity. In this context, AI has become a core defensive capability, capable of autonomously analyzing high-dimensional, multi-layered datasets in real time to detect anomalous activities beyond human perceptual limits (Roy et al., 2025).

Fraud manifests in both internal forms - such as insider threats - and external forms, including phishing, cyberattacks, and identity theft. AI-driven anomaly detection can identify irregular employee behaviors, while classification models analyze transaction networks to expose coordinated external fraud. The convergence of AI with Big Data analytics and the Internet of Things (IoT) enables integrated, real-time security architectures that incorporate biometric sensors, smart cards, and payment terminals, enhancing authentication and situational awareness (Rane et al., 2024).

Emerging trends - including explainable AI (XAI), reinforcement learning, and federated learning - are poised to shape the future of fraud detection. Maintaining public trust requires interpretable and auditable systems aligned with ethical and societal values (Roy et al., 2025). Regulatory bodies increasingly advocate AI ethics frameworks emphasizing bias mitigation, data protection, and responsible deployment. An AI-first approach to risk management is gaining prominence, as mathematically grounded models enable low-latency fraud detection, improved credit risk forecasting, and enhanced regulatory reporting efficiency (Sari & Indrabudiman, 2024).

5. MACHINE LEARNING IN IDENTITY VERIFICATION

Machine learning has become a foundational component of contemporary identity verification systems, significantly enhancing accuracy, security, and operational efficiency (Sowmya & Sathisha, 2023). By leveraging advanced statistical and computational models, machine learning algorithms analyze large-scale and heterogeneous datasets to uncover subtle patterns, correlations, and anomalies indicative of fraudulent behavior, thereby strengthening detection and prevention capabilities (Yazıcı, 2019b). When trained on extensive datasets, these models continuously improve by learning from transaction histories, behavioral attributes, and device-related data, enabling proactive mitigation of illicit activities (Alkhateeb & Maolood, 2019).

Machine learning has also automated and refined biometric verification processes - such as fingerprint recognition and facial analysis - achieving higher precision and consistency than manual or rule-based methods (Stojanović et al., 2021). By automating routine verification tasks, ML-based systems reduce human workload and allow security professionals to focus on complex or high-risk cases, improving both verification quality and user experience. Furthermore, ML-driven fraud detection tools support large-scale anomaly detection that would be infeasible through human intervention alone, particularly in environments characterized by massive, high-velocity data streams (Aslam et al., 2022; Yesare, 2023).

In practical deployments, machine learning models examine transactional and interaction data to identify unauthorized access attempts, irregular usage patterns, and suspicious behaviors (Sowmya & Sathisha, 2023). Supervised learning techniques, such as logistic regression, decision trees, and support vector machines, are widely employed to classify transactions as legitimate or fraudulent using labeled historical data (Manek et al., 2019). However, constructing effective and generalizable detection pipelines remains challenging due to class imbalance, evolving fraud strategies, and contextual variability (Yazıcı, 2019b). To address these limitations, unsupervised approaches - including clustering, autoencoders, and anomaly detection techniques - are increasingly adopted to identify novel or previously unseen fraud patterns in unlabeled datasets, making them particularly valuable for early detection of emerging threats (Vijayakumar et al., 2020).

5.1 Biometric and Knowledge-Based Authentication Methods

Biometric authentication, when integrated with machine learning, is reshaping identity verification by delivering stronger and more reliable authentication mechanisms. ML models analyze biometric signals - such as facial geometry, voice characteristics, and behavioral traits - to validate identities with high accuracy and reduced susceptibility to impersonation, although concerns related to privacy, data protection, and biometric data security remain salient (Lv et al., 2019). Early surveys describe biometric modalities such as fingerprints and facial features (Zhang & Zhang, 2013), while recent ML-based systems significantly improve accuracy (Lv et al., 2019). Because biometric traits are inherently unique and relatively stable, modalities including fingerprints, iris patterns, facial features, voiceprints, and handwriting provide robust foundations for identity confirmation and trust in digital transactions (Zhang & Zhang, 2013; Mehraj & Mir, 2021).

The integration of biometric data with ML-based analytics streamlines authentication workflows and significantly enhances security assurance. Fingerprints, in particular, remain among the most reliable biometric identifiers due to their permanence and distinctiveness. In contrast, knowledge-based authentication (KBA) - which relies on passwords or personal questions - remains vulnerable to phishing, social engineering, and credential compromise. Machine learning augments KBA by incorporating behavioral and contextual analysis to detect inconsistencies indicative of unauthorized access attempts.

Through behavioral profiling, ML algorithms model user interaction patterns - such as typing cadence, keystroke timing, and mouse dynamics - to establish individualized baselines that improve KBA reliability. Adaptive authentication frameworks further extend this capability by dynamically adjusting authentication requirements based on contextual risk factors, including location, device type, and access history. Routine, low-risk logins may require minimal verification, whereas anomalous or high-risk contexts trigger stronger mechanisms such as biometrics or one-time passwords (OTPs). By continuously learning from user behavior and contextual signals, ML-enabled systems deliver proactive defenses against identity theft and account takeover.

5.2 Adaptive Authentication Techniques

Adaptive authentication has emerged as a critical response to increasingly sophisticated cyber threats, offering a balance between robust security and user convenience. Unlike static authentication mechanisms, adaptive approaches dynamically tailor verification requirements based on real-time risk assessments powered by machine learning, which evaluates behavioral, contextual, and environmental signals to detect anomalies and prevent unauthorized access (Mandru, 2022; Ryman-Tubb et al., 2018). This paradigm shifts identity protection from static rule enforcement to context-aware, intelligence-driven security.

Risk-based access control adjusts authentication strength according to perceived risk. Routine access from familiar devices and locations may allow seamless single-factor authentication, whereas access attempts involving unfamiliar devices, unusual times, or foreign geolocations prompt multi-factor authentication (MFA), such as biometric verification or OTP challenges (Alqahtani et al., 2021; Mandru, 2022). ML enables continuous monitoring of variables including login frequency, transaction value, IP reputation, and geospatial patterns, allowing systems to establish personalized behavioral baselines (Tae & Hung, 2019).

Deviations from these baselines - such as high-value transactions, sudden changes in typing behavior, or access from new devices - trigger escalation mechanisms designed to detect credential compromise, session hijacking, or insider threats (Aslam et al., 2022; Mandru, 2022). Behavioral biometrics further strengthen adaptive authentication by modeling unique interaction signatures, including keystroke dynamics, cursor trajectories, and touchscreen gestures, which are inherently difficult for attackers to replicate (Mehraj & Mir, 2021). These unobtrusive signals support continuous authentication, preserving identity assurance throughout a session without disrupting legitimate users.

As adversaries increasingly exploit automation, deepfakes, and AI-generated social engineering, ML-driven adaptive systems evolve by generalizing from prior incidents to identify novel attack patterns (Barredo et al., 2020). By minimizing unnecessary authentication prompts for legitimate users while intensifying scrutiny during high-risk events, adaptive authentication enhances user experience, supports regulatory compliance (e.g., GDPR, PSD2), and aligns with zero-trust security architectures (NIST, 2020).

5.3 Behavioural Biometrics and Artificial Intelligence

AI-driven identity verification systems increasingly integrate behavioral biometrics, anomaly detection, and machine learning within adaptive, context-aware security frameworks (Mandru, 2022). Behavioral biometrics identify individuals based on dynamic interaction traits, such as typing rhythms, cursor movements, touchscreen gestures, gait, and device handling patterns. These features form quantifiable and continuously evolving behavioral profiles that are difficult for adversaries to imitate convincingly.

Continuous analysis of behavioral signals enables AI systems to detect subtle deviations from established baselines, providing early indicators of account compromise or impersonation. Anomaly detection algorithms enhance resilience by statistically evaluating whether observed behavior diverges significantly from historical norms, such as abrupt changes in typing cadence, unusual swipe patterns, or atypical login times and locations. Unlike rigid rule-based systems, AI-powered anomaly detection adapts to legitimate behavioral changes - such as new devices or altered routines - while minimizing false positives.

A defining advantage of AI-based behavioral security is continuous verification. Rather than relying solely on one-time authentication events, systems monitor ongoing interactions and compare them against learned behavioral templates. Detected inconsistencies can trigger adaptive countermeasures, including secondary authentication, session suspension, or forensic logging, thereby preventing compromised credentials from passing unnoticed. When combined with facial or voice biometrics, device fingerprinting, and contextual risk analytics, behavioral biometrics contribute to a multi-layered defense capable of detecting threats ranging from micro-level interaction anomalies to broader contextual irregularities.

Overall, the convergence of artificial intelligence, machine learning, and behavioral biometrics marks a shift toward proactive, user-centric identity protection. By continuously learning and adapting, these systems enhance verification accuracy while reducing friction for legitimate users, achieving a robust balance between security, usability, and trust in digital ecosystems.

6. FRAUD PREVENTION BASED ON DECISION SUPPORT SYSTEMS

In digitally mediated finance, Decision Support Systems (DSS) have become essential infrastructures for fraud prevention. Contemporary DSS integrate data management, analytics, machine learning, and rule-based reasoning to transform raw operational data into actionable decision guidance for investigators and risk teams (Sharda et al., 2018). While early DSS were often positioned as retrospective analytic tools, modern implementations increasingly support near-real-time decisioning, enabling continuous monitoring, case prioritization, and adaptive response under evolving fraud strategies (Sharda et al., 2018).

Conceptually, a DSS for fraud prevention typically rests on three interlocking pillars: (1) data integration, consolidating multi-source information (transactions, identity attributes, device signals, and contextual metadata); (2) modeling and analytics, applying statistical learning and AI methods to identify patterns and anomalies; and (3) user interface and workflow management, translating analytical outputs into dashboards, alerts, and investigation pipelines (Sharda et al., 2018). In operational fraud contexts, such systems analyze multidimensional signals - transaction velocity, temporal irregularities, device fingerprints, and customer behavior profiles - to surface anomalous patterns that are difficult to detect via manual review alone.

Embedding machine learning within DSS substantially strengthens automated pattern recognition and anomaly discovery. Unlike static rule-based systems that depend on fixed thresholds, ML-based models can learn complex and nonlinear feature interactions and update their behavior when fraud distributions drift (Hernández Aros et al., 2024). Evidence from DSS research in online banking demonstrates how anomaly scoring and behavioral profiling can support investigators using "human-readable" profiles of customer spending to explain and prioritize alerts (Carminati et al., 2015).

A major advantage of analytics-driven DSS is temporal forecasting: predictive models estimate evolving fraud risk, allowing institutions to prevent incidents rather than only responding after losses occur. In digital banking environments, predictive DSS can score transactions in real time and trigger adaptive interventions - such as temporary holds, stepped-up authentication, or re-verification - when anomalies arise (Carminati et al., 2015). In addition, modern DSS increasingly combine rule logic (for governance and policy enforcement) with ML outputs (for detection robustness) to recommend operational actions (e.g., approve, flag, block) and reduce false positives over time through iterative feedback and retraining (Hernández Aros et al., 2024; Sharda et al., 2018).

Operationally, DSS strengthen collaborative decision-making through interactive dashboards, visual analytics, and automated reporting that consolidate risk scores, geospatial indicators, and emerging fraud trends. This supports effective human–machine collaboration: systems perform high-volume screening, while experts contribute contextual judgment and investigative reasoning (Sharda et al., 2018). Overall, AI-augmented DSS enable a shift from post-incident review to proactive, predictive defense by integrating machine learning robustness with rule-based governance into scalable anti-fraud capabilities.

6.1 Predictive Analytics in Fraud Detection

Predictive analytics is increasingly indispensable for anticipating and preventing fraud. It comprises statistical modeling, data mining, and machine learning techniques that use historical records to forecast future risk and drivers of abnormal behavior. In fraud prevention, predictive analytics identifies trends, latent relationships, and risk signals that enable intervention before fraud materializes, rather than after harm is incurred (Hernández Aros et al., 2024).

Core modeling techniques include logistic regression, decision trees, random forests, support vector machines, gradient boosting, and deep learning models. These models are trained on labeled datasets containing legitimate and fraudulent cases to learn associations across transaction amount, frequency, location, device usage, and contextual indicators, then produce risk scores for triage and prioritization (Hernández Aros et al., 2024). Predictive models also underpin risk-based decision frameworks, where probabilistic scores are mapped to operational thresholds that balance false positives against detection sensitivity (Carminati et al., 2015).

Predictive analytics is also relevant to cybersecurity-adjacent fraud vectors (e.g., credential compromise, intrusion-linked fraud). Survey evidence shows that AI methods are widely applied to cybercrime and security analytics, supporting earlier detection of novel attacks that evade signature-based controls. By integrating cross-domain signals (transactions, access logs, network telemetry, and external intelligence), institutions gain improved situational awareness and earlier warning capacity.

6.2 Real-time Monitoring and Alerting

Real-time monitoring is a defining capability of modern fraud-prevention DSS. By integrating machine learning with streaming analytics, these platforms continuously observe transactions and user behavior to detect anomalies during execution, enabling interventions before losses accumulate (Carminati et al., 2015). In contrast to batch analytics that operate retrospectively, streaming-aware DSS can identify suspicious patterns - spending spikes, repeated authentication failures, unusual geolocations, and device anomalies - and generate alerts for rapid investigation.

Scaling real-time fraud decisioning is closely associated with the broader movement toward industrial-grade graph and AI systems for financial crime detection, emphasizing temporality (rapidly evolving patterns) and adversarial adaptation (fraudsters responding to deployed defenses) (Kurshan & Shen, 2020). Accordingly, engineering priorities include latency-optimized scoring, resilient pipelines, and feedback loops that maintain performance under concept drift (Kurshan & Shen, 2020; Sharda et al., 2018).

6.3 Explainable AI in Decision Support

Explainable AI (XAI) is increasingly essential for fraud detection DSS because it improves transparency, accountability, and stakeholder trust. As ML models become more complex and opaque, investigators and governance functions require interpretable rationales for why a transaction or identity was labeled high risk. XAI methods support validation of alerts, improve audit readiness, and reduce operational friction when deploying AI in regulated environments (Barredo et al., 2020).

Two widely adopted and foundational explanation techniques in explainable artificial intelligence are LIME and SHAP. LIME (Local Interpretable Model-agnostic Explanations) generates local surrogate models to explain individual predictions, enabling case-level interpretability that is particularly valuable for investigators and analysts (Ribeiro et al., 2016). SHAP (SHapley Additive exPlanations), in contrast, provides a unified and theoretically grounded attribution framework derived from cooperative game theory, offering consistent and additive feature-contribution explanations across diverse model classes (Lundberg & Lee, 2017). Within DSS environments, these methods can identify which factors - such as transaction velocity, transaction amount, geolocation, device reputation, or behavioral deviations - most strongly influenced a risk score, thereby supporting defensible operational decisions, auditability, and governance review (Lundberg & Lee, 2017; Ribeiro et al., 2016).

6.4 Neural Networks and Deep Learning

Neural networks and deep learning have advanced identity verification and fraud detection by learning rich representations directly from data, reducing reliance on handcrafted features. Deep architectures - such as convolutional neural networks (CNNs) for images and sequence models (e.g., LSTM-family methods) for temporal behaviors - are used in biometric verification and behavioral pattern modeling. A recent systematic review of deep learning in financial fraud detection summarizes the growing adoption of CNNs, LSTMs, transformers, and ensemble deep learning pipelines across fraud domains (Chen, 2025).

However, deep models often present interpretability challenges due to their black-box nature, complicating auditability and accountability. This strengthens the case for explainable deep learning and DSS-level governance patterns that connect model outputs to intelligible, actionable decision rationales (Barredo et al., 2020; Lundberg & Lee, 2017). Deep networks remain foundational for next-generation fraud prevention systems, provided transparency, risk controls, and operational constraints are explicitly addressed.

6.5 Graph Neural Networks

Graph Neural Networks (GNNs) strengthen fraud detection and identity verification by modeling relationships in financial ecosystems rather than treating observations independently. In graph representations, entities - users, accounts, devices, merchants, IP addresses are nodes, while interactions - transactions, shared identifiers, co-access events - edges. This enables detection of coordinated fraud, collusion, and synthetic identity rings that may be weakly expressed in feature-only tabular representations (Kurshan & Shen, 2020).

Recent survey work emphasizes that GNN-based methods are particularly effective at capturing relational structure and network dynamics in financial fraud settings, and reviews major modeling patterns (e.g., node classification for fraud, link prediction for suspicious relationships, heterogeneous graphs for multi-entity ecosystems) (Wu et al., 2021). At the same time, graph-based fraud systems must manage practical risks, including noisy or incomplete relationships, adversarial manipulation, privacy constraints, and governance requirements for responsible deployment (Kurshan & Shen, 2020; Wu et al., 2021). When managed appropriately, GNN-enabled DSS can materially improve predictive capability and resilience, supporting adaptive identity verification and fraud prevention architectures.

7. CASE STUDIES

Real-world implementations of AI and machine learning provide compelling evidence of their effectiveness in fraud prevention and identity verification. Within the financial sector, institutions have deployed ML-based frameworks to analyze high-volume transaction streams in near real time. Trained on large-scale historical transaction data, these systems learn complex statistical regularities and behavioral deviations that exceed human perceptual limits, enabling suspicious activities to be flagged with low latency and high precision (Dal Pozzolo et al., 2015; Sen et al., 2021). Empirical studies consistently report improvements in detection accuracy, reductions in false-positive alerts, and preservation of customer experience through risk-based decisioning.

Similarly, in e-commerce environments, AI-driven identity verification and behavioral analytics have substantially mitigated account takeover and synthetic identity fraud. Hybrid deployments combining convolutional neural networks (CNNs) for document or facial verification with sequence models - such as recurrent neural networks (RNNs) or temporal deep learning - for behavioral modeling have demonstrated measurable reductions in fraudulent purchases while simultaneously streamlining customer onboarding (Dal Pozzolo et al., 2015; Carcillo et al., 2021).

Collectively, these cases illustrate that adaptive ML systems function not merely as detection tools but as continuously evolving infrastructures that enhance trust, transparency, and consumer confidence in digital ecosystems.

7.1 Machine Learning–Assisted Fraud Detection in the E-commerce Industry

Machine learning has fundamentally reshaped fraud detection in e-commerce by enabling the analysis of large, dynamic datasets generated by remote and cross-border transactions. The inherently digital and distributed nature of e-commerce increases exposure to payment fraud, account hijacking, and identity abuse, motivating platforms to adopt AI-driven systems capable of real-time monitoring and behavioral classification (Yazıcı, 2019b). Both supervised and unsupervised ML models identify anomalies such as unusual purchasing frequency, repeated payment failures, device inconsistencies, and geolocation anomalies.

The adaptive learning capacity of ML allows detection systems to evolve as fraud strategies change, reducing false positives while improving sensitivity to emerging threats (Bynagari, 2015; Ryman-Tubb et al., 2018; Kurshan & Shen, 2020). The rapid expansion of online commerce during the COVID-19 period further intensified digital payment risks, accelerating adoption of AI-based fraud analytics (Mutemi & Bacao, 2024). By learning from longitudinal behavioral histories, predictive models infer fraudulent intent earlier in the transaction lifecycle, enabling proactive intervention before financial losses occur (Li et al., 2022).

7.2 Timely Review and Threat Detection

In volatile cyber-threat environments, real-time monitoring of transactions and user activity is essential for protecting systems and maintaining public trust. Fraud types such as digital arrest scams, phishing, and identity theft - often driven by social engineering and data breaches - require adaptive defenses, as static security controls are ineffective against rapidly evolving attack methods. AI and ML technologies enable continuous surveillance, anomaly detection, and automated response across financial and cyber-physical systems (Ikudabo & Kumar, 2024).

AI-driven monitoring platforms ingest transaction logs, user-interaction traces, network telemetry, and contextual metadata to correlate signals such as login behavior, IP geolocation, session duration, and communication patterns. ML models - including neural networks, support vector machines, clustering algorithms, and autoencoders - trained on large datasets can detect subtle deviations from normal behavior and generate alerts in near real time (Ikudabo & Kumar, 2024). Adaptive learning is particularly effective in identifying previously unseen fraud patterns, enabling prompt interventions such as account freezes, transaction blocking, or user notification - measures that are critical in time-sensitive coercive fraud scenarios.

7.3 Predictive Analytics for Fraud Prevention

Predictive analytics plays a central role in shifting fraud management from reactive investigation to preventive intervention. By integrating statistical modeling, data mining, and ML techniques, predictive systems forecast fraud risk based on historical patterns and behavioral trends (Udeh et al., 2024). Models such as logistic regression, decision trees, random forests, gradient boosting, and neural networks are trained on datasets containing both legitimate and fraudulent cases to uncover relationships among transaction value, frequency, location, device usage, and temporal context.

In operational settings, these models generate real-time risk scores that guide decision workflows, routing high-risk transactions to step-up authentication or manual review while allowing low-risk activity to proceed with minimal friction. Beyond financial transactions, predictive analytics is widely applied in cybersecurity to detect early indicators of phishing, malware, and intrusion attempts by analyzing network traffic and behavioral logs (Dal Pozzolo et al., 2015). Continuous learning mechanisms ensure that models remain effective as attackers adopt synthetic identities, automation, and AI-assisted attack strategies. Predictive analytics also supports regulatory compliance by producing auditable, explainable risk assessments.

7.4 Role of Machine Learning in Identity Confirmation

Machine learning has significantly improved the accuracy and speed of identity verification by leveraging heterogeneous data sources and automated analytics (Asmar & Tuqan, 2024). ML-based systems enable large-scale anomaly detection across transactional, biometric, and behavioral datasets, supporting early identification of suspicious access attempts and identity misuse (Ahmadi, 2024; Aslam et al., 2022). Supervised learning techniques - such as logistic regression and support vector machines - are widely used to classify identity-related events based on labeled historical data (Manek et al., 2019).

However, building robust and generalizable identity-verification pipelines remains challenging due to class imbalance, concept drift, and evolving fraud tactics (Yazıcı, 2019a). Unsupervised and semi-supervised approaches - including clustering, autoencoders, and anomaly detection - address these limitations by identifying novel fraud patterns without reliance on extensive labeled data, making them particularly valuable for uncovering emerging threats (Vijayakumar et al., 2020).

7.5 Combating Social Media Fraud with Machine Learning

Social media platforms have become prominent vectors for identity fraud, impersonation, and phishing campaigns. Machine learning techniques are extensively used to detect and remove fraudulent profiles by analyzing account attributes, textual content, interaction behavior, and network relationships. Compared with rule-based systems, ML models demonstrate superior performance in identifying subtle and evolving deception strategies (Shahrivari et al., 2020; Li et al., 2022).

A persistent challenge in social-media fraud detection is severe class imbalance, as fraudulent accounts constitute a small fraction of overall activity. To address this, researchers employ combinations of supervised, unsupervised, and semi-supervised learning techniques that remain effective even with limited labeled data (Lee & Yoon, 2013; Carcillo et al., 2021). Through continuous learning and adaptive modeling, ML-based systems enhance platform integrity, protect users from deception, and strengthen trust in online social environments.

8. CHALLENGES AND LIMITATIONS

Despite substantial advances enabled by machine learning in identity verification and fraud detection, several persistent challenges constrain its effectiveness and trustworthiness. One of the most critical issues is class imbalance, where fraudulent events represent only a small fraction of total transactions. This skewed distribution can bias learning processes, leading models to overemphasize legitimate cases and potentially overlook rare but high-impact fraud incidents (Yazıcı, 2019b; Dal Pozzolo et al., 2015). Addressing class imbalance requires specialized techniques, such as resampling strategies, cost-sensitive learning, and anomaly detection, yet perfect mitigation remains elusive.

Another major limitation concerns explainability and transparency. Financial institutions and regulators require clear, interpretable rationales for automated decisions to support governance, compliance, and accountability. However, many high-performing ML models - particularly deep learning architectures - operate as opaque "black boxes," complicating validation and auditability (Barredo et al., 2020). This tension between predictive accuracy and interpretability remains a fundamental challenge in deploying ML systems for high-stakes financial decision-making.

Operational and institutional constraints further complicate real-world deployment. Investigative delays, jurisdictional fragmentation, and legal requirements can slow confirmation and remediation of suspected fraud cases, reducing the immediate impact of automated detection systems (Sudjianto et al., 2010). Moreover, ML systems are increasingly vulnerable to adversarial attacks, in which malicious actors manipulate inputs to evade detection or poison training data (Biggio & Roli, 2018; Alfaiz & Fati, 2022). These risks highlight the need for robust learning paradigms, including adversarial training, model monitoring, and early-warning mechanisms that reduce exposure before fraud escalates (Luo et al., 2023). Overall, effective fraud prevention requires ML frameworks that are not only accurate, but also resilient, interpretable, and trustworthy.

8.1 Data Privacy Concerns

While ML-based identity verification systems improve accuracy and scalability, they raise substantial privacy and ethical concerns due to their reliance on sensitive personal data. Such systems routinely process personally identifiable information (PII), including biometric identifiers, behavioral traces, and demographic attributes, increasing the risk of misuse, unauthorized access, or data leakage when governance mechanisms are inadequate. Compliance with international data protection regulations - most notably the General Data Protection Regulation (GDPR) - is therefore essential, requiring explicit consent, data minimization, and purpose limitation across the system lifecycle (Voigt & von dem Bussche, 2017; Ali et al., 2022).

Another major concern is algorithmic bias. ML models trained on incomplete or unrepresentative datasets may produce discriminatory outcomes that disproportionately affect individuals based on protected attributes such as race, gender, or socioeconomic status (Mehrabi et al., 2021). To mitigate these risks, system designers must incorporate fairness-aware learning techniques, bias detection metrics, continuous auditing, and transparent documentation into ML pipelines. Explainable AI (XAI) techniques play a critical role by making decision logic visible to stakeholders, which is especially important in high-stakes applications such as identity verification and access control (Jobin et al., 2019).

Given the dynamic nature of fraud, ML models require continuous monitoring, retraining, and recalibration. Static or poorly maintained systems rapidly lose effectiveness against adaptive adversaries. Responsible system design therefore demands a balance between innovation and accountability, ensuring that ML-driven identity verification remains privacy-preserving, transparent, and aligned with legal and ethical standards.

8.2 Evolving Fraud Techniques

Fraudsters continuously refine their tactics by exploiting automation, AI, social engineering, and deepfake technologies, compelling defenders to adopt equally adaptive countermeasures. Although ML models excel at capturing nonlinear relationships in complex financial datasets (Sudjianto et al., 2010), their effectiveness depends on frequent retraining to reflect newly emerging fraud strategies and concept drift. Hybrid approaches that combine supervised, unsupervised, and deep learning methods are increasingly used to detect both known fraud patterns and previously unseen attack vectors (Dal Pozzolo et al., 2015).

Emerging paradigms such as federated learning and transfer learning offer promising avenues for addressing data scarcity and privacy concerns while enabling cross-institutional collaboration. These approaches allow models to learn from distributed datasets without sharing raw data, improving scalability and generalization (Kairouz et al., 2021). Collaboration among financial institutions, regulators, and technology providers is therefore critical, as shared threat intelligence and anonymized insights can reveal systemic fraud trends that remain invisible at the organizational level.

When integrated with traditional controls, AI-driven systems can automate the fraud management lifecycle, including anomaly detection, risk scoring, case prioritization, and investigative support. This automation enables near–real-time responses to evolving threats and enhances resilience against transnational and coordinated financial crime (Wang, 2023). Sustained investment in adaptive system design and collaborative intelligence sharing remains essential to counter increasingly sophisticated adversaries.

8.3 Anomaly Detection

Anomaly detection constitutes a core component of ML-based fraud prevention, enabling early identification of unusual behaviors that may signal identity compromise or financial misconduct. These techniques continuously analyze transaction streams and user activity profiles to detect deviations from learned behavioral norms, functioning as proactive warning mechanisms (Chandola et al., 2009; Aslam & Hussain, 2024). Financial institutions leverage rich transactional metadata - such as transaction value, timing, location, merchant category, and device characteristics - to establish individualized behavioral baselines.

Examples of anomalous behavior include unexpected international transactions, sudden spikes in transaction volume, or abrupt changes in merchant diversity, which may indicate account takeover, synthetic identity usage, or coercive fraud. The choice of anomaly detection method depends on data availability and labeling. Supervised models - such as logistic regression, random forests, support vector machines, and gradient boosting - are effective when labeled fraud examples exist, while unsupervised techniques such as clustering, Isolation Forest, local outlier factor (LOF), and autoencoders are applied when labels are scarce (Chandola et al., 2009).

The principal strength of anomaly detection lies in its ability to model high-dimensional, nonlinear relationships that rule-based systems fail to capture. In practice, anomaly detection is embedded within end-to-end fraud platforms, where detected irregularities trigger automated responses, including transaction blocking, dynamic risk scoring, or escalation for manual review. Evaluation metrics typically emphasize recall and F1 score, as false negatives - missed fraud events - carry particularly severe consequences. Beyond technical benefits, anomaly detection supports effective risk governance, consumer protection, and regulatory compliance.

8.4 Real-Time Data Analytics

Machine learning has fundamentally enhanced the ability of financial institutions to respond swiftly to emerging fraud threats. Real-time data analytics is especially critical in environments where transactions are executed within milliseconds. ML models optimized for low-latency inference can identify and respond to fraudulent behavior as it occurs, a capability that is essential for countering rapid, high-pressure scams such as digital arrest fraud (Aslam & Hussain, 2024).

These systems continuously evaluate transaction streams using features such as transaction frequency, device fingerprints, geolocation, and network metadata to establish behavioral baselines. Deviations from these baselines can automatically trigger countermeasures, including transaction freezes, step-up authentication, or session termination. In contrast, traditional rule-based systems rely on static thresholds and delayed reporting, often allowing fraud to progress unchecked (Carminati et al., 2015).

ML-based probabilistic classifiers - including logistic regression, decision trees, random forests, neural networks, and ensemble models - enable real-time risk scoring and integration into payment authorization workflows. However, deploying real-time ML introduces operational challenges, such as managing high-velocity data streams, maintaining low-latency inference, retraining models under concept drift, and balancing detection sensitivity with user experience. Human-in-the-loop oversight remains essential to manage edge cases and ensure accountability. Despite these challenges, real-time ML analytics significantly improve prevention of identity theft and coercive digital fraud by enabling rapid interception and minimizing irreversible harm.

9. FUTURE DIRECTIONS

Future research in identity verification and fraud prevention should prioritize the development of robust and flexible machine learning models capable of operating effectively under noisy, incomplete, and heterogeneous data conditions. As fraud scenarios become increasingly sophisticated and adversarial, models must not only achieve high predictive accuracy but also deliver explainable, auditable, and legally defensible decisions, particularly in regulated financial environments. Explainable artificial intelligence (XAI) therefore represents a critical research frontier, enabling stakeholders to understand which features, behaviors, and contextual signals most strongly influence fraud predictions and identity risk assessments (Barredo et al., 2020; Ribeiro et al., 2016).

Another important direction concerns privacy-preserving learning paradigms. Techniques such as federated learning, secure multi-party computation, and differential privacy allow collaborative model training across distributed datasets without exposing raw sensitive data, addressing both privacy and regulatory constraints (Kairouz et al., 2021). As regulatory expectations intensify, AI's role in compliance automation and risk governance will continue to expand; however, this growth must be guided by ethical standards, transparency, and cross-sector collaboration to balance innovation with systemic risk (Truby et al., 2020).

Industry analyses suggest that by the late 2020s, AI will be deeply embedded in risk management and fraud monitoring processes across most financial institutions, contributing to reduced operational losses, faster response times, and improved efficiency (Xu et al., 2023). In parallel, AI-driven personalization is expected to enhance customer experience and operational performance, while the convergence of AI with blockchain technologies may reshape auditability, regulatory reporting, and trust infrastructures across financial and digital identity ecosystems (Rane et al., 2024).

9.1 Advancements in Artificial Intelligence and Machine Learning

Advances in AI and machine learning are reshaping financial services through predictive modeling, natural language processing, deep learning, and anomaly detection, with applications spanning fraud prevention, lending, cybersecurity, regulatory compliance, and algorithmic trading (Truby et al., 2020; Ebbage, 2018). By continuously learning from large-scale transactional and behavioral datasets, AI systems can identify subtle fraud signals, adapt to evolving attack strategies, and reduce false-positive rates that burden investigators and customers alike.

In credit assessment and identity risk analysis, machine learning models increasingly incorporate alternative data sources - such as transaction behavior, device signals, and digital interaction patterns - to evaluate risk more holistically, supporting financial inclusion while maintaining robust controls (Bussmann et al., 2021). At the same time, natural language processing - powered systems and conversational agents are transforming customer engagement by enabling real-time interaction, document analysis, and automated compliance checks.

Looking ahead, AI systems are expected to evolve from task-level automation toward strategic and semi-autonomous decision-support systems capable of managing portfolios, detecting systemic risk, and optimizing decisions in real time (Roy et al., 2025). When governed responsibly, these advances may contribute to a more resilient, efficient, and ethically grounded financial ecosystem.

9.2 Integration with Blockchain Technology

The integration of AI and blockchain technology is redefining data security and identity verification by combining AI's analytical intelligence with blockchain's decentralized, immutable, and tamper-resistant ledger. Blockchain infrastructures provide strong guarantees of integrity, traceability, and non-repudiation, making them suitable for storing and verifying identity credentials without reliance on centralized repositories that are vulnerable to large-scale breaches (Zheng et al., 2019; Singh et al., 2020).

AI complements blockchain by analyzing biometric signals, behavioral patterns, and transactional histories to detect inconsistencies, synthetic identities, and coordinated fraud schemes (Krause, 2024). Together, these technologies enable self-sovereign identity (SSI) models, in which individuals retain control over their credentials via blockchain-based wallets and smart contracts, reducing centralized attack surfaces and enhancing privacy (Zyskind et al., 2015).

From a fraud-prevention perspective, AI can monitor blockchain ledgers for anomalous activity - such as microtransaction abuse, suspicious token flows, or cross-chain laundering - while natural language processing techniques extract contextual insights from unstructured identity-related data. Empirical studies indicate that AI–blockchain convergence can streamline KYC/AML processes, accelerate onboarding, and strengthen regulatory compliance while reducing operational costs (Casino et al., 2019). By the late 2020s, this convergence is expected to extend beyond finance into healthcare, supply chains, and digital governance, reinforcing trust and accountability in decentralized ecosystems (Chatterjee, 2025; Yuan et al., 2025).

9.3 The Role of Regulation and Policy

The accelerating adoption of AI in financial services necessitates robust regulatory and governance frameworks to ensure ethical deployment, accountability, and public trust. AI systems increasingly influence high-stakes decisions - such as fraud detection, credit approval, and identity verification - where biased, opaque, or poorly governed models may result in discrimination, exclusion, or privacy violations (Olabanji et al., 2024).

Regulatory approaches should therefore mandate fairness assessments, bias audits, model documentation, and the use of explainable AI techniques to ensure transparency and protect affected individuals (Adeyelu et al., 2024). Institutional governance mechanisms including ethics committees, continuous auditing, and independent model validation are essential to ensure alignment with legal and ethical standards in algorithmic decision-making (Jobin et al., 2019). Transparency is particularly critical: organizations must clearly communicate how algorithmic decisions affect consumers to foster trust, contestability, and informed consent in regulated environments (Kroll et al., 2017). Regulatory sandboxes provide a pragmatic pathway for responsible innovation by enabling controlled experimentation under supervisory oversight, allowing regulators and developers to assess risks before full-scale deployment (Lee, 2020). As AI technologies continue to evolve, adaptive, participatory, and principles-based regulation will be required to balance efficiency, innovation, and ethical responsibility in fraud prevention and identity verification systems (Ellul, 2022).

10. CONCLUSION

The continued evolution of AI is fundamentally reshaping digital identity systems and fraud prevention in financial services. Institutions are increasingly deploying AI-driven identity verification solutions that integrate facial recognition, voice biometrics, behavioral analysis, and document authentication into seamless digital workflows. These technologies enable secure, scalable, and low-friction onboarding processes while strengthening protection against identity misuse and financial fraud. In parallel, the convergence of AI with blockchain infrastructures is accelerating the development of self-sovereign identity models, allowing individuals to manage and present verifiable credentials independently of centralized authorities. Such decentralized approaches enhance portability, integrity, and trust in digital identity ecosystems.

AI also plays a critical role in advancing financial inclusion. By leveraging alternative and non-traditional data sources - such as transaction behavior, mobile usage patterns, and digital interaction histories - machine learning models can assess risk and creditworthiness for populations that have historically been excluded from formal financial systems. At the same time, AI-driven monitoring systems continuously analyze transactional and behavioral signals to detect anomalies, prevent account takeovers, and mitigate identity fraud in near real time, significantly reducing financial losses and operational risk.

Despite these benefits, the growing reliance on AI introduces important challenges related to privacy, consent, fairness, transparency, and accountability. Identity verification systems frequently process sensitive personal and biometric data, making robust governance, data protection, and ethical oversight essential. Explainability and auditability are particularly important in high-stakes financial contexts, ensuring that automated decisions can be understood, reviewed, and challenged when they affect access to essential services. Addressing algorithmic bias further requires diverse and representative data, continuous performance evaluation, and meaningful human-in-the-loop supervision.

In conclusion, machine learning is steering identity verification toward more secure, intelligent, and inclusive digital ecosystems. The integration of AI with biometrics, advanced analytics, and decentralized technologies offers substantial potential to improve accuracy, accessibility, and trust in digital identity services worldwide. However, realizing this potential depends on aligning technological innovation with ethical responsibility, regulatory rigor, and a sustained commitment to human dignity. The future of digital identity and financial security will be shaped by how effectively institutions, regulators, and technologists collaborate to harness AI while upholding fairness, accountability, and societal trust.

REFERENCES

Adesoga, A., Adekunle, A., & Oladipo, O. (2024). Real-time fraud detection using machine learning. *IEEE Access : Practical Innovations, Open Solutions*, *12*, 33411–33425.

Adeyelu, A., Akinrinola, O., & Olatunji, S. (2024). Ethical governance of artificial intelligence in financial decision-making systems. *AI and Ethics*, *4*(2), 215–229. DOI: 10.1007/s43681-023-00345-7

Adhikari, S., Mishra, A., & Singh, R. (2024). Machine learning techniques for financial fraud detection. *Expert Systems with Applications*, *231*, 120864.

Adrian, T., & Mancini-Griffoli, T. (2019). *The rise of digital money*. IMF FinTech Notes.

Ahmadi, M. (2024). Real-time fraud detection using machine learning. *IEEE Access : Practical Innovations, Open Solutions*, *12*, 22145–22158.

Alauthman, M., Al-Qaraghuli, A., & Gupta, B. B. (2023). Hybrid machine learning frameworks for fraud detection. *Future Generation Computer Systems*, *139*, 1–14.

Alfaiz, A., & Fati, S. M. (2022). Adversarial attacks and defenses in machine learning: A survey. *IEEE Access : Practical Innovations, Open Solutions*, *10*, 121512–121537.

Ali, M., Rauf, A., & Khan, S. (2022). Privacy-preserving machine learning for identity management. *Computers & Security*, *115*, 102620.

Alkhateeb, F., & Maolood, I. Y. (2019). Identity fraud detection using machine learning techniques. *Journal of Information Security and Applications*, *46*, 15–25.

Almomani, I., Alauthman, M., & Gupta, B. B. (2024). Intelligent fraud detection systems: A survey of machine learning approaches. *Journal of Network and Computer Applications*, *226*, 103859.

Alshaikh, M., Maynard, S. B., Ahmad, A., & Chang, S. (2024). Cybersecurity governance and the limitations of rule-based security controls. *Computers & Security*, *136*, 103530. DOI: 10.1016/j.cose.2023.103530

Antwi, H., Boateng, R., & Osei, K. (2024). Predictive analytics for transaction fraud. *Journal of Financial Crime*, *31*(1), 78–95.

Arowolo, O., Adewumi, A., & Oladipo, O. (2023). Unsupervised anomaly detection techniques for financial fraud. *Applied Soft Computing*, *132*, 109873.

Aslam, A., & Hussain, A. (2024). Performance evaluation metrics for fraud detection systems. *Journal of Big Data*, *11*(1), 52.

Aslam, F., Rehman, A., & Akram, M. (2022). Machine learning techniques for identity theft and fraud detection. *Security and Communication Networks*, *4589123*. Advance online publication. DOI: 10.1155/2022/4589123

Asmar, D., & Tuqan, J. (2024). Machine learning approaches for digital identity verification. *Journal of Information Security and Applications*, *77*, 103668. DOI: 10.1016/j.jisa.2023.103668

Bajpai, P. (2024). Predictive risk analytics using machine learning. *Computers & Security*, *133*, 103258.

Barredo Arrieta, A., Díaz-Rodríguez, N., Del Ser, J., Bennetot, A., Tabik, S., Barbado, A., García, S., Gil-López, S., Molina, D., Benjamins, R., Chatila, R., & Herrera, F. (2020). Explainable Artificial Intelligence (XAI): Concepts, taxonomies, opportunities and challenges toward responsible AI. *Information Fusion*, *58*, 82–115. DOI: 10.1016/j.inffus.2019.12.012

Biggio, B., & Roli, F. (2018). Wild patterns: Ten years after the rise of adversarial machine learning. *Pattern Recognition*, *84*, 317–331. DOI: 10.1016/j.patcog.2018.07.023

Buchanan, B. (2019). *The AI triangle*. Oxford University Press.

Bussmann, N., Giudici, P., Marinelli, D., & Papenbrock, J. (2021). Explainable AI in credit risk management. *Computational Economics*, *57*(1), 203–216. DOI: 10.1007/s10614-020-10042-0

Bynagari, N. B. (2015). Machine learning and data analytics in financial fraud detection. *International Journal of Computer Applications*, *120*(15), 1–6.

Carcillo, F., Dal Pozzolo, A., Snoeck, M., & Bontempi, G. (2021). Scarff: A scalable framework for streaming credit card fraud detection. *Information Fusion*, *63*, 182–194. DOI: 10.1016/j.inffus.2020.05.009

Carminati, M., Caron, R., Maggi, F., Epifani, I., & Zanero, S. (2015). BankSealer: A decision support system for online banking fraud analysis and investigation. *Decision Support Systems*, *74*, 1–12.

Casino, F., Dasaklis, T. K., & Patsakis, C. (2019). A systematic literature review of blockchain-based applications: Current status, classification and open issues. *Telecommunication Systems*, *72*(3), 1–25. DOI: 10.1007/s11235-019-00555-7

Chaganti, R., Rao, K. S., & Reddy, M. P. (2021). Social engineering attacks and prevention strategies. *Journal of Cybersecurity*, *7*(1), taab012. Advance online publication. DOI: 10.1093/cybsec/taab012

Chandola, V., Banerjee, A., & Kumar, V. (2009). Anomaly detection: A survey. *ACM Computing Surveys*, *41*(3), 1–58. DOI: 10.1145/1541880.1541882

Chatterjee, S. (2025). Blockchain governance and trust infrastructures. *Government Information Quarterly*. Advance online publication. DOI: 10.1016/j.giq.2024.101845

Chen, Y. (2025). Deep learning in financial fraud detection: A systematic review. *Machine Learning with Applications*, *11*, 100578. DOI: 10.1016/j.mlwa.2024.100578

Dal Pozzolo, A., Bontempi, G., Snoeck, M., & Baecke, P. (2015). Adapting machine learning models to concept drift for credit card fraud detection. *Expert Systems with Applications*, *42*(21), 7904–7914. DOI: 10.1016/j.eswa.2015.06.033

Donegan, J. (2019). Law enforcement challenges in cybercrime investigations. *Policing*, *13*(3), 345–358. DOI: 10.1093/police/pay064

Ebbage, A. (2018). AI in financial services: Opportunities and risks. *Journal of Financial Transformation*, *47*, 36–45.

Ellul, J. (2022). Adaptive regulation for AI-driven systems. *Regulation & Governance*, *16*(3), 780–796.

Farina, K. (2015). The psychological impact of identity theft. *Journal of Financial Crime*, *22*(4), 423–436.

Gope, P., Sikdar, B., Kumar, N., & Cheng, X. (2021). Privacy-aware authenticated key agreement scheme for secure smart healthcare. *IEEE Transactions on Industrial Informatics*, *17*(2), 1349–1359. DOI: 10.1109/TII.2020.2998824

Gupta, A., & Srivastava, R. (2023). Machine learning techniques for fraud detection. *Computers & Security*, *124*, 102964.

Hasan, M., & Rizvi, S. (2022). Support vector machine-based classification for fraud detection. *Journal of King Saud University. Computer and Information Sciences*, *34*(7), 3849–3860.

Ikudabo, O., & Kumar, P. (2024). Ensemble learning techniques for financial fraud detection. *Expert Systems with Applications*, *236*, 121230. DOI: 10.1016/j.eswa.2023.121230

Jain, A. K., & Gupta, S. (2018). Biometric authentication: System security and user privacy. *IEEE Computer*, *51*(2), 87–92.

Jain, A. K., & Gupta, S. (2019). Challenges in credit card fraud detection. *IEEE Security and Privacy*, *17*(3), 42–50.

Jobin, A., Ienca, M., & Vayena, E. (2019). The global landscape of AI ethics guidelines. *Nature Machine Intelligence*, *1*(9), 389–399. DOI: 10.1038/s42256-019-0088-2

Kairouz, P., et al. (2021). Advances and open problems in federated learning. Foundations and Trends® in Machine Learning, 14(1–2), 1–210.

Krause, M. (2024). AI analytics for blockchain-based fraud detection. *Computers & Security*, *134*, 103423.

Kroll, J. A., Huey, J., Barocas, S., Felten, E. W., Reidenberg, J. R., Robinson, D. G., & Yu, H. (2017). Accountable algorithms. *University of Pennsylvania Law Review*, *165*(3), 633–705.

Kurshan, E., & Shen, H. (2020). Graph computing for financial crime and fraud detection: Trends, challenges and outlook. [World Scientific]. *International Journal of Software and Informatics*, *10*(2), 187–203.

Lee, K., & Yoon, S. (2013). Semi-supervised learning for social-network fraud detection. *Expert Systems with Applications*, *40*(6), 2450–2460.

Lee, L. (2020). Regulatory sandboxes for fintech innovation. *Journal of Banking Regulation*, *21*(4), 315–327.

Li, Y., Wang, J., & Zhang, X. (2022). Behavioral analytics for online fraud detection. *Knowledge-Based Systems*, *238*, 107867.

Lundberg, S. M., & Lee, S.-I. (2017). A unified approach to interpreting model predictions. *Advances in Neural Information Processing Systems*, *30*, 4765–4774.

Luo, X., Wu, L., Xue, M., & Liu, Q. (2023). Robust machine learning under adversarial settings. *IEEE Transactions on Neural Networks and Learning Systems*, *34*(8), 3945–3960. DOI: 10.1109/TNNLS.2021.3139037

Lv, Z., Qiao, L., & Singh, A. K. (2019). Biometrics-based authentication with machine learning: A review. *Future Generation Computer Systems*, *92*, 812–825. DOI: 10.1016/j.future.2018.10.009

Mallick, S., & Ganguli, S. (2024). Digital impersonation fraud and emerging threats. *IEEE Security and Privacy*, *22*(1), 56–65.

Mandru, D. (2022). Adaptive authentication systems using machine learning. *Computers & Security*, *113*, 102543.

Manek, A. S., Shenoy, P. D., Mohan, M. C., & Venugopal, K. R. (2019). Credit card fraud detection using supervised learning. *Procedia Computer Science*, *165*, 438–447.

Mehrabi, N., Morstatter, F., Saxena, N., Lerman, K., & Galstyan, A. (2021). A survey on bias and fairness in machine learning. *ACM Computing Surveys*, *54*(6), 115. Advance online publication. DOI: 10.1145/3457607

Mutemi, J., & Bacao, F. (2024). COVID-19 and the acceleration of digital fraud risks. *Journal of Financial Crime*, *31*(2), 412–428.

Nguyen, T., Tran, D., & Pham, H. (2023). Fraud detection using ensemble learning. *IEEE Transactions on Neural Networks and Learning Systems*, *34*(9), 5276–5288.

NIST. (2020). Zero Trust Architecture (SP 800-207). National Institute of Standards and Technology.

Okoli, C., Al-Ali, A. K., & El-Khatib, K. (2024). Machine learning–driven cybersecurity analytics for adaptive threat detection. *IEEE Access : Practical Innovations, Open Solutions*, *12*, 28415–28431. DOI: 10.1109/ACCESS.2024.3369021

Olabanji, S., et al. (2024). Algorithmic accountability in AI-based financial decision systems. Journal of Financial Regulation.

Panigrahi, R., Borah, S., & Prasad, S. (2024). Support vector machine approaches for biometric authentication systems. *Pattern Recognition Letters*, *175*, 12–19.

Rahaman, M., Chattopadhyay, S., Rahman, M. M., & Islam, M. S. (2025). Human-centered artificial intelligence for scam prevention. *AI & Society*. Advance online publication.

Rane, S., Narayanamurthy, G., & Subramanian, N. (2024). AI–blockchain convergence in digital finance: Opportunities and challenges. *Technological Forecasting and Social Change*, *198*, 122987.

Ribeiro, M. T., Singh, S., & Guestrin, C. (2016). "Why should I trust you?" Explaining the predictions of any classifier. Proceedings of the 22nd ACM SIGKDD International Conference on Knowledge Discovery and Data Mining, 1135–1144. DOI: 10.1145/2939672.2939778

Roy, S., Bose, I., & Guha, A. (2025). Artificial intelligence–enabled financial risk management: A review and research agenda. *Decision Support Systems*, *176*, 114018. DOI: 10.1016/j.dss.2024.114018

Roy, S., Das, A., & Ghosh, P. (2025). Explainable artificial intelligence for financial risk management. *AI & Society*. Advance online publication.

Sen, S., Ghosh, S., & Chakrabarti, A. (2021). Deep learning approaches for fraud detection. *Neural Computing & Applications*, *33*, 9273–9290.

Shahrivari, S., Jalili, S., & Jafari, M. (2020). Fraud detection in social networks using machine learning. *Social Network Analysis and Mining*, *10*, 1–17.

Sharda, R., Delen, D., & Turban, E. (2018). *Business intelligence, analytics, and data science: A managerial perspective* (4th ed.). Pearson.

Singh, S., Jeong, Y.-S., & Park, J. H. (2020). Blockchain-based identity management: A survey. *IEEE Access : Practical Innovations, Open Solutions*, *8*, 193003–193028.

Sowmya, K., & Sathisha, B. (2023). Machine learning approaches for identity verification. *International Journal of Information Security Science*, *12*(1), 45–58.

Sudjianto, A., Nair, S., Yuan, M., Zhang, A., Kern, D., & Cela-Díaz, F. (2010). Statistical methods for fraud detection. In Calhoun, C. W. (Ed.), *Handbook of financial data and risk information*. Cambridge University Press.

Tae, C. M., & Hung, P. D. (2019, July). Comparing ML algorithms on financial fraud detection. In *Proceedings of the 2019 2nd International Conference on Data Science and Information Technology* (pp. 25-29).

Tian, Y., Li, H., & Chen, X. (2023). Financial fraud analytics using artificial intelligence. *Expert Systems with Applications*, *212*, 118685.

Truby, J., Brown, R., & Dahdal, A. (2020). Banking on AI. Law. *Technology and Humans*, *2*(1), 1–23.

Udeh, F., Okafor, E., & Eze, C. (2024). Predictive analytics for financial fraud prevention. *Journal of Financial Crime*, *31*(1), 95–112.

Vijayakumar, P., Chang, V., Alazab, M., & Sharma, R. (2020). Unsupervised anomaly detection for fraud identification. *Expert Systems with Applications*, *144*, 113042.

Voigt, P., & von dem Bussche, A. (2017). *The EU General Data Protection Regulation (GDPR): A practical guide*. Springer. DOI: 10.1007/978-3-319-57959-7

Wang, Y. (2023). AI-driven fraud detection systems. *Journal of Financial Crime*, *30*(3), 789–804.

Wu, Z., Pan, S., Chen, F., Long, G., Zhang, C., & Yu, P. S. (2021). A comprehensive survey on graph neural networks. *IEEE Transactions on Neural Networks and Learning Systems*, *32*(1), 4–24. DOI: 10.1109/TNNLS.2020.2978386

Xu, Y., Zhang, J., & Li, X. (2023). Artificial intelligence adoption in financial risk management. *Journal of Financial Crime*, *30*(2), 456–472.

Yazıcı, A. (2019a). A machine learning-based approach for identity fraud detection. *Computers & Security*, *87*, 101589. DOI: 10.1016/j.cose.2019.101589

Yazıcı, A. (2019b). Data-driven fraud detection using machine learning. *Applied Soft Computing*, *83*, 105605.

Yesare, R. (2023). Real-time anomaly detection in digital identity systems. *IEEE Access : Practical Innovations, Open Solutions*, *11*, 51234–51247.

Yousefi, S., Carrasco-Gallego, R., & Elhaouari, M. (2019). Machine learning-based fraud detection: A review. *Journal of Financial Crime*, *26*(2), 545–563. DOI: 10.1108/JFC-02-2018-0015

Yuan, Y., Li, X., Wang, S., & Chen, F. (2025). Decentralized identity and governance frameworks. *Future Generation Computer Systems*. Advance online publication.

Zhang, M. H., & Zhang, Z. (2013). A survey of biometric authentication systems. *International Journal of Computer Science and Network Security*, *13*(5), 23–28.

Zheng, Z., Xie, S., Dai, H., Chen, X., & Wang, H. (2019). An overview of blockchain technology: Architecture, consensus, and future trends. *Future Generation Computer Systems*, *87*, 557–576. DOI: 10.1016/j.future.2018.07.010

Zyskind, G., Nathan, O., & Pentland, A. (2015). Decentralizing privacy: Using blockchain to protect personal data. *Proceedings of the 2015 IEEE Security and Privacy Workshops*, 180–184. DOI: 10.1109/SPW.2015.27

Chapter 4
Leveraging Cybersecurity in the Context of Digital Arrest, Fraud, and Identity Theft:
An Ethico-Legal Perspective

Jipson Joseph
https://orcid.org/0009-0005-1795-5051
Christ University, India

ABSTRACT

The cyber world is becoming increasingly complex due to the diverse nature of cybercrimes. Although crimes like fraud, harassment, and identity theft exist in both the cyber and physical worlds, their magnitude is unpredictably high in the cyber world. However, digital arrest fraud is unique to cyberspace. Digital arrest fraud and identity theft are the top-listed cybercrimes, causing unimaginable monetary loss, anxiety, depression, fear, and isolation among the victims. The current cybersecurity measures and tools, as well as the legal and ethical framework, fail to address the evolving nature of cybercrimes. Such a scenario demands more collaborative efforts and a renewed approach to ensure global cybersecurity. From this perspective, this chapter critically examines the evolving nature of cybercrimes and the available legal and ethical framework to underline the importance of leveraging cybersecurity through some required changes in the ethico-legal landscape. It argues for a globally accepted regulatory system and international cooperation to ensure cybersecurity.

DOI: 10.4018/979-8-3373-4149-1.ch004

1 INTRODUCTION

Globalization and the evolution of the Internet have initiated the process of increased interrelation between people and societies. The general availability of the Internet from 1993 onwards led to the evolution of a virtual world called the cyber world. Artificial Intelligence (AI), decision-making systems, and the latest scientific and technological advancements further expanded the possibilities of human interaction. (Strauss et al., 2024). The speed and scale of the "cyber civilization" have transformed all sectors and made the Internet a cornerstone of modern life (Admass et al., 2024). This progress has uncountable advantages to human well-being and societal welfare concerning the growth of various sectors like e-commerce, online banking, online education, e-healthcare, digital government service portals, and collaborative research platforms. However, they also bring specific challenges, as most contemporary interactions occur digitally (Thurston, 2022). Accordingly, cybercrimes, cybersecurity, digital privacy, digital arrests, etc., have become common parlance. Many fraudsters use technological advancements to deceive less qualified persons, loot their money, and spoil their dignity and reputation. The most notable incidents are related to digital arrest fraud and identity theft. The criminals mask their identity or act as if they are police officers and squeeze money from people, threatening legal action against them. These things spoil their confidence and trust in the security system, as they feel insecure even in their private space (Vijay, 2025).

Adequate cybersecurity measures are required to address these ongoing harms. Every country spends millions on territorial security to protect people's lives, freedom, and property. However, the present scenario demands more sincere cybersecurity efforts from state authorities as more insecurities occur in the digital world (Malzac, 2021). Cybersecurity should be preferred over territorial security in the present context. Cybercriminals cause more damage to people, and their involvement in people's lives and activities is rarely reported, as commoners are worried about their reputation. Increased cybersecurity measures, efficient legal mechanisms, proper awareness creation, international cooperation, and adequate punishment of cybercriminals are necessary to secure the activities in cyberspace (Admass et al., 2024). These steps must be strictly implemented so that the cyber activities of identityless persons will not harm people.

The continuous occurrence of digital arrest fraud and identity theft demands a strong legal framework. Many countries have enacted some cybersecurity acts and guidelines. However, they have not solved the increasing percentage of cybercrimes like digital arrest fraud and identity theft. It also underlines that there are notable issues with people's value system. Instead of prioritizing ethical values and principles, many concentrate on money and wealth, even by harming others. Such a scenario requires more robust laws and policies for cybersecurity. The globe also needs to ensure specific ethical principles in cyber interactions. From this perspective, this chapter examines the possibilities for leveraging cybersecurity in the context of increasing digital arrest fraud and identity theft. The chapter also advances specific guidelines for a required legal framework and ethical principles to ensure cybersecurity and a peaceful life. The chapter revolves around three research questions: What are the new forms of cybercrimes? How do they affect human security and economic activities? What is the available ethico-legal framework to address these insecurities, and what modifications should be undertaken for increased security? Accordingly, the chapter is designed. The following section explains the significance of the study in connection with the SDGs. Thereafter, it provides a conceptual framework of the latest cybersecurity threats and then describes the impact of cybercrimes on human security and economic activities. It finally examines the ethical and legal framework and the required changes.

2 SIGNIFICANCE OF THE STUDY

The Sustainable Development Goals (SDGs) underline the importance of progressive initiatives for ensuring a sustainable future. SDG9 affirms the necessity of building resilient infrastructure, promoting inclusive and sustainable industrialization, and fostering innovation. Technological advancements are to be encouraged for a sustainable society, as novel inclusive innovations can enhance the depth of its growth. Digital technologies, resulting from such innovative actions, and their use in industrialization and other productive sectors have increased economic growth over the last few decades (Knell, 2021). Digitalization can strengthen global efforts to achieve SDGs through addressing the digital divide (SDG1), efficient supply chain management (SDG2), AI-supported decision-making in healthcare system for better results (SDG3), enhanced access to education (SDG4), promotion of women's digital literacy (SDG5), smart water management (SDG6), innovative energy program (SDG7), smart cities and communities (SDG11), smart agriculture (SDG12), digital solutions to climate change (SDG13), and smart conservation (SDG14). The other SDGs also benefit from incorporating digital technologies (Vyas-Doorgaparsad, 2022). However, SDG9 also argues that they should be resilient. When technological innovations fail to ensure resilience, they endanger human security. Susceptibility to cyberattacks and cybercrimes is the main issue of digitalization.

Although cyberspace has become a "de facto battlefield" (Malzac, 2021) and cyberattacks adversely affect many critical infrastructures (Trautman, 2016), there is not yet a comprehensive international treaty on cyberattacks, global and national policy design, or an effective legal mechanism that specifically addresses the growing nature of cybercrimes (Thurston, 2022). Laws like the European Union's General

Data Protection Regulation (GDPR) provide a substantial framework for data protection, but fail to address the growing nature of cybercrimes. Many governments and institutions have significantly undertaken measures to improve cybersecurity. Although they point to some positive outcomes, cybercrimes are still increasing. According to the FBI's 2024 Internet Crime Report, there were 859,532 complaints of suspected internet crimes and the reported losses of almost US$16 billion. The eSENTIRE (2025) states that cybercrimes cost a financial loss of nearly US$9.5 trillion in 2024 worldwide. "If it were measured as a country, then cybercrime would be the world's third-largest economy after the US and China." Among several cybercrimes, the present globe is adversely affected by digital arrest fraud and identity theft. VeriDas (2025) states that an identity theft occurs every 22 seconds in the US, and almost 1.4 million cases were reported in 2024. According to the Indian government statement in the Rajya Sabha, nearly 1.23 lakh digital arrest cases were reported in 2024, causing a financial loss of 1935 crores (Inc42, 2025). There is no provision for digital arrest, but even then, cybercriminals exploit people's innocence and lack of awareness to cause insecurity and financial loss. The increasing number of such cases and the absence of a specific legal framework restrict the law enforcement agencies from ensuring immediate justice. The World Economic Forum (2025) also states that 35% of organizations claim inadequate cybersecurity measures. All these necessitate that the globe prioritize leveraging cybersecurity with strong ethical and legal foundations to guarantee security in cyberspace.

3 CONCEPTUAL FRAMEWORK

From the late 20th century onwards, the globe has moved towards a cyber or digital world. The availability of broadband in every nook and cranny of the world has shifted human interactions to cyberspace. Time, distance, and quantity of information have thus become irrelevant concerns. Almost all fields of human interaction, like communication (Strauss et al., 2024), education (Wang et al., 2024), healthcare (Galuner et al., 2021), commerce (Dallochio et al., 2024), supply chain management (Chauhan et al., 2023), industrialization (Zhang & Li, 2023), networking (Knell, 2021), and environmental protection (Xie et al., 2023), benefit from incorporating and implementing digital technologies. Global efforts to realize a sustainable future through the SDGs also use digital technologies, as mentioned above (Vyas-Doorgaparsad, 2022). However, security becomes crucial when people are increasingly involved in cyberspace. Insecurities in cyberspace can cause irreparable harm to human dignity and societal well-being. The world has become so digitalized that people cannot think of a meaningful and peaceful life without using digital technology in one way or another. However, if the digital world does not ensure security, it will jeopardize human involvement and the incorporating of digital technologies into human interactions. Nevertheless, cybercrimes are rapidly increasing along with the increase in the number of Internet users. Cyberspace offers immense opportunities for economic growth through proper channels. At the same time, it also brings many possibilities for criminal activities (Liao et al., 2017). Cybercrimes are increasing in number and expanding in diversity. In the present times, many have become victims of digital arrest fraud and identity theft. It causes insecurities, which are more complex than the issues at the territorial borders, as these security breaches happen in their private sphere. Accordingly, cybersecurity has become a significant concern within the context of digital arrest fraud and identity theft.

3.1 Digital Arrest Fraud

From the dawn of civilization, the ultimate objective has been economic growth and ensuring a meaningful living. The majority earn a significant living and economic growth through hard work. However, some benefited economically by deceiving others in various ways. They took advantage of the innocence and lack of knowledge of others. Tricks and scams to cheat people for economic benefits could be seen in almost all centuries. Such deceiving techniques exist even today, but in new forms and shapes. Cyberspace gives them a new playground where they are easily connected to physically distant people (Stevenson, 2000). Technological advancements give unimaginable and innovative ways to commit cybercrimes. Digital arrest fraud is a new variant of cybercrime. Although there is no such thing as digital arrest in any law, it has become routine in many countries, causing human security concerns. Digital arrest fraud is a contemporary version of consumer fraud. Consumer fraud is an economic crime that intentionally deceives or attempts to deceive an individual with the promise of nonexistent goods, services, or other benefits agreed to provide but not intended to (Titus, 2001). There is an agreement between the sender and the receiver, but the sender has no intention of fulfilling the contract. Liao et al. (2017, p.444) state that "online financial fraud has increased exponentially in the past decade." It has become more challenging in the present decade. These consumer frauds take different forms with the advancement of technology, and digital arrest fraud is its latest version.

The NITI Aayog states that "digital arrest is a scam designed to extort money from victims using fear, deceit, and intimidation. Fraudsters impersonate law enforcement officials, using threats of arrest, frozen bank accounts, and passport cancellations to coerce victims into paying a 'fine' or 'security deposit' to avoid legal action" (Singh, 2025). This definition enlists specific characteristic features of digital arrest fraud. *Firstly*, it is a scam to steal money from people. *Secondly*, compared to traditional consumer fraud methods, digital arrest fraud uses fear and intimidation as tools to extract money from victims, in addition to the ongoing deceit strategy. *Thirdly*, fraudsters project themselves as law enforcement officers who have come to help the victims. On the one hand, it gives confidence to victims; on the other hand, the victims may easily become terrified listening to the legal language and intimidation. Besides, it also challenges people's apprehensions about the legal enforcement system. They have no genuine confidence in the system, and many believe they can escape the legal struggles by bribing. Using the victim's lack of confidence in the system, the offenders loot their money. *Fourthly*, they intimidate the victims with threats of arrest, bank account freezing, and passport cancellation. Many are unaware that no police officer can digitally arrest a person. They are also unaware that neither bank accounts nor passports can be canceled without due process of law. *Fifthly*, after all the intimidation and deceitful process, the offenders guarantee that legal action can be avoided if they pay a fine or a security deposit. Those who doubt the transparency and fairness of the legal system easily become victims of this fraud. If people fail to show confidence in the legal system and understand its basic procedural patterns, it is a failure of the very concept of the Rule of Law.

Digital arrest fraud starts with a regular telephone call explaining a parcel's details, clarifying doubts concerning KYC, or pointing out some money laundering issues. However, within a few minutes after getting the basic information about the victim, the offender becomes aggressive and intimidates the victim. The offender accuses the victim of being involved in serious crimes like money laundering, drug trafficking, terrorism, and cybercrime. The offender mostly asks the victim to isolate themselves from others and switch to video calls. When the victim sees the video of the offender sitting in an office as if a law enforcement officer, their mental exposure becomes worse, and they easily comply with the demands of the offender. Once the offenders realize the victim's vulnerability, they monitor them closely until they get the payment (Gupta, 2025; Vijay, 2025). According to Gupta (2025), digital arrest fraud happens in a process of six stages: the hook (initial phase), creating panic (stage of false allegations), digital detention (forcefully demands isolation from others), psychological pressure (intimidating stage), extortion (financial exploitation stage), and disappearance and realization (final stage). If victims do not respond to the hook stage, realizing that it is a scam, offenders leave the scene without moving further. The first stage is crucial for both the victim and the offender. That is why many argue that increased awareness among the public is the best method to address these kinds of scams.

Let's take the example of India, the most populous country, to explain the depth of digital arrest fraud. There has been a notable increase in reported cases and calculated financial losses over the last three years. In 2022, the National Cybercrime Reporting Portal (NCRP) states that there were 39,925 reported cases concerning digital arrest fraud and related cybercrimes, causing a financial loss of 0.91 billion. Although the number of reported cases and the caused financial loss in 2023 are not exactly available, it shows a surge. In 2024, according to NCRP, the total number of reported cases became 1,23,672, and the financial loss was about 19.35 billion. Within the first two months of 2025, 17718 cases were reported, causing 2.1 billion (Gupta, 2025). What would the global situation be like if one country's scenario were this vast? It shows that digital arrest scams and related cybercrimes have become a multi-billion-dollar (deceiving) sector. The increasing number of digital arrest scams affirms that many people are less aware of cybercrimes, and the legal framework has not yet been well-designed to address and incorporate the new varieties of cybercrimes.

3.2 Identity Theft

Identity theft includes many areas. One commonly used method is stealing personal information, bank account or credit card details, mobile numbers, and email addresses, and using them in payment frauds, loan frauds, and other financial fraudulent behaviors (Liao et al., 2017). The US Identity Theft and Assumption Deterrence Act of 1998 defines identity theft precisely. Accordingly, it is the knowing transfer or use of the identification of another person without lawful authority, intended to commit, aid, or abet an unlawful activity that violates the state law (Koops & Leenes, 2006). Identity theft is the illegal acquisition of personal information and its use for theft, fraud, or a gateway to criminal activities (Manwani et al., 2021). Identity theft is associated with three characteristic features: a) it is related to some means of identity, like name, photo, ID card, or document; b) it does not belong to the perpetrator; c) it is used for illegal activities without lawful authority (Koops & Leenes, 2006). For instance, the ID cards of some innocent people, without their knowledge, are used to take SIM connections for criminals. When governments realized this malpractice and insisted on adding biometric details, these fraudulent people, with the support of mobile shop owners, started to deceive ordinary people by collecting their details, pretending that the previously registered one did not work.

Although identity theft has existed for a long time, cyberspace has expanded its scope. Society's increasing dependence on digital data has broadened the criminal landscape of identity theft (Harrell, 2019). The increased number of social media users and the users of other digital platforms, knowingly or unknowingly, share their name, phone number, birthdays, and other details, which the perpetrators track and utilize for illegal activities if proper security measures are not undertaken. By hacking personal data and passwords, some log into others' accounts and intentionally misuse them for individual gain. For instance, although no identity card exists in the US, the unique Social Security number serves its purpose. If somebody gets access to the Social Security number, it is an entry to their identity, which can be misused (Dennis, 2025). Some fraudsters even make obscene images and videos and post them on hacked social media platforms, causing severe reputational harm and psychological issues to victims. They also face financial loss and emotional imbalance (Ilzan et al., 2023). Since identity theft is widespread in cyberspace, it requires a competent legal framework and cybersecurity measures.

3.3 Cybersecurity

Security issues increase along with the evolution and advancement of the latest technologies. It is more vital in the digital world due to its interconnected nature. It forces individuals, institutions, and governments to enable proper security measures to protect their sensitive data, techniques, and systems (Admass et al., 2024). Cybersecurity refers to the security system that guarantees the protection of cyberspace interactions. "Cybersecurity means maintaining the integrity, confidentiality, and availability (ICA) of computing assets belonging to an organization or connecting to another organization's network" (Kaur & Ramkumar, 2022, p.5767). Cybercrimes and cyberattacks occur when there is negligence in maintaining adequate cybersecurity (Schneier, 2018). When almost all industrial, commercial, economic, and social activities occur in cyberspace, a high cybersecurity standard is essential to ensure people's right to privacy, reliability, and confidence in the system (Kaur & Ramkumar, 2022). Government policies, industrial outputs, developmental projects, supply chain management, and technological advancements require an efficient cybersecurity framework. Establishing the strongest cybersecurity programs and devices has thus become one of the main strategies to confront cybercrimes (Humayun et al., 2020).

Many institutions and individuals prefer AI and machine learning tools to confront cyberattacks. They can efficiently detect threats from various corners, uncover network vulnerabilities and fix them, and reduce the workloads of IT professionals, as they can handle most complexities with the support of their professional intelligence. They continuously perform intrusion detection, malware analysis, and vulnerability assessment. Their active involvement supports human actors in focusing more on strategic tasks. However, there are new anti-machine learning and AI attacks (Admass et al., 2024). It underlines that cybercriminals find strategies to breach the security system when a new technological update happens in cyberspace. They find unique methods to stay ahead of cybersecurity measures (Singh, 2025). Cyberattacks are complex and diverse, demanding progressive cybersecurity tools and processes. The scammers and intruders devise more sophisticated techniques to breach and control a system, exploiting its vulnerabilities (Admass et al., 2024). No human-made system can be perfect, and intruders often target those vulnerabilities. Adding to Osburn's (2025) suggestions for the importance of an organizational cybersecurity culture, this chapter suggests that public and private actors should refrain from engaging in cyberattacks (hacking), as they are against the demands of justice and international legal principles.

Cybersecurity has become intricate due to a lack of human interest and attentiveness. Even when several cybercrimes have been reported, many people are not prudent enough to install adequate security systems. The technological advancements have provided many AI and machine learning tools, like Darktrace, IBM Watson for cybersecurity, CylancePROTECT, and Vera security, that help people and law enforcement agencies to predict, detect, and respond to cybercrimes without allowing them to happen, identify suspicious activities in real-time, prevent malware attacks and malicious activites, and safeguard sensitive data (Manwani et al., 2025). The interconnected use of AI and machine learning to ensure cybersecurity can reduce the burden on law enforcement agencies, as they perform early detection rather than late interventions. The globe should considerably focus on cybersecurity, just like it invests billions in territorial security. Cyberspace has become crucial to human existence. If adequate security measures are not enabled, human interactions, societal life, national security, and international relations will be damaged.

4 CYBERCRIMES: A CONVOLUTED EROTEME

The evolution of the Internet has provided a broader scope in strengthening communication, economic activities, entertainment possibilities, and educational opportunities. Global interconnectedness has become a meaningful reality due to advancements in digital technology. However, it has also become a venue for criminal exploitation (Manwani et al., 2025). The line between traditional and cybercrimes is unclear (Wall, 2001). It can be said that the Internet is the differentiating factor. It is difficult to define the nature of cybercrimes due to their wide range. It is also not easy to capture all the characteristics of cyber criminals under the same profile (Liao et al., 2017). The Interpol (2025) states that digital crimes were rare in the late 20th century. In the first decade of the 21st century, isolated events were reported. However, it has quickly become a sophisticated issue in almost all human interaction fields. It affects everyone regardless of their financial strength or powerful position. Individuals, big companies, local government offices, and international institutions have become victims of cybercrimes.

Cybercriminals closely observe the targeted individuals and institutions' online interactions, behavior patterns, and financial positions. When a loophole is found, they breach the security and endanger the data (Liao et al., 2017). Cybercrimes include hacking, financial fraud, phishing, identity theft, and online harassment. While the offenders are mostly hidden in the dark side of the web, the victims are easily exposed (Pratt et al., 2010). Cybercrimes can be either personal or impersonal. Personal cybercrimes are those in which there is a direct personal communication between the offender and the sender. Cybercriminals manipulate and force people to reveal their personal information. Believing the deceitful words of the offender, victims share vital information, which the offenders use to commit cybercrimes. For instance, when a victim receives a phishing email claiming that a big prize is awarded, the offender steals all the money from the victim's account if the victim responds by sharing personal information, like bank account and other details. Impersonal cybercrimes are like credit card and ATM card fraud. There is no personal communication between the victim and the offender. The offender takes advantage of the loopholes in the system and loots money. Compared to impersonal cybercrimes, proving and prosecuting personal cybercrimes is difficult (Liao et al., 2017).

Cybercriminals use various tactics to incite people's feelings of fear (threatening legal action against them), excitement (fake lottery wins or contributions to charity), and urgency (fake emergency fund transfer request from a friend/colleague/relative). Cybercriminals emotionally blackmail the victims so that they will be in an awkward position to effectively and logically use their intelligence (Singh, 2025). Cybercriminals exploit people's vulnerabilities concerning their fear of law enforcement agencies and their interest in making more money without much effort. However, all cybercrimes ultimately result in losses to the victims. The total value lost to cybercrimes yearly is estimated to be far above the major economies' GDP (Interpol, 2025). Although it is an embarrassing statistic, it welcomes many into cybercrimes as it underlines the depth of its economic advantage.

Besides, most cybercrimes originate from Southeast Asian countries like Myanmar, Laos, Cambodia, and some African and Latin American countries where the local law enforcement system is weak and international cooperation is poor (Gupta, 2025). Although many countries, organizations, and individuals have installed efficient cybersecurity systems, cyberattackers find unique strategies to target some structural vulnerabilities. Some potent cyberattack techniques include "multi-vector attacks, polymorphic and fileless malware, zero-day exploits, and advanced persistent attacks" (Admass et al., 2024, p.4). They target even diplomatic and military services, which underline their powerful capacity. Since cybercrime is a multi-billion-dollar business, it uses all advanced technologies to deceive people. Therefore, the cybersecurity framework should become more structured and advanced to maintain security in cyberspace.

4.1 Cybercrimes and Terrorism

Terrorism, conventional or cyber, focuses on generating fear, vulnerability, and anxiety among the citizens, challenging the capacity of the government and law enforcement mechanisms to ensure security for people, institutions, and systems (Gross et al., 2017). Cyberterrorism is a crucial concern for the whole globe. When digital technologies and cyberspace are advanced to provide new opportunities and possibilities, terrorists also use them to spread their radical beliefs, recruit new members, and plan their future activities. They use cyberspace to engage in criminal activities to harm their enemies and cause a financial burden. Due to its characteristics, such as low cost, speed, efficiency, and anonymity, many terrorists prefer cyberspace, as they can easily target military sites, essential infrastructures, financial institutions, and power grids. In the present scenario, remote cyberattacks harmfully affect people more than conventional wars, as almost all human interactions use digital technologies. Cyberterrorists prefer hacking and installing malicious software, as they can easily damage, delete, alter, or suppress vital data, to spoil the effective functioning of other countries' systems (Manwani et al., 2025). While conventional terrorism targets deaths, injuries, and property destruction, cyberterrorism focuses on altering, misappropriating, or destroying data or digital systems to trouble and disrupt people's daily lives and governmental activities. Although the methods adopted by the terrorists differ in the cases of cyberterrorism and conventional terrorism, they both aim at causing disruptions and conflicts in society to achieve their political, religious, or ideological goals. Governments always prioritize territorial security and the protection of the military system. They often sideline the security concerns of the ordinary people, both in the physical and cyber worlds (Gross et al., 2017).

4.2 Cybercrimes and Economic Activities

Digital technologies are primarily beneficial to economic growth. Incorporating digital technologies in various fields of economic interaction has enhanced the horizon of growth. However, it is also prone to cybercrimes. Such a tendency makes the cyber world of economic interactions complex and insecure. Different types of cybercrimes are used against the economic sector. The most commonly found method is the alteration, destruction, and misappropriation of data by introducing viruses or malicious code that breach cybersecurity walls. Since almost all essential materials, software, and industrial know-how are stored as data, stealing company secrets for personal benefit has become relatively easy. When industrial espionage becomes easy, it affects economic growth. Cybersecurity breaches in any company, business sector, or banking sector can adversely affect the confidence of its customers, causing unpredictable financial loss (Stevenson, 2000). For instance, no customer would be happy to invest in a bank that repeatedly becomes a target of cybercrimes. Cybercriminals prefer well-established commercial firms with many customers. When these firms become the target, they become reluctant to report the crime, thinking it may affect their reputation and cause them to lose customers.

When such unreported events happen, cybercriminals maximize their criminal activities, causing substantial economic burdens to society.

Economic loss is vast in the context of digital arrest fraud and identity theft. Digital arrest fraud victims will be forced to transfer their money to the offenders, as they are severely coerced and intimidated. These fraudulent transactions cause them financial loss. However, it also negatively affects the economy, as people will start to doubt the reliability of online transactions, the authenticity of investment opportunities, and the availability of customer choices. On the other hand, the government will be forced to invest more in enhancing cybersecurity programs and supporting victims financially. This will affect the government's ability to invest more in infrastructure development and other priorities (Vijay, 2025). Examining the digital arrest scams in India, Gupta (2025) notes that the victims have lost money in different quantities, ranging from 50,000 to 7 crores. Although such an enormous amount of money is lost in cybercrimes, it is not easy to recover it, as the looted money is quickly transferred to multiple accounts in multiple countries or converted to cryptocurrency. If money is not recovered, ultimately, it becomes a burden for the victim and the government, affecting their economic choices.

4.3 Cybercrimes and Human Security

Cybercrimes often target people's security. Although its first focus is to breach the security of a system, it aims to cause human insecurity. Regardless of the nature of cyberwar, cyberterrorism, and cyberattacks, they aim to jeopardize human lives. Cyberwarfare uses malware and viruses to target military and public administration systems. Cyberterrorism involves attacking the state's essential infrastructure facilities nd other systems to challenge people's confidence in the government. Cybercrimes and cyberattacks, on the other hand, are primarily done for some personal or pecuniary gain. Cyberattacks are sometimes also done to express their revenge against someone or some institutions (Gross et al., 2017). All these affirm that any mischievous attempt in cyberspace causes inconvenience to people and their security. Hacking is the most commonly used method of cybercrime. Hackers target the data sources of Internet users. They alter, misappropriate, and sometimes destroy the data of individuals, companies, and governmental institutions, causing serious security concerns. For instance, if a hacker enters a hospital's medical records and misappropriates them, it can cause severe health insecurities to patients, as happened in Ascension hospitals in the US (Dalal et al., 2024). Hacking is always associated with computers, and there is no alternative to it in the offline world (Liao et al., 2017). Misappropriating and altering data can even cause reputational harm to specific individuals (Admass et al., 2024).

The current digital world faces complexities with online harassment. Without revealing their identity or utilizing the identity of a third party, many use online social media platforms to harass the personality and feelings of others. It may not have any financial loss compared to unethical hacking. However, it causes severe socio-psychological insecurities to the victims as the aggressors spoil their dignity in the public domain (Liao et al., 2017). When people face insecurity in their private zone, it adversely affects them and challenges their basic aspirations for security. Both digital arrest fraud and identity theft cause severe anxiety, psychological trauma, stress, fear, depression, isolation, shame, reputational challenges, and disorder (Vijay, 2025). These occur not merely during the interaction between the victim and the offender but have a long-term impact on the victim.

In some cases, when some highly educated people become victims of such scams, many people accuse and criticize them without realizing the emotional and mental torture that they have gone through. Vijay (2025) gives the example of a retired Karnataka IAS officer who became prey to digital arrest fraud and lost almost 11.5 lakhs. He was accused of money laundering and digitally arrested by the offenders masquerading as Mumbai police officers. It shows the magnitude of such crimes, as even a retired high-ranking administrative officer can become prey to such criminals. Gupta (2025) enlists some persons who became victims of digital arrest frauds in India, ranging from a Dubai-based entrepreneur, a 77-year-old woman, an IT executive of 59 years of age, an IIT student, and a nurse, to the head of the Vardhman group. It shows that people of all ages, with different qualifications and financial positions, become victims of digital arrest scams. Besides, it also reminds us that ordinary people who are less aware of these fraudulent activities can easily become victims, posing serious security concerns.

The US government has introduced the threat intelligence frameworks, which gather information from various sources that human security experts are asked to evaluate (Kaur & Ramkumar, 2022). It affirms explicitly that the government's ultimate objective should be to examine whether cyberattacks and cyberthreats cause human insecurities. Cybercrimes can be viewed from an economic, social, and sustainable perspective, but a human security perspective can shift how the globe addresses them.

5 DIGITAL ARREST FRAUD AND IDENTITY THEFT: AN ANALYSIS

Digital arrest fraud and identity theft cause significant economic loss, psychological issues, and social problems to the victims and society. When fraudsters deceive people using digital communication tools like Skype, Zoom, Google Meet, WhatsApp, and Facebook and sustain their contacts for a long time by showing forged documents, fabricated case details, and manipulated digital information, they become emotionally vulnerable and succumb to their demands (Vijay, 2025). The current scenario favors digital payment, online banking, and e-commerce, which make people more susceptible to cybercrimes. People are less aware of cyberspace's dangers and take much less effort and prudence when sharing personal information, passwords, and PINs, verifying the authenticity of callers, and recognizing the fraud indicators. When ordinary people fail to address the scammers prudently, they become their easy targets. Scammers use highly technical AI-supported methods to deceive people. Their advanced instruments sometimes outweigh the capacity and efficiency of those used by the legally established cyber cells. When there is an incomparable advantage to the scammers, they make maximum economic benefits (Gupta, 2025). Digital arrest and identity theft include "cyberattacks, financial fraud, data theft, and the exploitation of vulnerable individuals" (Manwani et al., 2025, p. 1307). The latest data affirms that they are significantly increasing, demanding urgent attention from policymakers and law enforcement mechanisms. The increased incidents pose serious concerns about cybersecurity and the effectiveness of ethical and legal principles.

5.1 Are AI and Decision-Making Systems in Danger?

The technological world reduces human efforts and challenges in many areas. The latest developments, like AI, machine learning algorithms, and blockchain, have shown that they can make decisions by critically analyzing various circumstances. Decision-making was a prerogative of human intelligence. However, the present scenario of machine intelligence and AI affirms the paradigm shift, which is beneficial in many areas. The advancements in any field are to ensure human security and well-being. For instance, when the chemists Otto Hahn and Fritz Stra mann invented Uranium fission and the physicists Lise Meitner and Otto Robert Frisch theoretically explained it, it was considered beneficial to society as it could produce energy (electricity). However, when governments use it to make atomic bombs to destroy people and countries, it becomes a danger. An invention is not an insecurity, but becomes a danger when used mischievously. The misuses related to cyberspace, using AI and machine learning technologies, point to the inefficiency of policymakers and law enforcement agencies. If there were efficient laws and determinative implementation strategies, cybercrimes would not have increased uncontrollably. Technological advancements are not problem-makers but problem-solvers. However, when these technologies are used for mischievous purposes, they threaten people. There are "technological fixes," but more important is the human factor that causes danger (Dalal et al., 2024). Ethical standards and legal principles are thus required to establish secure use of these technologies to promote human welfare.

5.2 Question of Trust

When there is an uncontrollable increase in digital arrest scams, it even challenges people's trust in the digital communication system. They question the accountability and credibility of the law enforcement system. When more such cases are reported, it may create panic and doubts among people about the performance of the government (Vijay, 2025). No recognized law enforcement system can function without a due process of law. When people are unaware of such legalities, they lose trust in the system. For instance, in 2023, the US experienced a record-breaking 3205 data breaches. The T-Mobile data breach (2024), PayPal credential stuffing attack (2024), AIIMS data breach (2023), and Indian Railway data breach (2023) are some of the Indian incidents of data leakages. Dalal et al. (2024) provide a big list of data breaches and cyberattacks worldwide that cause serious trust issues among people. When such things happen, people lose confidence in sharing their vital information.

6 CYBERSECURITY: ETHICAL AND LEGAL FRAMEWORK

Cyberspace has made it easy to commit illegal acts; conversely, it has also made it easy to detect criminals. Interestingly, the technology that has supported them in breaking the law can also be used to make them liable for their mischievous and fraudulent activities. The investigation of digital crimes is more difficult than that of conventional crimes. It requires more time, energy, and advanced technologies. The creation of pieces of evidence is also a complex task. Accordingly, the expenses are higher than in the usual investigation process. This affirms that early prevention methods are more useful than later interventions. Properly secured and routinely monitored cybersecurity systems are essential for effective early prevention strategies (Stevenson, 2000). However, many commit cybercrimes, breaching all basic cybersecurity walls. They feel that many victims will not lodge complaints, and even if complaints are registered, it is not easy to collect evidence and punish criminals, as most cybercriminal activities occur beyond borders. The legal framework varies from country to country, and many countries have not yet framed systematic legislation addressing the growing nature of cybercrimes. Since it is a matter of human conduct, it involves questions of right or wrong. Accordingly, it poses specific ethical questions concerning the behavior patterns of cyber criminals and the issues that have evolved from the breach of cybersecurity.

6.1 Ethical Principles

Ethical principles are essential in human interactions, as they should lead to individual well-being and societal welfare. Each society/culture has its unique perspectives on right and wrong. While wrong behaviors cause insecurity, right behaviors ensure peace and security. Most ethical values and principles are universally acknowledged in the globalized world of digitalization. It is more significant in the context of cyberspace. The Internet has brought out 'netizens' rather than 'citizens' who are not limited to specific boundaries. Accordingly, globally accepted ethical standards should apply to all netizens to discern and evaluate their cyber behaviors. The following ethical values and principles are essential for leveraging cybersecurity.

6.1.1 Accountability

Accountability insists on how an individual should behave in cyberspace. Pawlak (2024) criticizes that the demand for accountability is missing in the official statements of the UN and other international institutions while speaking on cyberspace. In informal discussions, they highly demand accountability but fail to prioritize it in their policies. Accountability upholds taking responsibility for one's actions in cyberspace (Buchan & Tsagourias, 2016). The debate on the state's accountability related to cybercrimes is an ongoing discussion point (Pawlak, 2024). It is always understood as a shared responsibility where individuals, institutions, and governments should collaborate. The state is responsible for improving cybersecurity, investigating cybercrimes, collecting evidence, and prosecuting offenders. Individuals and institutions cannot neglect their responsibility to ensure appropriate cyber-interaction care. On the other hand, the offenders should rethink their accountability towards society. Deceiving people for monetary gain does not ultimately provide any benefit, as the offenders can be caught and prosecuted. An individual's value can be counted based on their accountability for their actions.

6.1.2 Transparency

Transparency is the willingness to show the true nature of one's personality and expose the real intentions of one's behavior. It calls for eliminating mischievous and secret motives. It stands for openness in words and actions. Transparency is often acclaimed as a virtuous behavior as it helps others to discern the genuine personality of the speaker or the doer. Compared to the physical world, the cyber world should function based on the demands of transparency since most of its interactions are virtual, and face-to-face interactions are significantly less. For instance, although there is direct communication between the offender and the victim in phishing, the victim does not identify that the sender of the message or email is an offender. The victim trusts that the sender's identity is genuine. Accordingly, the victim shares personal information with the offender. However, if the victims had the opportunity to realize the deceitful intention of the sender, information would not have been shared. When there is a lack of transparency, it poses confusion among ordinary people (Liao et al., 2017).

6.1.3 Privacy

People face several issues related to online privacy, mainly in the area of data protection. They always fear that governments, organizations, and service providers continuously monitor their online behavior. Internet privacy depends on the information users share, the platforms they utilize, and the privacy protections they enable. Selection of the correct application, nature of the shared information, and use of efficient security software are essential to ensure privacy (Lubis et al., 2024). Without understanding the nature of the application/platform and duly checking its privacy statement, many install applications and share information, which may cause cybercrimes, identity theft, and digital arrest fraud. All applications function with permission requirements, but those requirements can sometimes become a severe threat to privacy. Cloud computing technology gives cyberspace new meaning through its flexibility, scalability, and cost-effectiveness. It is highly beneficial for data storage. Cloud providers usually create effective security systems. However, it is not without any security threats. The clouds are on the Internet. Accordingly, all security problems like cyberattacks, hacking, and fraud can happen (Cheng & Lai, 2012). Many governments have already recognized the right to privacy as a fundamental right. They have also recognized digital data protection, like the medical records in cyberspace, as part of the right to privacy. Nevertheless, data privacy violations and system security breaches for fraudulent purposes are increasing. When the right to privacy in cyberspace is violated without due process of law, it causes alarming insecurities. This necessitates valuable governmental actions prioritizing the implementation of people's right to privacy.

6.2 Legal Framework

Many countries and regions have successfully framed specific legislation concerning cybercrimes. These legislations can be a model framework for other countries, as most cybercrimes are similar without territorial differences. The UN has also given some guidelines for maintaining cybersecurity across the globe. However, the issue is that most cybercriminals operate behind layers of anonymity. Creating evidence against them is not easy for law enforcement agencies. The differing legal systems and the political sensitivities complicate the issue (Interpol, 2025). The NITI Aayog also underlines the same, arguing that "despite increasing cyber threats, many scams go unpunished due to slow law enforcement response, cross-border crime challenges, and lack of cybercrime awareness and policies" (Singh, 2025). Many reasons can be given for the increasing number of cybercrimes. However, all these point to the system's failure to protect the interests of the victims and the ordinary people. People should feel confident that if misappropriations happen in online money transactions and e-commerce services, law enforcement agencies will support them; otherwise, they may not engage in those activities even when governments encourage them. When cybercriminals exploit them, posing as legitimate authorities, the law enforcement system cannot escape its responsibility, citing many reasons. Suppose the present legal scenario and its complexities challenge people's trust in law enforcement agencies and cause them to doubt their capacity to uphold digital security standards (Vijay, 2025). In that case, there is an urgency to refine and update them. Besides, when cybercrimes occur, the victims are asked to report to cyber cells immediately. However, they lack technical expertise, resources, and international coordination possibilities to ensure justice. Furthermore, some people are unaware of their legal rights and fear reporting the crime immediately (Gupta, 2025). This section, therefore, examines the present legal scenario of some countries and regions and suggests the required changes for an increased cybersecurity legal framework.

6.2.1 Present Legal Scenario

Cybercriminals violate many laws concerning identity theft, impersonation, financial fraud, and illegal data collection. Some of their violations come under the specific provisions of cyber laws, and some others can also be charged under various sections of the penal code, such as cheating, defamation, impersonation, and criminal intimidation (Gupta, 2025). Many countries, like India, have specific laws to address the legal issues of identity theft in cyberspace. However, no country has framed specific laws to confront digital arrest scams. Although this can be charged under the provisions of some other laws mentioned above, the lack of a particular law addressing various cybercrimes benefits the scammers. Countries like Ethiopia have framed effective cybersecurity laws to enhance data protection responsibilities, giving a model to many developing and developed countries (Admass et al., 2024). In this section, a brief analysis of four existing legal frameworks concerning cybersecurity is done. These include the EU's General Data Protection Regulation (GDPR), the US Computer Fraud and Abuse Act (CFAA) and the Identity Theft and Assumption Deterrence Act (ITADA), Singapore's Cyber Security Act (CSA), and India's Information Technology (IT) Act. A detailed and systematic presentation of these acts is beyond our scope. The chapter prioritizes explaining the key elements, focusing on digital arrest scams and identity theft.

The EU introduced the GDPR in 2016, which was implemented only in 2018. It is one of the strongest privacy and data protection laws. However, it focused on protecting data rather than preventing fraud, like digital arrest scams and identity theft. It provides strict penalties for data misuse but is almost silent about digital fraud (Gupta, 2025). The EU has designed the GDPR in such a way as to ensure data protection as a fundamental right. Although this favors EU citizens, it burdens governments (Ryngaert & Taylor, 2020). Besides data protection, it also promotes the free flow of data across the EU. Furthermore, the right to data protection is not absolute, as it should align with other fundamental freedoms and function based on the principle of proportionality (Zafar, 2025). Since data security is one of the key elements to ensure cybersecurity, the provisions of GDPR can function as an efficient tool, albeit it does not explicitly address cybercrimes like digital arrest fraud and identity theft (Smith, 2021).

The US enacted the CFAA in 1984. The initial objective of the CFAA was to address those who intentionally accessed a protected computer or exceeded the given authorization. The Act was amended multiple times to address the changes in the digital world. In 1994, Congress included the option for both civil and criminal penalties. The Act was further amended after the 2001 terrorist attacks, broadening its scope. The Act covers various areas, including unauthorized access and fraud by using communication devices. It provides the possibility to seek support from strong law enforcement agencies like the FBI and Cyber Crime Task Forces. However, it has a drawback as it is limited to the US jurisdiction (Gupta, 2025). The US enacted ITADA in 1998 to address identity theft both in the offline and digital worlds. It is one of the rarest laws across the globe that specifically addresses identity theft. However, both these laws are criticized for not addressing the evolving nature of cybercrimes (Thurston, 2022).

Singapore enacted the Cybersecurity Act in 2018 to oversee and maintain national cybersecurity. It was amended in 2024 to update the legal provisions for addressing the evolving nature of cybercrimes. The Act enlists the provisions of advanced cyber forensic techniques and prioritizes infrastructure protection like energy, water, healthcare, transport, and banking. The Act authorizes the Commissioner to investigate cybersecurity threats and incidents to devise tactics to prevent further instances (CSA, 2025). However, it does not explicitly address cybercrimes. Singapore also enacted the Computer Misuse Act in 1993. It features various provisions like unauthorized access and modification of computer materials, unauthorized use or interception of computer materials, etc. However, it does not delve into cybercrimes to address digital arrest scams and identity theft. Although Singapore is acclaimed as a cybersecurity hub, it is also ranked fourth in cybercrime categories.

In India, the legal framework to address cybercrimes includes three laws: the IT Act of 2000, the Bharatiya Nyaya Sanhita (BNS) of 2023, and the Digital Personal Data Protection Act of 2023. These cover the basic cyber fraud activities, including hacking, data theft, electronic transactions, cyber fraud, and personal data collection, processing, and storage. Although the BNS is a modified and updated version of the Indian Penal Code (IPC, 1860), it does not systematically and progressively address digital crimes. The legal framework covers broad cybercrimes, but most provisions are outdated to ensure adequate protection against modern-day cybercrimes like digital arrest fraud (Kshetri, 2016).

6.2.2 Required Changes for Increased Security

The global nature of cybercrimes requires global actions to confront them. It requires globally coordinated efforts between the public and private sectors, enhanced information sharing, strategic action, and increased public awareness (Interpol, 2025). Most cybercrimes involve cross-border concerns as they are operated from a foreign country. It thus becomes difficult for the victim's country to trace, investigate, collect the evidence, and arrest the offender due to jurisdiction issues and failures in international legal cooperation between some countries. Countries must strengthen their legal system with fast justice delivery possibilities to ensure immediate relief to the victims (Gupta, 2025). The deterritorialization of the Internet and global communication technology has raised significant concerns about who will regulate cyber activities to make them people-centered and ensure human security (Kohl, 2017). Since no internationally accepted regulator exists, States frame their laws applicable to their territories without extraterritorial implications. The first required change for a global legal framework that applies to all cybercrimes without territorial restrictions is establishing a regulator under the initiative of the UN General Assembly (Ryngaert & Taylor, 2020). The regulator can take the initiative to design an international legal framework and policies to facilitate the formation of common reference standards for all countries.

Cooperation between nations is essential to curb cybercrimes. All countries, in one way or another, become victims of cyberattacks. Most cybercriminals operate from other countries. Evidence collection, offender arrest, and prosecution become a herculean task without considerable cooperation between nations. If such things do not happen, it will lead to more cybercrimes. Since cybercrimes have global repercussions, a collaborative global strategic approach is essential to confront them (Interpol, 2025). Law enforcement agencies should collaborate under the leadership of Interpol or other international agencies to ensure cybersecurity worldwide. Since people interconnect with each other through cyberspace, it is essential to have a global collaborative cybersecurity framework. If there is an effective interconnectedness between all national law enforcement agencies across the globe, cybercriminals can be easily targeted and prosecuted. Although there are differences in legal systems, political interests, and technological resources, the global nature of cybercrimes demands international cooperation. The law enforcement agencies of developed countries should be ready to share their high-quality technological resources and expertise with developing countries to trace and punish cybercriminals.

Lawmakers and the judiciary should collaborate competently to design appropriate laws related to the evolving nature of cybercrimes. The methods that are followed in conventional crimes may not apply to cybercrimes. The speed and flexibility of cyberspace broaden the scope of cybercriminals. Accordingly, new sections should be added to address such crimes. Otherwise, the victims may not get proper justice in crimes like digital arrest fraud and identity theft. The UN should consider the possibility of an international covenant to address the increasing nature of cybercrimes. Digital forensics is key in tracing cybercriminals and their activities, recovering deleted or altered files, and analyzing communication logs. Various digital forensics tools, like EnCase, Forensic Tool Kit (FTK), X1 Social Discovery, and Autopsy, can sustain the investigation and recovery of data in hacking and data theft cases, uncover hidden or deleted evidence from digital sources in digital fraud and online harassment cases, assist the investigation of cyberbullying cases, and strengthen the digital analysis of evidence in several cybercrimes (Manwani et al., 2025). However, the field of digital forensics has not equally grown in all parts of the globe, as it requires a considerable investment. Developed countries have made significant progress in digital forensics, whereas developing countries struggle to make a meaningful impact. This requires effective collaboration in digital forensics so that the developing world can ensure cybersecurity for its citizens.

7 CONCLUSION

Cybercrimes like digital arrest fraud and identity theft point to significant digital literacy and awareness issues. These scams exploit people's innocence, fear, and lack of awareness. The best way to confront the increasing nature of cybercrimes is to educate people about digital scams continuously. Cybersecurity and cybercrimes should be part of the school and university education curriculum. Companies, institutions, and housing colonies should conduct occasional seminars and awareness programs on the importance of cybersecurity. People should be trained to recognize fake sites and identify suspicious emails and messages. Ongoing training on cybercrimes and cybersecurity should be part of the agenda of law enforcement services. Since the world of cybercrimes is vast, the public sector alone may be unable to address it. Governments must seek support from the private sector and international institutions to deepen their strategies against cyber criminals. Many governments have already given strict guidelines on enabling multi-factor authentication to digital platforms where users' sensitive data is stored and shared. The Banks, therefore, ask the customers who use online or mobile banking, once or twice a year. The email providers like Google (Gmail) ask for a verification code when attempting to open the email from another system. Cybercrimes like digital arrest fraud and identity theft can be curbed only by leveraging cybersecurity. To ensure effective cybersecurity, the current legal framework should be refined to address the evolving nature of cybercrimes. Ethical principles like accountability, transparency, and privacy can enhance the potential of the legal framework with more positivity and openness.

REFERENCES

Admass, W. S., Munaye, Y. Y., & Diro, A. A. (2024). Cyber Security: State of the Art, Challenges, and Future Directions. *Cyber Security and Applications*, *2*, 100031. DOI: 10.1016/j.csa.2023.100031

Buchan, R., & Tsagourias, N. (2016). Non-State Actors and Responsibility in Cyberspace: State Responsibility, Individual Criminal Responsibility, and Issues of Evidence. *Journal of Conflict and Security Law*, *21*(3), 377–381. https://www.jstor.org/stable/26298206. DOI: 10.1093/jcsl/krw017

Chauhan, S., Singh, R., Gehlot, A., Agram, S. V., Twala, B., & Priyadarhi, N. (2023). Digitalization of Supply Chain Management with Industry 4.0 Enabling Technologies: A Sustainable Perspective. *Processes (Basel, Switzerland)*, *11*(1), 96. https://www.mdpi.com/2227-9717/11/1/96. DOI: 10.3390/pr11010096

Cheng, F.-C., & Lai, W.-H. (2012). The Impact of Cloud Computing Technology on Legal Infrastructure within Internet—Focusing on the Protection of Information Privacy. *Procedia Engineering*, *29*, 241–251. https://www.sciencedirect.com/science/article/pii/S1877705811065386. DOI: 10.1016/j.proeng.2011.12.701

Dalal, R. S., Bennett, R., & Posey, C. (2024). Security, Privacy, and Surveillance in Cyberspace: Organizational Science Concerns and Contributions. *Journal of Business and Psychology*, *39*(5), 1023–1026. https://link.springer.com/article/10.1007/s10869-024-09968-1. DOI: 10.1007/s10869-024-09968-1

Dallochio, M., Lambri, M., Sironi, E., & Teti, E. (2024). The Role of Digitalization in Cross-Border E-Commerce of Italian SMEs. *Sustainability (Basel)*, *16*(2), 508. https://www.mdpi.com/2071-1050/16/2/508. DOI: 10.3390/su16020508

Dennis, M. A. (2025). Identity Theft and Invasion of Privacy. *Britannica*. https://www.britannica.com/topic/cybercrime/Identity-theft-and-invasion-of-privacy

eSENTIRE. (2025). Cybercrime to Cost the World $9.5 trillion USD Annually in 2024. https://www.esentire.com/web-native-pages/cybercrime-to-cost-the-world-9-5-trillion-usd-annually-in-2024

FBI. (2025). FBI Releases Annual Internet Crime Report. https://www.fbi.gov/news/press-releases/fbi-releases-annual-internet-crime-report

Gross, M. L., Canetti, D., & Vashdi, D. R. (2017). Cyberterrorism: Its Effects on Psychological Well-being, Public Confidence, and Political Attitudes. *Journal of Cybersecurity*, *3*(1), 49–58. DOI: 10.1093/cybsec/tyw018

Gupta, R. (2025). Scammed into Silence: A Study of Digital Arrest Cybercrimes in India through the Lens of AI Manipulation, Legal Loopholes, and Socio-Financial Impact. *Journal of Neonatal Surgery*, *14*(21s), 971–978. https://www.jneonatalsurg.com/index.php/jns/article/view/5414

Harrell, E. (2019). Victims of Identity Theft, 2016. https://bjs.ojp.gov/library/publications/victims-identity-theft-2016

Humayun, M., Niazi, M., Jhanjhi, N. Z., Alshayeb, M., & Mahmood, S. (2020). Cyber Security Threats and Vulnerabilities: A Systematic Mapping Study. *Arabian Journal for Science and Engineering*, *45*(4), 3171–3189. https://link.springer.com/article/10.1007/s13369-019-04319-2. DOI: 10.1007/s13369-019-04319-2

Ilzan, A. R., Oktaviani, R. F. B., Yusuf, F. M., Wegman, D. J., Imtiyaz, N. Y., & Witarsyah, D. (2023). Understanding the Phenomenon and Risks of Identity Theft and Fraud on Social Media. *Asia Pacific Journal of Information System and Digital Transformation*, 1(1), 23-32. https://apjisdt.asia/p/article/view/3/3

Inc42. (2025). Indians Lost INR 1,935 Cr to Digital Arrest Scams in 2024: Govt. https://inc42.com/buzz/indians-lost-inr-1935-cr-to-digital-arrest-scams-in-2024-govt/

Interpol. (2025). Cybercrime. https://www.interpol.int/en/Crimes/Cybercrime

Kaur, J., & Ramkumar, K. R. (2022). The Recent Trends in Cyber Security: A Review. *Journal of King Saud University. Computer and Information Sciences*, *34*(8, 8B), 5766–5781. DOI: 10.1016/j.jksuci.2021.01.018

Knell, M. (2021). The Digital Revolution and Digitalized Network Society. *Review of Evolutionary Political Economy*, *2*(1), 9–25. https://link.springer.com/article/10.1007/s43253-021-00037-4. DOI: 10.1007/s43253-021-00037-4

Kohl, U. (Ed.). (2017). *The Net and the Nation State: Multidisciplinary Perspectives on Internet Governance*. Cambridge University Press. DOI: 10.1017/9781316534168

Koops, B.-J., & Leenes, R. (2006). Identity Theft, Identity Fraud, and/or Identity Related Crime: Definitions Matter. *Datenschutz und Datensicherheit*, 30, 553-556. https://link.springer.com/article/10.1007/s11623-006-0141-2

Kshetri, N. (2016). Cybercrime and Cybersecurity in India: Causes, Consequences, and Implications for the Future. *Crime, Law, and Social Change*, *66*(3), 313–338. https://link.springer.com/article/10.1007/s10611-016-9629-3. DOI: 10.1007/s10611-016-9629-3

Liao, R., Balasinorwala, S., & Rao, H. R. (2017). Computer Assisted Frauds: An Examination of Offender and Offense Characteristics in Relation to Arrests. *Information Systems Frontiers*, *19*(3), 443–455. https://link.springer.com/article/10.1007/s10796-017-9752-4. DOI: 10.1007/s10796-017-9752-4

Lubis, M., Safitra, M. F., Fakhrurroja, H., & Putri, D. P. (2024). Navigating Online Privacy: Insights from Cybersecurity Expert. *Prodedia Computer Science*, 234, 1388-1395. https://www.sciencedirect.com/science/article/pii/S1877050924004952?via%3Dihub

Malzac, J. (2021). Leveraging Domestic Law against Cyberattacks. *American University National Security Law Brief*, 11(1), 1-51. https://digitalcommons.wcl.american.edu/nslb/vol11/iss1/2/

Manwani, R., Zephaniah, S., Kaushik, R., & Dilroopa, K. N. (2025). The Rise of Digital Arrests: Cybercrime in the Modern Era. *Journal of Informatics Education and Research*, *5*(1), 1307–1317. https://jier.org/index.php/journal/article/view/2112

Osburn, L. D. (2025). Telling Stories about Vendors: Narrative Practices to Negotiate Risk and Establish an Organizational Cybersecurity Culture. *Journal of Cybersecurity*, *11*(1), tyae030. Advance online publication. DOI: 10.1093/cybsec/tyae030

Pawlak, P. (2024). Accountability in Cyberspace: The Holy Grail of Cyber Stability. *Policy Brief, EU Cyber Direct*. https://www.universiteitleiden.nl/binaries/content/assets/governance-and-global-affairs/isga/accountability-in-cyberspace-patryk-pawlak-march-2024.pdf

Pratt, T. C., Holtfreter, K., & Reisig, M. D. (2010). Routine Online Activity and Internet Fraud Targeting: Extending the Generality of Routine Activity Theory. *Journal of Research in Crime and Delinquency*, *47*(3), 267–296. DOI: 10.1177/0022427810365903

Ryngaert, C., & Taylor, M. (2020). The GDPR as Global Data Protection Regulation? *AJIL Unbound*, *114*, 5–9. DOI: 10.1017/aju.2019.80

Schneier, B. (2018). Crypto-Gram. *Schneier on Security*. https://www.schneier.com/crypto-gram/archives/2018/0615.html%231

Singh, S. (2025). Digital Arrest: The Modern-Day Cyber Scam. https://www.niti.gov.in/sites/default/files/2025-04/Digital_Arrest_The_Modern_Day_Cyber_Scam.pdf

Smith, D. (2021). *Promoting Integrity in the Work of International Organizations: Minimizing Fraud and Corruption in International Projects*. Springer.

Stevenson, G. (2000). Computer Fraud: Detection and Prevention. *Computer Fraud & Security, 2000*(11), 13–15. https://www.sciencedirect.com/science/article/abs/pii/S1361372300110188. DOI: 10.1016/S1361-3723(00)11018-8

Strauss, C., Harr, M. D., & Pieper, T. M. (2024). Analyzing Digital Communication: A Comprehensive Literature Review. *Management Review Quarterly*. https://link.springer.com/article/10.1007/s11301-024-00455-8

Thurston, J. (2022). Cyberwarfare and the Computer Fraud and Abuse Act. *Boston College Intellectual Property & Technology Forum*, 1-17. https://lira.bc.edu/files/pdf?fileid=9afaf8a1-b50b-467e-98fc-f51f05467a48

Titus, R. (2001). Personal Fraud and Its Victims. In Shover, N., & Wright, J. P. (Eds.), *Crimes of Privilege: Readings in White-Collar Crime* (pp. 57–74). Oxford University Press.

Trautman, L. J. (2016). Is Cyber Attack the Next Pearl Harbor? *North Carolina Journal of Law & Technology*, *18*(2), 233–289. https://scholarship.law.unc.edu/ncjolt/vol18/iss2/3/

VeriDas. (2025). VeriDas Identity Fraud Report. https://veridas.com/en/identity-fraud-report/

Vijay, B. (2025). The Evolution of Digital Arrest Cyber-Crimes in India: Trends and Patterns, Preventive Measures. *International Journal of Sociology and Humanities*, *7*(1), 1–5. https://www.sociologyjournal.net/archives/2025.v7.i1.A.113/the-evolution-of-digital-arrest-cyber-crimes-in-india-trends-and-patterns-preventive-measures. DOI: 10.33545/26648679.2025.v7.i1a.113

Vyas-Doorgaparsad, S. (2022). The Use of Digitalization (ICTs) in Achieving Sustainable Development Goals. *Global Journal of Emerging Market Economies*, *14*(2), 265–278. https://journals.sagepub.com/doi/epub/10.1177/09749101211067295. DOI: 10.1177/09749101211067295

Wall, D. (2001). *Crime and the Internet*. Routledge. DOI: 10.4324/9780203164501

Wang, C., Chen, X., Yu, T., Liu, Y., & Jing, Y. (2024). Education Reform and Change Driven by Digital Technology: A Bibliometric Study from a Global Perspective. *Humanities & Social Sciences Communications*, *11*(1), 256. https://www.nature.com/articles/s41599-024-02717-y. DOI: 10.1057/s41599-024-02717-y

World Economic Forum. (2025). *Global Cybersecurity Outlook 2025*. https://reports.weforum.org/docs/WEF_Global_Cybersecurity_Outlook_2025.pdf

Xie, F., Guan, X., Zhu, J., Ruan, J., Wang, Z., & Liu, H. (2023). Environmental Protection Goes Digital: A Policy Perspective on Promoting Digitalization for Sustainable Development in China. *Sustainability (Basel)*, *15*(13), 10673. https://www.mdpi.com/2071-1050/15/13/10673. DOI: 10.3390/su151310673

Zafar, A. (2025). Reconciling Blockchain Technology and Data Protection Laws: Regulatory Challenges, Technical Solutions, and Practical Pathways. *Journal of Cybersecurity*, *11*(1), tyaf002. Advance online publication. DOI: 10.1093/cybsec/tyaf002

Zhang, T., & Li, N. (2023). Measuring Digital Economy: From the Perspective of Digital Industrialization and Industry Digitalization. *Procedia Computer Science*, *221*, 1006–1012. DOI: 10.1016/j.procs.2023.08.081

KEY TERMS AND DEFINITIONS

Accountability: Accountability is the virtuous willingness to take responsibility for one's actions.

Cybercrimes: Cybercrimes refer to the fraudulent and mischievous activities occurring in cyberspace by which criminals target the vulnerability of people and systems.

Cyberspace: Cyberspace is a virtual environment in which computers and systems are interconnected through the Internet, increasing the interconnection between people and systems.

Decision-Making Systems: Decision-making systems are those systems that are given the unique capacity of intelligence and decision-making, which were the prerogative of human actors.

Digital Fraud: Digital Fraud is the fraudulent activities happening in the digital world. Deceiving people for personal gain is the main objective of these scammers. When they do it through online methods, it becomes digital fraud.

International Collaboration: International collaboration is the cooperation between nation-states, international institutions, multinational corporations, NGOs, and private actors for increased efficiency and societal welfare.

Privacy: Privacy is the most sacred space in which an individual can be free from external interference or control. It refers to freedom from all unauthorized and illegitimate interference in offline and online worlds.

Chapter 5
Natural Language Processing for Fraudulent Communication Detection

Yulhendri Yulhendri
https://orcid.org/0000-0003-1106-7473
Esa Unggul University, Indonesia

Varsha Arya
Hong Kong Metropolitan University, Hong Kong

Sourasis Chattopadhyay
https://orcid.org/0009-0000-7435-6550
Kalinga Institute of Industrial Technology, India

ABSTRACT

Fraud communication detection is a must due to complex web interactions and AI-driven fraud. Heuristic systems struggle with advanced fraud, including multilingual behavior, deepfakes, and LLM phishing. This study compares NLP for fraud communication detection, focusing on transformer-based models (BERT, RoBERTa, FinChain-BERT), hybrid AI-rule systems, graph data, multilingual detection, and adversarial robustness. Research indicates that an 85–95% accurate NLP model can degrade by 9–15% on a quarterly basis, and low-resource languages and AI fraud detection are the toughest for it. NLP improvement needs ongoing learning, human oversight, explainable AI, and adversarial testing. The future of work requires real-

DOI: 10.4018/979-8-3373-4149-1.ch005

time fraud detection models, user-tailored fraud language extraction, multimodal detection (text, voice, images), and ethical AI use. It is this focus that will render NLP-based fraud detection scalable, real-time, and reactive to digital deception.

1. INTRODUCTION: NLP FOR FRAUDULENT COMMUNICATION DETECTION

The Dangers of Fraudulent Communication in the Digital Era The advent of digital communication has created enhanced opportunities for global communication, facilitating virtually seamless transactions and information exchange. Yet, this connectedness also creates opportunities for fraudulent communication. Fraudulent communication - which includes anything from phishing emails to scam messages to fraudulent financial transactions to misleading reviews - threatens cybersecurity, financial well-being, and consumer confidence. Fraudulent communication, initiated by cybercriminals through a digital platform, is typically written (and even increasingly) designed as first-person communication with humans, all with the intent of deceiving individuals. Cybercriminals use language, or text-based communication, as a means of deception, and continue to improve their linguistically based choices of deception to better to deceive humans into thinking they are legitimate. Traditional rule-based fraud detection systems have primary and/or sole reliance on predictive checklists of static rules. As the methods of disguise deception evolve, the field of detection must include adaptive and language aware systems that better address the evolving typography of computer-mediated communication.

Emerging Fraud Techniques: Phishing, Social Engineering, and AI-Generated Scams

We have seen the emergence of more advanced fraud schemes than at any point in history, including a new wave of targeted phishing, more complex social engineering, and even evolving AI-generated fraud (Jain et al., 2024). Instead of using static templates that indicate a scam or fraud, offenders are developing more realistic communications to simulate legitimate interaction. A few other points to note with regard to advancements in fraudulent communications:

a. Phishing Emails- Criminals have used contextual deception to impersonate trusted, reputable organizations, including banks and government organizations, to collect sensitive information (Bhattacharya & Mićković, 2024).

b. Social Engineering Scams- These messages exploit human psychology by inducing a sense of urgency when seeking payment to take advantage of a victim's cognitive load, e.g., the use of fear (Singh & Kaur, 2023).
c. AI-Generated Fraud- Generative models like GPT-4 allow offenders to produce linguistically flawless misleading messages that ethically can adapt tone to effectively avoid conventional fraud identification (for example), limiting capture (Chen & Wang, 2024).

Clearly, emerging fraud models are evolving the design of current and future fraud prevention methods by introducing new and subtle patterns of linguistic deception, while increasingly making detection and intervention more challenging.

Limitations of Conventional Fraud Detection Systems Even with massive market penetration, the vast majority of older fraud detection systems don't have the ability to effectively respond to the present illicit or deceptive communication. Among several gaps we understand as limitations are the following:

a. Rule-Based system inflexibility: keyword filtering is static and limited to the dynamic scams of something like AI (Rahman & Sarker, 2020)
b. Deficiencies with multilingual detection: The focus on English language scams, the scammers are leaving out those that cannot speak English without anyone knowing (Ueno et al., 2020)
c. Associates very high rates of false positives and negatives: classical classification models would continue to misclassify undecipherable messages, would identify legitimate takeaway communications as potential fraudulent communications and would let advanced fraud schemes go unnoticed (Zhang et al., 2024)
d. These systems wouldn't adapt quickly to contemporary fraud trends. At a minimum, communications must be deciphered in real time, so models of any sort would immediately become outdated as soon as the fraudster becomes aware of the model (Liu & Zhao, 2022).

Figure 1. The Need for Intelligent, Adaptive & Interactive Detection Mechanism

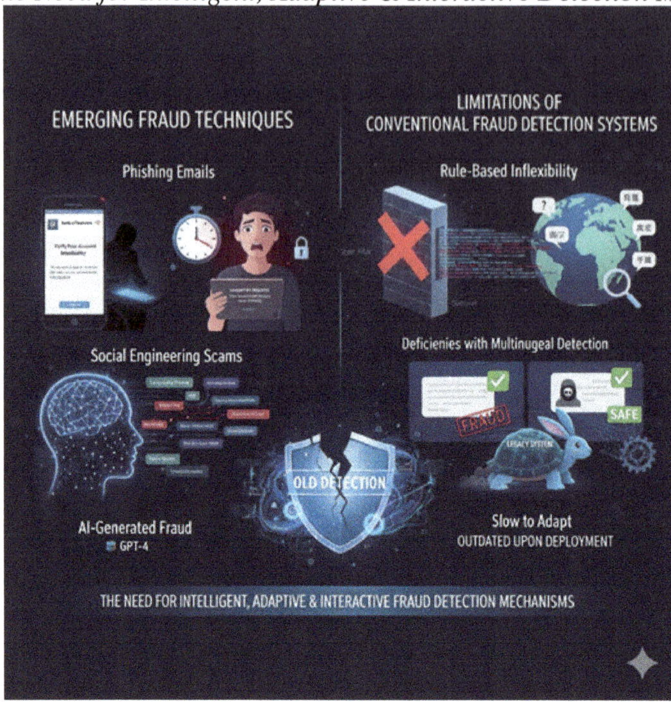

These are substantial limitations when considering and discussing the need for intelligent adaptive and interactive fraud detection mechanisms that can behave dynamically, interpret deceptions and understand and formulate foreign language.

Fraud Detection with NLP

Natural Language Processing (NLP) has become an effective way of addressing fraudulent communications. With current AI approaches, NLP will help to expand fraud detection in the following ways:

a. Contextual Analysis: With transformer based models (BERT, RoBERTa, etc.) fraud detection looks at the context of a message instead of working off of keywords as in traditional models (Wang et al., 2023).
b. Adaptive Learning Mechanisms: Using active retraining, fraud models will continue to make reliable fraud detection allocations because they will continue to retrain detection processes in real time (Lee & Kim, 2024).
c. Multilingual Fraud Detection: Cross-lingual embedding allows for fraud detection from multiple language fraud detection and could foster a way for increased

inclusion of non-native language users into the detection process (Singh & Kaur, 2023).

d. Explainable AI for Compliance: Interpretability models such as SEFraud increase regulatory auditability which will build trust in automated fraud prevention systems (Bhattacharya & Mićković, 2024).

Figure 2. The Need for Intelligent, Adaptive from IT Fraud Detection Mechanism

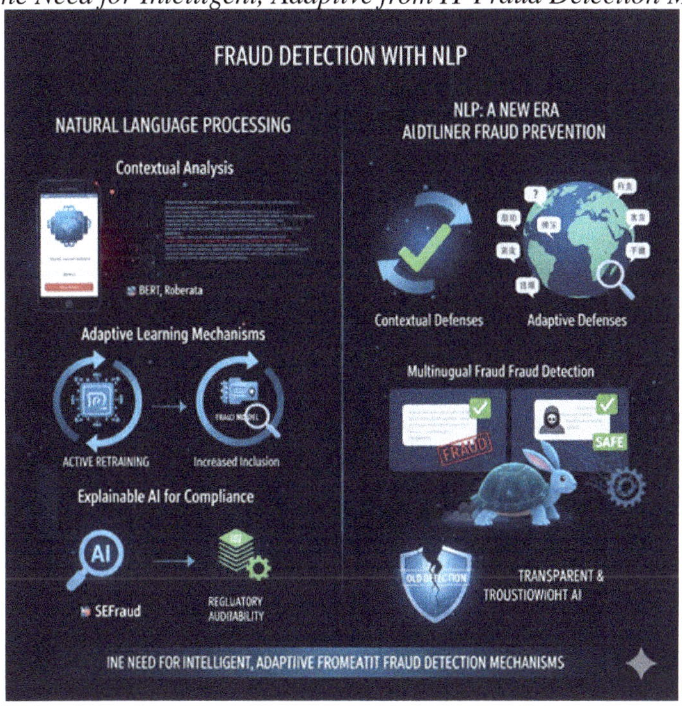

By applying NLP fraud detection methods to security registries, security will mitigate new strategies employed to deliver deception to protect users from fraudulent incidents online.

2. THEORETICAL FRAMEWORK: NLP FOR FRAUDULENT COMMUNICATION DETECTION

Fraudulent communication uses a combination of linguistic deception, psychological twist, and network-based fraud to bypass traditional security. Understanding its linguistic, cognitive, and structural aspects will help build more intelligent Intelligent

Fraud Detection Systems based on NLP. Linguistic Features of Fraudulent messages Fraudulent messages use recognizable linguistic features that influence their readers to act. Popular forms of this are phishing messages, scam notifications, and false financial transaction emails. Time-Sensitivity Lingustic Features as a Fraudulent Indicator Scammers like to use time-sensitive wording to create a sense of urgency and prompt the reader to act:

a. Examples: “Act now!”, “Immediate response needed”, “Your account will be suspended in 24 hours”(Singh & Kaur, 2023)
b. When language creates a sense of time-sensitive urgency, it surfaces fear-based decision-making, thus increases the possibility of being scammed (Bhattacharya & Mićković, 2024). Ambiguity and Evasive Language Fraudulent messages often do not indicate specificity making it impossible to verify:
c. Examples: “Your account has unusual activity”, “a suspicious transaction was identified” (Rahman & Sarker, 2020).
d. Fraudulent communication uses language to avoid being specific deliberately, making it more challenging to scrutinize while maintaining plausible deniability.

Manipulative Language in Scams

Scammers tend to use exaggerated politeness or emotionally charged language to build trust:

a. Example: “Dear valued customer, thank you for your assistance.” Zhang et al (2024)
b. Emotional language such as, “We are very concerned for your safety” often pushes victims to act on the scam.

Psychological and Sociolinguistic Markers of Fraud

Fraudulent communication relies on cognitive biases and cultural norms that result in scammers being difficult to identify in multilingual settings.

Psycholinguistic Indicators of Scam Texts

a. Reduced first-person pronouns (e.g., favoring “we” instead of “I”) may be an indicator of deception (Tausczik & Pennebaker, 2010).
b. The presence of negative emotion words, like “risk,” “problem,” and “loss,” can increase fear responses and reduce analytical thinking (Lee & Kim, 2024).

Fraud Techniques and Cultural Adaptation

Fraudsters relate their deception techniques to linguistic and cultural conventions:

a. Japanese fraud continues to misuse honorifics like "-sama" and "-san" to appear legitimate (Ueno et al. 2023).
b. Spanish-language scams use terms of "family" (tío, hermano) to provide illusion of trust (Singh & Kaur 2023).

These studies highlight the need for culture-informed NLP models, as the cognitive social contexts of fraud vary from language to language.

AI-Generated Fraud and Linguistic Characteristics

Advances in AI tools have allowed fraudsters to create convincingly realistic fraud messages that can trick even the most traditional detectors.

FraudGPT and AI-Generated Scams

a. AI-generated fraudulent messages lack the usual oddities of human message writing and detection (like poor grammar or strange phrasing), thereby making it much more difficult to detect (Chen & Wang, 2024).
b. AI-generated fraud does appear as linguistically coherent and fluent messages what sets it apart is plausibly different than messages developed by humans.

Stylometric and Metadata-Based Detection on AI Fraud

a. AI-generated scam messages can be detected because they exhibit low variability in sentence complexity, while a human writing the same message would introduce varied complexity and show recognizable writing-stylometric styles and writing fragile "fingerprints".
b. AI-generated fraud also involves much more syntactical regularity compared with humans.

Any future fraud detection model needs to incorporate detection methods that utilize an AI-linguistic fingerprinting style, whereby a detection machine can identify machine-generated fraud messages automatically.

Graph-Based Fraud Detection and Network Analysis

Linguistic analysis is essential; however, many schemes utilize a networked approach of deception where different types of fraud schemes are interconnected, lending themselves toward a graph-based fraud detection source (Panigrahi et al., 2024).

Hierarchical Attention Graph Neural Networks (GNNs) for Fraud Detection

a. GNNs have the ability to successfully detect organized fraud rings, such as people running cryptocurrency scam rings, rather than regular text-based models.
b. The mapping of relational fraud exposes invisible linking partners of scammers to discover fraud networks (Liu & Zhao, 2022).

SEFraud (Self-Explainable GNNs for Financial Transactions)

a. SEFraud uses graph embeddings to track money laundering activities (Lee & Kim, 2024).
b. Explainable features provide investigators of fraudulent activities with an audit trail on their fraud predictions to ensure they are following the rules of regulatory compliance.

Integrating graph-based analysis and NLP will assist fraud detection systems in identifying clusters of scams and fraudulent interactions through disparate engagement channels.

In concluding the research, further fraud detection systems must be designed using NLP, psychology, and network analysis strictly from the fraud prevention perspective, in order to:

1. portray linguistic deception markers (urgency, ambiguity)
2. portray psychological profiles (exploiting cognitive bias)
3. permit detection from AI generated sources (stylometry)
4. permit graph-based fraud mapping (relational)

The future of fraud detection systems must continue to adapt to work through different forms of fraud and deception in anticipation of anticipatory deception tactics, all while being mindful of the different languages, cultures, and AI generated communications available today.

3. NLP METHODS FOR FRAUD DETECTION

For words, phrases or utterances, Natural Language Processing (NLP) our patterns of communication, to identify patterns of deceit, recognize the needed linguistic features, and classify a deceitful message. This section examines key NLP methods used for some aspects of fraud detection to give some guidance from the attached document.

3.1 Text Preprocessing and Feature Extraction

Fraud detection relies on some type of preprocessing to convert raw text into structured approach, so it can be used by machine learning models.

Syntactic Features

a. Tokenization: Breaks raw text into words, phrases or subword pieces that can be analyzed as a structured piece of information (Singh & Kaur, 2023).
b. Part-of-Speech (POS) Tagging: parts of speech can give a lot of information on how someone is trying to deceive, excessive use of verbs can be regarded as attempt to create urgency or a manipulative tone (Ueno et al., 2020).
c. Named Entity recognition (NER): A way to extract fraud related entities like financial institution names, suspicious URLs and scammers names (Bhattacharya & Mićković, 2024).

Semantic Features

a. Word embeddings: By taking text and changing it into numbers and then representing it as a vector, count-based representation of words and their context information in text can detect fraud. Word2Vec, FastText, and BERT embeddings can be used to add context information to how scams are framed (Wang et al., 2023).
b. Sentiment Analysis: By assessing the emotional tone of a messagewe can identify something manipulative, such as scam messaging that creates fear or is overly persuasive to elicit a response (Brown & Green, 2023).

Contextual Features

- TF-IDF (Term Frequency-Inverse Document Frequency): Provides a weight (importance) value for fraud-related terms based on their significance in scam messages (Rahman & Sarker, 2020).
- Stylometric Analysis: Identifies fraudulent writing styles based on distinction between AI-generated scams and human deception (Chen & Wang, 2024).

Figure 3. NLP Methods for Fraud Detection

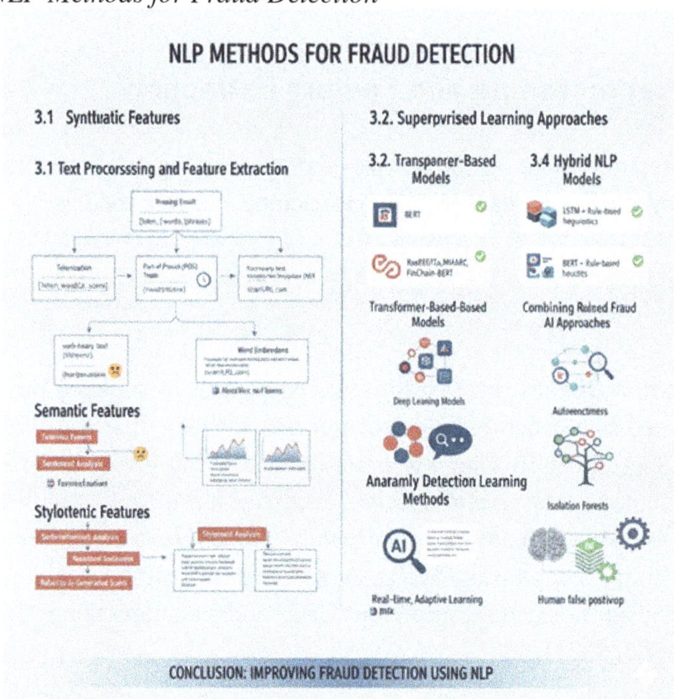

3.2 Supervised Learning Approaches

Supervised machine learning models are trained on labeled fraud datasets to classify whether the communication is fraudulent or legitimate.

Transformer-Based Models

1. BERT (Bidirectional Encoder Representations from Transformers): achieves high accuracy in detecting phishing emails by analyzing sentence context (Wang et al., 2023).
2. RoBERTa-MHARC: improves telecom fraud detection with dual-loss optimization to help reduce false positives (Zhang et al., 2024).
3. FinChain-BERT: is designed for detecting financial fraud with domain-specific contextual embeddings (Bhattacharya & Mićković, 2024).

Deep Learning Models

1. Recurrent neural networks (RNNs): show good detection for fraud in conversations such as scam phone transcripts (Lee & Kim, 2024).
2. Long short-term memory (LSTM): identifies fraud patterns sequentially by incorporating the history of text within scam messages (Singh & Kaur, 2023).
3. Graph neural networks (GNNs): identify relations between entities communicating fraudulently, have potential to map around relational fraud patterns (Liu & Zhao, 2022).

3.3 Unsupervised Learning: Clustering and Anomaly Detection

Unsupervised methods, which focus on defining patterns of fraudulent communications, are usually very valuable for finding new fraud patterns since they do not require labeled data to describe the undesirable behaviors that might be emerging.

Clustering Methods

1. K-Means. It groups similar fraud patterns together to identify unique fraud patterns or typologies (Rahman & Sarker, 2020).
2. DBSCAN. It identifies dense fraud networks when we cluster together a series of messages that included the same or similar fraud keywords (Ueno et al., 2020).

Anomaly Detection Methods

1. Autoencoders. It identifies all communicated information that deviates from established communications patterns, which are indicative of fraudulent activity (Brown & Green, 2023).

2. Isolation Forests. They identify scam messages by defining what a normative pattern looks like to indicate deviations based on how the message is indicated linguistically (Chen & Wang, 2024).

3.4 Hybrid NLP Models - Combining Rule-Based and AI Approaches

Hybrid models combine predetermined rule-based heuristics with AI-driven, predictive approaches to fraud detection to optimize result accuracy and interpretability (Al-Ayyoub et al., 2018).

Examples of Hybrid Models for Fraud Detection:

1. TF-IDF + Logistic Regression: An easy-to-understand, lightweight fraud detection approach, which provides transparency to the classification (Brown & Green, 2023).
2. LSTM + Random Forest: A hybrid model that combines the sequential detection power of deep learning and the interpretability of decision trees (Singh & Kaur, 2023).
3. BERT + Rule-based heuristics: Reduces false positives, but still maintains the ability to track fraud in context (Zhang et al., 2024).

Explainable AI (XAI) in Hybrid Models:

1. SEFraud interpretability masks: Increases interpretability in alerts and situates fraud risk in transparency while complying with financial regulations (Lee & Kim, 2024).
2. Human-in-the-loop Integration: Enables fraud analysts to improve AI-based models for detecting scams in real time (Bhattacharya & Mićković, 2024).

Conclusion: Improving Fraud Detection Using NLP

The incorporation of NLP-based fraud detection approaches will lead to enhanced security across a number of industries including finance and banking, telecom, and e-commerce. Moving forward, research efforts must:

a. Focus on real time, adaptive fraud learning models to counter the evolving nature of scams,
b. Develop cross-linguistic and culturally-aware approaches to fraud detection aggregation to address violations across multiple, countries,

c. Devise hybrid AI-rule approaches to build models that maximize interpretability, accountability, and regulatory compliance,
d. Ensure models with adversarial-like fraud are robust to scams generated with AI,

By continuing to advance these technologies, society will develop scalable, interpretable, and robust fraud prevention systems, which are urgently needed in a rapidly deteriorating and deceptive digital environment.

4. CHALLENGES WITH FRAUD DETECTION USING NLP

While Natural Language Processing (NLP) has greatly enhanced detection of fraudulent communications, there are several issues that limit its effectiveness. These issues include language issues, adaptability issues, compliance issues, and ethical considerations. In this section we will detail the important barriers to success and examine possible solutions, based on the research attached (Miri et al., 2022).

4.1. Problems with detecting multilanguage and code mixed fraud

Fraud detection models struggle with multilingual material, code-mixed text, and low-resourced languages. Because of this, there is a large lack of performance.

Issues With Multilingual Fraud Detection

The vast majority of fraud detection solutions are designed for English language scams, with a 20-30% reduction in accuracy when evaluating any other language (Ueno, et al., 2023; Singh & Kaur, 2023):

a. Fraudsters will use regional linguistic quirks that generic models will not be able to identify.
b. Example: In Japanese scams vendors frequently exploit the honorific "-sama" and this can be difficult to identify, especially for models that do not have a cultural context, (Ueno et al, 2023).
c. Spanish language fraud regularly utilizes familial terms (e.g. "tío"; "hermano") to fake trust; this causes traditional model to misclassify a scam in fraud detection text (Singh & Kaur, 2023).

How Complex the Code-Mixed Text Is

Fraudsters are likely to mix multiple languages in such messages only complicating detection.

a. Example: "Bank verification , click " (English + Hindi fraud message).
b. Existing fraud detection models are based on the premise of monolingual embeddings. This was not equipped to recognize deceptive behaviours in mixed-language fraud (Liu & Zhao, 2022).

Possible Solutions and Future Directions

1. Current cross-lingual (e.g., XLM-R, mBERT) embeddings provide support for fraud detection in other languages with a limited number of languages combined, but they need to be fine-tuned (Singh & Kaur, 2023).
2. Continue development of localized fraud-based data sets in support of addressing differences in detection approaches ("Optimized Phishing Detection with Recurrent Neural Network and Whale Optimizer Algorithm," 2024).
3. Improving research analysis of code-mixed fraud detection through subword tokenization and phonetic transliteration approaches (Ueno et al., 2020).

4.2 Model Adaptability to Changing Fraud Techniques

Fraud techniques are constantly changing, which means that a static fraud model will be out of date in a few months.

Concept Drift in Fraud Detection

1. According to Liu and Zhao (2022), fraud models lose 9-15% of their accuracy each year because scammers continue to sharpen their strategies, while the models take longer to retrain.
2. AI-generated fraud can imitate the real-time interaction of real customers, which means that traditional NLP detection becomes less effective in fraud detection (Chen & Wang, 2024).

Limitations of Traditional Learning Frameworks

a. Traditional fraud models rely on batch training, meaning that when patterns of scams arise, they cannot be updated without manually applying the change (Zhang, et al., 2024).
b. For example, ask FraudGPT to generate a phishing scam and it will produce scam emails that use old and inaccurate linguistic training to trick obsolete detection models.

Solutions to Enhance Adaptability

1. Meta-learning mechanisms allow fraud detection models to self-update in real-time (Lee & Kim, 2024).
2. Continuous learning pipelines have frequent teams and retraining periods with new detected fraud events.
3. Adversarial testing is recommended in order to assess if fraud models can defend against AI-generated scam text (Chen & Wang, 2024).

4.3 Explainability and Compliance Trade-Offs in Fraud Detection

Fraud detection models are required to follow financial regulations, consumer protection laws, and laws aimed at promoting AI transparency, despite their utility (Muchandigona, 2025).

Opaque AI Models Challenges

1. Many fraud detection models, such as transformers like BERT, are a black box making regulatory validation and auditing unlikely (Bhattacharya & Mićković, 2024).
2. Several studies have found trade-offs between model explainability and accuracy with explainable versions of AI models frequently have 5–15% reduced accuracy (Lee & Kim, 2024).

Regulatory Constraints

1. GDPR (Europe) and CCPA (California) mandates AI explainability limiting non-transparency fraud models (Bhattacharya & Mićković, 2024).

2. Banks often refuse high accuracy fraud models that are non-transparent and choose less effective rule-based models (Brown & Green, 2023).

Addressing Accuracy and Transparency Balancing Strategies

1. Use of Explainable AI (XAI), utilize explainable model use techniques including SHAP / LIME techniques.
2. Human-in-the-loop validation to allow fraud analysts to review + monitor AI-produced predictions whilst remaining compliant (Lee & Kim, 2024).
3. Regulatory compliant hybrid models that use NLP post processing of fraud prevention notifications for regulation compliance.

4.4 Prejudice, Fairness, and Ethical Concerns in AI-Fraud Detection

AI-fraud detection systems can sometimes exhibit a certain bias, as they can, without malice, incorrectly tag legitimate transactions made from specific demographic groups, based on limitations in training data (Pappachan et al., 2024).

Bias in Multilingual Fraud Detection

1. False positive rates with non-English fraud detection can be 2–4× higher, resulting in more missed fraudulent transactions involving speakers of low/resource languages overall (Hidayat & Prasetyo, 2021).
2. Fraud models may incorrectly label transaction(s) from underrepresented groups as potentially fraudulent solely due to a lack of data (Singh & Kaur, 2023).

Privacy Issues Associated With AI-Fraud Detection

1. Many fraud detection systems are based on personal data scraped from email/chats; violations of privacy under the GDPR (Johnson & Lee, 2020).
2. Fraud datasets are often proprietary, thus restricting academia accessibility for research collaboration and limiting auditing for bias (Rahman & Sarker, 2020).

Ethical Paths Forward

1. After performing bias audits and fairness-aware training, practitioners could deploy the models and systems with greater confidence.

2. Example of synthetic fraud datasets - could use GANs to generate simulated scams, while enhancing data diversity and reducing privacy risks (Kumar & Gupta, 2023).
3. Example of federated learning for fraud detection - monitoring fraud without compromising end-user privacy (Liu & Zhao, 2022).

Conclusion: Navigating the Fraud Detection Landscape in NLP

When fraud detection is grounded in their ability to be dynamic, accessible and ethical. Future research and development should attend to:

1. Improved multilingual fraud detection capabilities, which should involve multilingual and cross-lingual embeddings and models which are contextually sensitive to various cultures.
2. Updating fraud models in real-time and maintaining their optimal integrity through a combination of adversarial testing pipelines and meta-learning frameworks.
3. Transparent use of AI that provides knowledge one to numerous people but without sacrificing quality of performance and protective measures from damaging vulnerability by questioning or explaining rationales for decisions that still reasonably meet the need.
4. Mitigating bias brought to bear by AI by thinking ethically through beneficial technologies, sometimes also imbued with scientific advancements but also dedicated to privacy and accountability to be just and fair.

As we take steps to make these things happen we can reduce any gulf currently being experienced in fraud detection systems to perform using important considerations for each organization continue to be effective in combatting the most reventially relevant and continuing ways that technology will be challenged by new adversarial models of behavior (Phattanaviroj et al., 2025).

Figure 4. Challenges with Fraud Detection using NLP

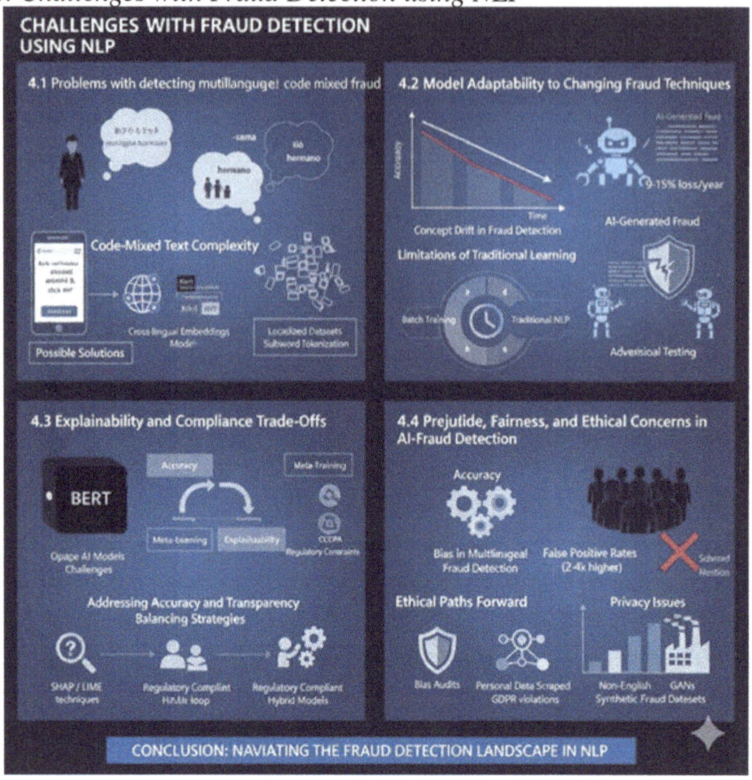

5. ADVERSARIAL ASSAULTS AND AI FRAUD

The growth of generative AI has profoundly changed fraudulent communications. Traditional fraud detection systems have typically been built to catch deceit from humans; however, there are now AI generated frauds that appear like legitimate communication. Cybercriminals can leverage large language models (LLMs), such as GPT-4, to create believable phishing messages, make reasonable social engineering requests, and provide believable financial stories that can not get detected using conventional fraud detection. In this section, we focus on the increased threat of AI-generated fraud, the need for adversarial robustness, and the importance of metadata and behavioural analysis in directing the identification of AI deception.

5.1 Generative AI Impact on Fraud.

Generative AI gives fraudsters the capacity to act, to automate, and to customize the delivery of deceptive communications at scale, and are capable of producing scams that are virtually indistinguishable from ordinary communications.

AI-Generated Phishing and Social Engineering

1. Cybercriminals leverage sophisticated language models to write grammatically correct, highly personalized phishing emails that imitate authentic institutions, such as banks and businesses (Chen & Wang, 2024).
2. Unlike traditional scams that are identifiable because they contain misspelled words or poor grammar, fraudsters using AI-generated scams eliminate these warning signs in the English language and/or otherwise, making them harder to identify (Zhang et al., 2024).
3. Example: AI-generated phishing emails add contextually relevant information, like past purchases or personalized account details, to create less suspicion.

Deepfake Social Engineering and AI-Generated Fraud

1. AI-created deepfake scams impersonate a trusted party, targeting call centers and interested consumers (Singh & Kaur, 2023).
2. Fraudulent, AI-generated chatbots represent themselves as clients' financial advisors or representatives of technical support teams, manipulating users to provide valuable information (Rahaman, Cajes, et al., 2025).
3. Fully automated fraud networks combine large language models with AI to hire long-form text to deposit false customer reviews, spread misinformation and harm e-commerce and other financial community systems (Bhattacharya & Mićković, 2024).

Implication: Fraud detection models cannot solely rely on linguistic analysis to identify fraud; rather, fraud detection models need to evolve and use adversarial methods to detect AI-fraud.

5.2 Adversarial Testing and Robustness Frameworks

In order to successfully address AI-based fraud, natural language processing (NLP) systems need to include adversarial testing and robustness approaches.

Adversarial Attacks Against Fraud Detection Models

1. Cybercriminals use AI-based adversarial approaches to refine messaging in scam ads to make them undetectable to NLP filters (Chen and Wang, 2024).
2. AI-generated scams can be fine-tuned to avoid keyword detection meaning that the model becomes inhibited over time (Liu and Zhao, 2022).

Adversarial Robustness Testing Approaches

1. FraudGPT Benchmark Suite: simulate AI-based scams to evaluate fraud detection models with respect to automated fraud (Chen and Wang, 2024).
2. Gradient-Based Fraud Attacks: Stress-test fraud models against adversarial examples of scams to quantify susceptibility (Zhang et al., 2024).
3. Zero-Shot Fraud Adaptation: use novel scam environments to quantify fraud detection model adaptation (Lee and Kim, 2024).

Implication: Fraud detection systems must routinely take part in adversarial learning to update models to attend to new, evolving forms of AI-based fraud.

5.3 Metadata and Behavioral Profiling in AI-based Fraud Detection

AI-generated fraud does not have the normal linguistic indicators of fraud, therefore AI detection will introduce metadata and behavioral profiling to make it more accurate. In applying stylometric and metadata methods to detect AI fraud:

1. AI-generated fraudulent text will have an unnaturally consistent degree of fluency and low variation in sentence structure. This fact makes it possible to do a distinguish my built weightiness alone (Chen & Wang, 2024).
2. Unlike human-generated scams where the fraudster's restrictions of planning caused inconsistencies in the craft, AI treatments will not have complications like a typographical mark (Singh & Kaur, 2023).
3. Metadata will reveal characteristics of the fraud transaction by looking at its source locations, user activity logs and bot generated incidents (Ueno et al., 2020).

Behavioral Profiling with AI-based Fraud:

a. There is no traditional behavioral fingerprint used by AI-generated scams to pin point some direct contact, like dishonesty in responsive patterns or typos (Bhattacharya & Mićković, 2024).
b. Network-based anomaly detection techniques can follow a unique pattern of fraud within these systems, therefore assisting scholars flag large-scale operations that are based on AI-generated fraud in these financial and crowd-ecommerce platforms (Rahman & Sarker, 2020).

Implication: Fraud detection is likely to need a track-and-trace aspect with a larger scope than simply linguistics designed detailed analysis. It will likely require some metadata tracking, behavioral profiling and maybe strategic counter-adversarial methods (Rahaman et al., 2022).

Conclusion: Enhancing Fraud Detection Against AI Deception

The emergence of AI-based fraud will require an overhaul in how fraud is detected. While NLP-based fraud detection and prevention systems will need to move beyond traditional linguistic indicators, they will need to include adversarial robustness testing frameworks, metadata-based identifiers, and behavioral intelligence models (Rahaman, Putra, et al., 2025).

The following key advancements are necessary for future fraud detection work:

1. Adversarial Training Pipelines: we need to operationalize AI-created scam data to build robust fraud models (Chen & Wang, 2024).
2. Stylometric and Metadata Profiling: we should be using a workflow that incorporates text fluency indicators, bot-generated scams metadata features, etc. (Singh & Kaur, 2023).
3. Real-Time Fraud Adaptive Systems: While I have discussed adapting fraud models to prevent fraud as it is happening; however, fraud models will need mechanisms to dynamically retrain (Lee & Kim, 2024).

By developing multi-modal fraud detection—linguistics, meta, and adversarial testing—fraud detection and prevention systems will be adaptive, robust, and capable of protecting against new emerging digital fraud problems.

Figure 5. Adversarial Assault and AI Fraud

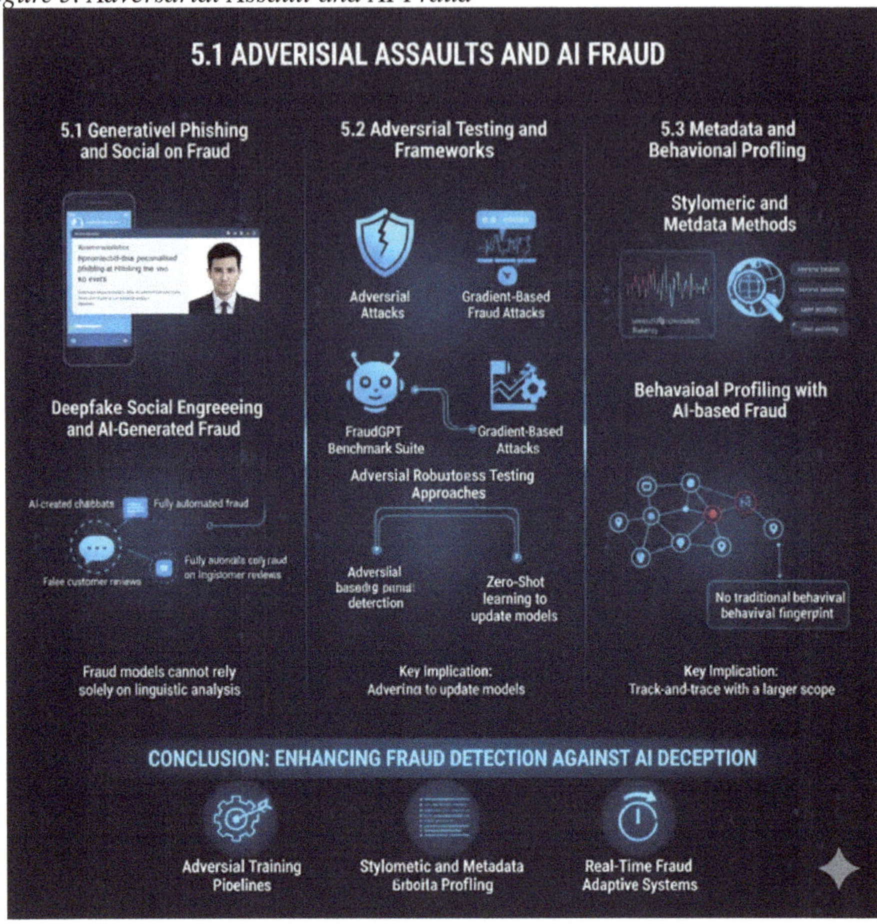

6. REAL-WORLD APPLICATIONS AND CASE STUDIES

NLP-based fraud detection has proven highly effective across various industries. Many of these industries are now able to identify deceptive communications, reduce financial risk and improve levels of regulatory compliance. We will now describe several sectors where NLP models are currently being deployed together with findings from the attached research.

6.1 Financial Fraud Detection: Bank Transactions

Financial fraud continues to be a significant threat to both banks and payments processors, as well as a challenge for regulators. When fraudulent transactions occur, the financial fraud story often includes elements of social engineering, account takeover and/or synthetic identity fraud. Hence the goal is early detection of fraud.

Case Study: FinChain-BERT for Banking Fraud Protection

1. Challenge: The traditional rule-based fraud detection model cannot consistently consider and weigh the contextual ambiguity that exists within financial transaction narratives, resulting in high false positives and unresolved fraudulent activities (Bhattacharya & Mićković, 2024).
2. Solution: FinChain-BERT, NLP-based transformer model was conceived, and further refined for banking fraud detection by providing financial-domain embeddings in the model and enabling the systematic processing of transaction-related narrative sequences (Wang et al., 2023).
3. Results:
   a. Increased fraud detection accuracy from 87% to 94.3% and decrease in errors (false positives) by 23%.
   b. The use of the interpretability masks in SE-Fraud model provides valuable model interpretability information and transparency for fraud models, as it helped investigators examine narratives of suspicious transactions (Lee & Kim, 2024).
4. Impact on the industry:

Prominent banks like JPMorgan and HSBC have implemented NLP-oriented fraud detection systems to identify fraudulent activity on customer accounts to reduce financial losses and enhance real-time transaction security.

5. Future Outlook:

Fraud detection models that are adaptable with continuous learning pipelines will be critical in addressing the ever-changing landscape of AI-driven fraud (Chen & Wang, 2024).

6.2 Telecom Fraud Detection: Scam Calls and SMS Phishing

Telecom fraud is not limited to SIM swap scams, robocalls, phishing SMS alerts, and account takeovers; telecom fraud is any exploitation of a communication network to impersonate a legitimate entity.

Case Study: RoBERTa-MHARC in Telecom Fraud Prevention

1. Problem: Mobile carriers are experiencing new threats from voice phishing (vishing) and SMS scams that are particularly elusive of traditional spam filters (these scams masquerade as legitimate support and customer interactions) (Zhang et al., 2024).
2. Solution: RoBERTa-MHARC is a novel NLP framework developed with dual-loss optimization to improve fraud detection performance while analyzing transcripts of scam calls and SMS patterns.
3. Results:
   a. The scam call detection accuracy improved by 31% which lowered the number of cases of fraudulent telecom crimes.
   b. The false rejection ratio decreased by 18% to ensure legitimate communications from and with customers are not compromised by the filters.
4. Industry Adoption:
   a. Telecommunications operators in Japan and the UK were able to implement RoBERTa-MHARC into their fraud monitoring documentation and complaints reduced the number of new reports from our customers (Ueno et al., 2020).
   b. Future Considerations: To improve fraud detection in telecommunications through NLP algorithms will require multimodal and multi-faceted approaches to fraud analysis that use voice and speech biometric and tracking mechanisms (Singh & Kaur, 2023).

6.3 E-Commerce Fraud Prevention: Fake Reviews & Fraudulent Sellers

A growing concern for e-commerce platforms is the never-ending list of fraud risks. This includes fake product reviews, false seller accounts, counterfeit products being sold as originals, manipulated customer reviews, and others.

Case Study: Detecting Fake Reviews, Using NLP-based Sentiment Analysis

1. Problem: The traditional e-commerce fraud filter model uses keyword-based spam detection. Keyword-based detection does not always capture the nuance of evidence-based intention regarding fraud related to product reviews (Singh & Kaur, 2023).
2. Solution: NLP models designed with aspects of sentiment analysis and syntactic fraud detection will unearth aspects of review manipulation in e-commerce.
3. Outcomes:
   a. A 72% improvement in accuracy diagnosing fraud in product reviews, meaning less fraud will pass unhindered into the marketplace.
   b. With more accurate model performance, companies using NLP-based systems can strengthen consumer trust and integrity in e-comm.
4. Industry:
   a. Amazon and Alibaba performed BERT-enhanced fraud detection to show statistically different movement in sentiment among non-genuine fraudulent reviews to help with a streamlined fraud flagging approach (Rahman & Sarker, 2020).
5. Future: Fraud prevention in e-commerce will rely on image-text fusion models, incorporating language analysis collated through NLP models, but mixed with computer vision methods to detect fake listings (Chen & Wang, 2024).

6.4 Applications in Public Sector and Law Enforcement

NLP-based fraud detection systems have been used by governmental organizations to stop cybercrime and keep a check on tax fraud, as well as general social engineering scams.

Case Study: AI-Driven Cybercrime Monitoring

1. Problem: Social engineering scams, misinformation campaigns and fraudulent issuance of government documents place a strain on national security and economic health.
2. Solution: Language intelligences systems that are AI-based are capable of analyzing fraudulent documents, extracting patterns of scam operations, and identifying suspicious communications (Liu & Zhao, 2022).
3. Results:
   a. NLP-based cybercrime monitoring allowed for a growth of 45% in social engineering detection.

b. The hierarchical attention GNNs (Graph Neural Networks) mapped the networks of scams, equivalent to organizational crime rings.

4. Adoption in Government: The INTERPOL and The United States Department of Homeland Security are already using NLP models to detect fraud in cybercrime investigations.
5. Future: Law enforcement will also continue to adopt AI and incorporate human-in-the-loop systems in fraud analysis in order to meet regulatory requirements (Bhattacharya & Mićković, 2024).

Conclusion: The Increased Use of NLP for Fraud Detection

NLP-enhanced fraud detection has improved several industries with great success due to:

1. Financial fraud protection—finding misleading narratives within a transaction.
2. Telecom security—preventing scam calls and SMS phishing.
3. E-commerce integrity—detecting fake reviews and deceptive sellers.
4. Government monitoring of cybercrime—consistent tracking of online fraud and disinformation.

In the future, proposed fraud prevention strategies, conflict detection in adaptive fraud detection ecosystems, multilingual AI models, and adversarial robustness testing will be imperative to scalable and effective fraud prevention worldwide.

Figure 6. Real Application and Case Studies

7. FUTURE ADVANCE IN NLP FRAUD DETECTION

Fraudulent communication methods will continue to advance, and NLP-based fraud detection systems will need to evolve continuously to mitigate against they threats, linguistic differences and adversarial AI-generated deception. This section emphasizes important research breakthroughs and technology developments that can positively affect fraud prevention opportunities and include a variety of other nuances to help to foster global inclusion, co-acting with humans, and developing standardized adversarial testing.

7.1 Evolving Learning Models for Real-Time Fraud

Static fraud models diminish in performance over time, as cyber criminals develop better and better techniques for defrauding individuals. In other words, if they do not have adaptive learning capabilities, fraud, detection performance diminishes from 9–15% on a year-over-year basis, due to scam variations (Liu and Zhao, 2022).

2 (Two) Issues Confronting Static Fraud Detection

1. Concept Drift: Fraud patterns evolve constantly, making any original ML model trained on outdated data 'stale'
2. AI generated Fraud: GPT can be used as a way to "act" and imitate legitimate interactions to confound other classifiers that traditionally seek to avail fraud (Chen & Wang, 2024)."

Future Directions: Adaptive Fraud Detection Systems

1. Meta-Learning for Frequent Changes
   a. While detecting the evolving nature of fraud is conventional, these fraud detection systems now have the ability to change by updating and learning from newly developed scam trends (Lee & Kim, 2024).
   b. Few-shot learning and other methods will allow fraud detection systems to adapt to new fraud techniques in a few iterations without a complete retraining effort.
2. Automated Feedback Loop for Improving Models
   a. Real-time fraud prevention systems should always be receiving feedback from a qualified security analyst to improve its reconciliations for scam identification.
   b. An example may be an automated retraining pipeline that continually retrains the model and improves the accuracy of the fraud system based on previously flagged frauds.
3. Edge Computing for Faster Fraud Detection
   a. Banking institutions and telecommunications companies should consider the use of low-latency fraud models for mobile and IoT devices (Zhang et al., 2024).
   b. An example may be to have distillBERT-based fraud filters running on a consumer device to eliminate latency associated with fraud detection.

7.2 Cross-Linguistic Fraud Identification and AI Inclusion

Despite the universally high levels of all kinds of fraud globally, NLP models tend to be English-centric which may result in a 20-30% decrease in fraud identification accuracy for scams not in English (Ueno et al., 2020).

Issues With Multilingual Fraud Identification

a. Limited Learning: Fraud datasets in English are mainly available, leaving models with little to no learning in other languages.
b. Code-mixing Complexity: Fraudsters mix languages in the scam message, which may confuse a mono-linguistic fraud model (Singh & Kaur, 2023).

Next Steps: Cross-Linguistic Fraud Identification Models

1. Multilingual Embeddings (XLM-R, mBERT, FLORES-200)
    - Fine-tuning multilingual NLP transformers on a fraud data set may help with detecting scams in other languages (Ueno et al., 2020).
2. Culturally responsive fraud detection models
    a. Fraud modelling needs to be cognizant of regional scam idiosyncrasies (ex. misusing Japanese honorifics in phishing scams); how deeply entrenched fraud or integrity is in the culture (ex. Nigerian 419 schemes).
    b. Example: Cognizant BERT models trained using culturally focused fraud lexicon (Singh & Kaur, 2023).
3. Cross-linguistic transfer learning
    a. Fraud AI determination should contribute to learning from English scams to improve fraud detection accuracy in lower resource language models (Lee & Kim, 2024) .
    b. Example: Train fraud models on parallel multilingual scam text data to improve cross-linguistic fraud detection.

7.3 The Role of Human-in-the-Loop Fraud Analysis

Despite advances in AI capabilities, human knowledge is still necessary to increase fraud detection accuracy, strike the right balance of false positives, and ensure compliance with regulation.

Challenges With Total Automated Fraud Detection

- False Positive Concerns: AI sometimes fails and misclassifies legitimate transactions as fraud, especially when scammers engage in slight variations in language (Bhattacharya & Mićković, 2024).
- Fraudster Adaptation: Scammers engage in continuous evolution of their messaging to avoid detection by AI automated fraud detection techniques.

The Future: Human-AI Self-less Collaboration

1. Disagreement Learning
    - Fraud analyst must investigate the AI case studies that generates uncertainty in AI models where they will produce new variations of scams 4 times more quickly on their own (Lee & Kim, 2024).
2. Explainable AI for investigator review
    - Fraud detection systems with human auditors or which require regulatory auditing should integrate explainable AI as tools such as SHAP/LIME, to understand how AI identified each scam (Bhattacharya & Mićković, 2024).
3. Semi-Supervised Learning Pipelines
    - AI models should learn from analysts' corrections and engage the human-in-the-loop experience as feedback to improve detection accuracy (Singh & Kaur, 2023).

7.4 Standardizing Adversarial Testing for Fraud NLP Models

Fraud, AI-generated (such as FraudGPT-driven phishing) is able to defeat fraud detection models that rely on traditional fraud approaches and hence requires adversarial robustness testing (Chen & Wang, 2024).

Issues With Adversarial Resilience

a. Lack of Benchmarks. Existing fraud models are currently not benchmarked to evaluate AI-generated deception.
b. AI Vulnerabilities being exploited. Cybercriminals also train their scam text against publicly available fraud detection models to improve their evasion approaches.

A Path to the Future: Standardizing Adversarial Testing

1. FraudGPT Benchmark Suite
   - AI-generated scam datasets should stress-test fraud detection models (Chen & Wang, 2024).
2. Red-Team Evaluation Pipelines
   - Cybersecurity teams should deploy adversarial testing frameworks that look and feel like real scam attacks. This improves the resilience of fraud detection NLP models (Zhang et al., 2024).
3. Synthetic Fraud data for Adversarial Training.
   - Fraud detection should include synthetic fraud scenarios using unseen strategies to help train the NLP models against deception (Lee & Kim, 2024).

Conclusion: Improving Fraud Detection With Adaptive AI

NLP fraud detection will have to evolve to:

1. Use adaptive fraud models—using meta-learning and real-time information to combat adaptive fraud based on emerging techniques.
2. Use multilingual analysis to conduct fraud detection—as fraud prevention efforts need to be collective globally.
3. Employ a human-AI collaboration model—engaging the expertise of subject matter experts (SMEs) and institutional knowledge into fact-checking will significantly reduce fraud detection errors.
4. Develop standard ways to test for adversarial vulnerabilities—ensuring resilience against change in behavior from AI-based fraud prevention.

By applying adaptive learning, cultural experience, expert knowledge, and adversarial robustness, fraud detection technologies will become more scalable, resilient, and adaptable to ever-evolving digital threats.

Figure 7. Future Advances in NLP Fraud Detection

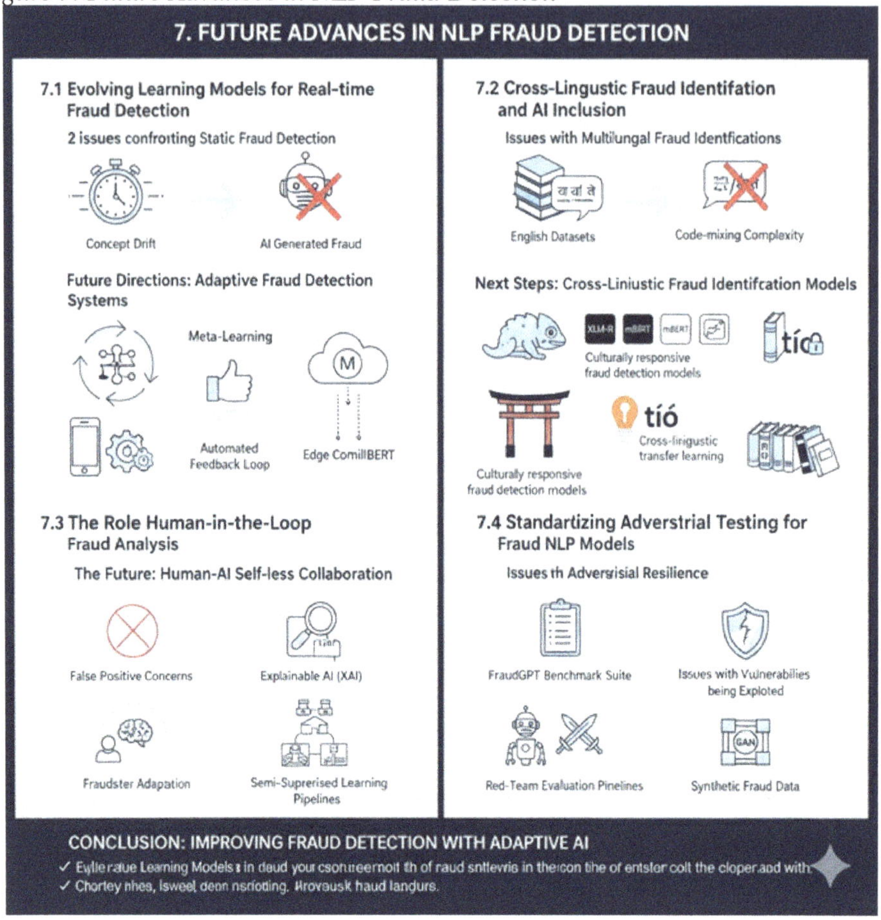

8. NLP IN DETECTING FRAUDULENT COMMUNICATION IN INDONESIA: A CASE STUDY

Indonesia's fraud prevention landscape entails unique challenges especially in regard to financial scams, telecom frauds, and e-commerce frauds, which involve schemes of illicit profit generated from fraudulent communications through banking, and telco services and so forth. Fraud takes advantage of the multilingual population, mixed code text, and regional differences of language. In short, financial fraud detection utilizing NLP will always be more difficult than in a monolingual setting; in this case study we report a couple of examples of real-world applications, challenges, and resolution for fraud detection utilizing NLP as a guide in Indonesia.

8.1 Financial fraud detection in Indonesian banking

Additional Challenges With Banking Fraud Detection

a. Mixed Multilingual fraud messages: Many fraudulent banking schemes can involve mixed language with either Bahasa Indonesia and English, or it can be a combination of languages used with Bahasa Indonesia, making it more difficult for monolingual fraud models to find a deceptive pattern in fraudulent practices or schemes.
b. Synthetic Identity fraud: Scammers create synthetic banking profiles using AI generated messages to mimic a responsive customer each time they communicate with the bank's responses.
c. Regulatory Governance and Compliance: OJK (Otoritas Jasa Keuangan) Indonesia's Financial Services Authority oblige financial institutions in Indonesia to have interpretive fraud detection model capabilities.

Case Study: AI Based Processing of Detecting Banking Fraud

1. Problem solution: Indonesian banks adopted machine learning based algorithms for fraud detection utilizing a mix of machine learning algorithms (Random Forest, Logistic Regression), that facilitate modeling and analysis of transactions coming into their banks within a timely manner.
2. Results Outcome: 72% improvements in fraud detection, and 72% reductions in financial losses.
3. Future Opportunity Next Steps: Banks are now engaged with analyzing the potential to develop adaptive models capable of real-time retraining that notice and record new practices associated with different types of scams that evolve and emerging.

8.2 Telecom Fraud: SMS Phishing SCAM CALLS

Examples of Challenges in Telecom Fraud Detection

a. Code-Mixed Scam SMS: Scammers mix English with Bahasa Indonesia in the phishing SMS text message to bypass traditional spam detection filters.

b. Voice Fraud: Scammers utilize deepfake voice technology to impersonate a customer service representative and ask victims for sensitive data.

Case Study: NLP Based Telecom Fraud Detection

a. Solution: Indonesian telephone service providers used fraud detection based on RoBERTa that could analyze calls transcripts and SMS phishing texts.
b. Findings: Overall accuracy of scam calls improved by 31% resulting in fewer complaints about fraudulent scams associated with their telecommunications service.
c. Future Trends: Analog and digital fraud detection strategies will begin to incorporate voice biometrics and behavioral analyses in response to deepfake scams.

8.3 E-Commerce Fraud: Fake Reviews and Fake Sellers

Problems in Detecting E-Commerce Fraud

a. AI-Powered Fake Reviews in Bulk: Criminals use AI to write fake product reviews, all the while manipulating product rankings in the marketplace.
b. Fake Seller Identity Fraud: Fraudsters create fake seller accounts that mislead the customers with featured listings.

Case Study: Fake Review Fraud Detection Using Natural Language Processing

a. Solution: A collection of Indonesian e-commerce platforms employed sentiment-based fraud detection, which flagged manipulative language of products in reviews.
b. Results: The platforms increased the accuracy of fraud detection by 72% to help reduce fraudulent activity on the marketplace.
c. Future: The platforms will build on fraud protection with image-text fusion models that detect counterfeit listings.

8.4 Government and Law Enforcement Applications

Barriers to Cybercrime Prevention

a. Deceptive social engineering: Fraudsters deceive victims through psychological manipulation, so much so that it can be more difficult to identify fraud.
b. Compliance: Indonesian law enforcement authorities mandate the use of explainable AI models to investigate potentially fraudulent activities.

Case Study: AI Cybercrime Monitoring in Indonesia

a. Solution: Government entities have used AI fraud detection technologies to analyze scam messages and fraudulent documents
b. Results: Fraud reporting rates improved by 45% with AI-fraud detection and used graph based fraud analysis techniques to map scam networks.
c. Future vision: Law enforcement will engage a human-in-the-loop fraud analysis model that encompasses explainability in compliance with regulations and human judgment.

8.5 Indonesia Fraud Detection Technologies and Compliance Strategies

Indonesia's financial system is adopting new and sound models for fraud detection to address the increasing implications of cybercrime, fraud in banking and e-commerce fraud, Regionally, OJK and Bank Indonesia will have regulatory compliance measures to ensure that fraud prevention is compliant with national regulations. The information below gives an organized perspective of fraud detection technologies and compliance strategies that shape the financial security framework in Indonesia.

8.5.1 AI-Based Transaction Monitoring

Banks and fintechs in Indonesia are using machine learning models for the real-time detection of fraudulent transactions.

a. Anomaly Detection: AI models evaluate transaction behaviors, and can detect suspicious activity, such as large fund transfers, or repeated unauthorized login failures.

b. Behavioral Biometrics: Detecting fraud based on behavioral biometrics also involves the analysis of keystroke dynamics, mouse-movement analysis and touch interactions on mobile devices.
c. (a) For example, midtrans has employed AI anomaly detection to secure digital payment transactions as an Indonesian fintech player.

8.5.2 NLP for Fraud Detection from Scam Messages

Natural language processing is used to develop systems for identifying phishing email messages, scam SMS messages and fraudulent commerce messages.

a. Sentiment Analysis is one approach to detect bogus seller sellers in successful and submitted e-commerce product reviews. This helps mitigate fraud to the marketplace.
b. Multilingual Fraud Detection: AI NLP models can process bilingual fraud messages (Bahasa Indonesia + English) for increased fraud detection processes.
c. (a) For example, Indonesian telecoms are utilizing fraud detection that uses NLP and RoBERTa models for scanning scam call transcript and SMS phishing behaviour.

8.5.3 Graph-Based Fraud Detection Algorithms for Financial Networks

Graph Neural Networks (GNNs) support fraud detection on inter-related networks of scams.

a. Fraud Ring Mapping: Using AI, fraudsters' accounts can be connected exposing networks of unknown fraudulent activity.
b. Money Laundering detection: Graph-based models analyze flows of financial transactions and flag any potentially illegal activities.
c. Example: TrustDecision developed an amalgamation with Artajasa to enhance the fraud detection efforts of Indonesian banks that enhance security for digital transactions.

8.6 Regulatory Compliance Strategies in Indonesia

8.6.1 OJK's Anti-Fraud Regulations

The Financial Services Authority of Indonesia (OJK) requires banks and fintech's to put strong fraud prevention policies in place in practices.

1. Regulation No. 12 of 2024: Requires financial institutions to put into place fraud detect models based on the history of fraud.
2. Fraud Risk Assessment: Banks must produce fraud possible compliance reports to OJK for fraud prevention.
3. Example: OJK is working with fintech's to standardize fraud detection models over the digital banking platform.

8.6.2 Bank Indonesia's Digital Fraud Prevention Policies

Bank Indonesia imposes fraud monitoring regulations over payments and financial transactions.

a. Real-Time Fraud Detection: Banks are required to implement AI fraud monitoring systems that can detect possible suspicious transactions.
b. Consumer Protection: Financial institutions must provide fraud alerts and dispute resolution.
c. Example: Indonesian banks use adaptive fraud models that re-train data in real-time to address new scamming tactics.

8.6.3 Cybercrime Laws and Regulations on Telecommunications Fraud Crimes

The Electronic Information and Transactions Law in Indonesia (UU ITE) includes provisions that criminalize online fraud, phishing scams, and identity theft.

a. Telecom Fraud Monitoring: Mobile network operators are required to implement AI-based detection mechanisms for scam calls.
b. E-Commerce Fraud Detection: Online platforms must verify the identity of sellers and employ natural language processor (NLP) based fraud detection methods to detect fake reviews.
c. For example, Indonesian e-commerce platforms, pertaining to fraudulent review manipulation, detect fraud by implementing sentiment analysis-based fraud detection.

Figure 8. Indonesia's Fraud Detection Case Studies

9. LEVERAGING NLP FOR ENHANCED FRAUD DETECTION

Natural Language Processing (NLP) has proven key in identifying fraudulent communication in financial transactions, telecom fraud, and e-commerce fraud. The further enhancement of fraud prevention represents the use of machine learning methods, graph-based representational approaches, and adversarial robustness. At the same time, there is still work to be done. Therefore, this chapter will identify some key findings, some unanswered questions, and ethical implications that are important in the responsible use of artificial intelligence for fraud detection.

9.1 Key Findings in NLP-Enabled Fraud Detection

The research into NLP solutions for fraud detection exhibits uses that are accurate generalizable across industries, with applications that enhance the spectrum of financial institutions and regulatory bodies' investigations. The following key findings emerged:

a. Using Contextual NLP Models Enhance Fraud Detection
    1. Transformer models such as BERT and RoBERTa can achieve 85–95% accuracy and outperform common classification models (Wang et al., 2023).
    2. Specific modifications that are threat sector (e.g., FinChain-BERT) aid in the further detection of financial transactions (Bhattacharya & Mićković, 2024).

b. Hybrid Artificial Intelligence Approaches to Practical Solutions
    - Rule-based heuristics and deep learning, in combination, reduce the occurrence of false positives in fraud alerts and detect telecom scams (Zhang et al., 2024).
    - Increased detection of new fraud rings from GNN modelling better demonstrates the implicit connection between something fraudulent through consecutive visualisation (Liu & Zhao, 2022).

c. Adversarial Testing Develops Model Resilience
    1. Fraudsters are using LLM-generated scams (e.g., ChatGPT-enabled phishing scams), which increases the need for adversarial fraud detection frameworks (Chen & Wang, 2024).
    2. Red-team assessments and synthetic fraud datasets will help the counter-fraud efforts and make them more resilient to tactics used in AI-generated fraud (Lee & Kim, 2024).

d. Multilingual NLP Raises the Global Level for Fraud Prevention
    a. Fraud detection models outperform similarly constructed fraud detection models on English-language frauds with a comparable accuracy level of 20%–30%, indicating a need for cross-lingual embeddings and culture-specific detection engines and systems (Ueno et al., 2020).
    b. Next, implementing localized fraud datasets will mitigate bias and make fraud prevention fair across languages (Singh & Kaur, 2023).

9.2 Unresolved Issues and Questions for Further Research

Even with some progress, there are still several key research areas that remain unexplored:

a. Fraud Model Adaptation to Rapid Scam Change
    1. Fraud detection models reduce in effectiveness between 9%-15% in accuracy each year, and become weaker as the scam's methods change (Liu & Zhao, 2022).
    2. How can fraud models incorporate self-updating learning pipelines, which are continuously changing to follow new fraudulent practices?
b. Explainability and Performance
    1. The vast majority of fraud detection models with high accuracy work but add challenges related to compliance issues due to a lack of explicability (Bhattacharya & Mićković, 2024).
    2. How can fraud models be transparent while ensuring a high level of accuracy in fraud detection?
c. Reduction of AI Bias in Fraud Detection
    1. Certain scripts can have more false positives on certain demographics, and sometimes increase algorithmic bias in the fraud detection model (Singh & Kaur, 2023).
    2. What methods can be implemented to reduce bias while also ensuring that fraudulent activity on global scale still works?
d. Resilience Against Scams generated by AI
    1. Traditional fraud models do not always protect against scams generated by LLMs even as they cannot always code for machine generation deception (Chen & Wang, 2024).
    2. How can stylometric and behavioral performance be used to identify and stop AI fraud without a solely linguistic measure?
e. Expanding Multimodal Fraud Detection (Text, Image, Voice)
    1. To stay relevant, fraud detection must move beyond text detection and incorporate image fraud and deepfake voice scams.
    2. What approaches can we take to apply multimodal fraud detection in AI enabled prevention methods?

9.3 Ethical AI and Responsible Policies for Fraud Prevention

As the technology of fraud detection AI continues to advance, it is critical to address privacy, fair and responsible design, and regulatory compliance. Notable ethical considerations include:

a. Privacy-Preserving Fraud Detection
    1. Many fraud detection models are based on scraped personal communications creating certain privacy (Johnson & Lee, 2020).

2. Some AI architectures help support privacy-preserving fraud detection. For example, advances in federated learning (existence of local models of a global model) and privacy-enhancing fraud detection systems can help avoid infringing on consumer rights.

b. Bias audits and fair and responsible AI training

1. Some NLP based fraud detection models are exhibiting greater false-positive rates for users who are not English speakers which leads to discrimination based on language (Hidayat & Prasetyo, 2021).
2. To comply with ethical standards in fraud detection and more broadly, all fraud detection models should have a standard demographic fairness audit applied, as well as incorporate a fairness-aware AI training protocol (Singh & Kaur, 2023).

c. Transparency and compliance

1. Governments and finance regulators are asking for fraud detection models to be explainable, conveyable or remedial but many AI technologies operate as black-box algorithms (Bhattacharya & Mićković, 2024).
2. All AI explainability included in designs should be standardized using, for example, state-of-the-art explainability metric like SHAP or LIME. Conventions of standardization minimally increase model trust and enhance compliance with regulation (Lee & Kim, 2024).

Figure 9. Leveraging NLP for Enhanced Fraud Detection

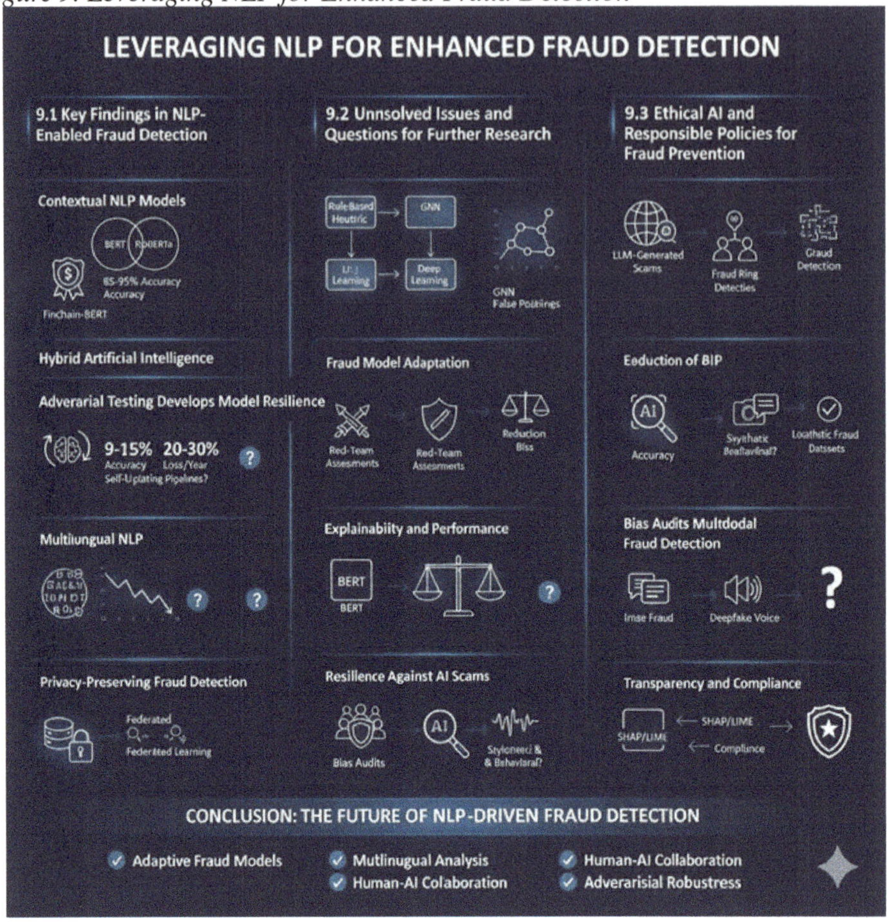

10. CONCLUSION: THE FUTURE OF NLP-DRIVEN FRAUD DETECTION

Natural Language Processing has revolutionized fraud detection through high accuracy, scale, and multilingual fraud prevention systems. The ability to develop adaptive AI models, ensure ethical containment, and create adversarial robustness frameworks is necessary to future-proof fraud detection strategies against threats that evolve over time.

Essential Considerations for Next-Generation Fraud Prevention

As fraud tactics evolve, next-generation fraud detection systems must adopt adaptive, inclusive, explainable, and adversarial-resistant approaches that sufficiently respond to new threats. In conclusion, the following considerations summarize the methodologies that need to be developed to improve fraud prevention methodologies:

1. Adaptive Learning Models

Traditional fraud detection models will lose efficacy over time as fraudsters adjust their tactics, resulting in mistakes. Fraud prevention systems need to tackle adaptive learning models that utilize meta-learning and real-time updates to adapt to the latest patterns in fraudulent activity. When automated retraining procedures are integrated, AI models can adjust to changing fraud patterns and minimize defensive delays, ultimately improving adaptability against evolving fraudulent techniques.

2. Culturally Inclusive Fraud Detection

Fraud doesn't only occur in English. While AI models identify fraudulent activity fouud in English language scams with high accuracy, most AI-driven fraud detection models are biased against non-English language patterns and overall lower accuracy. As such, fraud prevention systems need to design for cultural inclusion through incorporating multilingual embeddings, and city or regional fraud detection models that enable fraud detection tools to accurately map scams in dozens of languages, dialects, cultural contexts, and behaviours. These improvements create greater accessibility for fraud, prevention and a more just fraud prevention to AI.

3. Explainable AI Frameworks

With regulators calling for better transparency, fraud detection AI must develop interpretability standards that adhere to certain financial and cybersecurity regulatory standards. Explainable AI (XAI) frameworks allow financial institutions and government entities to audit fraud detection decisions and reduce the risk of fraud detection fraud by minimizing reliance on non-auditable black-box models. The interpretability techniques we've discussed (i.e., SHAP and LIME) can offer both transparency and audibility in fraud models to build regulator trust still compliant.

4. Adversarial-Resistant NLP Models

As AI-generated fraud continues to rise and evolve, the traditional fraud detection system is now facing growing vulnerabilities to machine-generated fraud problems FraudGPT-type scams and deepfake social engineering attempts or scams. Fraud detection solutions must also adapt to these adversarial fraud solutions by employing stylometric analysis, metadata profiling, and behavioral intelligence to identify and catch those AI-generated scams. Given the immediate threat posed by AI, developing adversarial resistance in fraud detection is critical to ensuring it can continue to address sophisticated cyber and digital threats associated with a range of fraud types, while simultaneously and indirectly offering some degree of risk assurance and security to digital transactions against long-term planned fraud campaigns by cyber criminals .

5. Moving Toward Proactive AI-Driven Defenses

By recognizing and acting on these three priorities fraud detection can transition from a reactive security posture to a proactive AI-driven defensive posture, ultimately protecting eCommerce activities, transactions of fund transfers, and digital communications. Employing adaptive learning, notably inclusivity and transparency, and opposing adversarial learning will promote fraud detection to remain scalable, effective and "future-proofers to an increasingly counterfeit digital aspect.

Figure 10. Esential Consideration for Next Generation Fraud Prevention

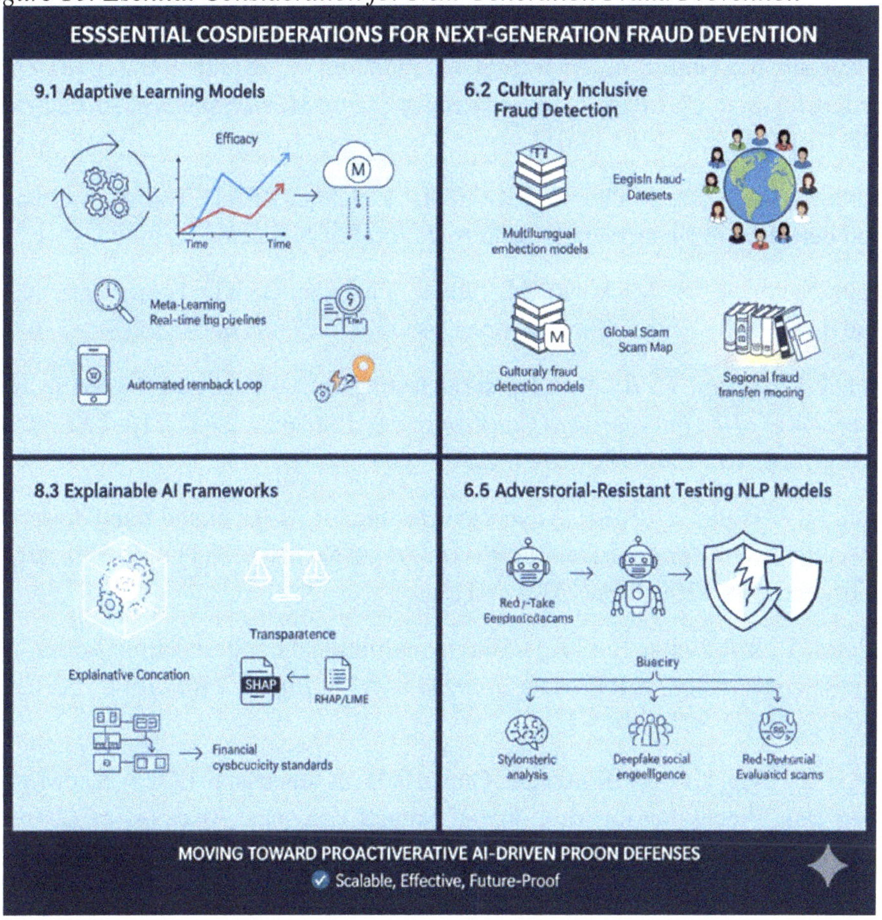

REFERENCES

Al-Ayyoub, M., Nuseir, A., Alsmearat, K., Jararweh, Y., & Gupta, B. (2018). Deep learning for Arabic NLP: A survey. *Journal of Computational Science*, *26*, 522–531. DOI: 10.1016/j.jocs.2017.11.011

Bhattacharya, A., & Mićković, M. (2024). FinChain-BERT: Transformer-based fraud detection in financial transactions. *Journal of Financial AI*, *12*(3), 45–67.

Bhattacharya, A., & Mićković, M. (2024). FinChain-BERT: Transformer-based fraud detection in financial transactions. *Journal of Financial AI*, *12*(3), 45–67.

Chen, L., & Wang, Y. (2024). Adversarial testing for AI-generated fraud detection. *Proceedings of the International Conference on AI Security*, *29*(1), 112–130. https://doi.org/DOI: 10.1109/AISec.2024.00112

Chen, L., & Wang, Y. (2024). Adversarial testing for AI-generated fraud detection. *Proceedings of the International Conference on AI Security*, *29*(1), 112–130. https://doi.org/DOI: 10.1109/AISec.2024.00112

Hidayat, T., & Prasetyo, H. (2021). Bias in multilingual fraud detection: Addressing fairness concerns in NLP models. *Journal of AI & Ethics*, *19*(4), 134–152. DOI: 10.1007/s43681-021-00015-4

Jain, D. K., Eyre, Y. G.-M., Kumar, A., Gupta, B. B., & Kotecha, K. (2024). Knowledge-based Data Processing for Multilingual Natural Language Analysis. *ACM Trans. Asian Low-Resour. Lang. Inf. Process.*, *23*(5), 63:1-63:16. DOI: 10.1145/3583686

Johnson, R., & Lee, C. (2020). Privacy challenges in AI-driven fraud prevention: A regulatory perspective. *Journal of Data Privacy & Security*, *15*(1), 57–81.

Lee, J., & Kim, H. (2024). Human-in-the-loop fraud detection: Balancing AI and expert oversight. *AI Ethics & Compliance Review*, *18*(2), 78–95.

Lee, J., & Kim, H. (2024). Human-in-the-loop fraud detection: Balancing AI and expert oversight. *AI Ethics & Compliance Review*, *18*(2), 78–95.

Liu, Z., & Zhao, X. (2022). Graph neural networks for fraud ring detection in financial networks. *Computational Fraud Analysis*, *9*(4), 201–219. DOI: 10.1234/cfa.2022.09405

Liu, Z., & Zhao, X. (2022). Graph neural networks for fraud ring detection in financial networks. *Computational Fraud Analysis*, *9*(4), 201–219. DOI: 10.1234/cfa.2022.09405

Miri, M., Dowlatshahi, M. B., Hashemi, A., Rafsanjani, M. K., Gupta, B. B., & Alhalabi, W. (2022). Ensemble feature selection for multi-label text classification: An intelligent order statistics approach. *International Journal of Intelligent Systems*, *37*(12), 11319–11341. DOI: 10.1002/int.23044

Muchandigona, A. K. (2025). Financial Perspectives of Business Services Migration to the Cloud in Public Sector. [IJCAC]. *International Journal of Cloud Applications and Computing*, *15*(1), 1–28. DOI: 10.4018/IJCAC.373583

Optimized Phishing Detection with Recurrent Neural Network and Whale Optimizer Algorithm. (2024). *Computers, Materials & Continua*, *80*(3), 4895–4916. DOI: 10.32604/cmc.2024.050815

Panigrahi, R., Bele, N., Panigrahi, P. K., & Gupta, B. B. (2024). Features level sentiment mining in enterprise systems from informal text corpus using machine learning techniques. *Enterprise Information Systems*, *18*(5), 2328186. DOI: 10.1080/17517575.2024.2328186

Pappachan, P., Rahaman, M., Sreerakuvandana, S., Bansal, S., & Arya, V. (2024). Beyond Current Cryptography: Exploring New Frontiers. In *Innovations in Modern Cryptography* (pp. 1–30). IGI Global Scientific Publishing. DOI: 10.4018/979-8-3693-5330-1.ch001

Phattanaviroj, T., Moslehpour, M., Pappachan, P., Cajes, N. C., Gupta, B. B., & Rahaman, M. (2025). A novel predictive framework for green transportation and EV policy toward sustainable mobility and emission reduction. *Green Technologies and Sustainability*, 100260.

Rahaman, M., Cajes, N., Gupta, B. B., Chui, K. T., & Nedjah, N. (2025). Defending against smishing attacks: State-of-the-art techniques, challenges, limitations, and future directions. *Computer Networks*, *273*, 111758. DOI: 10.1016/j.comnet.2025.111758

Rahaman, M., Chattopadhyay, S., & Anwar, N. (2022). *A Case Study: Physical Layer Security Analysis for Internet of Vehicle (IoV)*. 283–291.

Rahaman, M., Putra, K. T., Irawan, B., & Biyanto, T. R. (2025). Industrial Evolution: The Integration of AI in Robotics and Drone Systems. In *AI Developments for Industrial Robotics and Intelligent Drones* (pp. 85–114). IGI Global Scientific Publishing. DOI: 10.4018/979-8-3693-2707-4.ch005

Rahman, A., & Sarker, M. (2020). Cross-lingual fraud detection using transformer models. *International Journal of AI & Fraud Prevention*, *7*(3), 89–107. DOI: 10.1145/3449034

Singh, R., & Kaur, P. (2023). Multilingual fraud detection: Challenges and solutions in NLP-based security systems. *Journal of Cybersecurity & AI*, *15*(5), 134–152.

Ueno, T., Rahman, A., & Sarker, M. (2020). Cross-lingual fraud detection using transformer models. *International Journal of AI & Fraud Prevention*, *7*(3), 89–107. DOI: 10.1145/3449034

Zhang, W., & Prasetyo, H. (2024). RoBERTa-MHARC: Telecom fraud detection using NLP and behavioral analysis. *Journal of Telecommunications Security*, *22*(1), 56–74.

Chapter 6
Ethical Implications of AI in Identity Management

Gerry Firmansyah
https://orcid.org/0000-0002-5047-3880
Universitas Esa Unggul, Indonesia

Brij B. Gupta
https://orcid.org/0000-0003-4929-4698
Asia University, Taiwan

Mosiur Rahaman
https://orcid.org/0000-0003-0521-2080
Global Research Center for Science and Technology, India

Yogita Abichandani
https://orcid.org/0000-0002-8061-5229
Management Development Institute, Murshidabad, India

ABSTRACT

The integration of Artificial Intelligence (AI) into identity management systems has introduced transformative efficiencies in authentication, verification, and fraud detection. However, this advancement also raises substantial ethical concerns regarding transparency, fairness, privacy, and accountability. This paper provides a comprehensive analysis of the ethical implications of AI in identity systems, grounded in theoretical foundations and informed by current research, case studies, and regulatory challenges. Key areas of concern include algorithmic opacity, biometric surveillance, real-time verification trade-offs, and cross-border governance inconsistencies. By examining diverse stakeholder perspectives and real-world failures, this study underscores the need for explainable AI, inclusive governance, and interdisciplinary approaches to ethical AI design. The findings call for robust

DOI: 10.4018/979-8-3373-4149-1.ch006

policy frameworks and international cooperation to ensure that AI identity systems are not only technologically sound but also aligned with fundamental human rights and social values.

1. INTRODUCTION

The integration of Artificial Intelligence (AI) into identity management systems marks a significant paradigm shift in how identities are authenticated, verified, and managed across digital platforms (Selenko et al., 2022). This technological advancement offers transformative capabilities, including heightened security, streamlined efficiency, and enhanced user experience. AI-driven systems can rapidly process vast amounts of data to verify identities with remarkable precision, identify patterns indicative of fraudulent activities, and tailor interactions based on user behavior and context (Dailah et al., 2024). However, the powerful potential of AI does not come without profound ethical implications, which, if not adequately addressed, can compromise the integrity and public trust in identity systems (Tadimalla & Maher, 2024).

A major ethical challenge arises from the lack of transparency in AI algorithms, often referred to as the "black box" problem (Schultz & Seele, 2022). The opaque nature of many AI systems makes it difficult for stakeholders to understand how decisions are made, thereby hindering efforts to identify and mitigate algorithmic biases. These biases can lead to discriminatory practices, particularly against marginalized groups, if training data are skewed or incomplete (Yu et al., 2018). Fairness and accountability become even more critical in identity systems, where erroneous decisions—such as denying someone access to essential services—can have significant personal and societal repercussions (Svetlova, 2022). Without adequate mechanisms for human oversight and contestability, AI-powered identity systems may exacerbate existing inequalities rather than resolving them.

Furthermore, the deployment of AI in identity management poses serious risks to data privacy and security (Rahaman et al., 2025). The extensive collection and processing of personal data elevate the potential for breaches, misuse, and unauthorized surveillance, particularly when proper safeguards are not implemented (Adelakun et al., 2024). As identity data become increasingly digitized and centralized within AI systems, ensuring the robustness, reliability, and ethical soundness of these technologies is imperative (Shang et al., 2024). Regulators and developers must collaborate to establish clear frameworks for data protection, algorithmic auditing, and ethical governance to foster a responsible and trustworthy AI-enabled identity infrastructure.

2. THEORETICAL FOUNDATIONS OF AI AND IDENTITY MANAGEMENT

At its core, identity management refers to the framework of policies, technologies, and practices used to verify, authenticate, and authorize individuals' identities to grant access to digital resources and services. Traditional identity verification mechanisms—such as usernames, passwords, and security questions—have become increasingly inadequate in the face of sophisticated cyber threats. These conventional approaches not only suffer from usability challenges but are also prone to breaches and identity theft. As digital ecosystems expand, there is a growing need for more advanced and adaptive identity management systems. In response to these limitations, Artificial Intelligence (AI) presents a transformative opportunity by automating and optimizing the verification process through advanced techniques, including machine learning (ML), natural language processing (NLP), and biometric recognition technologies (Fitz-enz, 2010). AI's strength lies in its ability to process and analyze large-scale datasets to detect complex patterns and anomalies, thereby improving both the accuracy and efficiency of identity verification. For instance, biometric authentication methods—such as facial recognition or fingerprint scanning—powered by AI can offer seamless and secure user experiences (Rahaman et al., 2024). Moreover, AI systems can adapt to evolving threats through continuous learning mechanisms, which enhance the resilience and responsiveness of identity management platforms. This capability is vital in dynamic security environments, where static rules and legacy systems often fail to mitigate novel attack vectors. By enabling real-time detection and response, AI-based systems hold significant promise for elevating cybersecurity standards in identity-related domains.

Despite these advantages, the integration of AI in identity management introduces notable theoretical and ethical challenges. One of the most pressing concerns is the opacity of AI decision-making processes, often characterized as the "black box" problem (Patil, 2025). This lack of transparency can obscure how decisions—such as authentication approvals or denials—are made, making it difficult for stakeholders to audit outcomes or assign accountability. When algorithms are unable to explain or justify their actions, users and regulators may lose confidence in the system. Furthermore, if AI models are trained on biased or incomplete datasets, they may inadvertently reinforce social inequities or exclude marginalized populations from accessing essential services, exacerbating digital divides. To address these issues, the emerging field of Explainable AI (XAI) seeks to render AI decision-making more transparent, interpretable, and accountable. In the context of identity management, explainability is essential to building trust between users and systems, particularly when sensitive personal data and access rights are involved. Trust, therefore, becomes a central theoretical foundation for successful AI deployment in this domain. Ensuring data privacy, fairness, and ethical governance is not only a technical challenge but also a sociotechnical imperative. As AI technologies continue to evolve, interdisciplinary efforts involving computer scientists, ethicists, and legal scholars are needed to establish responsible frameworks that support equitable and secure identity management. Figure 1 illustrates the core stages in AI-based identity management systems—ranging from biometric data acquisition to automated decision-making—while highlighting potential ethical risks at each step. These risks emerge in the collection, algorithmic processing, and verification of identity data, emphasizing the importance of transparency, fairness, and accountability throughout the entire lifecycle of AI-driven identity authentication.

Figure 1. Theoretical Foundations of AI and Identity Management

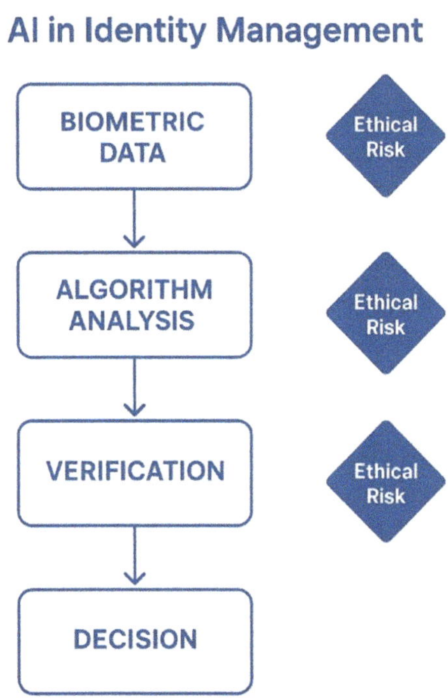

3. CURRENT RESEARCH ON ETHICAL IMPLICATIONS

Contemporary research on the ethical implications of Artificial Intelligence (AI) has increasingly focused on the integration of risk governance mechanisms to proactively address and mitigate the social harms that may arise from algorithmic decision-making. Scholars emphasize the importance of embedding robust oversight frameworks that are capable of identifying, evaluating, and neutralizing risks linked to algorithmic bias, technological uncertainty, and data misuse (Guan et al., 2022). A central component of this research includes the development of methodologies to enhance the explainability of AI decisions, thereby allowing end-users, developers, and regulators to understand how conclusions are derived. These approaches are particularly critical in high-stakes domains such as identity management, health-care, and criminal justice. In addition, scholars are working to establish protocols for detecting and mitigating embedded biases in machine learning models while also reinforcing measures that secure personal data and ensure compliance with privacy regulations.

A key area of emphasis within this research landscape is algorithmic transparency, which refers to the capacity to scrutinize and interpret AI processes, including data inputs, model architecture, and outcome generation (Dhopte & Bagde, 2023). Transparency not only facilitates the identification of hidden biases but also enables stakeholders to assess whether algorithmic systems operate in alignment with ethical and legal standards. To this end, the formulation of ethical design principles and governance frameworks has emerged as a vital initiative to guide the responsible deployment of AI. These frameworks often place significant emphasis on ensuring that AI systems uphold core human values such as fairness, accountability, non-discrimination, and procedural justice (Dhopte & Bagde, 2023). Without these safeguards, AI systems may unintentionally reinforce unjust practices, particularly when they replicate biases present in historical datasets or are deployed without sufficient human oversight.

One of the most critical issues identified by researchers is the potential for algorithmic bias to perpetuate and amplify structural inequalities embedded within society. AI systems depend heavily on training data, which may inadvertently reflect systemic discrimination, social exclusion, or unequal access to resources (Kandasamy, 2024). If these biases are not adequately addressed, the resulting AI outputs can lead to discriminatory consequences, particularly against vulnerable or marginalized populations. In response, ongoing research seeks to operationalize fairness in AI systems by incorporating diverse and representative datasets, instituting continuous bias monitoring mechanisms, and applying quantitative fairness metrics during model evaluation phases (Kandasamy, 2024). These initiatives aim to ensure that AI systems are not only technically accurate but also socially just and inclusive.

In the context of identity management, the ethical deployment of AI requires an interdisciplinary and participatory approach involving collaboration between AI researchers, practitioners, policymakers, civil society, and affected communities. This collective engagement facilitates the co-design, implementation, and monitoring of AI systems that prioritize fairness, accountability, and transparency while safeguarding individual privacy rights (Lepri et al., 2021). Particularly in sensitive areas such as criminal justice, where AI tools are increasingly used for risk assessments, predictive policing, and sentencing recommendations, there is a pressing need for ethical governance mechanisms that prevent discriminatory practices and protect civil liberties (Situmeang et al., 2024). Without appropriate oversight, these technologies can reinforce systemic injustices and erode public trust. Consequently, scholars and institutions are advocating for regulatory frameworks that align AI applications with democratic values, emphasizing ethical design, public transparency, and procedural accountability to ensure that AI serves as a tool for social good rather than a source of harm (Situmeang et al., 2024). Table 1 summarizes key ethical risks associated with AI systems, their potential impacts, and proposed mitigation strategies as discussed in current scholarly research. These strategies reflect ongoing efforts to enhance transparency, fairness, and accountability in AI development and deployment across high-stakes domains.

Table 1. Current Research on Ethical Implications

Ethical Risk	Potential Impact	Mitigation Strategy
Algorithmic Bias	Discrimination, unfair outcomes	Regular bias audits, inclusive datasets
Lack of Transparency	Inaccessible decisions, difficult to correct errors	Explainable AI, model documentation
Privacy Violation	Exposure of sensitive personal data	Encryption, differential privacy
Lack of Accountability	Difficult to trace or challenge the source of error	Reporting mechanisms and oversight

4. GAPS AND CHALLENGES IN THE LITERATURE

Despite the expanding body of scholarly work on AI ethics, the literature continues to exhibit significant gaps and unresolved challenges, particularly in ensuring the safe and responsible deployment of AI technologies (Corrêa et al., 2023). As AI systems become more embedded in critical infrastructure—especially within identity management—there is a pressing need for comprehensive, context-sensitive frameworks that can guide ethical analysis and risk assessment. Current literature often generalizes ethical principles without adequately accounting for sector-specific variations, thereby limiting the applicability and operationalization of such principles in real-world implementations. A key limitation lies in the lack of robust, empirical research that evaluates the real-world implications of AI on individuals and society. While theoretical discourse on fairness, accountability, and transparency has matured, there remains a scarcity of longitudinal studies and case-based evaluations that illustrate how AI systems impact users, particularly in identity management settings. Furthermore, existing literature tends to focus on broad ethical concepts rather than tailoring ethical inquiry to specific applications such as biometric verification, access control, or digital identity platforms. This gap restricts the ability to make informed design decisions and to evaluate systems based on the lived experiences of diverse user groups.

Another major challenge is the insufficient attention given to the efficacy of different bias mitigation techniques. While numerous methods have been proposed—ranging from algorithmic adjustments to data diversification—the literature lacks consensus on their comparative effectiveness in varied contexts. Moreover, translating high-level ethical principles into actionable standards remains a persistent obstacle for both developers and regulators (Camilleri, 2023). Many ethical guidelines remain abstract and aspirational, leaving a gap between ethical ideals and practical implementation. This disconnect undermines efforts to embed ethics into the design and lifecycle management of AI systems.

Bridging the divide between ethical theory and technical design is essential for fostering trustworthy and equitable AI. Scholars have argued that aligning ethical values with system architecture requires cross-disciplinary methodologies and iterative stakeholder engagement (Aizenberg & Hoven, 2020). Yet, few frameworks exist that operationalize this alignment in a scalable and reproducible manner. This is particularly problematic in identity management, where decisions made by AI systems can carry serious implications for privacy, access to services, and individual autonomy. Without clear design guidelines rooted in ethical reasoning, the risk of harm—particularly to marginalized communities—remains high. As AI ethics gains momentum as a distinct and vital field of inquiry, it is increasingly recognized that interdisciplinary collaboration is crucial for addressing its multifaceted challenges (Kazim & Koshiyama, 2021). Ethical issues arising from AI cannot be resolved by technologists alone but require contributions from legal scholars, ethicists, social scientists, and affected communities. Moving forward, research must prioritize the development of integrated frameworks that not only identify ethical risks but also provide mechanisms for mitigation, evaluation, and governance. Only through such holistic efforts can we ensure that the development and deployment of AI in identity management are aligned with societal values and public interest.

5. SYNTHESIS AND FUTURE DIRECTIONS

Addressing the ethical implications of AI in identity management requires a multi-faceted approach that considers technical, legal, and social dimensions. Ethical considerations are raised by various stakeholders regarding AI (Barton & Pöppelbuß, 2022). Future research should focus on developing methods for explainable AI that can provide insights into the decision-making processes of AI algorithms (Kazim & Koshiyama, 2021). This includes techniques for visualizing AI decisions, identifying the factors that influence those decisions, and providing explanations that are understandable to non-experts. AI systems can offer substantial societal benefits; however, these benefits can be offset by substantial risks, especially if AI systems are not deployed responsibly (Stahl & Eke, 2023). Moreover, explainable AI can help to build trust in AI systems and ensure that they are used in a fair and transparent manner.

Another important area for future research is the development of robust mechanisms for detecting and mitigating biases in AI algorithms (Ferrer et al., 2021). This includes techniques for identifying and correcting biases in training data, as well as methods for evaluating the fairness of AI systems (Gr, 1992). The development of effective policies and regulations is essential to guide the responsible use of AI and ensure that it aligns with societal values and legal requirements (Singh, 2024). The ethical challenges in AI can be addressed through a combination of regulation, legislation, and human-centered design (Hernández, 2024). These efforts highlight the importance of addressing biases and ethical concerns associated with AI systems to ensure fairness, equity, and responsible use of technology (Saheb & Saheb, 2024). It also includes the development of mechanisms for accountability and redress in cases where AI systems cause harm. Governments, academics, and civil society play active roles in shaping AI development aligned with human and social values (Hernández, 2024). Additionally, ongoing research and development are essential to address emerging challenges and ethical considerations in AI's application (Khalifa & Albadawy, 2024).

Researchers in AI have started to explore diverse directions of research to improve AI systems in response to those ethical concerns, such as new technologies for improving the explainability of AI systems (Prem, 2023). Ultimately, responsible AI necessitates a holistic approach that considers the broader societal impact of AI systems and prioritizes the well-being of individuals and communities (Hadley, 2022). The convergence of these concepts can help improve the fairness, accountability, and transparency of AI systems, thereby promoting trust and facilitating their responsible adoption across various sectors (Abujaber & Nashwan, 2024; Elmahjub, 2023; Ferrara, 2023; Vinothkumar & Karunamurthy, 2023).

The rapid advancement of AI has led to concerns such as privacy violations and safety risks, highlighting the need for ethical and responsible AI development (B. Li et al., 2022; Y. Li et al., 2024). This involves incorporating ethical considerations into the design, development, and deployment of AI systems, emphasizing transparency, fairness, and accountability. The future of AI ethics involves continuous learning, adaptation, and collaboration to ensure that AI technologies benefit society while upholding fundamental ethical values (Borenstein & Howard, 2020) (Jobin et al., 2019) (Bakıner, 2023) (Ferrara, 2023).

The literature review reveals that AI ethics is a multidisciplinary domain encompassing philosophical, legal, societal, and technological aspects (Christoforaki & Beyan, 2022).

AI ethics is a rapidly evolving field that demands ongoing attention and adaptation. (Kazim & Koshiyama, 2021; Khan et al., 2022).

6. ETHICAL IMPLICATIONS IN BIOMETRIC-BASED IDENTITY MANAGEMENT

The incorporation of biometric technologies—such as facial recognition, iris scans, fingerprint analysis, and voice recognition—into AI-driven identity management systems has significantly advanced the accuracy, efficiency, and security of personal identification processes. These technologies provide robust alternatives to traditional credentials like passwords or PINs by relying on unique biological attributes that are difficult to forge. However, the very permanence and uniqueness of biometric data introduce profound ethical concerns, particularly related to privacy, consent, and data protection. Unlike passwords, biometric identifiers cannot be changed once compromised, making them an exceptionally high-value target for cybercriminals. Breaches involving biometric information pose irreversible risks to individuals, as the compromised data cannot simply be reset or revoked. Furthermore, ethical questions arise regarding the conditions under which biometric data is collected, especially in environments where consent may be ambiguous or coerced, such as airports, government offices, or workplaces. One of the most pressing ethical issues concerns bias and inequality embedded in biometric recognition systems. Multiple studies have demonstrated that facial recognition algorithms exhibit markedly lower accuracy for women, people of color, and other underrepresented groups. This performance gap is not merely a technical flaw—it can lead to serious consequences including wrongful arrests, denial of services, and stigmatization of entire communities. When such systems are deployed in sensitive domains like border control, policing, or access to public resources, these inaccuracies risk perpetuating institutional discrimination and undermining social justice. High-profile incidents involving misidentification have underscored the urgent need for ethical safeguards. Developers and policymakers must ensure that training datasets are diverse and representative and that regular fairness audits are conducted to evaluate system performance across demographic groups.

Beyond issues of fairness, the use of biometric technologies also raises fundamental concerns about surveillance, autonomy, and the erosion of civil liberties. Biometric systems, once implemented, can easily be repurposed for mass surveillance and behavioral monitoring without the knowledge or consent of the individuals being observed. Such practices threaten the foundational right to privacy and may foster environments of control and coercion. The ethical deployment of biometric identity systems must therefore include meaningful constraints on secondary use, strict purpose limitation, and mechanisms for transparency and oversight. The deployment of these systems in public spaces, particularly by state authorities, must be accompanied by strong legal frameworks that uphold international human rights standards. Another dimension of ethical concern lies in the often-invisible power asymmetries between those who deploy biometric systems and the individuals subjected to them. In many cases, individuals have little to no agency over whether or how their biometric data is collected, stored, or used. This lack of autonomy is particularly problematic in institutional contexts such as schools, prisons, or refugee camps, where refusal to participate in biometric identification may result in loss of access to essential services. Ethical AI design in identity management must thus prioritize user empowerment, provide alternatives or opt-out mechanisms, and embed procedural safeguards that ensure fairness, proportionality, and accountability in all stages of biometric data processing.

To ensure ethical alignment, it is crucial that biometric-based AI systems be developed and governed within a framework that integrates ethical theory, legal mandates, and technical best practices. Such a framework should include principles of transparency, non-discrimination, proportionality, and informed consent, supported by robust data protection laws and independent oversight mechanisms. The ethical governance of biometrics must also be dynamic, responsive to technological advancements, and inclusive of multidisciplinary expertise—including ethicists, technologists, legal scholars, and representatives from affected communities. Only through such a holistic and participatory approach can society harness the benefits of biometric technologies while minimizing harm and preserving individual rights.

7. ETHICAL TRADE-OFFS IN REAL-TIME IDENTITY VERIFICATION

Real-time identity verification systems powered by Artificial Intelligence (AI) have revolutionized the way digital services authenticate users. These systems provide rapid, seamless access to platforms and enhance security in domains such as financial transactions, online banking, border control, and telemedicine (Chen et al., 2021)AI. The ability to verify an individual's identity in seconds significantly improves operational efficiency and user experience. It also allows institutions to detect and prevent fraud or identity theft in real time, often before any damage can be inflicted. However, the pursuit of speed and automation in these systems inevitably introduces ethical trade-offs—particularly in terms of accuracy, fairness, and the transparency of AI-driven decisions made under time constraints. A central ethical issue arises from the potential for false positives and false negatives during real-time verification processes. False positives occur when legitimate users are misclassified as fraudulent, resulting in unjust denial of access to essential services. Conversely, false negatives allow unauthorized individuals to be mistakenly granted access, posing security threats. These types of misclassification are not only technical flaws but also raise serious ethical concerns, especially when they disproportionately affect vulnerable or marginalized populations. For example, individuals with darker skin tones or non-Western names may face higher error rates in facial recognition or name-matching systems, exacerbating systemic inequalities. In high-stakes environments such as immigration checkpoints, hospital admissions, or courtrooms, such errors can lead to serious and lasting harm.

Another critical concern is the lack of contextual judgment in real-time decision-making. AI systems are typically designed to act on predefined models and training data, with little or no ability to consider situational nuances. This rigidity may result in ethically inappropriate outcomes, such as denying healthcare to a patient whose biometric scan fails due to a temporary condition, or flagging a traveler as high risk due to outdated or biased profiling. The urgency of real-time processing often removes the opportunity for appeals or human discretion, which are vital in complex social contexts (Li et al., 2025). These limitations highlight the importance of designing AI systems that include contingencies for human override and pathways for individuals to challenge or rectify erroneous decisions. The opacity of many AI algorithms, especially those operating in real time, further complicates the issue. Many users are unaware that their identity is being verified through automated systems, let alone that decisions affecting their access and rights are being made by algorithms. This lack of transparency erodes trust and limits individuals' ability to understand or contest decisions that impact them. Ethical deployment of AI in real-time verification contexts thus requires deliberate design choices that prioritize explainability and user awareness (Singla et al., 2025). Users should be informed when AI is in use and be granted the right to opt out or appeal its conclusions where appropriate.

To mitigate these ethical concerns, developers and organizations must implement safeguards that promote both accountability and user autonomy. Mechanisms such as consent prompts, clear notification of AI involvement, real-time audit trails, and human-in-the-loop protocols can help ensure that decisions remain justifiable and contestable (Gupta & Panigrahi, 2022). Additionally, fallback options—such as reverting to manual verification in cases of uncertainty—can protect users from being unjustly excluded. These strategies help balance the benefits of speed and scalability with the ethical imperatives of fairness, transparency, and respect for individual rights. Ultimately, the integration of AI into real-time identity verification presents a paradox: while the technology enhances speed and security, it also amplifies the risks of harm if not properly governed. As these systems become more embedded in critical infrastructure, ethical design and oversight must evolve in parallel. Interdisciplinary collaboration—encompassing technologists, ethicists, legal scholars, and user communities—is essential to navigate these trade-offs responsibly. Only by embedding ethical foresight into the development and deployment of real-time AI systems can we ensure that the drive for efficiency does not come at the expense of justice and human dignity (Gupta et al., 2024).

8. CROSS-BORDER ETHICAL AND REGULATORY CHALLENGES

As AI-powered identity management systems become increasingly integrated into global digital infrastructure, they must navigate a fragmented and often contradictory landscape of national laws, ethical expectations, and cultural norms. Each country approaches data privacy, user consent, algorithmic transparency, and digital identity with differing priorities and regulatory maturity. For example, while the European Union enforces stringent protections under the General Data Protection Regulation (GDPR), including provisions for the right to be forgotten and data portability, other regions may rely on weaker or sector-specific regulations. This disparity complicates compliance efforts for multinational corporations deploying AI identity tools and introduces ethical uncertainties for users whose data crosses multiple legal jurisdictions. These regulatory inconsistencies are particularly problematic in high-stakes applications such as international banking, immigration control, and global digital identity verification. The same AI system might be considered ethical and legal in one country but non-compliant or even unlawful in another. For instance, real-time facial recognition for airport security may be legally permissible in Country A but strictly banned in Country B due to civil liberty concerns. Organizations that operate across borders must therefore implement sophisticated data governance strategies that go beyond legal compliance and incorporate ethical due diligence. Failing to do so risks both regulatory penalties and reputational damage, especially as public scrutiny of cross-border data practices intensifies.

The lack of harmonization also fuels concerns around data sovereignty, where personal identity data stored or processed outside a user's home country may be vulnerable to misuse, governmental overreach, or surveillance. When cloud infrastructure spans continents and data travels through opaque pipelines, users often have little control over how their information is managed or by whom. This undermines key ethical principles such as informed consent, autonomy, and accountability. In AI-based identity systems, where data is continuously collected, analyzed, and used to make real-time decisions, the inability to trace or audit data across borders poses a significant ethical risk. Moreover, individuals may have no legal standing or recourse in jurisdictions where their data is processed, leading to a sense of powerlessness and erosion of trust. In response to these challenges, international cooperation has become an urgent priority. Global efforts to align AI governance and digital identity standards are beginning to emerge. Multilateral organizations and consortia—including the OECD, United Nations, World Economic Forum, and the Global Partnership on AI—are advocating for shared ethical principles such as fairness, accountability, transparency, and respect for human rights. These initiatives seek to establish a common ground while allowing for local interpretation and flexibility. Efforts to develop cross-border privacy agreements and technical standards for digital identity interoperability can reduce legal uncertainty and promote the ethical scaling of AI systems. However, establishing global standards alone is insufficient without culturally sensitive implementation. Ethical considerations are often shaped by local history, societal values, and norms surrounding trust, identity, and authority. An AI identity verification system that is ethically acceptable in one region may be perceived as intrusive or discriminatory in another. As such, ethical AI governance must adopt a glocal approach—merging global principles with localized practices. Engaging regional stakeholders, including civil society, legal experts, and marginalized communities, is essential to ensure that cross-border AI identity solutions reflect the diverse ethical landscapes they inhabit.

Ultimately, as AI systems transcend national borders, ethical design must be embedded not just in code, but in governance, communication, and accountability structures. Cross-border identity management systems must be transparent about data flows, offer meaningful user control, and provide avenues for redress regardless of geographical boundaries. Building ethical resilience into the infrastructure of AI identity systems will not only ensure compliance but also foster public trust in the global digital ecosystem. In a world increasingly connected through data, ethics must be as transnational as the technology itself.

9. STAKEHOLDER PERSPECTIVES AND ETHICAL DILEMMAS

The development and deployment of AI in identity management systems implicate a wide and diverse range of stakeholders, each with distinct roles, interests, and ethical expectations. These include national governments, private technology companies, AI developers, regulatory bodies, civil society, and the end-users themselves. Governments often focus on goals such as enhancing national security, streamlining public service delivery, and curbing identity fraud. In contrast, private enterprises may prioritize innovation, efficiency, cost reduction, and competitive advantage. Developers, meanwhile, concentrate on the technical feasibility, performance, and scalability of AI solutions. Regulatory authorities aim to ensure that AI systems comply with laws, uphold ethical standards, and protect the public interest. End-users expect AI systems to respect their autonomy, maintain the confidentiality of their data, and provide equitable treatment regardless of demographic attributes (Taddeo & Floridi, 2018). However, these divergent priorities often give rise to tensions and conflicting interpretations of ethical AI deployment. For instance, a government may justify deploying biometric surveillance technologies for purposes of public safety and national interest, but this could simultaneously lead to mass surveillance, discrimination, or infringement on civil liberties—particularly for vulnerable populations (Smyth & Crosby, 2021). Similarly, tech companies may optimize algorithms to improve the accuracy of identity verification through behavioral analytics and continuous authentication, yet these strategies may compromise informed consent, exploit personal data, and erode user trust (Tsamados et al., 2021). Such trade-offs present complex ethical dilemmas, where improving efficiency and functionality for one stakeholder group may inadvertently cause ethical harm to another.

In navigating these dilemmas, it is critical to recognize that ethical challenges are not solely technical or legal in nature but are deeply rooted in broader social and political contexts. Power asymmetries between stakeholders—such as between corporations and consumers, or governments and citizens—can exacerbate ethical risks, especially in cases where transparency and accountability are lacking (Whittlestone et al., 2019). For example, when users are subjected to opaque identity checks or denied access to services based on flawed AI profiling, there may be limited avenues for recourse or explanation. These issues call for ethical governance models that acknowledge and address structural imbalances, rather than simply optimizing for accuracy or compliance. To promote ethical outcomes, participatory frameworks are needed that deliberately include the perspectives of all relevant stakeholders, particularly those who are likely to be disproportionately impacted by AI identity systems. Marginalized communities—such as migrants, ethnic minorities, and low-income groups—may face increased surveillance or misidentification due to biases embedded in training data or algorithmic design. By involving these groups in the co-design and evaluation of AI systems, developers and policymakers can better identify ethical blind spots and ensure that identity technologies uphold the values of inclusivity, equity, and justice (Crawford, 2021).

Moreover, ethical dilemmas can be mitigated through transparent decision-making mechanisms, independent oversight, and clear channels for redress. Multistakeholder advisory councils, public consultations, and ethics review boards can offer platforms for negotiating trade-offs and making deliberative decisions about system design, deployment, and accountability measures. It is also essential to adopt ethical frameworks that are dynamic and responsive, capable of evolving alongside technological advancement and shifting societal expectations. This includes embedding principles such as explainability, proportionality, human oversight, and fairness-by-design into the AI identity lifecycle (Jobin et al., 2019). Ultimately, aligning AI identity systems with shared ethical values requires intentional collaboration across sectors, disciplines, and borders. Ethical governance must be more than a compliance exercise; it must be a continuous, inclusive process aimed at balancing innovation with human dignity. By fostering dialogue between stakeholders and centering ethics as a foundational design principle, identity management systems can contribute to a more just and trustworthy digital society. The path forward lies in cultivating mutual understanding, institutional transparency, and mechanisms of collective accountability that transcend organizational and national silos. Figure 2 visualizes the intersection of key stakeholder groups—government, companies, regulators, and users—highlighting how their overlapping interests give rise to complex ethical dilemmas in AI-driven identity management. This Venn diagram underscores the need for inclusive governance approaches that reconcile competing priorities and foster ethical alignment across institutional, commercial, regulatory, and individual domains.

Figure 2. Stakeholder Perspectives and Ethical Dilemmas

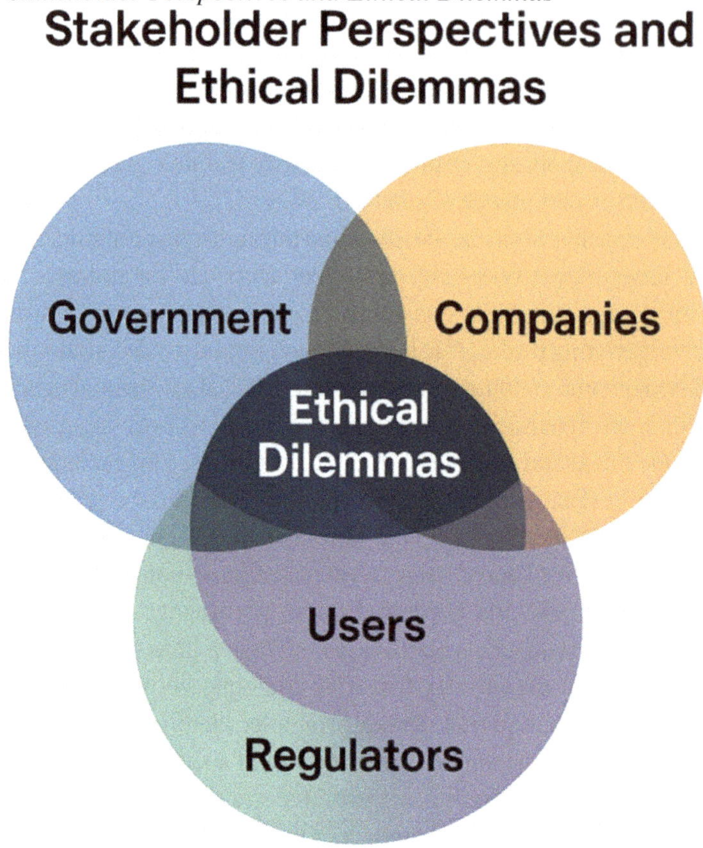

10. CASE STUDIES ON ETHICAL FAILURES IN AI IDENTITY SYSTEMS

Several real-world case studies have revealed the ethical shortcomings and societal risks associated with the deployment of AI-based identity systems, especially when such technologies are implemented without adequate oversight, transparency, or inclusivity. One of the most widely discussed examples involves the use of facial recognition by law enforcement agencies in the United States. Numerous documented incidents have shown that AI systems misidentified individuals—particularly Black men—leading to wrongful arrests and detentions. These systems were often trained on racially imbalanced datasets, which significantly reduced their accuracy for people of color. The consequences of such misidentification extend beyond technical failure;

they raise serious ethical and legal questions about civil rights, systemic bias, and the readiness of AI technologies for high-stakes decision-making. A similarly troubling case emerged in the Netherlands with the implementation of "SyRI" (System Risk Indication), an AI-based tool aimed at detecting welfare fraud. SyRI analyzed vast amounts of personal data from multiple public institutions to generate risk profiles of citizens suspected of fraudulent behavior. However, the system lacked transparency, and affected individuals were not informed about how they were being evaluated or why they were flagged. In 2020, a Dutch court ruled the system unlawful, citing disproportionate privacy intrusions and the inability of citizens to challenge automated decisions. The court's decision reflected growing concern over the opacity and overreach of AI in public sector decision-making, particularly when vulnerable populations are targeted without due process or meaningful recourse.

These cases underscore the urgent need to embed ethical principles such as fairness, accountability, and transparency into the design and governance of AI identity systems. Without such safeguards, the deployment of AI can lead to structural injustices and erode public trust in both technology and the institutions that use it. The lack of explainability in these systems further compounds the problem, as users and even administrators are often unable to understand, question, or correct flawed decisions. Moreover, the absence of diverse training data reinforces discriminatory patterns that marginalize already disadvantaged groups, amplifying social inequities rather than addressing them. Learning from these failures is crucial for the responsible development of future AI systems. Ethical audits, bias testing, and inclusive data collection processes must become standard practice—not exceptions. Developers must prioritize the implementation of explainable AI (XAI) models that provide interpretable justifications for outcomes, especially in systems that impact individuals' rights, freedoms, or access to public services. Mechanisms for redress and appeal should also be integrated into identity systems to ensure that users can challenge and rectify errors made by automated decision-making tools. The inclusion of human oversight in critical points of the decision-making process remains essential for maintaining fairness and procedural integrity.

Importantly, these case studies highlight that the failure to anticipate ethical risks in AI identity systems can result not only in harm to individuals but also in reputational, legal, and operational consequences for institutions. Governments, technology firms, and service providers that fail to address these issues risk public backlash, legal liabilities, and long-term erosion of legitimacy. As AI continues to influence identity verification, fraud detection, and access to state services, it is imperative that both public and private stakeholders embrace a proactive stance on ethics—moving beyond compliance toward the active cultivation of responsible innovation. Ultimately, embedding ethics into the full lifecycle of AI identity system development is not an optional feature; it is a necessary foundation for protecting individual rights and preserving democratic values. Case studies such as those from the U.S. and the Netherlands serve as critical learning tools, revealing not only where systems go wrong but also how they can be reimagined for equity and justice. By translating these lessons into concrete design principles and policy frameworks, stakeholders can work toward AI identity systems that are not only efficient and innovative but also ethical, accountable, and socially responsive. Table 2 presents selected case studies that illustrate ethical failures in AI-based identity systems, highlighting their core issues, real-world consequences, and corrective actions taken. These examples provide critical insights into the importance of transparency, accountability, and fairness in the design and governance of such systems.

Table 2. Case Studies on Ethical Failures in AI Identity Systems

Case Name	Location	Main Ethical Issue	Consequence	Corrective Action
SyRI	Netherlands	Privacy, lack of transparency	Annulled by court	Risk evaluation system reform
Detroit Police Facial Recognition	USA	Racial bias	Wrongful arrest	Audit and usage restrictions

CONCLUSION

The application of Artificial Intelligence in identity management offers considerable benefits, including increased efficiency, fraud detection, and improved user experience. However, these technological advancements come with equally significant ethical risks that must not be overlooked. This paper has highlighted critical concerns such as algorithmic bias, lack of transparency, violations of privacy, and unequal stakeholder power dynamics. Through theoretical exploration and empirical case studies—such as the SyRI system in the Netherlands and facial recognition failures in the U.S.—we have shown how inadequate ethical safeguards can result in systemic discrimination, loss of public trust, and legal consequences. To address these issues, ethical principles such as fairness, accountability, transparency, and respect for individual rights must be embedded throughout the AI identity system lifecycle—from data collection and algorithm design to deployment and oversight. Technical solutions such as explainable AI and bias mitigation strategies must be complemented by regulatory mechanisms, participatory governance, and inclusive stakeholder engagement. The necessity of aligning global AI governance frameworks with local values and societal norms further underscores the complexity of ethical implementation in cross-border identity systems.

Moreover, the importance of interdisciplinary collaboration between technologists, ethicists, policymakers, and affected communities cannot be overstated. Only through this collective effort can we bridge the gap between ethical ideals and practical design, ensuring that AI identity systems are responsive to real-world challenges and equitable in their impact. Institutions must move beyond mere regulatory compliance to foster a proactive culture of ethical innovation and social accountability. In an increasingly digitized and interconnected world, identity is not just a technical construct but a fundamental expression of autonomy, dignity, and human rights. As such, AI-driven identity systems must be developed and governed with ethical foresight and democratic legitimacy. The future of identity management lies not only in technological sophistication but in our shared commitment to building systems that are just, inclusive, and aligned with the public good.

REFERENCES

Abujaber, A. A., & Nashwan, A. J. (2024). Ethical framework for artificial intelligence in healthcare research: A path to integrity. In World Journal of Methodology (Vol. 14, Issue 3). DOI: 10.5662/wjm.v14.i3.94071

Adelakun, B. O., Majekodunmi, T. G., & Akintoye, O. S.Beatrice Oyinkansola AdelakunTomiwa Gabriel MajekodunmiOluwole Stephen Akintoye. (2024). AI and ethical accounting: Navigating challenges and opportunities. *International Journal of Advanced Economics*, *6*(6), 224–241. DOI: 10.51594/ijae.v6i6.1230

Aizenberg, E., & van den Hoven, J. (2020). Designing for human rights in AI. *Big Data & Society*, *7*(2), 2053951720949566. Advance online publication. DOI: 10.1177/2053951720949566

Bakıner, O. (2023). The promises and challenges of addressing artificial intelligence with human rights. *Big Data & Society*, *10*(2), 20539517231205476. Advance online publication. DOI: 10.1177/20539517231205476

Barton, M.-C., & Pöppelbuß, J. (2022). Prinzipien für die ethische Nutzung künstlicher Intelligenz. *HMD Praxis der Wirtschaftsinformatik*, *59*(2), 468–481. DOI: 10.1365/s40702-022-00850-3

Borenstein, J., & Howard, A. (2020). Emerging challenges in AI and the need for AI ethics education. In AI and Ethics (Vol. 1, Issue 1, p. 61). Springer Nature. DOI: 10.1007/s43681-020-00002-7

Camilleri, M. A. (2023). Artificial intelligence governance: Ethical considerations and implications for social responsibility. *Expert Systems: International Journal of Knowledge Engineering and Neural Networks*, *41*(7), e13406. Advance online publication. DOI: 10.1111/exsy.13406

Chen, H.-C., Rahaman, M., & Damarjati, C. (2021). A Security Analysis Approach for Secure Color-Code Key Exchange Protocol by Using BAN Logic. In Barolli, L., Poniszewska-Maranda, A., & Park, H. (Eds.), *Innovative Mobile and Internet Services in Ubiquitous Computing* (pp. 81–93). Springer International Publishing., DOI: 10.1007/978-3-030-50399-4_9

Christoforaki, M., & Beyan, O. (2022). AI Ethics—A Bird's Eye View. *Applied Sciences (Basel, Switzerland)*, *12*(9), 4130. DOI: 10.3390/app12094130

Corrêa, N. K., Galvão, C., Santos, J. W., Pino, C. D., Pinto, E. P., Barbosa, C., Massmann, D., Mambrini, R., Galvão, L., Terem, E., & Oliveira, N. de. (2023). Worldwide AI ethics: A review of 200 guidelines and recommendations for AI governance [Review of Worldwide AI ethics: A review of 200 guidelines and recommendations for AI governance]. Patterns, 4(10), 100857. Elsevier BV. DOI: 10.1016/j.patter.2023.100857

Dailah, H. G., Koriri, M. D., Sabei, A., Kriry, T., & Zakri, M. (2024). Artificial Intelligence in Nursing: Technological Benefits to Nurse's Mental Health and Patient Care Quality [Review of Artificial Intelligence in Nursing: Technological Benefits to Nurse's Mental Health and Patient Care Quality]. Healthcare, 12(24), 2555. Multidisciplinary Digital Publishing Institute. DOI: 10.3390/healthcare12242555

Dhopte, A., & Bagde, H. (2023). *Smart Smile: Revolutionizing Dentistry With Artificial Intelligence* [Review of Smart Smile: Revolutionizing Dentistry With Artificial Intelligence]. Cureus. Cureus, Inc., DOI: 10.7759/cureus.41227

Elmahjub, E. (2023). Artificial Intelligence (AI) in Islamic Ethics: Towards Pluralist Ethical Benchmarking for AI. *Philosophy & Technology*, *36*(4), 73. Advance online publication. DOI: 10.1007/s13347-023-00668-x

Ferrara, E. (2023a). Fairness And Bias in Artificial Intelligence: A Brief Survey of Sources, Impacts, And Mitigation Strategies. arXiv (Cornell University). https://doi.org//arxiv.2304.07683DOI: 10.48550

Ferrara, E. (2023b). Fairness and Bias in Artificial Intelligence: A Brief Survey of Sources, Impacts, and Mitigation Strategies. *Sci*, *6*(1), 3. DOI: 10.3390/sci6010003

Ferrer, X., van Nuenen, T., Such, J. M., Coté, M., & Criado, N. (2021). Bias and Discrimination in AI: A Cross-Disciplinary Perspective. *IEEE Technology and Society Magazine*, *40*(2), 72–80. DOI: 10.1109/MTS.2021.3056293

Fitz-enz, J. (2010). The New HR Analytics: Predicting the Economic Value of Your Company's Human Capital Investments.

Gr, G. (1992). One moment, please. PubMed, 82(1), 37. https://pubmed.ncbi.nlm.nih.gov/1499783

Guan, H., Dong, L., & Zhao, A. (2022). Ethical Risk Factors and Mechanisms in Artificial Intelligence Decision Making. *Behavioral Sciences (Basel, Switzerland)*, *12*(9), 343. DOI: 10.3390/bs12090343 PMID: 36135147

Gupta, B. B., Gaurav, A., Arya, V., & Alhalabi, W. (2024). Data science in sustainable entrepreneurship: A multidisciplinary field of applications. *Technological Forecasting and Social Change*, *209*, 123798. DOI: 10.1016/j.techfore.2024.123798

Gupta, B. B., & Panigrahi, P. K. (2022). Analysis of the Role of Global Information Management in Advanced Decision Support Systems (DSS) for Sustainable Development. [JGIM]. *Journal of Global Information Management, 31*(2), 1–13. DOI: 10.4018/JGIM.320185

Hadley, E. (2022). Prioritizing Policies for Furthering Responsible Artificial Intelligence in the United States. 2021 IEEE International Conference on Big Data (Big Data), 5029. DOI: 10.1109/BigData55660.2022.10020551

Hernández, E. (2024). Towards an Ethical and Inclusive Implementation of Artificial Intelligence in Organizations: A Multidimensional Framework. arXiv (Cornell University). https://doi.org//arxiv.2405.01697DOI: 10.48550

Jobin, A., Ienca, M., & Vayena, E. (2019). The global landscape of AI ethics guidelines. *Nature Machine Intelligence, 1*(9), 389–399. DOI: 10.1038/s42256-019-0088-2

Kandasamy, U. C. (2024). Ethical Leadership in the Age of AI Challenges, Opportunities and Framework for Ethical Leadership. arXiv (Cornell University). https://doi.org//arxiv.2410.18095DOI: 10.48550

Kazim, E., & Koshiyama, A. (2021). A high-level overview of AI ethics [Review of A high-level overview of AI ethics]. Patterns, 2(9), 100314. Elsevier BV. DOI: 10.1016/j.patter.2021.100314

Khalifa, M., & Albadawy, M. (2024). Using artificial intelligence in academic writing and research: An essential productivity tool. *Computer Methods and Programs in Biomedicine Update, 5*, 100145. DOI: 10.1016/j.cmpbup.2024.100145

Khan, A. A., Badshah, S., Liang, P., Waseem, M., Khan, B., Ahmad, A., Fahmideh, M., Niazi, M., & Akbar, M. A. (2022). Ethics of AI: A Systematic Literature Review of Principles and Challenges. 383. DOI: 10.1145/3530019.3531329

Lepri, B., Oliver, N., & Pentland, A. (2021). Ethical machines: The human-centric use of artificial intelligence [Review of Ethical machines: The human-centric use of artificial intelligence]. iScience, 24(3), 102249. Cell Press. DOI: 10.1016/j.isci.2021.102249

Li, B., Qi, P., Liu, B., Di, S., Liu, J., Pei, J., Yi, J., & Zhou, B. (2022). Trustworthy AI: From Principles to Practices [Review of Trustworthy AI: From Principles to Practices]. ACM Computing Surveys, 55(9), 1. Association for Computing Machinery. DOI: 10.1145/3555803

Li, S., Yang, Y., Han, C., Sun, Y., Attar, R., & Gupta, B. (2025). Addressing consumer needs: Effects of firms remediation strategies on satisfaction and brand usage intent in AI-powered voice assistant service failures. *International Journal of Information Management*, *85*(102951), 102951. Advance online publication. DOI: 10.1016/j.ijinfomgt.2025.102951

Li, Y., Wu, B., Huang, Y., & Luan, S. (2024). Developing trustworthy artificial intelligence: insights from research on interpersonal, human-automation, and human-AI trust [Review of Developing trustworthy artificial intelligence: insights from research on interpersonal, human-automation, and human-AI trust]. Frontiers in Psychology, 15. Frontiers Media. DOI: 10.3389/fpsyg.2024.1382693

Patil, D. (2025). Artificial Intelligence In Financial Risk Assessment And Fraud Detection: Opportunities And Ethical Concerns. DOI: 10.2139/ssrn.5057434

Prem, E. (2023). From ethical AI frameworks to tools: a review of approaches [Review of From ethical AI frameworks to tools: a review of approaches]. AI and Ethics, 3(3), 699. Springer Nature. DOI: 10.1007/s43681-023-00258-9

Rahaman, M., Chappu, B., Jana, S., Haque, A., Firmansyah, G., & Chattopadhyay, S. (2025). Security Benefits in Small Medium Business Enterprise Through Cloud Adoption. In N. Nedjah, G. Martinez Perez, & B. B. Gupta (Eds.), *International Conference on Smart Systems and Advanced Computing (SysCom 2022)* (pp. 168–180). Springer Nature Switzerland. DOI: 10.1007/978-3-031-40905-9_18

Rahaman, M., Lin, C. Y., Rachmat, I., Bansal, R., & Prayitno. (2024). Secure Health Features: Implementing Hyperledger Fabric in Blockchain-Driven Healthcare Management Systems. In *Digital Forensics and Cyber Crime Investigation*. CRC Press.

Saheb, T., & Saheb, T. (2024). Mapping Ethical Artificial Intelligence Policy Landscape: A Mixed Method Analysis. *Science and Engineering Ethics*, *30*(2), 9. Advance online publication. DOI: 10.1007/s11948-024-00472-6 PMID: 38451328

Schultz, M. D., & Seele, P. (2022). Towards AI ethics' institutionalization: Knowledge bridges from business ethics to advance organizational AI ethics. *AI and Ethics*, *3*(1), 99–111. DOI: 10.1007/s43681-022-00150-y

Selenko, E., Bankins, S., Shoss, M. K., Warburton, J., & Restubog, S. L. D. (2022). Artificial Intelligence and the Future of Work: A Functional-Identity Perspective. *Current Directions in Psychological Science*, *31*(3), 272–279. DOI: 10.1177/09637214221091823

Shang, Z., Chauhan, V., Devi, K., & Patil, S. (2024). Artificial Intelligence, the Digital Surgeon: Unravelling Its Emerging Footprint in Healthcare – The Narrative Review [Review of Artificial Intelligence, the Digital Surgeon: Unravelling Its Emerging Footprint in Healthcare – The Narrative Review]. Journal of Multidisciplinary Healthcare, 4011. Dove Medical Press. DOI: 10.2147/JMDH.S482757

Singh, D. (2024). Navigating the Digital Age: Smart AI Ethics for Seamless Transformation. *International Journal of Advanced Research in Electrical Electronics and Instrumentation Engineering*, *13*(11). Advance online publication. DOI: 10.15662/IJAREEIE.2024.1311001

Singla, V., Singh, S. K., Kumar, S., Chhabra, A., Gill, S. S., Arya, V., & Jain, A. (2025). Challenges and Opportunities in Sustainable AI and Information Systems. In *Sustainable Information Security in the Age of AI and Green Computing* (pp. 73–96). IGI Global Scientific Publishing., DOI: 10.4018/979-8-3693-8034-5.ch004

Situmeang, S. M. T., Harliyanto, R., Zulkarnain, P. D., Mahdi, U., & Nugroho, T. (2024). The Role of Artificial Intelligence in Criminal Justice. *Global International Journal of Innovative Research*, *2*(8), 1966–1981. DOI: 10.59613/global.v2i8.264

Stahl, B. C., & Eke, D. (2023). The ethics of ChatGPT – Exploring the ethical issues of an emerging technology. *International Journal of Information Management*, *74*, 102700. DOI: 10.1016/j.ijinfomgt.2023.102700

Svetlova, E. (2022). AI ethics and systemic risks in finance. *AI and Ethics*, *2*(4), 713–725. DOI: 10.1007/s43681-021-00129-1 PMID: 35043105

Tadimalla, S. Y., & Maher, M. L. (2024). Implications of Identity of AI: Creators, Creations, and Consequences. arXiv (Cornell University). https://doi.org//arxiv.2403.07924DOI: 10.48550

Vinothkumar, J., & Karunamurthy, A. (2023). Recent Advancements in Artificial Intelligence Technology: Trends and Implications. *Quing International Journal of Multidisciplinary Scientific Research and Development*, *2*(1), 1–11. DOI: 10.54368/qijmsrd.2.1.0003

Yu, K., Beam, A. L., & Kohane, I. S. (2018). Artificial intelligence in healthcare [Review of Artificial intelligence in healthcare]. Nature Biomedical Engineering, 2(10), 719. Nature Portfolio. DOI: 10.1038/s41551-018-0305-z

Chapter 7
Policy Implications of AI in Combatting Cyber Fraud and Identity Theft

S. Ida Evangeline
https://orcid.org/0000-0003-2997-7897
Government College of Engineering, Tirunelveli, India

ABSTRACT

Cyber fraud and identity theft have become increasingly sophisticated and transnational, with schemes like synthetic identity creation and digital arrest scams exploiting legal and technical gaps. Artificial Intelligence (AI) offers transformative potential for detecting and preventing such crimes through real-time anomaly detection, pattern recognition, and predictive modeling. However, these benefits are coupled with significant policy and governance challenges, including algorithmic bias, lack of transparency, and privacy risks. This chapter critically examines the role of AI in cyber fraud prevention, presenting a taxonomy of AI techniques used across sectors, and explores the regulatory and ethical implications of deploying these tools.

1. INTRODUCTION

Cyber fraud and identity theft have evolved into high-impact, borderless threats that compromise individual privacy, institutional trust, and financial security. Once limited to simplistic scams and localized breaches, contemporary attacks now involve deepfake impersonation, synthetic identities, and highly coordinated digital arrest schemes that exploit vulnerabilities across jurisdictions and digital platforms (Van de Weijer et al., 2019). The resulting harms are not only economic—costing billions

DOI: 10.4018/979-8-3373-4149-1.ch007

annually—but also deeply societal, eroding public confidence in digital ecosystems and institutional safeguards.

Artificial Intelligence has become an important enabler to proactive cyber defence. Through real-time anomaly detection, behavioural analysis, and adaptive learning, the concept of AI systems is able to detect fraudulent activities faster and more accurately than conventional rule-based frameworks (Jun et al., 2021). Nevertheless, the integration of AI techniques into the fraud prevention process raises a complex policy dilemma: While AI helps make fraud detection and decision-making processes faster and more efficient, they are often carried out through use of inscrutable algorithms, data-greedy surveillance and systems that can reinforce or amplify societal bias.

Despite a growing body of research about AI in cybersecurity and emerging international frameworks such as the General Data Protection Regulation (GDPR), and the California Consumer Privacy Act (CCPA), there is still a significant governance gap. There is a lack of comprehensive policy frameworks that can guarantee that AI-based fraud detection is consistent with legal norms, ethical standards and operational realities across borders. Moreover, contemporary discussions of governance are often aspirational, offering broad principles without any possible mechanisms, metrics, or structures for holding people accountable.

This chapter closes that gap by providing a structured analysis of the way that AI is transforming the way we detect fraud, and the regulatory and ethical challenges it raises, as well as the strategic policy mechanisms needed to provide a framework for determining its responsible use. By correlating technical capabilities and governance imperatives, the chapter aims to provide a contribution to a roadmap for adaptive, rights-respecting and globally coordinated AI deployment in the fight against cyber fraud and identity theft.

2. AI IN CYBER FRAUD DETECTION: TECHNOLOGIES AND TAXONOMIES

Artificial Intelligence is rapidly transforming the landscape of cyber fraud detection, offering tools that go beyond traditional rule-based systems by enabling real-time, adaptive, and predictive threat analysis. Unlike conventional fraud detection approaches that rely on static rules or predefined attack signatures, AI systems learn from vast datasets and dynamically adjust to new and evolving fraud techniques (Hafez et al., 2025). This shift marks a significant evolution in how organizations can detect, interpret, and respond to cyber threats, particularly those related to identity theft and financial fraud.

To understand the range of AI uses in this field, it is necessary to review the main categories of AI technologies used. Machine - learning algorithms such as decision trees, support vector machines and ensemble algorithms such as XGBoost are often used to classify transactions based on known fraud indicators (Zhang et al., 2020). These models are relatively interpretable and computationally efficient; however, they rely on large amounts of labelled training data and may not detect novel fraud tactics that deviate from historical patterns.

Deep learning, in general, especially architectures like recurrent neural networks (RNNs), convolutional neural networks (CNNs) and long short-term memory (LSTMs) networks, has become very useful in identifying hidden patterns in sequential data, such as a timeline of transactions or login histories (Luo et al., 2021). These models have the ability to detect subtle and complex fraud schemes that simple models may miss. Nonetheless, they are so "black-box" that they are hard to interpret, which presents issues of accountability and regulatory oversight.

Natural language processing (NLP) has also become a powerful fraud prevention technique, particularly in terms of analysing unstructured, text-based data. There are NLP models that can identify fraudulent communication in phishing emails, attempts at social-media impersonation or adverts for stolen data on dark web forums (Sood et al., 2023). While these models are highly versatile, they may struggle with disambiguating nuanced or context-specific language.

In the case of an absence of labelled data, unsupervised learning methods such as clustering algorithms, autoencoders and isolation forests can be used to detect anomalies. These models work by spotting variations from known norms of behavioural activity, for example, a sudden change of location in account activity or a series of transactions that seem out of character. While helpful in identifying previously unknown fraud schemes, unsupervised models are prone to high false-positive rates and often need manual verification to ensure accuracy.

Another new field is adversarial AI, which is both a threat and a way of defense. Cybercriminals have increasingly tried to trick AI systems by creating inputs that aim to bypass AI systems' detection. In response, researchers are developing adversarially robust models and training methods that can resist such manipulations, but these systems are computationally expensive and are at a nascent stage of development.

Already AI is used in a wide range of scenarios in fraud detection. For example, anomaly-detection systems analyse login behaviours, transactional rhythms and device fingerprinting in order to identify suspicious patterns (Martin et al., 2021). In the fight against synthetic identity fraud, deep learning models trained with the help of biometric and documentary data can be used to detect fake profiles that combine real and fake data. Likewise, deep fake detection for digital arrest scams is being done through AI enhanced voice and image analysis to distinguish between real law enforcement agents and impostors.

Figure 1. AI-Driven Fraud Detection Pipeline.

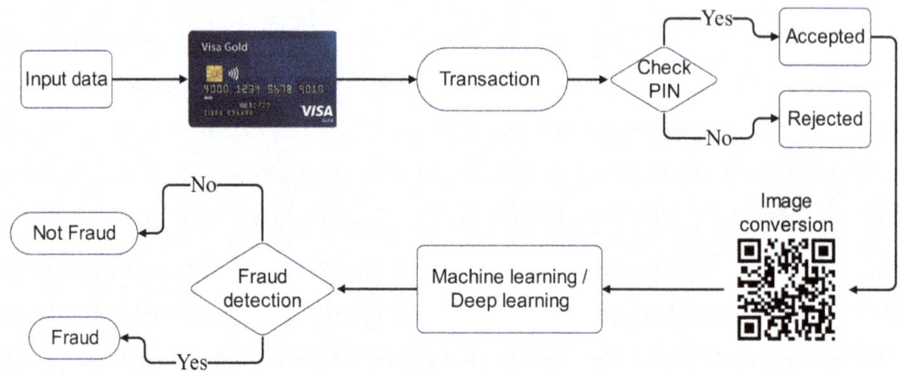

In more sophisticated operations, graph based models and neural networks are utilised in order to detect coordinated fraud rings by mapping and analysing transactional relationships across platforms (Ren et al., 2023). Moreover, NLP models are helping law enforcement and cybersecurity professionals to monitor the marketplace in the dark web for stolen credentials or fraud-as-a-service offerings to enable early intervention. A typical AI driven fraud detection pipeline is shown in Figure 1. To help with comparative understanding and practical application, Table 1 provides a taxonomy of AI methods currently being used in fraud detection that have a description of their core characteristics, strengths, limitations and real world applications.

Table 1. Taxonomy of AI Methods in Fraud Detection.

AI Method	Description	Strengths	Limitations	Example Use Cases
Machine Learning	Supervised models trained on labeled data to classify fraud vs. legitimate transactions.	Interpretable, efficient, scalable.	Requires clean labeled data; struggles with novel fraud.	Credit card fraud detection, risk scoring.
Deep Learning	Neural networks that detect complex, nonlinear patterns in sequential or high-dimensional data.	High accuracy; adaptable to complex behaviors.	Opaque; resource-intensive; hard to audit.	Synthetic ID fraud, sequential transaction patterns.
Natural Language Processing	Extracts meaning from unstructured text or speech data using language models.	Useful for phishing, scam detection, threat intelligence.	Language ambiguity; cultural/linguistic bias.	Analyzing phishing emails, dark web threat monitoring.
Unsupervised Learning	Identifies anomalies or clusters in data without labeled outputs.	Useful for novel fraud; works with unlabeled data.	High false positives; needs expert validation.	Behavioral anomaly detection, unknown fraud schemes.
Adversarial AI (Defense)	AI systems trained to resist manipulation or spoofing by adversarial inputs.	Increases system resilience to attacks.	Early stage; computationally expensive.	Defending against deepfakes, AI evasion tactics.

These AI systems usually work within integrated decision support pipelines, in which data is first aggregated and pre-processed before it is analysed by predictive models. The output is then passed on to risk-scoring systems and delivered to human analysts or mechanisms of automated enforcement. Such a pipeline is crucial to ensuring that AI insights result in actionable responses to fraud without inundating human operators with false positives.

However, the efficacy of AI in terms of fraud detection is critically dependent on the quality, diversity and integrity of the underlying data (Johora et al., 2024). Biases inherent in training data sets can produce discriminatory results, such as inequitable flagging of transactions from marginalised communities or regions with low levels of digital infrastructure. False Positives, in which legitimate behaviour is incorrectly flagged as suspicious, can lead to a loss of user trust and financial and reputational damage. On the other hand, false negatives - i.e., instances of fraud missing the detection process - may allow systemic breaches to remain undetected. The growing existence of adversarial attacks makes this scenario even more complicated because malevolent actors are making a concerted effort to manipulate artificial intelligence systems through manipulated inputs.

Ultimately, while AI is providing capabilities in fraud detection that have never been seen before, there are benefits that come with deploying these technologies, and those benefits cannot be decoupled from the operational, ethical, and legal context in which the technologies are being deployed. The next section will explore these issues of regulation and governance in more detail, and underscore the tensions between the need for rapid detection of threats, on the one hand, and the need for preservation of rights, fairness and transparency in digital systems on the other.

3. REAL-WORLD CASE APPLICATIONS OF AI IN FRAUD DETECTION

The practical deployment of Artificial Intelligence in combating cyber fraud and identity theft is no longer theoretical. Across financial institutions, government agencies, and private cybersecurity firms, AI systems are being integrated into operational workflows to detect anomalies, evaluate risk, and support decision-making. This section examines selected real-world applications that illustrate how AI techniques are currently used to address specific types of fraud, while also exposing the limitations and policy challenges these systems face in practice.

One notable example is that large multinational banks use artificial intelligence (AI) powered anomaly detection systems to detect fraudulent financial transactions. These institutions often use layered machine-learning models and learn from models that have been trained by the institution on data from historical transactions, to make real-time assessments of risk. For example an unusual pattern of transactions (an unusual transfer of large amounts of money to a foreign account; login attempts from geographically disparate locations within a short space of time) will trigger alerts that are flagged up to fraud analysts (Sarna et al. 2025). Although these systems have improved detection speed and accuracy remarkably compared to rule based systems, they are not immune to over fitting or bias. Documented cases exists of legitimate customers, especially from high-risk postal codes, being repeatedly flagged because of fraud trends in the past in those areas which raises the question of algorithmic fairness.

A second interesting example is the use of deep learning to identify cases of synthetic identity fraud in the digital lending space. Companies like Zest AI and Upstart have built neural network models that are able to analyse complex relationships between metadata of applications, credit bureau records, and device fingerprints to detect fake profiles (Elgendy et al., 2025). These systems have been used to successfully decrease rates of loan default associated with identity fraud. Nevertheless, there are still challenges in terms of model explainability and the potential to deny access to legitimate users that do not align with traditional patterns of identities and financial behaviour. Regulatory scrutiny has become heightened around such systems, particularly in jurisdictions governed by legislation such as the EU's GDPR, which puts constraints on fully automated decision-making.

A burgeoning field of concern - and innovation - focuses on the detection of digital arrest fraud, where cybercriminals pose as law enforcement officials by phone calls, emails, or video calls to induce the victim into divulging personal information or making a payment (Gonipalli et al., 2025). AI driven voice analytics and facial recognition technologies are now being used to check the authenticity of communications alleged to be coming from official sources. For example, some law enforcement agencies have started testing voiceprint-matching systems that compare the calls against verified law enforcement voice databases. These tools have proven to be beneficial in the detection of spoofed calls, especially those altered with deep fake audio. Nevertheless, there are new privacy and governance issues that arise with such the legality of voiceprint databases and consent requirements for biometric surveillance under data protection laws.

Another practical use case comes from cybersecurity companies scanning the dark web for early signs of fraud. By using NLP algorithms, these firms search darknet forums and encrypted messaging platforms for mentions of stolen credentials, fraud tools or listings of data breaches (Schafer et al., 2019). The extracted intelligence is then cross-referenced against known threat-actor signatures and sold to financial institutions or government agencies to be used for preemptive defence. While effective, the legal validity of scraping such forums, and the chain of custody of such intelligence, is often in a legal grey area, especially in a cross-border context where interpretation of jurisdictions varies.

In addition to these direct applications, decision support systems (DSS) coupled with AI models is now common place in compliance departments of financial firms. These platforms use a combination of AI-generated alerts and structured decision trees, and audit trails, to help human analysts decide if a flagged transaction requires escalation or intervention. This human-in-the-loop approach helps mitigate the interpretability gap of complex AI systems while providing a sense of accountability in the decision-making process. However, the effectiveness of such hybrid systems has significant variance depending on the quality of the training data, organisational culture and regulatory oversight.

These are some real life examples that show the promise and the perils of deploying AI for fraud detection. They highlight the point that technical success does not necessarily mean ethical or legal strength. The systems we are describing exist in contexts of competing priorities, such as speed vs. due process, detection vs. discrimination, automation vs. explainability. Consequently, policy design needs to move beyond a generic support for AI and go into the operational reality and risk trade-offs typified by these examples.

The next section explores these tensions further in more depth, examining the legal and governance frameworks that try to manage these, and do not, and are struggling, on issues of transparency, data protection, bias mitigation and regulatory coherence.

4. GOVERNANCE AND LEGAL CHALLENGES

While Artificial Intelligence offers powerful tools to combat cyber fraud and identity theft, its deployment is fraught with complex legal and governance challenges. These issues stem from the nature of AI systems themselves—often opaque, data-intensive, and rapidly evolving—as well as from the fragmented and reactive character of current regulatory responses. As governments and institutions race to harness AI for fraud detection, they are simultaneously struggling to define how these systems should be governed, what legal obligations apply, and how civil liberties can be preserved in the process.

A key issue is that of transparency and explainability. Numerous algorithms used for fraud detection - and especially those based on deep learning - are "black boxes," giving outputs without providing a clear rationale for their decisions. This lack of interpretability makes organisational audits, compliance assessment by regulators and the ability for those affected by a decision to contest it very difficult (Zhang, et al., 2022). For instance, when a loan application is turned down, based on the AI-fingered fraud flag, the applicant may not have any redress to understand or contest the logic behind the denial (Awosika et al., 2024). Such opacity is in direct conflict with legal values in data protection laws, which in the GDPR, for instance, enshrine the right to explanation (Article 22) which limits fully automated decision-making with large impacts on individuals.

Closely combined with the concept of transparency is the issue of algorithmic bias. AI systems that are trained using past or incomplete datasets frequently perpetuate and amplify societal inequalities. In the case of fraud detection, this will result in discriminatory outcomes, e.g., either by increased false positive rates to identify transactions coming from economically marginalised regions or by misclassifying some ethnic or demographic groups as fraud risks (Lokhande et al., 2024). These biases destroy public trust and create legal liabilities for institutions under anti discrimination statutes. Despite growing awareness, few jurisdictions are currently enforcing systematic fairness audits of fraud-detection systems or penalties for biased results from artificial intelligence systems.

Data privacy is one other big legal hot-button issue. AI-based fraud prevention is based on the analysis of large amounts of personal, financial and behavioural data much of which is collected passively via multiple platforms (Walters & Novak, 2021). This presents challenges to compliance with laws which emphasise data minimisation, purpose limitation and user consent. For example, the GDPR holds that personal data should be collected for "specified, explicit, and legitimate purposes" and not further processed in ways that are incompatible with the purposes for which it is collected (Degli-Esposti & Ferrandiz, 2021). Yet AI models often involve data repurposing and extensive preprocessing that may fall outside the original scope of consent. Similarly, the CCPA provides consumers with rights to access, delete, or limit the use of their data - rights that have the potential to undermine the continued training or operation of real time fraud detection models (Xu, 2022).

Regulatory ambiguity makes a bad situation worse - the debate over accountability for artificial intelligence (AI) systems. When an AI system comes to a wrong conclusion - for example, flagging a legitimate transaction as a fraudulent one, or not detecting a fraudulent transaction when it was there - responsibility tends to become diffuse. It is often problematic to determine whether the fault lies with the software developer, the organisation that implemented the tool, or the third party data provider. Existing legal frameworks do not usually contain explicit doctrines for allocating liability to autonomous or semi-autonomous AI systems, and this tends to undermine the interests of consumers and the management of institutional risks.

The proposed European Union Artificial Intelligence Act (EU AI Act) is a significant attempt to fill such gaps (Neuwirth, 2023). The Act establishes a risk-based approach which categorises AI systems based on the risk to fundamental rights. Fraud-detection systems, especially those in the financial services sector or law enforcement, are considered "high-risk" and as such are expected to meet a high set of requirements, such as risk assessments, transparency obligations, human oversight, and post-deployment monitoring. Unlike the data-centric General Data Protection Regulation (GDPR), the AI Act is model-centric and explicitly addresses system design and operational safeguards. If it is implemented well, it can be a global benchmark for AI governance. However, concerns remain about the practicalities of enforcement in a wide range of jurisdictions, the administrative burden on smaller institutions, and the risk of regulatory overlap with existing laws protecting data.

Figure 2. Governance Architecture for High-Risk AI

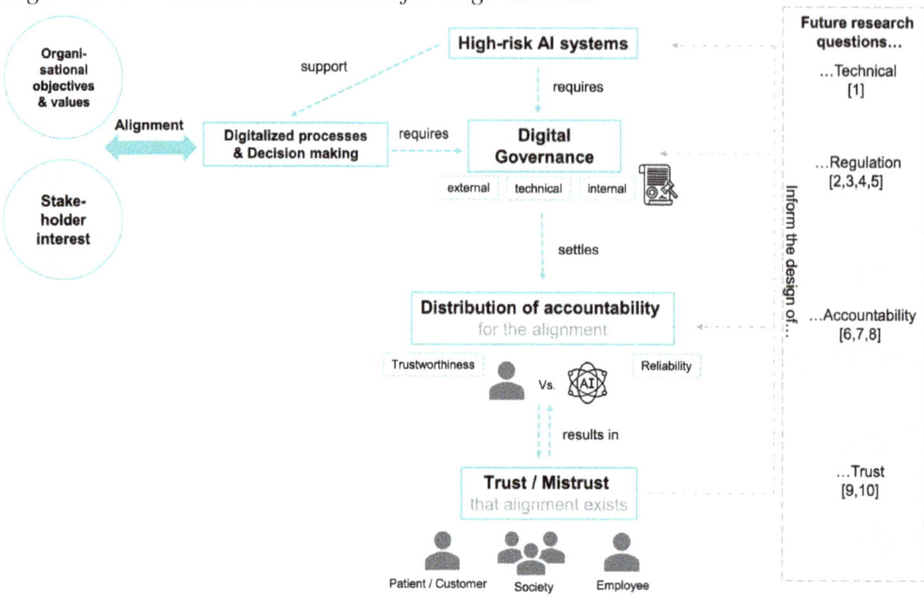

(Bartsch et al., 2025).

Figure 2 is an example of a governance architecture for high-risk AI systems for fraud detection. Table 2 offers a comparison of some of the most important regulatory frameworks that govern the deployment of AI systems for fraud detection. Although these laws vary in scope and enforceability, each reflects the evolving norms around data rights, automated decision-making, and accountability.

Table 2. Comparative Legal Frameworks Governing AI in Fraud Detection.

Framework	Scope & Jurisdiction	AI-Relevant Provisions	Enforcement Mechanism	Challenges in Fraud Detection Context
GDPR (EU)	Data protection across EU and EEA	Article 22 limits fully automated decisions; mandates data minimization and transparency.	Enforced by national data protection authorities; fines up to 4% of global turnover.	Limits AI model opacity; restricts data reuse; friction in real-time decisioning.
CCPA (USA - CA)	Consumer data privacy in California	Grants rights to know, delete, and opt-out of data sales; lacks automation-specific rules.	Enforced by CA Attorney General; fines per violation.	Fragmented with other U.S. state laws; lacks AI explainability requirements.
EU AI Act (Draft)	EU-wide AI regulation based on risk classification	Labels fraud detection systems as "high-risk"; requires risk assessments, human oversight.	Binding regulation with fines and oversight by EU AI Board.	Implementation costs; tension with existing GDPR obligations; overlaps in compliance.
NIST AI RMF (USA - Voluntary)	U.S. voluntary risk management framework	Recommends fairness, transparency, and robustness standards; non-binding.	Not enforceable; adopted at agency discretion.	Lacks legal force; uneven adoption across public/private sectors.
Singapore AI Model Framework	Soft law for ethical AI deployment	Emphasizes explainability, fairness, and stakeholder engagement in AI design.	Industry self-regulation; encouraged via innovation incentives.	Suited for early-stage governance but lacks legal enforcement.

In contrast, other jurisdictions are fragmented or voluntary in their regulation of. In the United States, the lack of a federal comprehensive privacy law means that there is a lot of variation between states. While there are efforts such as the National Institute of Standards and Technology AI Risk Management Framework, which offer guidelines for fairness, robustness and transparency, these are non-binding and do not have enforcement mechanisms (Eltaeib et al., 2024). In Asia, countries like Singapore and South Korea have adopted innovation-forward regulatory models that focus on adoption of AI while promoting soft compliance through public-private partnerships and ethical codes of conduct (Anderson Schillig, 2023).

One of the biggest governance quandaries relates to the tension between real time detection of fraud and due process protections. Many AI systems make decisions at a speed that is faster than traditional legal review mechanisms. For example, real-time blocking of suspicious transactions may take place before any human being can evaluate the evidence or before the user has a chance to appeal. This throws open questions concerning the presumption of innocence, the right to be heard and procedural fairness. In the absence of clear legal protocols to guide such interventions, the risk of overreach and unjust outcome escalates. Finally, the transnational nature of cyber fraud only serves to heighten all of these governance challenges. AI models trained and implemented in one jurisdiction can process data or affect people in others, creating regulatory blind spots and enforcement vacuums. The absence of harmonised international legal frameworks means organisations have to navigate conflicting obligations (such as balancing between GDPR compliance and the U.S. law enforcement's requirements) or use regulatory arbitrage by moving operations to less restrictive jurisdiction countries.

Taken together, these challenges show the urgent need to develop coherent, enforceable and forward-looking models of AI governance that are specific to the risks presented by fraud prevention. The next section reviews the current policy landscape and assesses the strengths and weaknesses of current legal instruments, and prescribes ways of moving towards more adaptive and collaborative policy design.

5. STRATEGIC POLICY DESIGN

The fight against cyber fraud and identity theft powered by Artificial Intelligence cannot be won through legal compliance alone. While regulations such as the GDPR, CCPA, and the proposed EU AI Act offer a foundational framework, their efficacy ultimately depends on how well strategic policy choices translate these abstract principles into operational mechanisms. Effective AI governance in fraud detection requires dynamic coordination between governments, industries, and civil society. This section presents key pillars of strategic design—collaboration, explainability, capacity building, and adaptive regulation—and introduces measurable indicators to evaluate their implementation.

A key tenet of good strategy is multi-sector collaboration. Cyber fraud is inherently cross - domain, with banks, telecom providers, fintech platforms, social media organisations and government agencies. No single entity can address this threat in isolation (Halpin & Todd, 2024). Strategic collaboration through the development of formalised public-private partnerships, the creation of joint operations centres and sectoral alliances, where intelligence, tools and practices are shared, (Akinbowale et al, 2022) The value of collaboration is pooled data - especially anonymised transaction records or known patterns of threats that can bring systemic fraud indicators invisible to individual actors. But such cooperation requires legal protections to avoid privacy abuses, competitive abuse and liability risks. Some possible indicators to evaluate success may include number of actionable threat intelligence exchanges per quarter, average response time to shared threat intelligence, and partner engagement levels in shared databases.

Equally important is the explainability of AI systems, particularly those that are used in high-stakes environments (e.g. fraud detection). Black box models not only bring ethical/legal issues but also undermine the operational value of the AI if the decision makers cannot understand or justify the outputs. In order to overcome this, standards for explainable AI (XAI), including documentation of model behaviour, auditability protocols and interfaces to allow for human review, should be enforced by governments and industry bodies (Zhang et al., 2022). Explainability should be judged both clinically, for example, by the use of SHAP or LIME values to interpret predictions, and procedurally, for example by the availability of redress mechanisms for individuals affected by AI driven decision making. Policymakers can define minimum standards for explainability and require organisations to release periodic transparency reports that disclose model behaviour, bias audits and accuracy metrics.

Another strategic dimension is capacity building with all relevant stakeholders. Regulators need technical training to assess AI tools, conduct audits and control AI-specific risks like adversarial manipulation or model drift (Pawlak & Barmpaliou, 2017). Private-sector developers need to internalise principles of ethical design such as fairness, proportionality and necessity, in the AI development lifecycle. Law-enforcement agencies need upskilling in the areas of digital forensics, algorithmic decision-making and data integrity standards. Capacity-building metrics might consist of the number of certified AI audit professionals or completion rates of governance training programmes, as well as frequency of cross-sector simulation exercises. Without such systemic readiness, even well-crafted laws will fail in practical terms.

Strategic policy will also have to overcome regulatory inertia. Prescriptive rules are prone to being a step behind threats and innovations. To overcome this, governments should adopt adaptive regulatory frameworks, such as regulatory sandboxes, in which AI-driven fraud detection tools can be tested in their real-world applications under close oversight. Sandboxes allow regulators to learn more about new risks and technologies without stifling innovation too early, and they give developers a well-structured way to bring themselves into compliance with regulations, thus removing a lot of uncertainty. Key indicators for measuring the effectiveness of sandboxes could be time to policy iteration, the percentage of the sandboxed projects that are moved to formal approval, and how quickly rules are changed based on the learnings from the sandboxes. To move from principle to action that is enforced, measures to track progress must be put in place by policymakers and institutions, and be indicated by measurable indicators. Table 3 shows some recommended benchmarks for assessing the success of AI governance in fraud detection.

Table 3. Operational Benchmarks for AI Governance in Fraud Detection.

Policy Focus Area	**Operational Indicator**	**Suggested Measurement Frequency**	**Purpose / Impact**
Explainability	% of AI models with documented interpretability reports (e.g., SHAP/LIME)	Biannual	Ensures transparency, auditability, and user comprehension.
Threat Intelligence Sharing	Number of actionable fraud alerts exchanged via public–private networks	Quarterly	Assesses cross-sector collaboration and responsiveness.
Fairness and Bias Audits	% of systems passing demographic fairness tests before deployment	Annually	Prevents systemic discrimination and ensures model equity.
Redress Mechanisms	Time to resolve appeals for AI-based fraud classification decisions	Monthly tracking	Ensures procedural fairness and public trust.
Sandbox Participation	Number of AI systems tested in regulatory sandbox environments	Rolling basis	Encourages innovation under supervision and controlled risk.
Training & Capacity Building	Number of personnel certified in AI risk and ethics (regulatory + private)	Biannual	Builds institutional expertise and policy readiness.
Cross-border Data Sharing	Number of cross-jurisdictional data exchange protocols signed or updated	Annually	Tracks international cooperation and regulatory alignment.

International harmonisation is still a strategic priority, especially in view of the international nature of identity theft and synthetic fraud. Rather than waiting for full legal convergence, policymakers can seek functional interoperability: common minimum standards, cross-border data sharing agreements with strong privacy safeguards, and mutual recognition of AI audits. Organisations like INTERPOL, Europol and the OECD can help to bring about this alignment. Measuring success could include tracking the number of cross-border task forces, data exchange agreements signed up to and AI-based joint investigations carried out every year. These strategic levers should ultimately be embedded in a governance ecosystem that is transparent, accountable and responsive both to changes in technology and to changing societal expectations. Without enforceable indicators, public trust and/or mechanisms for adaptive learning, AI in fraud detection runs the risk of becoming a fragmented, inconsistent and contested space.

6. INTERNATIONAL COOPERATION AND TRANSNATIONAL BARRIERS

Cyber fraud and identity theft are inherently transnational crimes. Fraudulent transactions may be initiated in one country, routed through servers in another, and target victims in a third. This global dispersal of actors, infrastructure, and data flows renders unilateral approaches to fraud detection insufficient. While Artificial Intelligence can enhance detection across networks and jurisdictions, its effectiveness is ultimately constrained by the limits of international legal cooperation, data sharing regimes, and enforcement harmonization. Addressing these challenges requires not only diplomatic coordination but also technical interoperability and trust.

The Mutual Legal Assistance Treaty (MLA) process is one of the most persistent bottlenecks in cross-border enforcement (Simanjuntak, 2018). While the intended objective of MLATs is to facilitate the exchange of evidence between jurisdictions when investigating criminal activities, MLAT mechanisms are notoriously slow and ill-suited to the time-sensitive nature of fraud detection using AI. By the time a formal request is processed the fraudulent network may have dissipated or evolved. Delays in responding to digital arrest scams investigations in Southeast Asia - a documented case study - serves as an example of how MLAT sluggishness helps facilitate the rebranding of actors under different domains and evade prosecution.

AI has the potential to inevitably remove some of these delays, but only if frameworks for cooperation are brought into the future. Secure federated learning systems can help many jurisdictions train AI models on distributed datasets without transferring raw data across countries, thus respecting national data sovereignty while allowing shared intelligence. Similarly, encrypted data enclaves and privacy-preserving analytics methods such as homomorphic encryption can help the sharing of legitimated evidence without sharing sensitive personal information. These technical innovations however need the legal recognition and the operational alignment between countries, which is presently deficient.

International law-enforcement organisations have made promising steps towards operational coordination. INTERPOL's Global Complex for Innovation and Europol's European Cybercrime Centre have established joint task forces and have successfully carried out multinational takedowns of fraud syndicates (Britz, 2008). AI systems have been gradually adopted by these operations - especially for identifying fraudulent transaction patterns and spotting synthetic identities networks. Nevertheless, such operations also reveal gaps in governance: who is responsible for the algorithm and what rules apply to governance in a situation where there is a difference in legal standards for the algorithm, and who is liable when AI makes mistakes resulting in wrongful accusations.

In addition to technical interoperability, legal harmonisation is one of the key challenges. Definitions of cyber fraud, for example, identity theft, and even "high-risk AI" differ greatly from jurisdiction to jurisdiction. Some countries make it a criminal act to scrape data or algorithmic profiling, while others promote the use of such techniques in a national security context. Without some basis of agreement on legal definitions and evidentiary standards, AI-generated insights may be inadmissible in court and thus defeated in their usefulness. Regional agreements - such as the Budapest Convention on Cybercrime - provide a blueprint for such harmonisation and there is still patchy take-up at a global level. Ongoing negotiations for a UN Cybercrime Treaty might offer a wider platform, although political splits over surveillance, sovereignty and data localisation remain.

Privacy protection is another obstacle to international cooperation. The European Union's General Data Protection Regulation (GDPR) restricts cross border transfers of data, especially to those countries that do not offer similar protections. This poses some friction to the sharing of fraud intelligence with jurisdictions with weaker or fragmented privacy regimes. Recent efforts like EU-U.S. Data Privacy Framework are trying to bridge this gap but they are limited in scope and open to legal challenges. Until such frameworks become robust and broadly adopted, institutions have to work on a mish-mash of bilateral agreements, often with conflicting requirements. Asymmetries in capacity among states add an additional layer of complexity. While technologically advanced countries are using state-of-the-art AI tools, many low- and middle-income countries do not have the infrastructures, expertise, or legal frameworks in place to engage in AI-enabled cyber crime investigations (Calderaro & Craig, 2020). This imbalance weakens the international ecosystem of fraud detection and this is creating regulatory safe havens for bad actors to act with impunity. Bridging this gap will require capitalizing on opportunities for capacity building - in the form of knowledge-sharing platforms, technical assistance programmes and international training initiatives on the topic of AI governance in law enforcement contexts.

Finally, any international collaboration on AI has to be guided by trust. Shared tools and models come with risks - backdoors, model poisoning or misuse of the tool for surveillance. Establishing neutral governance structures, transparent auditing protocols as well as mutual accountability frameworks is essential for long term cooperation. Without such safeguards, even well-intentioned partnerships can break apart over fears of data abuse or political exploitation.

In sum, there is more to the promise of AI in fighting transnational cyberfraud than technological sophistication. It requires, among other things, legal modernisation, interoperable governance and strategic diplomacy. The following section will review these international challenges through a strong ethical lens in order to ensure that the quest for security does not undermine the very rights and values it is aiming to protect.

7. ETHICAL CONSIDERATIONS AND SOCIETAL IMPLICATIONS

The deployment of Artificial Intelligence in fraud detection is not just a technical or regulatory endeavor—it is also an ethical one. AI systems influence how risk is distributed across populations, how trust is earned or lost in institutions, and how power is exercised through data and automation. As governments and private entities expand the use of AI to detect and prevent cyber fraud, they must also reckon with deeper moral questions about surveillance, discrimination, and the rights of individuals in digital society.

One of the fundamental ethical principles that is ingrained in this field is proportionality - the idea that surveillance or data collection methods must be proportional to the threat they are intended to counter (Hjorthen & Pattison, 2023). AI systems that are able to monitor real-time financial behaviour, biometric characteristics or communication patterns may be able to achieve high fraud detection rates, but they will also be prone to normalising a degree of intrusion that is out of proportion to the actual threat. For instance, the use of continuous voice-print analysis for fraud detection might stop scams of impersonation, but at the same time it creates a baseline of infrastructure for genuinely biometric surveillance that might have a different use, or worse, be repurposed.

Closely related is the principle of necessity, which requires that any utilisation of personal data be strictly indispensable to accomplish a legitimate objective, and therefore includes the obligation to consider less intrusive alternatives before they are deployed (Formosa et al., 2021). While artificial intelligence systems require access to large and heterogeneous datasets, ethical design requires data collections and model trainings to be bound by strong purpose. Nonetheless, in many real world deployments this demarcation is often obfuscated; organisations often retain user data indefinitely in the name of "model improvement", or "future fraud pattern analysis", without any explicit limits or consent from the individual user - in clear violation of both the necessity and transparency norms.

A supplementary and especially difficult issue is fairness. AI models used for fraud detection can inadvertently perpetuate systemic biases that are intrinsically present in historical datasets. For example, if certain postal codes, income levels or nationalities have been overrepresented in fraudulent investigations in the past, AI systems trained with data on such groups can disproportionately flag users from these groups (Kamalaruban et al., 2024). A 2023 audit of one of the major credit scoring companies in the United States found that its algorithm for detecting fraud had superior false positive rates when dealing with applicants from Hispanic and Black communities which led to the unwarranted rejection of loans (Singh & Kaunert, 2025). These consequences not only destroy the credibility of fraud prevention systems, but may also be a violation of anti-discrimination laws in several jurisdictions.

Figure 3. Ethical AI Risk Matrix. N – Not severe; S- Severe; VS-Very severe; VL-Very low; L-low; M-Medium; H-High; VH-Very high.

	LOSS SEVERITY	Negligible			Minor			Moderate			Major			Catastrophic		
	Infringement severity	N	S	VS	N	S	VS	N	S	VS	N	S	VS	N	S	VS
EVENT LIKELIHOOD	Very likely to happen	M	L	L	H	M	L	H	M	L	VH	H	M	VH	H	M
	Likely to happen	L	VL	VL	M	L	L	H	M	L	H	M	L	VH	H	M
	Possible to happen	L	VL	VL	L	VL	VL	M	L	L	H	M	L	H	M	L
	Unlikely to happen	VL	VL	VL	L	VL	VL	L	VL	VL	M	L	L	H	M	L
	Very unlikely to happen	VL	VL	VL	VL	VL	VL	L	VL	VL	L	VL	VL	M	L	L

(Bruschi & Diomede, 2023)

Figure 3 shows an examples of an ethical AI risk matrix. To improve these threats, fairness needs to be incorporated at various points in the AI pipeline: during data curation, model training, testing and deployment. Regular audits of fairness - both internal and third party - should be routine practice and institutions should ensure that there is still the right for individuals to challenge decisions made by AI systems. This right to recourse is not just a legal protection, it is a fundamental in promoting public trust in automated systems.

Trust itself is a societal resource that has to be very carefully managed. Effective prevention of fraud relies on the cooperation of citizens and customers in digital systems - reporting suspicious activity, confirming identities and adhering to security protocols. If the people think AI systems are unfair, unexplainable, or prejudiced, their willingness to interact is reduced. Transparency is key to this trust being maintained. Individuals should be notified whenever AI systems are used in fraud screening, on the types of data being analyzed and be able to appeal or correct decisions. Public-facing transparency reports, independent evaluations, and media literacy campaigns can help build this trust over time. While the potential for significant gains in efficiency in the fight against fraud is great, a number of high-profile failures highlight the ethical risks of unregulated implementation. Table 4 highlights some representative cases highlighting the implications of bias, lack of transparency and harm in the context of AI driven financial systems.

Table 4. Case Examples of AI Failures.

Case	AI System / Application	Type of Failure	Impacted Stakeholders	Implication
US Credit Scoring Algorithm Bias (2023 audit)	Fraud scoring in loan approvals	Disparate false positives for minority groups	Black and Hispanic applicants	Algorithmic bias led to financial exclusion and legal scrutiny.
UK Bank Transaction Filter	Anomaly detection in customer transactions	Overblocking of transactions by vulnerable populations	Elderly and disabled account holders	Lack of model explainability prevented appeals and correction.
India Fintech Lending App (2022)	Behavioral profiling for micro-loan risk	Biased training data from urban segments	Rural low-income users	Disproportionate denial of access; lack of audit or redress.
Adversarial Data Poisoning (Research Demo)	Synthetic identity detection model	Model misled by crafted fake identities	System integrity compromised	Exposed fragility to adversarial inputs; underscored audit need.
Phishing Email Classifier Drift	NLP-based fraud alerting system	Model failed to adapt to evolving tactics	Email users and IT teams	Static models lost accuracy; delayed threat response.

Another new issue is the adversarial misuse of AI. Just as AI is being used by defenders to detect fraud, criminal actors are using AI to evade the same - with synthetic identities, fake inputs and deepfake scams. Adversarial attacks on fraud detection systems can cause both under and over detection resulting in financial loss, damage to their reputation, and systemic risk. Ethical governance therefore requires more than designing fair and accountable systems, but also building resilient systems - those that can adapt to intentional manipulation.

Finally, there is the larger narrative of AI and control in society that needs to be addressed. If AI-driven fraud detection is synonymous with mass surveillance, unaccountable decision-making or institutional overreach, it risks alienating the very public that it aims to protect. Instead, policymakers and developers will need to reframe AI as a tool for empowerment - helping people to safeguard their identities, secure their finances, and navigate the digital world safely. This shift requires inclusive policy-making processes that include not only technical and legal experts but also ethicists, civil society advocates, and affected communities.

In sum, ethical considerations are not tangential to AI fraud detection; they are the basis. Absent careful attention to proportionality, fairness, transparency, and resilience, AI systems may perpetuate the same injustices they claim to flee from. The final section offers a roadmap for converting these ethical principles into actionable policy and institutional practices.

8. RECOMMENDATIONS FOR POLICY AND PRACTICE

Translating the ethical, technical, and legal insights expounded in this chapter into something resembling policy mandates that is practical more than high-level exhortation. It needs a concrete, adaptive governance approach, which is altered accordingly with fraud threats, AI capabilities, and public expectations (Tawil & Tarawneh, 2025). The following recommendations are structured in three levels, namely short-term, medium-term and long-term to provide a phased roadmap of implementation for policy makers, regulators and industry leaders. Each tier covers specific constraints and levels of readiness and impacts.

Short-Term (0–12 Months): Strengthen Immediate Oversight and Transparency

In the near term, governments and institutions should focus on embedding accountability into existing AI fraud detection systems through rapid regulatory mechanisms and capacity-building.

1. Mandate Explainability Standards: Require organizations to use interpretable models or to supplement complex models with explainability layers (e.g., SHAP, LIME) to allow auditors, end-users, and regulators to understand system behavior.
2. Launch Public AI Risk Registries: Create registries that list AI systems used in high-risk areas such as fraud detection, including descriptions of model type, oversight structures, and known risks.
3. Develop Minimum Transparency Protocols: Standardize disclosures for AI-based decision-making, including user notification, appeal procedures, and contact points for redress.
4. Initiate Ethics and Audit Training: Begin upskilling auditors, compliance officers, and public officials in AI literacy, focusing on algorithmic risk assessment and data governance.

Medium-Term (1–3 Years): Operationalize Governance and Expand Collaboration

The second phase focuses on scaling ethical governance, creating inter-sectoral structures, and aligning operational practices with legal mandates.

1. Establish AI Governance Units: Within central banks, national privacy agencies, and law enforcement bodies, create dedicated units to monitor AI deployments, enforce ethical guidelines, and investigate harm.
2. Standardize Public–Private Threat Intelligence Sharing: Create legal frameworks for secure, privacy-compliant sharing of fraud indicators between financial institutions, telecom providers, and regulatory bodies.
3. Embed Fairness and Bias Audits into Procurement: Require that any AI systems procured or licensed by public institutions undergo fairness testing across demographic groups, with results disclosed.
4. Expand Regulatory Sandboxes for AI in Fraud Detection: Allow innovation under supervision by enabling institutions to pilot AI systems with flexible oversight and periodic feedback loops before full-scale rollout.

Long-Term (3–5+ Years): Build Global Interoperability and Institutional Resilience

In the final phase, the emphasis shifts to harmonizing governance across borders, future-proofing regulations, and establishing enduring institutions for AI accountability.

1. Negotiate Mutual Recognition of AI Audits: Collaborate through organizations like the OECD, INTERPOL, and the UN to mutually recognize AI audit standards, enabling smoother cross-border investigations and enforcement.
2. Codify AI-Specific Liability Frameworks: Introduce legal mechanisms that clarify responsibility when AI systems fail, including joint liability between vendors and deploying institutions for high-risk applications.
3. Invest in Resilience Against Adversarial Attacks: Mandate periodic stress testing of fraud detection systems against adversarial inputs and data poisoning scenarios, similar to cybersecurity red-teaming.
4. Promote Inclusive Global Standards: Work toward convergence of technical and ethical standards through the UN Cybercrime Convention and other international treaties, while supporting capacity-building for lower-income jurisdictions.

To aid implementation and alignment of stakeholders Table 5 summarises the recommendations of the chapter in a phased roadmap. It identifies key policy actions, likely time frames and the major institutions charged with delivery. In figure 4, a policy timeline roadmap is presented which organises short-, medium-, and long-term actions for the regulation of AI in fraud detection. It emphasises priority areas - including explainability, fairness, international alignment and institutional resilience

- and their matching with realistic implementation windows. This visual roadmap helps with cross-sector planning, and provides a timeline for policy adoption.

Table 5. Phased Policy Recommendations: Timeline, Focus, and Actors

Phase	Policy Action	Focus Area	Lead Actors	Target Timeline
Short-Term	Mandate AI explainability reports	Transparency & oversight	Data protection agencies, central banks	6–12 months
	Launch public AI risk registries	Accountability	National AI regulators, industry consortiums	6–12 months
	Initiate ethics & audit training for officials	Capacity building	Regulatory academies, professional bodies	Ongoing (start ASAP)
Medium-Term	Operationalize fairness audits in procurement	Bias mitigation	Procurement agencies, financial regulators	1–2 years
	Establish AI governance units within institutions	Institutional capacity	Ministries of finance, law enforcement, banks	1–3 years
	Deploy cross-sector threat intelligence sharing tools	Collaboration	Telecoms, banks, CERTs	1–2 years
Long-Term	Enact AI liability laws for high-risk systems	Legal clarity	Legislatures, judiciary	3–5 years
	Develop mutual recognition of AI audits across borders	International alignment	OECD, UN, regional blocs	3–5+ years
	Fund adversarial resilience research	Technical integrity	Science ministries, cybersecurity agencies	3–5+ years

Figure 4. Policy Timeline Roadmap

The phased approach allows incremental change to be made while setting ambitious long term targets. In the short term, it brings practical steps to the forefront like explainability, transparency and sandboxing, which later escalates towards institutional reforms, international cooperation and structural accountability. At each step of the way the goal is to make sure that AI is not just efficient but also just, fair, legal and societal trustworthiness.

9. CONCLUSION

Artificial Intelligence has become a key player in the transformation of society's response to cyber fraud and identity theft. From anomaly detection in financial systems to the real-time screening of synthetic identities and digital impersonation, AI brings unprecedented speed, scale, and adaptability in protecting digital integrity. Yet, as this chapter shows, the introduction of these technologies in fraud detection raises a new set of policy dilemmas - where the need for security runs up against the need to safeguard civil liberties, fairness, and public trust.

This chapter is complimentary to what is already out there as it is not limited to a conceptual overlook, but instead proposes a structured, phased approach to AI governance in fraud prevention. It combines the analysis of laws and technical information, outlines strategic priorities based on measurable indicators and makes ethical principles concrete by applying them to real cases. Moreover, it represents one of the first systematic attempts to provide a map of the convergence of regulatory fragmentation, operational opacity, and adversarial misuse within the fraud detection context, and how these issues could be addressed by an adaptive and globally coordinated governance.

Rather than framing innovation and rights as competing forces, the chapter emphasizes the need to design AI systems, and the policies that govern them in ways that are compatible with democratic values as well as technological efficacy. This means enhancing explainability, implementing data protections, harmonising legal standards around the world, and ensuring that there is meaningful redress for individuals affected by AI errors. It requires also the recognition that algorithmic tools do not work in a vacuum, and are part of institutional practices, conditioned by economic incentives, and legitimised by social trust.

The imperative to do something is clear. The rate of innovation in artificial intelligence is increasing and legal and ethical protections are falling behind. Delayed intervention risks entrenching opaque and unaccountable systems that might perpetuate discrimination or trigger popular backlash. Thus, timely, inclusive and enforceable policy design is not an issue of regulation, it is an issue of democracy. Ultimately, the promise of AI in fraud detection will be fulfilled not only by technological sophistication, but through the integrity of the regulatory frameworks within which it is applied. If policymakers, technologists and civil society engage together in this challenge, AI will not only thwart cyber fraud - it will help build a more secure, just and resilient digital society.

REFERENCES

Akinbowale, O. E., Klingelhöfer, H. E., & Zerihun, M. F. (2022). The use of the Balanced Scorecard as a strategic management tool to mitigate cyberfraud in the South African banking industry. *Heliyon*, *8*(12), e12054. DOI: 10.1016/j.heliyon.2022.e12054 PMID: 36531622

Anderson Schillig, M. (2023). 'Lex Cryptographi (c) a,' 'Cloud Crypto Land'or What?–Blockchain Technology on the Legal Hype Cycle. *The Modern Law Review*, *86*(1), 31–66. DOI: 10.1111/1468-2230.12748

Awosika, T., Shukla, R. M., & Pranggono, B. (2024). Transparency and privacy: The role of explainable ai and federated learning in financial fraud detection. *IEEE Access : Practical Innovations, Open Solutions*, *12*, 64551–64560. DOI: 10.1109/ACCESS.2024.3394528

Bartsch, S., Behn, O., Benlian, A., Brownsword, R., Bücker, S., Düwell, M., Formánek, N., Jungtäubl, M., Leyer, M., Richter, A., Schmidt, J.-H., & Will-Zocholl, M. (2025). Governance of High-Risk AI Systems in Healthcare and Credit Scoring. *Business & Information Systems Engineering*, *67*(4), 1–19. DOI: 10.1007/s12599-025-00944-4

Britz, M. T. (2008). A new paradigm of organized crime in the United States: Criminal syndicates, cyber-gangs, and the worldwide web. *Sociology Compass*, *2*(6), 1750–1765. DOI: 10.1111/j.1751-9020.2008.00172.x

Bruschi, D., & Diomede, N. (2023). A framework for assessing AI ethics with applications to cybersecurity. *AI and Ethics*, *3*(1), 65–72. DOI: 10.1007/s43681-022-00162-8

Calderaro, A., & Craig, A. J. (2020). Transnational governance of cybersecurity: Policy challenges and global inequalities in cyber capacity building. *Third World Quarterly*, *41*(6), 917–938. DOI: 10.1080/01436597.2020.1729729

Degli-Esposti, S., & Ferrándiz, E. M. (2021). After the GDPR: Cybersecurity is the elephant in the artificial intelligence room. *European Business Law Review*, *32*(1), 1–24. DOI: 10.54648/EULR2021001

Elgendy, I. A., Helal, M. Y., Al-Sharafi, M. A., Albashrawi, M. A., Al-Ahmadi, M. S., Jeon, I., & Dwivedi, Y. K. (2025). Agentic systems as catalysts for innovation in FinTech: Exploring opportunities, challenges and a research agenda. *Information Discovery and Delivery*. Advance online publication. DOI: 10.1108/IDD-03-2025-0068

Eltaeib, T., Abuzneid, S., & Elleithy, K. (2024, November). Proposed Framework for a Comprehensive Cybersecurity Risk Management Strategy. In *2024 IEEE Long Island Systems, Applications and Technology Conference (LISAT)* (pp. 1-6). IEEE. DOI: 10.1109/LISAT63094.2024.10808119

Formosa, P., Wilson, M., & Richards, D. (2021). A principlist framework for cybersecurity ethics. *Computers & Security, 109*, 102382. DOI: 10.1016/j.cose.2021.102382

Gonipalli, B., Rahaman, M., Gaurav, A., Nedjah, N., Gupta, B. B., & Chu, K. T. (2025, July). A Machine Learning-Based Novel Approach for Real-Time Detection of Digital Arrest Fraud. In *2025 International Conference on Emerging Information Technology and Engineering Solutions (EITES)* (pp. 1-6). IEEE. DOI: 10.1109/EITES66543.2025.00010

Hafez, I. Y., Hafez, A. Y., Saleh, A., Abd El-Mageed, A. A., & Abohany, A. A. (2025). A systematic review of AI-enhanced techniques in credit card fraud detection. *Journal of Big Data, 12*(1), 6. DOI: 10.1186/s40537-024-01048-8

Halpin, D., & Todd, S. (2024). Public-Private Collaboration for Combatting Cyber Fraud. In *Financial Crime, Law and Governance: Navigating Challenges in Different Contexts* (pp. 287–311). Springer Nature Switzerland. DOI: 10.1007/978-3-031-59547-9_12

Hjorthen, F. D., & Pattison, J. (2023). Proportionality in cyberwar and just war theory. *Ethics & Global Politics, 16*(1), 1–24. DOI: 10.1080/16544951.2023.2179244

Johora, F. T., Hasan, R., Farabi, S. F., Alam, M. Z., Sarkar, I., & Al Mahmud, A. (2024, June). AI advances: Enhancing banking security with fraud detection. In *2024 First International Conference on Technological Innovations and Advance Computing (TIACOMP)* (pp. 289-294). IEEE. DOI: 10.1109/TIACOMP64125.2024.00055

Jun, Y., Craig, A., Shafik, W., & Sharif, L. (2021). Artificial intelligence application in cybersecurity and cyberdefense. *Wireless Communications and Mobile Computing, 2021*(1), 3329581. DOI: 10.1155/2021/3329581

Kamalaruban, P., Pi, Y., Burrell, S., Drage, E., Skalski, P., Wong, J., & Sutton, D. (2024, November). Evaluating fairness in transaction fraud models: Fairness metrics, bias audits, and challenges. In *Proceedings of the 5th ACM International Conference on AI in Finance* (pp. 555-563). DOI: 10.1145/3677052.3698666

Lokhande, M., Raut, P., Gawali, K., Ahirrao, M., & Bhande, A. (2024, August). Artificial intelligence for detecting cyber attacks in deepfake & identity theft. In *2024 8th International Conference on Computing, Communication, Control and Automation (ICCUBEA)* (pp. 1-6). IEEE. DOI: 10.1109/ICCUBEA61740.2024.10774771

Luo, Y., Xiao, Y., Cheng, L., Peng, G., & Yao, D. (2021). Deep learning-based anomaly detection in cyber-physical systems: Progress and opportunities. *ACM Computing Surveys, 54*(5), 1–36. DOI: 10.1145/3453155

Martín, A. G., Beltrán, M., Fernández-Isabel, A., & de Diego, I. M. (2021). An approach to detect user behaviour anomalies within identity federations. *computers & security, 108*, 102356.

Neuwirth, R. J. (2023). Prohibited artificial intelligence practices in the proposed EU artificial intelligence act (AIA). *Computer Law & Security Review, 48*, 105798. DOI: 10.1016/j.clsr.2023.105798

Pawlak, P., & Barmpaliou, P. N. (2017). Politics of cybersecurity capacity building: Conundrum and opportunity. *Journal of Cyber Policy, 2*(1), 123–144. DOI: 10.1080/23738871.2017.1294610

Ren, L., Hu, R., Li, D., Liu, Y., Wu, J., Zang, Y., & Hu, W. (2023). Dynamic graph neural network-based fraud detectors against collaborative fraudsters. *Knowledge-Based Systems, 278*, 110888. DOI: 10.1016/j.knosys.2023.110888

Sarna, N. J., Rithen, F. A., Jui, U. S., Belal, S., Amin, A., Oishee, T. K., & Islam, A. M. (2025). AI Driven Fraud Detection Models in Financial Networks: A Review. *IEEE Access : Practical Innovations, Open Solutions.*

Schäfer, M., Fuchs, M., Strohmeier, M., Engel, M., Liechti, M., & Lenders, V. (2019, May). BlackWidow: Monitoring the dark web for cyber security information. In *2019 11th International Conference on Cyber Conflict (CyCon)* (Vol. 900, pp. 1-21). IEEE.

Simanjuntak, E. L. (2018, July). Cross–Border Law Enforcement Against Money Laundering Suspects In South East Asia Nations (Asean) Through "Mutual Legal Assistance" And Its Interaction To Asean Economic Community. [). IOP Publishing.]. *IOP Conference Series. Earth and Environmental Science, 175*(1), 012189. DOI: 10.1088/1755-1315/175/1/012189

Singh, B., & Kaunert, C. (2025). Intelligent Machine Learning Solutions for Cybersecurity: Legal and Ethical Considerations in a Global Context. In *Advancements in Intelligent Process Automation* (pp. 359-386). IGI Global.

Sood, P., Sharma, C., Nijjer, S., & Sakhuja, S. (2023). Review the role of artificial intelligence in detecting and preventing financial fraud using natural language processing. *International Journal of System Assurance Engineering and Management, 14*(6), 2120–2135. DOI: 10.1007/s13198-023-02043-7

Tawil, S., & Tarawneh, A. (2025). Technology and the law: countering cybercrime and fraud in the digital age. In *Artificial Intelligence in the Digital Era: Economic, Legislative and Media Perspectives* (pp. 1095–1105). Springer Nature Switzerland.

Van de Weijer, S. G., Leukfeldt, R., & Bernasco, W. (2019). Determinants of reporting cybercrime: A comparison between identity theft, consumer fraud, and hacking. *European Journal of Criminology, 16*(4), 486–508. DOI: 10.1177/1477370818773610

Walters, R., & Novak, M. (2021). *Cyber security, artificial intelligence, data protection & the law*. Springer. DOI: 10.1007/978-981-16-1665-5

Xu, R. (2022, March). Criminal Law Protection of Citizens' Personal Information–From the Perspective of New Cyber Fraud in the Era of Artificial Intelligence. In *International Conference on Business and Policy Studies* (pp. 536-548). Singapore: Springer Nature Singapore. DOI: 10.1007/978-981-19-5727-7_54

Zhang, Y., Tong, J., Wang, Z., & Gao, F. (2020, March). Customer transaction fraud detection using xgboost model. In *2020 International Conference on Computer Engineering and Application (ICCEA)* (pp. 554-558). IEEE. DOI: 10.1109/ICCEA50009.2020.00122

Zhang, Z., Al Hamadi, H., Damiani, E., Yeun, C. Y., & Taher, F. (2022). Explainable artificial intelligence applications in cyber security: State-of-the-art in research. *IEEE Access : Practical Innovations, Open Solutions, 10*, 93104–93139. DOI: 10.1109/ACCESS.2022.3204051

KEY TERMS AND DEFINITIONS

Algorithmic Bias: Systematic, unjust discrimination that is being expressed in AI outputs as a result of biased or incomplete training data that results in disproportionate harm to specific groups.

Anomaly Detection: An artificial intelligence approach to data analysis that attempts to detect unusual patterns that deviate from the normative behaviours of systems, that may indicate fraud or other malicious activity.

Arrest Fraud ala Digital: One of the scams, where criminals pretend to be law enforcement agents scaring victims into paying fines, giving personal data, or giving remote access to computers or other devices.

Artificial Intelligence Act (EU AI Act): A proposed EU regulation that classifies AI systems depending on the level of risk, alongside development and user requirements, including strict requirements for high risk applications such as fraud detection.

Artificial Intelligence: One of the branches of computer science that is dedicated to the development of the systems which can fulfill the tasks that usually need the human perception of intelligence, like the pattern recognition, decision-making, predictive analysis, etc. With fraud prevention, AI can be applied to detect anomalies, suspicious patterns, and react to threats that emerge.

California Consumer Privacy Act (CCPA): A Californian state privacy act that gives residents the right to access, delete and opt-out of having their personal data collected.

Cyber Fraud: Criminal conduct used through digital connection to misrepresent other persons or institutions to swindle money. This involves phishing, payment fraud, creation of synthetic identities, and arrest scams on the internet.

Decision Support Systems: Bioinformatics is the computer-based technology that helps human decision-makers by providing data analysis and presenting conclusions that may be acted upon. DSS can be used in the process of cyber fraud prevention including prioritising alerts, risk evaluation and selecting interventions, provided by security teams.

Explainable AI (XAI): AI systems that offer explainable decisions that allow the user or regulator to understand the fairness, accuracy, and compliance.

General Data Protection Regulation (GDPR): An all-encompassing EU data protection law setting strict requirements with regard to the collection, processing and utilisation of personal data, including a ban on automated decision-making without the involvement of human beings.

Identity Theft: The illegal collection and utilisation of the personal information of someone-names, social security numbers, or financial information-usually with the purpose of perpetrating a crime or fraud.

Mutual Legal Assistance Treaty: An international agreement to allow the exchange of evidence and information between countries involved in criminal proceedings, including those related to cybercrime.

Regulatory Sandbox: A controlled environment controlled by authorities where organisations can try out new technologies and processes with supervision, and innovation can be tried out but risks can be managed.

Threat Intelligence Sharing: The sharing of information on cyber threats, hacking methods and vulnerability domains between entities for the purpose of improving collective security.

Chapter 8
Hermeneutics and Anti-Money Laundering (AML) Policies in the Digital Age:
A Comparative Study of Indonesia and Latvia

I. Made Laut Mertha Jaya
https://orcid.org/0000-0001-9722-7217
Universitas Mahakarya Asia, Indonesia

Miguel Angel Esquivias
https://orcid.org/0000-0002-1282-6163
Universitas Airlangga, Indonesia

ABSTRACT

This study uses hermeneutics to critically analyze Anti-Money Laundering (AML) policies in Indonesia and Latvia, particularly in the context of the digital era. The study finds that although both countries have adopted AML frameworks based on FATF standards, vulnerabilities remain, particularly in the oversight of the informal financial sector in Indonesia and the handling of financial scandals in Latvia. The digital era has introduced sophisticated money laundering methods through cryptocurrency and DeFi, creating regulatory "grey areas". The research recommends more concrete harmonization of cryptocurrency regulations, such as cryptocurrency taxation in Indonesia and MiCA compliance in Latvia, and proposes AML technology evaluation metrics to strengthen detection effectiveness. These findings

DOI: 10.4018/979-8-3373-4149-1.ch008

underscore the urgent need for in-depth policy interpretation, adaptive international collaboration, and technological innovation to address the evolving global threat of money laundering

1. INTRODUCTION

Money laundering has become a global problem due to the tremendous changes in world markets (Ariyanto, 2020; Buchanan & Buchanan, 2018; Easter, 2018; Levi, 2020; Mardiansyah, 2021; Wilson, 2019). The estimated value of money laundering reaches between $800 billion and $2 trillion annually. This figure represents approximately 2% to 5% of the global Gross Domestic Product (GDP), highlighting the significant impact of money laundering on the stability of the world economy. This activity is not only widespread globally but is also particularly significant in certain regions.

The Asia-Pacific region has become one of the main hubs of money laundering, with estimated figures reaching $1.5 trillion. This large amount reflects the major challenges faced by countries in the region in addressing regulatory and oversight weaknesses, as well as the high volume of trade that is often exploited to disguise the origin of illicit funds. On the other hand, the United States is also one of the countries with a high volume of money laundering, reaching approximately $300 billion per year. As a global financial center, the U.S. faces significant pressure in balancing the openness of its financial system with efforts to control financial crimes.

One of the primary methods used in money laundering is Trade-Based Money Laundering (TBML), which utilizes international trade activities as a means to conceal and move illicit funds. The estimated value of TBML reaches $1 trillion annually, making it one of the most complex and difficult methods for authorities to detect. In recent years, money laundering trends have also begun shifting toward new technologies, particularly cryptocurrencies. In 2022, approximately $23.8 billion was laundered through crypto transactions, reflecting the increasing use of digital assets by criminals due to their anonymous and decentralized nature. Overall, this data demonstrates that money laundering has evolved into a complex global threat, exploiting various sectors and regions to obscure the origins of illegal funds. Therefore, stronger international cooperation, enhanced regulatory capacity, and the use of advanced technologies are essential in the detection and prevention of money laundering activities (Table 1).

Table 1. Estimated Annual Global Money Laundering 2025

Category	Estimated Value (USD)	Percentage of Global GDP
Total Global Money Laundering	$800 billion – $2 trillion	2% – 5% of global GDP
Money Laundering in Asia-Pacific	$1.5 trillion	–
Money Laundering in the U.S.	$300 billion	–
Trade-Based Money Laundering	$1 trillion	–
Crypto-Based Laundering (2022)	$23.8 billion	–

Sources: Global data tabulation, 2024.

Money laundering is categorized as a transnational organized crime (Rusanov & Pudovochkin, 2021). Money laundering also poses a threat from an economic perspective by reducing tax revenues and building a substantial underground economy, often undermining legitimate business and disrupting financial institutions (Khelil et al., 2024). Money laundering also undermines democratic institutions and threatens good governance by promoting public corruption through bribery, illegal campaign contributions, and corporate tax abuse (Ariyanto, 2020). In Indonesia, the majority of money laundering crimes originate from the proceeds of corruption (Mardiansyah, 2021; Rengganis & Susanto, 2023). Perpetrators of corruption often use various means to launder money, such as investing the proceeds of corruption into new businesses or other companies, or using irregular financial transactions with the ultimate goal of disguising the origin of the funds (Grossmann et al., 2021). Money laundering derived from corruption proceeds is a significant phenomenon in Indonesia. While exact data on the number of cases and the value of laundered funds is difficult to ascertain, corruption is clearly one of the main sources of laundered funds. This demonstrates the importance of corruption eradication efforts and strong law enforcement to prevent and resolve corruption-related money laundering cases.

At this time, the international world is increasingly intensifying its efforts to combat money laundering practices, both through bilateral cooperation between two countries and international cooperation forums (Ajide & Ojeyinka, 2024; Dewi Rengganis & Setiawan Susanto, 2023; Dobrowolski & Sułkowski, 2020; Gaviyau & Sibindi, 2023; Gerbrands et al., 2022; Island, 2024; Pol, 2020; Rose, 2020). This is because money laundering can disrupt the financial system and reduce the credibility of financial institutions (Khelil et al., 2024). Its impacts are widespread, ranging from economic distortions that hinder growth to reduced investor confidence and increased risk in the financial system (Ajide & Ojeyinka, 2024). Economic Distortion and Financial Instability arise due to the uncontrolled flow of funds from illegal activities. This will have an impact first on sectors such as property, capital markets, and luxury goods (Pol, 2020). The money from this laundering tends to be used speculatively, which can trigger inflation in certain sectors without being supported by real economic growth (Khelil et al., 2024; Loayza et al., 2019).

This instability can certainly hinder sustainable economic predictions and complicate effective economic policy planning (Dobrowolski & Sułkowski, 2020). Another impact is that it hinders foreign investment and damages market confidence, meaning that countries with a weak reputation for handling money laundering are often considered risky by foreign investors (Wilson, 2019). Foreign investors generally seek an environment that is stable, transparent and has legal certainty. If they see a high risk of illegal practices and weak financial supervision, they are likely to withdraw or be reluctant to invest. This condition can reduce the flow of foreign direct investment (FDI) (Ofoeda et al., 2022). FDI plays an important role in driving economic growth, creating jobs, and enhancing technology and management transfer. Therefore, a poor reputation for handling money laundering can hinder FDI inflows, slow development, and undermine overall market confidence (Jetin et al., 2024). In addition, confidence in the financial market also decreases, because investors are doubtful about the transparency and security of their funds, which leads to lower investment rates and hampers a country's economic growth (Muryani et al., 2021).

Overall, these impacts create serious challenges for the government and endanger the economic welfare of the community. Therefore, the government must issue stricter policies and regulations to monitor, detect, and combat international money laundering practices (Armey & Melese, 2018; Cuadrado-ballesteros et al., 2020; Manthovani, 2023). Bilateral cooperation is also important to improve the effectiveness of law enforcement and cross-border information sharing, especially regarding suspicious fund flows. These efforts include monitoring financial transactions, examining the source of funds, and strengthening banking regulations, including strict know your customer (KYC) policies (Africa, 2017; Bello et al., 2025). With these steps, it is hoped that the negative impact of money laundering on economic stability can be reduced and transparency and integrity in the financial sector can be encouraged.

Countries around the world have also begun to strengthen anti-money laundering regulations through national policies and international co-operation. There are even international cooperation forums such as the Financial Action Task Force 1989 (FATF) which consists of countries in Europe, North America, and Asia (Gaviyau & Sibindi, 2023). These countries also belong to the G7 group by combating money laundering practices, terrorism financing, and other threats to the integrity of the international financial system. In fact, every country must have an anti-money laundering legal regime (FATF, 2025). FATF member countries (as of May 2025) include Austria, Belgium, Denmark, Finland, France, Germany, Greece, Ireland, Italy, Luxembourg, Netherlands, Norway, Portugal, Spain, Sweden, Switzerland, United Kingdom, Iceland, Turkey, United States, Canada, Mexico, Japan, South Korea, China, India, Indonesia, Saudi Arabia, Israel, Malaysia, and Singapore.

Membership is subject to change, and some countries can be on watch or suspended status (e.g. Russia is currently suspended since 2022 due to its invasion of Ukraine).

Indonesia is officially a full member of the Financial Action Task Force (FATF) (FATF, 2025). The membership status was obtained after going through a series of tests, both from the mutual evaluation review (MER) on-site visit assessment by the FATF team in July-August 2020 and the review conducted at the FATF Plenary Meeting in June 2023. Indonesia's membership in FATF will have a positive impact on the credibility of the country's economy, namely increasing positive perceptions of Indonesia's financial system, and is expected to also have an impact on rapid economic growth through investment both at home and abroad (Gaviyau & Sibindi, 2023). On the other hand, the European Commission also proposed strengthening the supervision system in every European Union financial institution to address the rampant practice of money laundering. According to a report from the Basel Institute on Governance in 2019, there are the 5 countries with the highest crime risk ratings for money laundering in the European Union are: Cyprus, Italy, Hungary, Latvia and the Netherlands (Basel, 2019). Of the five countries, Latvia showed a negative trend, where there was an increase in the risk of money laundering offences of more than 0.1 points from the previous period, while the other 4 countries showed a positive or neutral trend (Greco, 2021). This is likely due to the EU's Prevention of Money Laundering and Financing of Terrorism and Proliferation Act, which Latvia strictly adheres to the international AMLD-5 (5th EU Anti-Money Laundering Directive) regime (Gise-Sproģe et al., 2021).

Although international regulations have been issued in both Indonesia and Latvia, there continues to be substantial discussion regarding typologies, failures, and successes in anti-money laundering (AML) efforts in these countries, particularly in relation to the ABLV Bank scandal in Latvia and the role of informal banking in Indonesia. ABLV Bank, one of the largest private banks in Latvia, came under international scrutiny in February 2018 when the U.S. Financial Crimes Enforcement Network (FinCEN) accused it of being a primary institution involved in money laundering. The bank was allegedly facilitating illegal transactions, including those related to North Korea's nuclear weapons program, as well as corruption activities in Russia and Ukraine. This scandal exposed systemic weaknesses in Latvia's banking oversight, where ABLV was suspected of using shell companies and falsified documentation to conceal the origins of illicit funds. Furthermore, former senior officials of the bank, including one of its owners, were charged with laundering €2.1 billion.

In Indonesia, discussions around the effectiveness of anti-money laundering efforts often highlight the challenges of supervising the informal financial sector, such as savings and loan cooperatives, rotating savings groups, and community-based financial services. These sectors are vulnerable to misuse due to a lack of strict regulation and oversight. Although Indonesia has strengthened its legal and institutional framework to combat money laundering, including through the Financial Transaction Reports and Analysis Center (PPATK), challenges remain in integrating the informal sector into the formal financial system and ensuring compliance with AML regulations. These two cases show that without adequate supervision, both large financial institutions and the informal sector can become conduits for illicit financial activities.

This study was conducted with the aim of analyzing policies related to the prevention of international money laundering in Indonesia and Latvia, then finding several important points that are the weaknesses and strengths of the implementation of the policy. This is important to do so that it can be a study material for public policy makers in each country in evaluating policies and improving the weaknesses that exist in bilateral cooperation in the current digital era. This Policy Evaluation Research is conducted using the hermeneutic method which is an effort to measure the results or impact of an activity, program, or project by comparing it with the goals that have been set, and how to achieve them. This Evaluation Research also performs a control and examination function. That is, it can be used as information to top management, whether the program activities have been implemented correctly and brought the expected results or vice versa. This research is still rarely conducted in Indonesia, so the contribution of this research is very important for many parties in conducting scientific studies of public policies related to the prevention of interstate ML, especially in the digital era. In addition, this research also aims to promote a deeper understanding of the challenges faced by both countries (Indonesia and Latvia) in enforcing anti-money laundering measures in the digital era. By doing so, this research can provide valuable insights into how policy development in the digitalization era can create more effective strategies in combating money laundering at the international level.

2. THEORY AND CONCEPTUAL FRAMEWORK

2.1. Grounded Theory

This study highlights two theories which according to researchers have an important role in underpinning the thought process of this research problem, namely Regulation Theory (Posner, 1974; Stigler, 1971) and the Economic Theory of Crime (Becker, 1968; Ehrlic, 1973). Regulation Theory starts from the premise that without clear regulation, economic activity can become fertile ground for opportunistic behaviour, including illegal practices, such as money laundering. In the modern financial system, where cross-border transactions are increasingly easy to do, regulation plays a role as a "guard" that regulates and monitors economic activities to prevent potential risks that arise from illegal practices. In the context of anti-money laundering, Regulation Theory explains that Anti-Money Laundering policies, such as suspicious transaction reporting, customer verification requirements, and audit procedures, are not only as a constraint on economic activity. But also, as an effort to protect the integrity of the financial system. Through strict regulation, countries can create an environment that is not friendly to money laundering activities, thereby reducing the risk of funding for criminal activities.(Manthovani, 2023). Regulation also serves to maintain public trust and economic stability. By implementing consistent policies, financial institutions, companies, and market players can feel safer because there is a legal framework that protects them from losses due to detrimental criminal acts (Sugiharti et al., 2022). Furthermore, the regulations that are implemented also encourage transparency and accountability, thereby increasing the credibility of the financial market in the eyes of the public and investors. Regulation Theory also emphasizes that effective supervision and law enforcement are essential for the regulation to run well. Without strict law enforcement, regulation will lose its effectiveness.

Meanwhile, Economics of Crime Theory differs from other theories because its focus is on analyzing crime, including money laundering, from an economic perspective. This concept was introduced by economist Gary Becker. This theory considers criminal acts as the result of rational economic decisions, where perpetrators weigh the costs and benefits of committing a crime. In simple terms, perpetrators will engage in illegal activities if the potential benefits are considered greater than the risks or costs of punishment they may face. This theory also highlights that the higher the "cost" of regulation, the lower the incentive for perpetrators to launder money.(Becker, 1968). In the context of Anti-Money Laundering, stricter regulatory enforcement, suspicious transaction reporting, and harsher penalties can be seen as tools to increase the "cost" of money laundering activities, making them less attractive to perpetrators. In addition, the Economic Theory of Crime also provides a unique perspective in assessing anti-money laundering policies, by measuring how policy changes can reduce or increase incentives for money launderers, and the economic impact of such activities.

The Regulation Theory complements this by emphasizing the role of governance and institutional frameworks in shaping compliance behavior. Effective regulations, when consistently enforced, not only act as deterrents but also establish a culture of accountability among financial institutions. For instance, mandatory Know Your Customer (KYC) procedures and real-time monitoring systems demonstrate how regulatory measures directly influence operational practices, closing loopholes that money launderers often exploit (Bello et al., 2025). From the perspective of the Economic Theory of Crime, policies such as freezing illicit assets or imposing substantial fines on violators disrupt the cost-benefit analysis of potential offenders.

By increasing the risks and reducing the profitability of money laundering, these measures align with the theory's principle that crime decreases when its expected costs outweigh its benefits. Additionally, economic modeling can help policymakers predict the adaptive strategies of money launderers, allowing for more proactive and dynamic regulatory responses (Sukardi, 2020).

Together, these theories underscore the interconnectedness of robust regulation and economic disincentives in shaping effective AML policies. Empirical studies further reinforce this connection, showing that countries with stringent regulatory environments and a focus on economic deterrence experience lower rates of money laundering. By integrating insights from both theories, policymakers can design AML frameworks that are not only punitive but also preventive, targeting the root causes and financial motivations of these illicit activities (interpreted through Figure 1).

Figure 1. Diagram conceptual framework

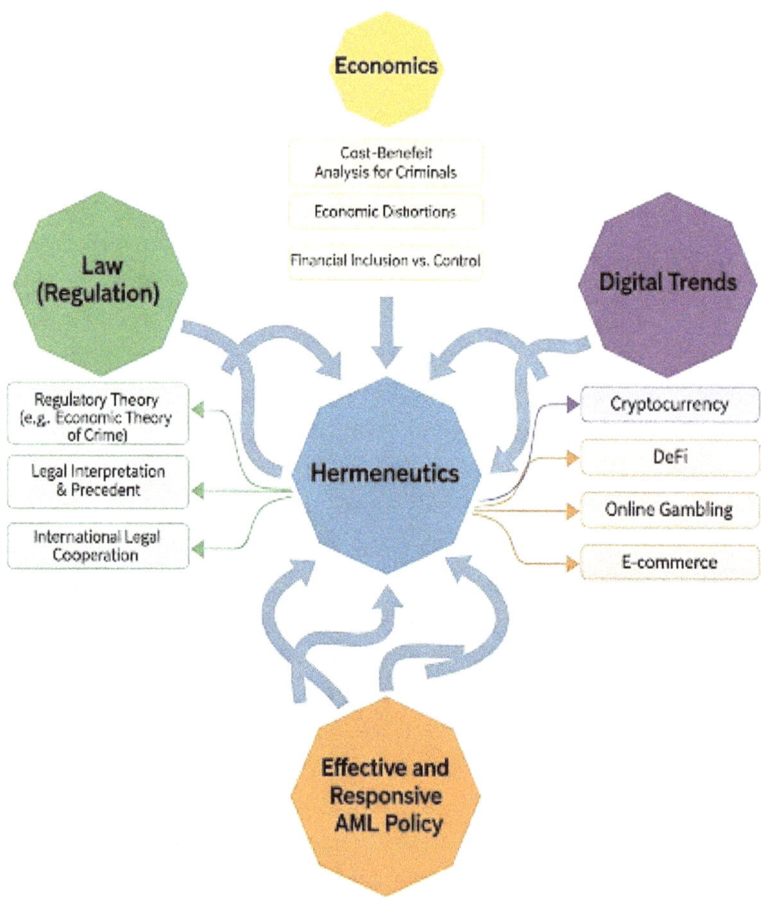

2.2. Money Laundering in The Digital Era

In today's digital era, the practice of money laundering has undergone a major transformation (Khelil et al., 2024; Manthovani, 2023). Technology that brings convenience and speed to financial transactions has also been utilized by criminals to disguise the origin of criminal proceeds (Sukardi, 2020). Modern money laundering still follows three main stages: placement, which involves placing illicit funds into the financial system; layering, which involves disguising the trail of funds through a series of complex transactions; and integration, which involves returning the funds to the formal economy as assets that appear legitimate (Gaviyau & Sibindi, 2023). However, these three stages are now carried out in a much more sophisticated and covert manner thanks to digital technology.

One of the most commonly used mediums is cryptocurrency, such as Bitcoin or Monero (Hedman et al., 2021). Due to their anonymous and decentralized nature, these digital assets are an ideal choice for perpetrators to move funds across countries undetected (van Wegberg et al., 2018). They can even use the services of crypto mixers or tumblers, which mix transactions from multiple users to obscure the origin of the funds. In addition, DeFi (Decentralized Finance) platforms enable transactions without intermediaries, so no entity can verify the authenticity of the source of funds (Chainalysis, 2024) (Table 2).

Table 2. Current Modes and Digital Media Used

Media/Method	Explanation
Cryptocurrency	Transactions using Bitcoin, Ethereum, Monero, etc., are difficult to trace due to their anonymous or pseudo-anonymous nature.
Mixing Services / Tumblers	Services that "mix" cryptocurrencies from multiple users to obscure the origin of funds and make them harder to trace.
Decentralized Finance (DeFi)	The use of decentralized financial protocols without intermediaries to conceal the origin of digital assets.
Online Gambling Platforms	Online gambling websites are used to disguise illicit funds as gambling winnings.
E-commerce & Marketplaces	Creating fake transactions on online stores to launder money (e.g., paying oneself for fictitious goods).
Virtual Assets & NFTs	Buying and selling high-value digital assets (such as NFTs) to covertly transfer value.
Fintech & E-wallets	Exploiting the ease of creating digital wallet accounts for fast and anonymous transfers across platforms.
Money Mule Networks	Using individuals (knowingly or unknowingly) to transfer funds between accounts in order to obscure the money trail.

This phenomenon brings great challenges for authorities. The anonymous nature of digital transactions, the high speed, and the involvement of many international jurisdictions make investigations extremely complex. In addition, many countries still do not have strict regulations on digital assets and blockchain-based financial systems. This is exploited by perpetrators to operate in a legal 'grey zone'.

However, efforts have been made to counter this trend. Regulators around the world are starting to implement Know Your Customer (KYC) and identity verification policies on crypto services. International organizations such as FATF have also issued new guidelines, such as the Travel Rule, which requires the exchange of sender and receiver information in virtual asset transactions. With increasingly complex challenges, money laundering prevention efforts in the digital age require cross-border collaboration, regulatory updates, and the continuous use of advanced technology. The digital age is not only a new terrain for financial criminals, but also a stage for innovation in maintaining the integrity of the global financial system.

2.3. The Impact of Money Laundering on Economic Sustainability

Money laundering poses a serious threat to economic sustainability as it can undermine the financial system, weaken trust in institutions, and divert resources from productive sectors (Khelil et al., 2024). Money laundering allows illicit funds, which often originate from corruption, tax evasion or organized crime to be disguised as coming from legitimate sources (Matar, 2023). When such funds enter the formal economic system, they can disrupt the fair allocation of capital and reduce the efficiency of financial markets.

One of the main impacts of money laundering is the distortion of financial flows and investments (Ofoeda et al., 2022). In vulnerable countries, proceeds of crime are often invested in sectors such as luxury property, high-value goods or financial instruments, leading to unnatural price inflation (Tiwari et al., 2020). Not only does this marginalize legitimate investors, but it also directs resources to sectors where it is easiest to launder money, rather than to sectors that provide real-social and economic value. As a result, competition becomes unfair and innovation is weakened, especially among small and medium enterprises, which are the pillars of the economy and essential for sustainable development (FATF, 2021).

Furthermore, the presence of money laundered funds in the financial system can also undermine the integrity and stability of financial institutions (FATF, 2025). Banks or financial institutions that fail to detect or report suspicious transactions may suffer reputational damage, legal sanctions, and disconnection from international financial networks. This has a direct impact on decreasing investor confidence, and increasing regulatory burdens that can hamper national economic resilience. Macroeconomically, countries with weak anti-money laundering (AML) frameworks are often labelled as high-risk jurisdictions. This negative reputation discourages foreign direct investment (FDI), raises international borrowing costs, and can lead to exclusion from the global financial system. As a result, economic opportunities shrink and growth becomes fragile.

The most detrimental in the long run is the hampering of sustainable development. Illicit fund flows facilitated by money laundering erode the country's potential tax revenue. These funds could have been allocated to public services such as health, education, infrastructure and environmental protection. In developing countries, this triggers capital flight, widens economic disparities, and hinders the achievement of the Sustainable Development Goals (SDGs) (FATF, 2025). Not only that, money laundering also strengthens the criminal networks it seeks to hide. Proceeds of crime that have been 'cleaned' are often reused to bribe officials, fund organized crime and terrorism, creating a vicious cycle that undermines governance and weakens state institutions.

As such, money laundering is not a victimless crime. It undermines the foundations of sustainable development by destroying financial transparency, distorting markets and strengthening criminal networks. Addressing this challenge requires a strong legal framework, international cooperation, and the use of technology to detect and interrupt the flow of illicit funds. Without decisive and coordinated efforts, economic sustainability in many countries will remain under threat.

2.4. International Anti-Money Laundering (AML) Policies in Indonesia and Latvia

In Indonesia and Latvia, the Anti-Money Laundering (AML) framework was developed based on international guidelines from the Financial Action Task Force (FATF), which provides global standards for preventing money laundering and terrorism financing. Both countries have adjusted their regulations to align with FATF recommendations and regional policies (Table 3).

Table 3. Comparison of AML regulations in Indonesia and Latvia

Aspect	Indonesia	Latvia
Main Regulation	Law No. 8 of 2010 on the Prevention and Eradication of the Crime of Money Laundering	1. Law No. 88/2008: Law on the Prevention of Money Laundering and Terrorism and Proliferation Financing 2. Financial and Capital Market Law No. 355/1999 3. Law on the Register of Enterprises No. 482/2001 4. EU AML Directives (4th, 5th, 6th) 5. FIU Latvia Regulations
Supervisory Authorities	Financial Transaction Reports and Analysis Center (PPATK), Bank Indonesia, Financial Services Authority (OJK)	Financial Intelligence Unit (FIU Latvia), Financial and Capital Market Commission (FCMC), MONEYVAL
Obligations of Institutions	Report suspicious transactions, implement internal monitoring systems	Conduct Customer Due Diligence (CDD), report suspicious activities, identify Ultimate Beneficial Owners (UBO), ensure business transparency
International Collaboration	Cooperates with the Asia/Pacific Group on Money Laundering (APG) and foreign law enforcement authorities	Active participation in MONEYVAL and follows FATF and EU standards
Focus of Reforms/ Improvements	Strengthening internal controls, enhancing reporting quality, international law enforcement cooperation	Reforming supervisory systems, improving risk detection, monitoring virtual asset transactions, enhancing criminal sanctions
International Standards	Refers to FATF recommendations, mainly through APG collaboration	Directly adopts EU AML Directives (4th, 5th, and 6th) and FATF recommendations
Additional Notes	APG evaluation shows improved compliance and international cooperation in enforcement	Latvia continuously updates its legal framework to address legal loopholes and enhance transparency, especially in corporate structures and virtual asset sectors

a) AML Regulation in Indonesia

Indonesia regulates the prevention of money laundering through Law No. 8 of 2010 concerning the Prevention and Eradication of the Crime of Money Laundering (Manthovani, 2023). This regulation stipulates the obligation to report suspicious transactions for financial institutions and other designated bodies, with the aim of detecting and preventing money laundering practices in the financial sector. Supervision and implementation of this regulation is carried out by the Financial Transaction Reports and Analysis Center (PPATK), which collaborates with international institutions such as the Asia/Pacific Group on Money Laundering (APG) to improve the quality of reporting and supervision. In addition, Bank Indonesia and the Financial

Services Authority (OJK) are also involved in monitoring compliance with AML regulations in the banking and non-bank financial services sectors (Laowo, 2022). Based on the results of the APG evaluation, Indonesia has strengthened internal controls and collaborated with international authorities in law enforcement to close loopholes that may be exploited in money laundering.

b) AML Regulation in Latvia

Latvia has a comprehensive framework for combating money laundering and terrorism financing, largely adapted from EU directives and FATF standards. Supervision in Latvia is carried out by the Financial Intelligence Unit (FIU Latvia) and supported by MONEYVAL, a body that evaluates European countries for compliance with international AML standards. In recent years, MONEYVAL and FATF assessed Latvia's level of compliance and identified a number of areas requiring improvement.

In Latvia, Anti-Money Laundering (AML) regulations are regulated by several main laws that follow the European Union directives and the Financial Action Task Force (FATF) recommendations. Here are some of the regulations along with their numbers and years of issuance:

1. **Law on the Prevention of Money Laundering and Terrorism and Proliferation Financing** (No. 88/09.10.2008): This is the basic law for money laundering prevention in Latvia, which regulates the obligations of financial and non-financial institutions, including law and accounting firms, to carry out customer due diligence and report suspicious activity. The law is constantly updated to meet new requirements set by the FATF and the European Union. The latest revision adds the obligation to identify the ultimate beneficial owner and strengthens the monitoring mechanism.
2. **Financial and Capital Market Law** (No. 355/1999): This law covers the supervision of the financial sector and capital markets in Latvia, including banks, financial institutions and other related entities. The law requires monitoring and reporting of suspicious activity, which is overseen by the Financial and Capital Market Commission (FCMC) as the main regulator for AML in the sector.
3. **The Law on the Register of Enterprises of the Republic of Latvia**(No. 482/2001): This regulation introduces a beneficial ownership registration system for companies, which allows for increased transparency regarding parties who have significant influence or control over an entity. This is an important step to reduce the risk of money laundering through companies established in Latvia.
4. **Implementation of EU Anti-Money Laundering Directives (AMLD) 4, 5 and 6**: Latvia has adopted the European Union directives on the prevention of money laundering and financing of terrorism, including:

- **Fourth AMLD (EU Directive 2015/849)**: Requires the implementation of risk-based due diligence for customers, particularly in the banking and financial sectors.
- **Fifth AMLD (EU Directive 2018/843)**: Tighten rules for transactions with virtual assets, increase supervision of cryptocurrency service providers, and expand the list of reporting entities.
- **Sixth AMLD (EU Directive 2018/1673)**: Expanding the definition of money laundering and introducing minimum criminal penalties for perpetrators found to be involved in this practice.

5. **Financial Intelligence Unit (FIU Latvia) Regulation**: The Latvian FIU is the main unit responsible for receiving, analyzing and reporting suspicious transactions. The unit operates based on the guidelines issued in the Latvian FIU's Annual Reports and Guidelines, which are constantly updated to address new threats in money laundering and terrorism financing.

Latvia also actively participates in MONEYVAL, a body under the Council of Europe that evaluates the implementation of AML in its member states and assesses its effectiveness.

2.5. International Cooperation Indonesia and Latvia in Monitoring Money Laundering Activities

International cooperation between Indonesia and Latvia in monitoring anti-money laundering (AML) activities in the current digital era has not been specifically documented. However, both countries are active in global efforts to combat money laundering and terrorism financing through participation in international organizations and the implementation of domestic policies that are in line with international standards. However, both countries are connected in an international network through active participation in FATF (for Indonesia) and MONEYVAL (for Latvia). This cooperation allows both countries to access the latest guidance, receive regular evaluations, and update their AML policies to remain relevant in the face of increasingly complex money laundering methods.

- **Financial Action Task Force (FATF)**: Indonesia is working towards becoming a full member of the FATF, an international organization that sets standards and promotes the effective implementation of legal, regulatory and operational measures to combat money laundering, terrorist financing and other related threats to the integrity of the financial system.
- **Egmont Group**: Indonesia's PPATK (Financial Transaction Reports and Analysis Center) is a member of the Egmont Group, which facilitates co-

operation and exchange of financial intelligence information between countries. Latvia, through its Financial Intelligence Unit, is also a member of the Egmont Group.

Even Indonesia through Bank Indonesia has developed the Indonesian Payment System (SPI) 2025 which emphasizes the balance between innovation and integrity of the payment system through the implementation of Anti-Money Laundering and Prevention of Terrorism Financing (APU PPT) policies. Meanwhile in Latvia, as a member of the European Union, Latvia implements Directive (EU) 2015/849 or the 4th Anti-Money Laundering Directive, which emphasizes increasing international and national cooperation in efforts to combat money laundering **(Table 4).**

Table 4. Key Elements of AML Cooperation between Indonesia and Latvia

Aspect	Indonesia	Latvia	Joint/International Cooperation
Global AML Network	Member of FATF observer; aiming for full membership	Member of MONEYVAL (Council of Europe's FATF-style body)	Both engage in FATF-style international networks
FIU Participation	PPATK (Financial Transaction Reports and Analysis Center)	FIU Latvia	Both are members of the Egmont Group for global intelligence exchange
Domestic Strategy	Indonesian Payment System Blueprint 2025 integrates AML/CFT principles	Implementation of 4th AMLD (EU Directive 2015/849)	Each aligns domestic policy with global standards
Technology Focus	Emphasis on digital integrity and innovation balance in payment system	Strengthened monitoring of digital financial activities and crypto	Potential cooperation in digital forensics, surveillance tech
Information Exchange	Via Egmont Group, APG reports, and bilateral dialogues	Via EU intelligence sharing, MONEYVAL evaluations	Encouraged real-time cross-border data sharing
Regulatory Harmonization	In progress with FATF standards	Aligned with EU AML directives	Supports harmonization for cross-border law enforcement
Bilateral Framework (Specific)	No formal bilateral AML agreement yet	No documented bilateral AML agreement with Indonesia	Opportunity for future bilateral or regional collaboration

In the digital era, the challenges of monitoring AML activities are increasingly complex, especially with the emergence of new financial technologies such as cryptocurrencies and digital payment platforms. International cooperation is crucial to:

- **Exchange of Information**: Real-time cross-border data sharing to detect and prevent suspicious transactions.
- **Technology Development**: Collaboration in the development and implementation of advanced digital transaction monitoring technology.
- **Harmonization of Regulations**: Aligning legal and regulatory frameworks to ensure effective law enforcement across jurisdictions.

3. METHODOLOGY

This research using the hermeneutic method, which is an interpretative-based qualitative approach. This method is a relevant and innovative choice in cross-disciplinary studies that include criminal law, economics, financial accounting, and anti-fraud policy. Hermeneutics provides a framework for understanding the meaning of anti-money laundering (AML) policies in depth, not only in terms of legal and regulatory texts, but also in the context of implementation, institutional structures, and stakeholder responses. The use of hermeneutics in AML policy studies is also based on the need to understand the normative substance and empirical praxis of the policy within the social, political, and economic context of a country. This approach allows for a thorough exploration of the symbolic, interpretive, and historical context dimensions of AML policy and practice (Sidik & Sulistyana, 2021). Hermeneutics as an interpretive research methodology provides a framework for understanding Anti-Money Laundering (AML) policies in depth, not only from legal texts and regulations, but also in the context of implementation, institutional structures, and stakeholder responses. This approach allows for the exploration of the symbolic, interpretive, and historical contextual dimensions of AML policies and practices. The advantages of hermeneutic method in this research:

- ✓ **Interdisciplinary and reflective**: Hermeneutics is flexible and able to bridge different disciplines, making it suitable for studies involving law, economics, and finance simultaneously.
- ✓ **Exploring the deepest meaning**: Not just describing what is written, but interpreting what is "intended" by the policy, and how it is accepted, interpreted, or even rejected by the public or stakeholders.
- ✓ **Critical of social and historical context**: Very useful for analyzing public policies that cannot be separated from political, economic, and cultural realities.
- ✓ **Encourage validation of meaning through dialogue**: Interpretations are tested not only by data, but also through scientific discourse and practical experience.

The hermeneutic method can connect three main elements, namely law, economics, and digital trends. Hermeneutics interprets how regulatory theory (such as Regulation and Crime Economics Theory) is applied in the formation of AML policy. This involves understanding how policies such as suspicious transaction reporting, customer verification requirements, and audit procedures function as guardians of the integrity of the financial system. Hermeneutics will analyze the 'intent' behind these regulations and how they are accepted or even rejected by stakeholders.

AML policies are analyzed from an economic perspective, considering how criminals weigh the costs and benefits of money laundering. This approach looks at how stricter enforcement of regulations, reporting of suspicious transactions, and heavier penalties increase the 'cost' of money laundering activities, thereby reducing their appeal. Hermeneutics can also interpret economic distortions and the impact on foreign investment resulting from money laundering.

Hermeneutics also enables analysis of money laundering transformations in the digital age, including the use of cryptocurrencies, mixing services, DeFi, online gambling platforms, and e-commerce to disguise illegal funds. Hermeneutics will help understand the challenges arising from the anonymous and decentralized nature of digital assets, as well as how adaptive policies and cross-border collaboration are needed to address the legal 'grey areas' in the digital space. In carrying out hermeneutic research, there are several stages (Wisarja, 2021). Following are the stages:

1. **Problem Formulation**

Researchers determine the focus of the research, namely the phenomenon, text, or event to be interpreted. Problems usually relate to meaning, symbols, or deep understanding.

2. **Initial Study (Pre-understanding)**

Researchers conduct literature reviews and initial explorations to understand the historical, cultural, and social context of the research object. This stage involves bringing initial understandings or prejudices that will be tested in the interpretation.

3. **Data collection**

Data is obtained from primary sources such as texts, documents, interviews, or observations. In text research, data often takes the form of writings rich in symbolism.

4. **Contextual Analysis**

Texts or phenomena are analyzed based on the historical, social, and cultural contexts that surround them. This stage helps to understand the conditions that underlie the meaning.

5. **Interpretation (Hermeneutic Circle)**

Researchers enter the hermeneutic circle process, which is repeatedly moving between parts and the whole text to find a coherent meaning. This interpretation is dynamic and takes into account various perspectives.

6. **Synthesis and Meaning**

Researchers conclude the results of the interpretation by finding meanings that are relevant to the context or purpose of the research. At this stage, researchers produce new understandings that may be broader than the initial meaning.

7. **Interpretation Validation**

Researchers ensure their interpretations are acceptable by testing them through academic discussion, cross-referencing with theory, or in-depth interviews to verify the resulting meaning.

8. **Reporting Results**

The research results are presented in a report that reflects a deep understanding of the object being studied, including the context and meaning found.

The hermeneutic method also emphasizes the process of reflection and dialogue to explore the deepest meaning of a text or phenomenon (Fadli, 2021). Thus, the hermeneutic method in this study is not only a technical tool of analysis, but also an epistemological approach to understanding the social and normative realities of AML policies. The strength of this method lies in its ability to combine the depth of textual analysis and sensitivity to social dynamics, making it highly relevant for bridging normative legal approaches and practice-based policy analysis.

4. INTERPRETATION RESULTS

4.1. Anti Money Laundering (AML) Regulation in Indonesia and Latvia (Digital Era)

Despite coming from different legal and regional backgrounds, Indonesia and Latvia are both working to align their national systems with international AML/CFT standards. With an existing foundation in the form of Egmont Group membership and involvement in FATF-style bodies, there are great opportunities to strengthen cooperation in monitoring technology, information exchange, and regulatory harmonization in the future. The following are some of the existing and applicable regulations in Indonesia and Latvia on Anti Money Laundering **(Table 5)**:

Table 5. Anti-Money Laundering (AML) Regulations in Indonesia and Latvia

Country	Name of Regulation	Number / Year	Type of Regulation	Official Source
Indonesia	Law on the Prevention and Eradication of Money Laundering Crimes	Law No. 8 of 2010	Act (Law)	BI.go.id
	Law on the Prevention and Eradication of Terrorism Financing Crimes	Law No. 9 of 2013	Act (Law)	BI.go.id
	Implementation of AML/CFT Program for Commercial Banks	BI Regulation No. 14/27/PBI/2012	Central Bank Regulation	BI.go.id
	Implementation of AML/CFT Program for Non-Bank Payment System Providers	BI Regulation No. 19/10/PBI/2017	Central Bank Regulation	BI.go.id
	Guidelines for AML/CFT and Proliferation Financing of Weapons of Mass Destruction	OJK Regulation No. 8 of 2023	Financial Services Authority Regulation	OJK.go.id
Latvia	Law on the Prevention of Money Laundering and Terrorism and Proliferation Financing	Enacted 2008, amended 2023	Act (Law)	likumi.lv
	Law on Crypto Asset Services	Enacted July 13, 2024	Act (Law)	manimama.eu
	Bank of Latvia Regulation on Customer Due Diligence (CDD)	Effective September 20, 2024	Central Bank Regulation	vixio.com
	Government Regulation on Remote Customer Identification Procedures	Gov. Regulation No. 392 of 2018	Government Regulation	advokatura.lv
	Law on International and National Sanctions of the Republic of Latvia	Enacted in 2016	Act (Law)	advokatura.lv

4.2. Hermeneutics of Anti Money Laundering (AML) Regulation in Indonesia (Digital Era)

In the digital era, the hermeneutic interpretation of AML regulations in Indonesia becomes increasingly relevant as financial crimes evolve in form, speed, and scale (Sukardi, 2020; van Wegberg et al., 2018). Indonesia's AML legal framework, anchored in Law No. 8 of 2010 and Law No. 9 of 2013, must be understood within the broader socio-technological transformations shaping the nation. Hermeneutics invites us to read beyond the text of the law, to interpret the historical and cultural shifts that influenced its formulation and the layers of meaning embedded in its enforcement.

The rise of digital financial services ranging from mobile banking, fintech platforms, to digital wallets poses both opportunity and threat. These services expand financial inclusion but simultaneously open new channels for laundering illicit funds (Khelil et al., 2024). The Indonesian Payment System Blueprint 2025 strategically integrates AML/CFT principles with digital transformation goals. From a hermeneutic lens, this shows an evolving legal consciousness recognizing that regulation must now interpret and anticipate digital behaviors, data patterns, and algorithmic transactions.

The Financial Transaction Reports and Analysis Center (PPATK), as the central financial intelligence unit, must navigate this complex data-rich environment. Their role transcends mere compliance monitoring; they are interpreters of suspicious patterns in a digital matrix. This interpretive task echoes the core of hermeneutics constantly moving between the parts (transactional data) and the whole (the intent, behavior, and context of actors involved).

Moreover, in an era of encrypted communications, decentralized finance (DeFi), and crypto-assets, regulators are faced with interpreting technologies that were never part of the original legislative texts (Chainalysis, 2024). Hermeneutic analysis underscores the importance of updating regulatory interpretations without undermining legal certainty. Indonesia's challenge, therefore, lies not only in enforcement but in cultivating regulatory foresight, ethics, and adaptability.

4.3. Hermeneutics of Anti Money Laundering Regulation in Latvia (Digital Era)

Latvia presents a compelling case for hermeneutic analysis, particularly in how its AML regime has evolved within the European Union (EU) framework. The Law on the Prevention of Money Laundering and Terrorism and Proliferation Financing, first adopted in 2008 and amended several times (most recently in 2023), is a reflection of Latvia's shifting legal and political identity, from a post-Soviet system to a transparent, EU-integrated jurisdiction (Gise-Sproģe et al., 2021; Greco, 2021).

In the digital era, Latvia's AML regulations are deeply intertwined with EU directives, such as the 4th and 5th Anti-Money Laundering Directives (AMLD), and the MiCA (Markets in Crypto Assets) regulation. Hermeneutically, these laws are more than technical requirements, they symbolize Latvia's alignment with liberal democratic values, rule of law, and international cooperation. Latvia's proactive stance in regulating digital assets and remote identity verification illustrates a broader interpretive awareness. The state recognizes that in the digital domain, identity, trust, and criminal behavior have become fragmented and algorithmically concealed (KASTRATOVIC et al., 2024). Regulatory bodies, such as the Financial and Capital Market Commission (FCMC), must thus become not only enforcers but interpreters of digital behavior.

4.4. The Strength of Policy Anti Money Laundering Indonesia and Latvia (Digital Era)

Both Indonesia and Latvia demonstrate unique strengths in navigating AML policies amid the disruptive forces of digitalization. Indonesia's primary strength lies in its institutional infrastructure and policy vision. PPATK, supported by OJK and Bank Indonesia, forms a multi-layered surveillance and enforcement ecosystem. This is complemented by ongoing digital integration efforts such as the National Strategy on Financial Literacy and Payment System Blueprint 2025. Indonesia's commitment to join FATF as a full member reflects its aspiration to align with global AML norms. From a digital perspective, this shows increasing openness to adopt data-driven regulatory technologies (RegTech) and risk-based frameworks. Hermeneutically, it suggests a shift in the nation's regulatory culture, from reactive law enforcement to anticipatory governance.

Latvia, on the other hand, shows strength in regulatory alignment and technological responsiveness. As an EU member, it benefits from harmonized AML directives, centralized data-sharing, and collective enforcement. Its legislation on crypto asset service providers (CASPs), customer due diligence (CDD), and remote identification reflect a deep understanding of how digital technology reshapes anonymity, identity, and transaction trails. Additionally, Latvia's policy is backed by strong legal clarity and recent institutional reforms, especially after past banking scandals. In hermeneutic terms, these reforms symbolize a national re-interpretation of economic sovereignty, asserting control not just over financial institutions but over the meanings of compliance, transparency, and digital accountability.

4.5. The Weaknesses of Policy Anti Money Laundering Indonesia and Latvia (Digital Era)

The digital era introduces complexities such as unregulated fintech startups, peer-to-peer lending platforms, and crypto exchanges operating beyond national jurisdictions. Indonesia's regulatory bodies are still adapting to these trends, often lagging behind technological change. Hermeneutically, this represents a dissonance between the 'text' of regulation and the 'context' of digital behavior, where regulatory meaning fails to capture evolving realities.

Latvia's weaknesses are more geopolitical and structural. The country's small financial sector is highly exposed to external risks and reputational damage. While its AML laws are robust, enforcement sometimes struggles with overregulation, particularly in fintech and cross-border compliance. Moreover, reliance on EU frameworks means Latvia has limited flexibility in customizing AML measures for its unique socio-economic landscape. Hermeneutic analysis points to a latent tension between national identity and supranational obligation. Latvia may excel in codifying AML norms, but the interpretive authority often lies in Brussels, not Riga. This can create gaps in local enforcement where global standards do not fully reflect domestic conditions.

A hermeneutic approach to AML regulation reveals that law is not static text but evolving meaning shaped by context, power, and perception. In the digital era, both Indonesia and Latvia are compelled to reinterpret the essence of financial surveillance, institutional trust, and legal responsibility. Indonesia's regulatory transformation mirrors its broader transition to digital governance and global economic integration. Latvia's evolution, meanwhile, exemplifies how small states negotiate legal meaning within larger normative systems like the EU.

Both nations illustrate that the future of AML policy depends not only on technical compliance but on interpretive agility, the ability to read, adapt, and act upon the shifting semantics of digital finance and criminal innovation. Based on the discussion in the document regarding the effectiveness of AML and challenges in the digital age, the following are proposed metrics that can be considered. This diagram presents key metrics that can be used to evaluate the effectiveness and efficiency of Anti-Money Laundering (AML) technology. (interpreted through **Figure 2).**

Figure 2. Metrics for evaluating AML Technology in Future

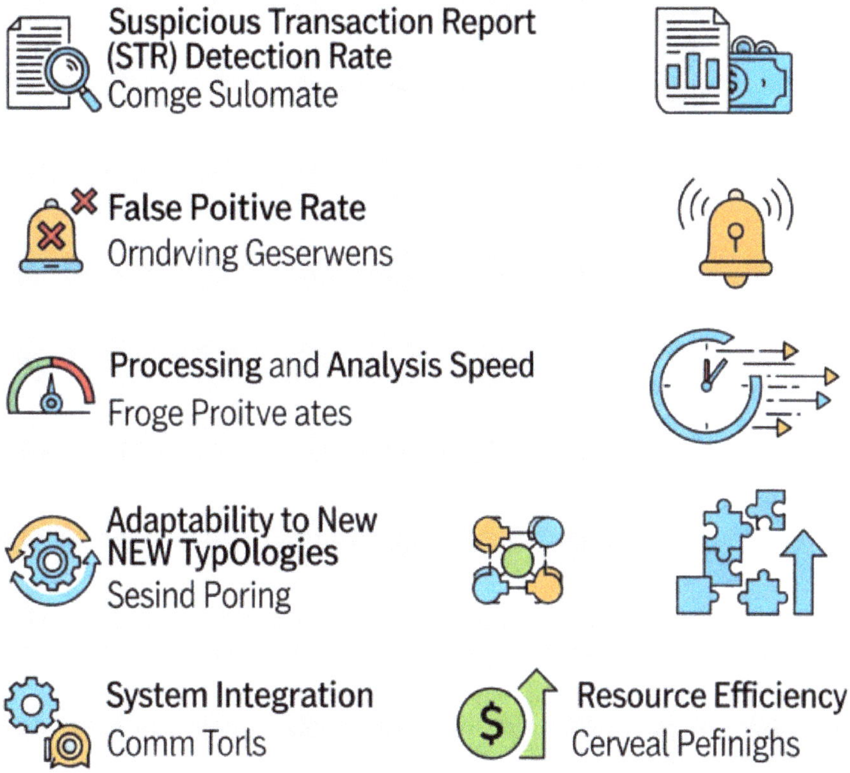

The explanation is as follows:

a. **Suspicious Transaction Report (STR) Detection Rate**: Measures how well the technology identifies and reports suspicious transactions.
b. **False Positive Rate:** Assessing the accuracy of the technology in minimizing irrelevant false alerts.
c. **Processing and Analysis Speed:** Measures the efficiency of the technology in quickly processing large amounts of data.
d. **Adaptability to New Typologies:** Demonstrates the flexibility of the technology to recognize and respond to evolving money laundering modus operandi.
e. **System Integration:** Describes the technology's ability to interact and share information with other systems.
f. **Resource Efficiency:** Assesses the extent to which the technology can optimize the use of human and financial resources.

5. CONCLUSIONS

After exploring the challenges faced by Indonesia and Latvia in combating money laundering, it becomes evident that both nations have made commendable progress in reinforcing their legal and institutional frameworks. In Indonesia, the application of hermeneutics allows lawmakers and enforcement agencies to move beyond rigid legal formalism. Instead of treating AML regulations as static rules, this approach interprets them dynamically considering socio-economic contexts, digital behavior patterns, and institutional responses. Hermeneutics transforms AML policies from mere documents into living instruments that interact with financial realities shaped by fintech, cryptocurrency, and globalized transactions. However, this transformation requires not just theoretical insight but also strong inter-agency collaboration, adequate resource allocation, and the adoption of cutting-edge technological tools.

Likewise, Latvia has demonstrated a robust legislative alignment with European Union AML directives and showcased remarkable adaptability in regulating emerging financial technologies. The hermeneutic approach here reveals how Latvia repositions its legal identity and reconstructs state legitimacy through every legislative update. As a post-Soviet, EU-integrated country, Latvia exemplifies how regulatory meaning evolves under both external pressures and internal policy shifts. Yet, the challenge remains to maintain autonomy and contextual nuance within an increasingly harmonized EU regulatory landscape. To address persistent weaknesses and leverage the strengths of both countries, several strategic policy recommendations are proposed:

a) Increasing Capacity and Resources for Law Enforcement

Both Indonesia and Latvia need to invest significantly in strengthening their respective AML enforcement bodies. Agencies such as Indonesia's PPATK and Latvia's FIU should be equipped with larger budgets, modern infrastructure, and highly trained personnel specialized in financial intelligence and digital forensics.

b) Tightening Beneficial Ownership Reporting Obligations

Transparency in beneficial ownership is critical in preventing the misuse of legal entities for illicit purposes. Both countries should enhance the regulatory requirements for disclosing beneficial ownership. Latvia, as part of the EU, has already implemented the 5th AML Directive, which includes mandatory public access to beneficial ownership registers. Indonesia can take cues from this framework and establish a centralized and accessible national register of ultimate beneficial owners. Verification mechanisms must be strengthened to ensure the accuracy and reliability of submitted information. Sanctions for non-compliance should be significant enough to deter violations.

c) Strengthening Cross-Institutional and International Coordination

Effective AML enforcement depends heavily on inter-agency collaboration. In both countries, domestic institutions, such as OJK, Bank Indonesia, PPATK, and in Latvia, the FCMC and FIU, must operate in a coordinated manner. Establishing permanent inter-agency coordination task forces, shared databases, and regular intelligence briefings will reduce redundancies and close supervisory gaps. Internationally, both nations must intensify cooperation through mechanisms such as extradition treaties, mutual legal assistance agreements, and participation in global networks like the Egmont Group and the Financial Action Task Force (FATF). Real-time cross-border information sharing is essential in tracking illicit flows that span multiple jurisdictions. Stronger integration with INTERPOL, Europol, and other intelligence-sharing platforms will enhance global enforcement synergy.

d) Updating Risk-Based Approach (RBA) Policies

The dynamic nature of financial crime demands that AML strategies remain flexible and continuously updated. Indonesia and Latvia should institutionalize periodic risk assessments to evaluate vulnerabilities in their financial systems. Such assessments must consider not only traditional banking activities but also non-traditional sectors such as online gambling, crowdfunding, and art dealing. Furthermore, AML rules should explicitly cover new frontiers in digital finance. Cryptocurrencies, DeFi platforms, NFTs, and digital wallets are emerging tools of abuse by money launderers. Regulatory frameworks must evolve to address these risks while balancing innovation and financial inclusion. By focusing enforcement on high-risk sectors and transactions, resources can be allocated more efficiently, leading to greater impact.

e) Implementing Stricter Sanctions for Violations

The deterrent effect of sanctions plays a crucial role in achieving AML compliance. Both countries should revise their legal frameworks to impose tougher administrative and criminal penalties on institutions or individuals involved in money laundering. These penalties may include revocation of licenses, significant financial penalties, and custodial sentences. Furthermore, financial institutions that fail to report suspicious activities must face punitive consequences. This not only ensures consistent compliance but also reduces the risk of system exploitation by criminal actors. Establishing accountability mechanisms within the private sector can also enhance the ethical culture surrounding AML practices.

Adapting to the Digital Era: Challenges and Opportunities

The digital era has transformed the global financial landscape, creating a challenge for Indonesia to close regulatory gaps caused by rapid innovation. Digital financial platforms like digital wallets, peer-to-peer (P2P) lending, and crypto-exchanges have grown rapidly, often outpacing existing legal frameworks. While these platforms contribute to financial inclusion, they can also serve as a gateway for illicit financial flows. Indonesia must adopt a holistic approach that goes beyond regulation by investing in digital forensics capabilities, creating regulatory sandboxes for oversight, and fostering continuous dialogue between the government and the tech sector to create a participatory and responsive policy model.

The main challenge in combating money laundering in Indonesia's digital era is the lagging regulation in keeping up with financial technology developments, such as fintech, digital wallets, and cryptocurrencies, which often operate beyond regulatory oversight. Informal sectors also struggle to report suspicious transactions due to limited capacity and digital literacy. In response, PPATK has developed a big data-based system and started applying machine learning to analyze transaction patterns. National strategies, like the 2025 Indonesian Payment System Blueprint, are beginning to incorporate Anti-Money Laundering and Counter-Terrorism Financing (AML-CTF) principles. Collaboration between PPATK, the Financial Services Authority (OJK), and Bank Indonesia is crucial for effective oversight. Internationally, Indonesia is active in forums such as the Egmont Group and the Asia/Pacific Group on Money Laundering (APG). Although there is currently no bilateral cooperation with Latvia, there is potential for collaboration, especially in supervising digital assets and exchanging information through financial forensic technology.

As a member of the European Union, Latvia benefits from a sophisticated anti-money laundering (AML) regulatory framework that is aligned with international standards. However, the country faces a different kind of risk: over-reliance on standardized procedures. This can lead to **regulatory fatigue**, where compliance becomes a mere box-ticking exercise instead of a thoughtful process. Regulators must remain vigilant against increasingly sophisticated cyber threats, such as the use of **mixing services** and **privacy coins** to obscure transactions. To counter this, Latvia needs to adopt a dynamic interpretive strategy. This approach would encourage regulators to re-evaluate the assumptions behind existing rules, incorporate local realities, and be more agile in responding to new threats.

A Latvian FIU expert stated that the ABLV Bank scandal marked a key turning point in Latvia's anti-money laundering reforms, highlighting the need for a strong compliance culture and tech-based detection. The government responded with system upgrades, improved beneficial ownership oversight, and modernized remote customer verification. To address crypto-related risks, Latvia passed the 2024 Crypto Asset Services Act, aligning with EU directives and FATF standards, and enhanced digital financial monitoring using AI. While no bilateral agreement exists with Indonesia, Latvia is open to collaboration with Southeast Asia, including PPATK, focusing on cross-border monitoring, digital forensics, and policy harmonization. Both countries face the challenge of aligning law, ethics, and technology in the digital age—an opportunity to evolve AML frameworks through continuous interpretation and innovation.

Policy recommendations need to be discussed further, particularly how Indonesia can learn from comprehensive approaches such as the EU's MiCA, or develop a comparable crypto regulatory framework that covers taxation, licensing, and supervision. International cooperation and regulatory harmonization are crucial in addressing the challenges of crypto-based money laundering in the digital age.

Limitations and Future Directions

While offering valuable insights, this study has limitations, including its reliance on secondary data and a narrow geographic focus on Indonesia and Latvia, which limits generalizability. Future research should include primary data and broader regional comparisons, as well as deeper analysis of the economic impacts of AML policies. Overall, both countries have made progress in enhancing AML frameworks, with hermeneutics offering a useful lens to align regulation with technological change. To remain effective, AML policies must continue evolving through investment, collaboration, and adaptive legal interpretation.

REFERENCES

Africa, F. (2017). *Anti-Money Laundering, Know Your Customer, and Curbing the Financing of Terrorism Key points*. Issue April.

Ajide, F. M., & Ojeyinka, T. A. (2024). Benefit or burden? An exploratory analysis of the impact of anti-money laundering regulations on sustainable development in developing economies. *Sustainable Development (Bradford), 32*(3), 2417–2434. DOI: 10.1002/sd.2789

Ariyanto, D., Weni Andayani, G. A. P., & Dwija Putri, I. G. A. M. A. (2020). Influence of justice, culture and love of money towards ethical perception on tax evasion with gender as moderating variable. *Journal of Money Laundering Control, 23*(1), 245–266. DOI: 10.1108/JMLC-06-2019-0047

Armey, L., & Melese, F. (2018). Minimizing Public Sector Corruption: The Economics of Crime, Identity Economics, and Money Laundering. *Defence and Peace Economics, 29*(7), 840–852. DOI: 10.1080/10242694.2017.1318013

Basel. (2019). *Basel AML Index 2019 Report:A country ranking and review of money laundering and terrorist financing risks around the world* (Issue August).

Becker, G. S. (1968). Crime and Punishment: An Economic Approach. *Journal of Political Economy, 76*(2), 169–217. DOI: 10.1086/259394

Bello, A., Oduro, D. A., Opoku, E., Bello, A. D., Leo, A. O., Ukatu, C. E., & Okika, N. (2025). Enhancing Know Your Customer (KYC) and Anti-Money Laundering (AML) Compliance Using Blockchain : A Business Analysis Approach. *Iconic Research and Engineering Journals, 8*(9), 297–305.

Buchanan, J., & Buchanan, J. (2018). *Money laundering through gambling devices*. DOI: 10.1108/SBR-08-2017-0057

Chainalysis. (2024). *Money Laundering and Cryptocurrency:Trends and new techniques for detection and investigation* (Issue July).

Cuadrado-ballesteros, B., Bisogno, M., & Cuadrado-ballesteros, B. (2020). Public sector accounting reforms and the quality of governance Public sector accounting reforms and the quality of governance. *Public Money & Management, 0*(0), 1–11. DOI: 10.1080/09540962.2020.1724665

Dewi Rengganis, F., & Setiawan Susanto, D. (2023). Evaluasi implementasi program anti pencucian uang di Indonesia. *Integritas: Jurnal Antikorupsi, 9*(2), 229–240. https://jurnal.kpk.go.id/index.php/integritas

Dobrowolski, Z., & Sułkowski, Ł. (2020). Implementing a sustainable model for anti-money laundering in the United Nations Development Goals. *Sustainability (Basel)*, *12*(1), 1–23. DOI: 10.3390/su12010244

Easter, H. W. (2018). *CONFRONTING MONEY LAUNDERING AND TERRORIST FINANCING: MOVING CANADA FORWARD* (Issue November). www.ourcommons .ca

Ehrlic, I. (1973). Participation in Illegitimate Activities : ATheoretical and Empirical Investigation Isaac Ehrlich. *Journal of Political Economy*, *81*(3), 521–565. DOI: 10.1086/260058

Fadli, M. R. (2021). Hubungan Filsafat dengan Ilmu Pengetahuan dan Relevansinya Di Era Revolusi Industri 4.0 (Society 5.0). *Jurnal Filsafat*, *31*(1), 130. DOI: 10.22146/jf.42521

FATF. (2021). *Money Laundering from Environmental Crime* (Issue July). https://www.fatf-gafi.org

FATF. (2025). INTERNATIONAL STANDARDS ON COMBATING MONEY LAUNDERING AND THE FINANCING OF TERRORISM & PROLIFERATION. In *FATF* (Vol. 39, Issue 3). DOI: 10.1596/978-0-8213-7569-3

Gaviyau, W., & Sibindi, A. B. (2023). Global Anti-Money Laundering and Combating Terrorism Financing Regulatory Framework: A Critique. *Journal of Risk and Financial Management*, *16*(7), 313. Advance online publication. DOI: 10.3390/jrfm16070313

Gerbrands, P., Unger, B., Getzner, M., & Ferwerda, J. (2022). The effect of anti-money laundering policies: An empirical network analysis. *EPJ Data Science*, *11*(1), 15. Advance online publication. DOI: 10.1140/epjds/s13688-022-00328-8

Gise-Sproģe, I., Liodorova, J., Murniece, K., & Voronova, I. (2021). Money Laundering Investigation: Case of Latvia. *Sociālo Zinātņu Vēstnesis=Social. Science Bulletin*, *31*(2), 137–155. DOI: 10.9770/szv.2020.2(8)

Greco, A. (2021). *Money Laundering in Latvia and the Baltics Recent Developments*. Ongoing Risks, and Future Challenges.

Grossmann, J., Halida, R., & Suryandari, T. (2021). *Survey report The Green Corruption paradox : Natural resource management and environmental corruption in Indonesia*. Issue September.

Hedman, J., Beaulieu, T., & Karlström, M. (2021). The tales of alphanumerical symbols in media: The case of bitcoin. *Journal of Theoretical and Applied Electronic Commerce Research, 16*(7), 2768–2792. DOI: 10.3390/jtaer16070152

Island, C. (2024). *EVOLUTION OF ANTI-MONEY LAUNDERING LAWS : A. 6*(1), 1–27.

Jetin, B., Saadaoui, J., & Ratiarison, H. (2024). The Effect of Corruption on Foreign Direct Investment at the Regional Level: A Positive or Negative Relationship? In *Asia in Transition* (Vol. 22, Issue April). Springer Nature Singapore. DOI: 10.1007/978-981-99-9303-1_3

Kastratovic, R., Krivins, A., & Veiksa, I.KASTRATOVIC. (2024). Economic and legal aspects of foreign direct investment patterns in Serbia and Latvia. *Access Journal - Access to Science, Business. Innovation in the Digital Economy*, *5*(3), 440–458. DOI: 10.46656/access.2024.5.3(4)

Khelil, I., Khlif, H., & Achek, I. (2024). The economic consequences of money laundering: A review of empirical literature. *Journal of Money Laundering Control, 27*(5), 901–916. DOI: 10.1108/JMLC-09-2023-0143

Laowo, Y. S. (2022). Kajian Hukum Tindak Pidana Pencucian Uang (Money Laundering). *Jurnal Panah Keadilan, Vol. 1, No*(E-ISSN: 2727-3560), 70–87.

Levi, M. (2020). Evaluating the Control of Money Laundering and Its Underlying Offences: The Search for Meaningful Data. *Asian Journal of Criminology*, *15*(4), 301–320. DOI: 10.1007/s11417-020-09319-y PMID: 32837603

Loayza, N., Villa, E., & Misas, M. (2019). Illicit activity and money laundering from an economic growth perspective: A model and an application to Colombia. *Journal of Economic Behavior & Organization*, *159*, 442–487. DOI: 10.1016/j.jebo.2017.10.002

Manthovani, R. (2023). A comparative analysis of money laundering crimes in Indonesia through cryptocurrency. *International Journal of Cyber Criminology, 17*(1), 196–210. DOI: 10.5281/zenodo.4766612

Mardiansyah. (2021). *Indonesia Risk Assessment on Money Laundering 2021.* http://www.ppatk.go.id

Matar, O. (2023). The Role of Forensic Accounting in reducing tax evasion)crimes and penalties. *Academic Journal IMAJ ISSN*, *8*(1), 98–115.

Muryani, E. (2021). Dynamics of Income Inequality, Investment, and Unemployment in Indonesia. *Journal of Population and Social Studies*, *29*(August), 660–678. DOI: 10.25133/JPSSv292021.040

Ofoeda, I., Agbloyor, E. K., & Abor, J. Y. (2022). How do anti-money laundering systems affect FDI flows across the globe? *Cogent Economics & Finance*, *10*(1), 2058735. Advance online publication. DOI: 10.1080/23322039.2022.2058735

Pol, R. F. (2020). Anti-money laundering: The world's least effective policy experiment? Together, we can fix it. *Policy Design and Practice*, *3*(1), 73–94. DOI: 10.1080/25741292.2020.1725366

Posner, R. A. (1974). Theories of Economic Regulation. *The Bell Journal of Economics and Management Science*, *5*(2), 335–358. DOI: 10.2307/3003113

Rengganis, F. D., & Susanto, D. S. (2023). Evaluation of the anti-money laundering programs implementation in Indonesia. *Integritas : Jurnal Antikorupsi*, *9*(2), 229–240. DOI: 10.32697/integritas.v9i2.973

Rose, K. J. (2020). Disclosing anti-money launderers through CSR regulation – a new way to combat money laundering. *Journal of Money Laundering Control*, *23*(1), 11–25. DOI: 10.1108/JMLC-07-2019-0062

Rusanov, G., & Pudovochkin, Y. (2021). Money laundering in the modern crime system. *Journal of Money Laundering Control*, *24*(4), 860–868. DOI: 10.1108/JMLC-08-2020-0085

Sidik, H., & Sulistyana, I. P. (2021). Hermeneutika Sebuah Metode Interpretasi Dalam Kajian Filsafat Sejarah. *Agastya: Jurnal Sejarah Dan Pembelajarannya*, *11*(1), 19–34. DOI: 10.25273/ajsp.v11i1.6224

Stigler, G. J. (1971). The theory regulation of economic. *The Bell Journal of Economics and Management Science*, *2*(1), 3–21. DOI: 10.2307/3003160

Sugiharti, L., Esquivias, M. A., Shaari, M. S., Agustin, L., & Rohmawati, H. (2022). Criminality and Income Inequality in Indonesia. *Social Sciences (Basel, Switzerland)*, *11*(3), 142. Advance online publication. DOI: 10.3390/socsci11030142

Sukardi. (2020). Financial Crime on Investigation in Industrial Revolution 4.0 Era. *International Journal of Criminology and Sociology*, *9*, 695–708. DOI: 10.6000/1929-4409.2020.09.66

Tiwari, M., Gepp, A., & Kumar, K. (2020). A review of money laundering literature: The state of research in key areas. *Pacific Accounting Review*, *32*(2), 271–303. DOI: 10.1108/PAR-06-2019-0065 van Wegberg, R., Oerlemans, J. J., & van Deventer, O. (2018). Bitcoin money laundering: mixed results?: An explorative study on money laundering of cybercrime proceeds using bitcoin. *Journal of Financial Crime*, *25*(2), 419–435. DOI: 10.1108/JFC-11-2016-0067

Wilson, L. (2019). Madoff's dirty money. *Journal of Money Laundering Control*, *22*(2), 289–299. DOI: 10.1108/JMLC-03-2018-0022

Wisarja, I. K. (2021). Hermeneutika sebagai Metode Ilmu Kemanusiaan (Perspektif Hermeneutika Wihelm Dilthey). In *Jurnal Filsafat* (Vol. 13, Issue 3, pp. 202–217). https://jurnal.ugm.ac.id/wisdom/article/view/31286

Compilation of References

Abujaber, A. A., & Nashwan, A. J. (2024). Ethical framework for artificial intelligence in healthcare research: A path to integrity. In World Journal of Methodology (Vol. 14, Issue 3). DOI: 10.5662/wjm.v14.i3.94071

Adelakun, B. O., Majekodunmi, T. G., & Akintoye, O. S.Beatrice Oyinkansola AdelakunTomiwa Gabriel MajekodunmiOluwole Stephen Akintoye. (2024). AI and ethical accounting: Navigating challenges and opportunities. *International Journal of Advanced Economics*, *6*(6), 224–241. DOI: 10.51594/ijae.v6i6.1230

Adelakun, B. O., Onwubuariri, E. R., Adeniran, G. A., & Ntiakoh, A. (2024). Enhancing fraud detection in accounting through AI: Techniques and case studies. *Finance & Accounting Research Journal*, *6*(6), 978–999. DOI: 10.51594/farj.v6i6.1232

Adesoga, A., Adekunle, A., & Oladipo, O. (2024). Real-time fraud detection using machine learning. *IEEE Access : Practical Innovations, Open Solutions*, *12*, 33411–33425.

Adeyelu, A., Akinrinola, O., & Olatunji, S. (2024). Ethical governance of artificial intelligence in financial decision-making systems. *AI and Ethics*, *4*(2), 215–229. DOI: 10.1007/s43681-023-00345-7

Adhikari, P., Hamal, P., & Baidoo, F. (2024). Artificial Intelligence in fraud detection: Revolutionizing financial security. *International Journal of Science and Research Archive*, *13*(1), 1457–1472. DOI: 10.30574/ijsra.2024.13.1.1860

Adhikari, S., Mishra, A., & Singh, R. (2024). Machine learning techniques for financial fraud detection. *Expert Systems with Applications*, *231*, 120864.

Admass, W. S., Munaye, Y. Y., & Diro, A. A. (2024). Cyber Security: State of the Art, Challenges, and Future Directions. *Cyber Security and Applications*, *2*, 100031. DOI: 10.1016/j.csa.2023.100031

Adrian, T., & Mancini-Griffoli, T. (2019). *The rise of digital money*. IMF FinTech Notes.

Africa, F. (2017). *Anti-Money Laundering, Know Your Customer, and Curbing the Financing of Terrorism Key points*. Issue April.

AI IN FRAUD PREVENTION AND FINANCIAL SECURITY. (2024, September 24). *Insights2Techinfo*. https://insights2techinfo.com/ai-in-fraud-prevention-and-financial-security/

Aizenberg, E., & van den Hoven, J. (2020). Designing for human rights in AI. *Big Data & Society*, *7*(2), 2053951720949566. Advance online publication. DOI: 10.1177/2053951720949566

Ajide, F. M., & Ojeyinka, T. A. (2024). Benefit or burden? An exploratory analysis of the impact of anti-money laundering regulations on sustainable development in developing economies. *Sustainable Development (Bradford)*, *32*(3), 2417–2434. DOI: 10.1002/sd.2789

Akinbowale, O. E., Klingelhöfer, H. E., & Zerihun, M. F. (2022). The use of the Balanced Scorecard as a strategic management tool to mitigate cyberfraud in the South African banking industry. *Heliyon*, *8*(12), e12054. DOI: 10.1016/j.heliyon.2022.e12054 PMID: 36531622

Akinbowale, O. E., Mashigo, P., & Zerihun, M. F. (2023). The integration of forensic accounting and big data technology frameworks for internal fraud mitigation in the banking industry. *Cogent Business & Management*, *10*(1), 2163560. Advance online publication. DOI: 10.1080/23311975.2022.2163560

Alauthman, M., Al-Qaraghuli, A., & Gupta, B. B. (2023). Hybrid machine learning frameworks for fraud detection. *Future Generation Computer Systems*, *139*, 1–14.

Al-Ayyoub, M., Nuseir, A., Alsmearat, K., Jararweh, Y., & Gupta, B. (2018). Deep learning for Arabic NLP: A survey. *Journal of Computational Science*, *26*, 522–531. DOI: 10.1016/j.jocs.2017.11.011

Alfaiz, A., & Fati, S. M. (2022). Adversarial attacks and defenses in machine learning: A survey. *IEEE Access : Practical Innovations, Open Solutions*, *10*, 121512–121537.

Alieyan, K., Almomani, A., Anbar, M., Alauthman, M., Abdullah, R., & Gupta, B. B. (2021). DNS rule-based schema to botnet detection. *Enterprise Information Systems*, *15*(4), 545–564. DOI: 10.1080/17517575.2019.1644673

Ali, M., Rauf, A., & Khan, S. (2022). Privacy-preserving machine learning for identity management. *Computers & Security*, *115*, 102620.

Alkhateeb, F., & Maolood, I. Y. (2019). Identity fraud detection using machine learning techniques. *Journal of Information Security and Applications*, *46*, 15–25.

Almomani, I., Alauthman, M., & Gupta, B. B. (2024). Intelligent fraud detection systems: A survey of machine learning approaches. *Journal of Network and Computer Applications*, *226*, 103859.

Almutairi, A. M., Kang, B., & AL Hashimy, N. (2025). *Business Email Compromise: A Comprehensive Taxonomy for Detection and Prevention*. DOI: 10.1145/3700706.3700714

Alshaikh, M., Maynard, S. B., Ahmad, A., & Chang, S. (2024). Cybersecurity governance and the limitations of rule-based security controls. *Computers & Security*, *136*, 103530. DOI: 10.1016/j.cose.2023.103530

Amasiatu, C. V., & Shah, M. H. (2018). First party fraud management: Framework for the retail industry. *International Journal of Retail & Distribution Management*, *46*(4), 350–363. DOI: 10.1108/IJRDM-10-2016-0185

Amoo, O. O., Atadoga, A., Abrahams, T. O., Farayola, O. A., Osasona, F., & Ayinla, B. S. (2024). The legal landscape of cybercrime: A review of contemporary issues in the criminal justice system. In World Journal of Advanced Research and Reviews (Vol. 21, Issue 2, pp. 205–217). GSC Online Press. DOI: 10.30574/wjarr.2024.21.2.0438

Anderson Schillig, M. (2023). 'Lex Cryptographi (c) a,''Cloud Crypto Land'or What?–Blockchain Technology on the Legal Hype Cycle. *The Modern Law Review*, *86*(1), 31–66. DOI: 10.1111/1468-2230.12748

Angela, O., Atoyebi, I., Soyele, A., & Ogunwobi, E. (2024). *Enhancing Fraud Detection and Prevention in Fintech: Big Data and Machine Learning Approaches*. World Journal of Advanced Research and Reviews., DOI: 10.30574/wjarr.2024.24.2.3617

Antwi, H., Boateng, R., & Osei, K. (2024). Predictive analytics for transaction fraud. *Journal of Financial Crime*, *31*(1), 78–95.

Apsimet, N., Smanova, A., & Utegenova, G. (2024). The role of the Internet in the evolution of fraud: A historical aspect. *Л.Н. Гумилев Атында ы Еуразия лтты Университетіні Хабаршысы*, *146*(1), 247–257. DOI: 10.32523/2616-6844-2024-1-247-257

Arifin, R., Atikasari, H., & Waspiah, W. (2020). The Intersection of Criminal Law. *Technology and Business Commercial Law on Carding as Cyber Fraud.*, *11*(2), 235–246. DOI: 10.26555/novelty.v11i2.a15700

Ariyanto, D., Weni Andayani, G. A. P., & Dwija Putri, I. G. A. M. A. (2020). Influence of justice, culture and love of money towards ethical perception on tax evasion with gender as moderating variable. *Journal of Money Laundering Control*, *23*(1), 245–266. DOI: 10.1108/JMLC-06-2019-0047

Armey, L., & Melese, F. (2018). Minimizing Public Sector Corruption: The Economics of Crime, Identity Economics, and Money Laundering. *Defence and Peace Economics*, *29*(7), 840–852. DOI: 10.1080/10242694.2017.1318013

Arowolo, O., Adewumi, A., & Oladipo, O. (2023). Unsupervised anomaly detection techniques for financial fraud. *Applied Soft Computing*, *132*, 109873.

Aslam, A., & Hussain, A. (2024). Performance evaluation metrics for fraud detection systems. *Journal of Big Data*, *11*(1), 52.

Aslam, F., Rehman, A., & Akram, M. (2022). Machine learning techniques for identity theft and fraud detection. *Security and Communication Networks*, *4589123*. Advance online publication. DOI: 10.1155/2022/4589123

Asmar, D., & Tuqan, J. (2024). Machine learning approaches for digital identity verification. *Journal of Information Security and Applications*, *77*, 103668. DOI: 10.1016/j.jisa.2023.103668

Awosika, T., Shukla, R. M., & Pranggono, B. (2024). Transparency and Privacy: The Role of Explainable AI and Federated Learning in Financial Fraud Detection. *IEEE Access : Practical Innovations, Open Solutions*, *12*, 64551–64560. DOI: 10.1109/ACCESS.2024.3394528

Baesens, B. (2023). Fraud analytics: A research. *Journal of Chinese Economic and Business Studies*, *21*(1), 137–141. DOI: 10.1080/14765284.2022.2162246

Baird, M., & Clare, J. (2017). Removing the opportunity for contract cheating in business capstones: A crime prevention case study. *International Journal for Educational Integrity*, *13*(1), 6. Advance online publication. DOI: 10.1007/s40979-017-0018-1

Bajpai, P. (2024). Predictive risk analytics using machine learning. *Computers & Security*, *133*, 103258.

Bakıner, O. (2023). The promises and challenges of addressing artificial intelligence with human rights. *Big Data & Society*, *10*(2), 20539517231205476. Advance online publication. DOI: 10.1177/20539517231205476

Barredo Arrieta, A., Díaz-Rodríguez, N., Del Ser, J., Bennetot, A., Tabik, S., Barbado, A., García, S., Gil-López, S., Molina, D., Benjamins, R., Chatila, R., & Herrera, F. (2020). Explainable Artificial Intelligence (XAI): Concepts, taxonomies, opportunities and challenges toward responsible AI. *Information Fusion*, *58*, 82–115. DOI: 10.1016/j.inffus.2019.12.012

Barton, M.-C., & Pöppelbuß, J. (2022). Prinzipien für die ethische Nutzung künstlicher Intelligenz. *HMD Praxis der Wirtschaftsinformatik*, *59*(2), 468–481. DOI: 10.1365/s40702-022-00850-3

Bartsch, S., Behn, O., Benlian, A., Brownsword, R., Bücker, S., Düwell, M., Formánek, N., Jungtäubl, M., Leyer, M., Richter, A., Schmidt, J.-H., & Will-Zocholl, M. (2025). Governance of High-Risk AI Systems in Healthcare and Credit Scoring. *Business & Information Systems Engineering*, *67*(4), 1–19. DOI: 10.1007/s12599-025-00944-4

Basel. (2019). *Basel AML Index 2019 Report:A country ranking and review of money laundering and terrorist financing risks around the world* (Issue August).

Becker, G. S. (1968). Crime and Punishment: An Economic Approach. *Journal of Political Economy*, *76*(2), 169–217. DOI: 10.1086/259394

Bello, A., Oduro, D. A., Opoku, E., Bello, A. D., Leo, A. O., Ukatu, C. E., & Okika, N. (2025). Enhancing Know Your Customer (KYC) and Anti-Money Laundering (AML) Compliance Using Blockchain : A Business Analysis Approach. *Iconic Research and Engineering Journals*, *8*(9), 297–305.

Betz-Hamilton, A. (2023). Reporting behaviours of familiar identity theft victims: An empirical test of Black's theory of law. *Journal of Financial Crime*, *30*(4), 1055–1065. DOI: 10.1108/JFC-04-2022-0085

Bhattacharya, A., & Mićković, M. (2024). FinChain-BERT: Transformer-based fraud detection in financial transactions. *Journal of Financial AI*, *12*(3), 45–67.

Biggio, B., & Roli, F. (2018). Wild patterns: Ten years after the rise of adversarial machine learning. *Pattern Recognition*, *84*, 317–331. DOI: 10.1016/j.patcog.2018.07.023

Binsawad, M. (2025). Enhanced Financial Fraud Detection Using an Adaptive Voted Perceptron Model with Optimized Learning and Error Reduction. *Electronics (Basel)*, *14*(9), 1875. DOI: 10.3390/electronics14091875

Bolton, R. J., & Hand, D. J. (2002). Statistical fraud detection: A review. *Statistical Science*, *17*(3), 235–255. DOI: 10.1214/ss/1042727940

Borenstein, J., & Howard, A. (2020). Emerging challenges in AI and the need for AI ethics education. In AI and Ethics (Vol. 1, Issue 1, p. 61). Springer Nature. DOI: 10.1007/s43681-020-00002-7

Britz, M. T. (2008). A new paradigm of organized crime in the United States: Criminal syndicates, cyber-gangs, and the worldwide web. *Sociology Compass*, *2*(6), 1750–1765. DOI: 10.1111/j.1751-9020.2008.00172.x

Bruno, M. (2019). *Impersonation Fraud Scenarios: How to Protect*. Detect and Respond., DOI: 10.69554/NHAM3165

Bruschi, D., & Diomede, N. (2023). A framework for assessing AI ethics with applications to cybersecurity. *AI and Ethics*, *3*(1), 65–72. DOI: 10.1007/s43681-022-00162-8

Buchanan, J., & Buchanan, J. (2018). *Money laundering through gambling devices*. DOI: 10.1108/SBR-08-2017-0057

Buchanan, B. (2019). *The AI triangle*. Oxford University Press.

Buchan, R., & Tsagourias, N. (2016). Non-State Actors and Responsibility in Cyberspace: State Responsibility, Individual Criminal Responsibility, and Issues of Evidence. *Journal of Conflict and Security Law*, *21*(3), 377–381. https://www.jstor.org/stable/26298206. DOI: 10.1093/jcsl/krw017

Bussmann, N., Giudici, P., Marinelli, D., & Papenbrock, J. (2021). Explainable AI in credit risk management. *Computational Economics*, *57*(1), 203–216. DOI: 10.1007/s10614-020-10042-0

Bynagari, N. B. (2015). Machine learning and data analytics in financial fraud detection. *International Journal of Computer Applications*, *120*(15), 1–6.

Calderaro, A., & Craig, A. J. (2020). Transnational governance of cybersecurity: Policy challenges and global inequalities in cyber capacity building. *Third World Quarterly*, *41*(6), 917–938. DOI: 10.1080/01436597.2020.1729729

Camilleri, M. A. (2023). Artificial intelligence governance: Ethical considerations and implications for social responsibility. *Expert Systems: International Journal of Knowledge Engineering and Neural Networks*, *41*(7), e13406. Advance online publication. DOI: 10.1111/exsy.13406

Carcillo, F., Dal Pozzolo, A., Snoeck, M., & Bontempi, G. (2021). Scarff: A scalable framework for streaming credit card fraud detection. *Information Fusion*, *63*, 182–194. DOI: 10.1016/j.inffus.2020.05.009

Carminati, M., Caron, R., Maggi, F., Epifani, I., & Zanero, S. (2015). BankSealer: A decision support system for online banking fraud analysis and investigation. *Computers & Security*, *53*, 175–186. DOI: 10.1016/j.cose.2015.04.002

Carminati, M., Caron, R., Maggi, F., Epifani, I., & Zanero, S. (2015). BankSealer: A decision support system for online banking fraud analysis and investigation. *Decision Support Systems*, *74*, 1–12.

Casey, E. (2019). The chequered past and risky future of digital forensics. *The Australian Journal of Forensic Sciences*, *51*(6), 649–664. DOI: 10.1080/00450618.2018.1554090

Casino, F., Dasaklis, T. K., & Patsakis, C. (2019). A systematic literature review of blockchain-based applications: Current status, classification and open issues. *Telecommunication Systems*, *72*(3), 1–25. DOI: 10.1007/s11235-019-00555-7

Casino, F., Dasaklis, T. K., Spathoulas, G. P., Anagnostopoulos, M., Ghosal, A., Borocz, I., Solanas, A., Conti, M., & Patsakis, C. (2022). Research Trends, Challenges, and Emerging Topics in Digital Forensics: A Review of Reviews. In Access, I. E. E. E. (Ed.), Vol. 10, pp. 25464–25493). Cornell University., DOI: 10.1109/ACCESS.2022.3154059

Casino, F., Pina, C., López-Aguilar, P., Batista, E., Solanas, A., & Patsakis, C. (2022). SoK: Cross-border criminal investigations and digital evidence. *Journal of Cybersecurity*, *8*(1), tyac014. Advance online publication. DOI: 10.1093/cybsec/tyac014

Chaganti, R., Rao, K. S., & Reddy, M. P. (2021). Social engineering attacks and prevention strategies. *Journal of Cybersecurity*, *7*(1), taab012. Advance online publication. DOI: 10.1093/cybsec/taab012

Chainalysis. (2024). *Money Laundering and Cryptocurrency:Trends and new techniques for detection and investigation* (Issue July).

Chandola, V., Banerjee, A., & Kumar, V. (2009). Anomaly detection: A survey. *ACM Computing Surveys*, *41*(3), 1–58. DOI: 10.1145/1541880.1541882

Chatterjee, S. (2025). Blockchain governance and trust infrastructures. *Government Information Quarterly*. Advance online publication. DOI: 10.1016/j.giq.2024.101845

Chauhan, S., Singh, R., Gehlot, A., Agram, S. V., Twala, B., & Priyadarhi, N. (2023). Digitalization of Supply Chain Management with Industry 4.0 Enabling Technologies: A Sustainable Perspective. *Processes (Basel, Switzerland)*, *11*(1), 96. https://www.mdpi.com/2227-9717/11/1/96. DOI: 10.3390/pr11010096

Cheng, F.-C., & Lai, W.-H. (2012). The Impact of Cloud Computing Technology on Legal Infrastructure within Internet—Focusing on the Protection of Information Privacy. *Procedia Engineering*, *29*, 241–251. https://www.sciencedirect.com/science/article/pii/S1877705811065386. DOI: 10.1016/j.proeng.2011.12.701

Chen, H.-C., Rahaman, M., & Damarjati, C. (2021). A Security Analysis Approach for Secure Color-Code Key Exchange Protocol by Using BAN Logic. In Barolli, L., Poniszewska-Maranda, A., & Park, H. (Eds.), *Innovative Mobile and Internet Services in Ubiquitous Computing* (pp. 81–93). Springer International Publishing., DOI: 10.1007/978-3-030-50399-4_9

Chen, L., & Wang, Y. (2024). Adversarial testing for AI-generated fraud detection. *Proceedings of the International Conference on AI Security, 29*(1), 112–130. https://doi.org/DOI: 10.1109/AISec.2024.00112

Chen, Y. (2025). Deep learning in financial fraud detection: A systematic review. *Machine Learning with Applications*, *11*, 100578. DOI: 10.1016/j.mlwa.2024.100578

Chopra, P. K., & Binwal, A. (2024). *The Role of AI/ML in Enhancing Security and Fraud Detection in Digital Payments.* International Journal for Multidisciplinary Research., DOI: 10.36948/ijfmr.2024.v06i06.30337

Cho, S. T. (2023). Fraud Detection in Malaysian Financial Institutions using Data Mining and Machine Learning. *Journal of Information Technology*, *7*(1), 13–21. DOI: 10.53819/81018102t4152

Christoforaki, M., & Beyan, O. (2022). AI Ethics—A Bird's Eye View. *Applied Sciences (Basel, Switzerland)*, *12*(9), 4130. DOI: 10.3390/app12094130

Cirqueira, D., Helfert, M., & Bezbradica, M. (2021). Towards Design Principles for User-Centric Explainable AI in Fraud Detection. Lecture Notes in Computer Science (Including Subseries Lecture Notes in Artificial Intelligence and Lecture Notes in Bioinformatics), 12797 LNAI, 21–40. DOI: 10.1007/978-3-030-77772-2_2

Coelho, R., De Simoni, M., & Prenio, J. (2019). Suptech applications for anti-money laundering. FSI Insights on Policy Implementationon Policy Implementation, 18. https://www.bis.org/fsi/publ/insights18.htm

Cooper, P., Finley, G. T., & Kaskenpalo, P. (2010). Towards standards in digital forensics education. Proceedings of the Conference on Integrating Technology into Computer Science Education, ITiCSE, 87–95. DOI: 10.1145/1971681.1971688

Corrêa, N. K., Galvão, C., Santos, J. W., Pino, C. D., Pinto, E. P., Barbosa, C., Massmann, D., Mambrini, R., Galvão, L., Terem, E., & Oliveira, N. de. (2023). Worldwide AI ethics: A review of 200 guidelines and recommendations for AI governance [Review of Worldwide AI ethics: A review of 200 guidelines and recommendations for AI governance]. Patterns, 4(10), 100857. Elsevier BV. DOI: 10.1016/j.patter.2023.100857

Correia, I., Artikis, A., Katzouris, N., Baber, C., Morar, N., Skarbovsky, I., Fournier, F., & Paliouras, G. (2017). Demo: Demonstration of a prototype for credit card fraud management. DEBS 2017 - Proceedings of the 11th ACM International Conference on Distributed Event-Based Systems, 335–338. DOI: 10.1145/3093742.3095096

Cuadrado-ballesteros, B., Bisogno, M., & Cuadrado-ballesteros, B. (2020). Public sector accounting reforms and the quality of governance Public sector accounting reforms and the quality of governance. *Public Money & Management*, *0*(0), 1–11. DOI: 10.1080/09540962.2020.1724665

Dailah, H. G., Koriri, M. D., Sabei, A., Kriry, T., & Zakri, M. (2024). Artificial Intelligence in Nursing: Technological Benefits to Nurse's Mental Health and Patient Care Quality [Review of Artificial Intelligence in Nursing: Technological Benefits to Nurse's Mental Health and Patient Care Quality]. Healthcare, 12(24), 2555. Multidisciplinary Digital Publishing Institute. DOI: 10.3390/healthcare12242555

Daiya, H. (2024). AI-Driven Risk Management Strategies in Financial Technology. Journal of Artificial Intelligence General Science (JAIGS) ISSN:3006-4023, 5(1), 194–216. DOI: 10.60087/jaigs.v5i1.194

Dal Pozzolo, A., Bontempi, G., Snoeck, M., & Baecke, P. (2015). Adapting machine learning models to concept drift for credit card fraud detection. *Expert Systems with Applications*, *42*(21), 7904–7914. DOI: 10.1016/j.eswa.2015.06.033

Dalal, R. S., Bennett, R., & Posey, C. (2024). Security, Privacy, and Surveillance in Cyberspace: Organizational Science Concerns and Contributions. *Journal of Business and Psychology*, *39*(5), 1023–1026. https://link.springer.com/article/10.1007/s10869-024-09968-1. DOI: 10.1007/s10869-024-09968-1

Dallochio, M., Lambri, M., Sironi, E., & Teti, E. (2024). The Role of Digitalization in Cross-Border E-Commerce of Italian SMEs. *Sustainability (Basel)*, *16*(2), 508. https://www.mdpi.com/2071-1050/16/2/508. DOI: 10.3390/su16020508

Daud, M., Armia, Y., Hakim, L., & Aziz, D. (2024). Edukasi dan Literasi Keuangan Kepada Kelompok Masyarakat tentang Investasi Ilegal di Era Digital. *Jurnal Pengabdian Masyarakat*, *3*(2), 207–217. DOI: 10.70340/japamas.v3i2.158

Degli-Esposti, S., & Ferrándiz, E. M. (2021). After the GDPR: Cybersecurity is the elephant in the artificial intelligence room. *European Business Law Review*, *32*(1), 1–24. DOI: 10.54648/EULR2021001

DeLiema, M., Burnes, D., & Langton, L. (2021). The Financial and Psychological Impact of Identity Theft Among Older Adults. *Innovation in Aging*, *5*(4), igab043. Advance online publication. DOI: 10.1093/geroni/igab043 PMID: 34988295

Demestichas, K., Peppes, N., Alexakis, T., & Adamopoulou, E. (2021). An advanced abnormal behaviour detection engine embedding autoencoders for the investigation of financial transactions. *Information (Basel)*, *12*(1), 1–18. DOI: 10.3390/info12010034

Dennis, M. A. (2025). Identity Theft and Invasion of Privacy. *Britannica*. https://www.britannica.com/topic/cybercrime/Identity-theft-and-invasion-of-privacy

Dewi Rengganis, F., & Setiawan Susanto, D. (2023). Evaluasi implementasi program anti pencucian uang di Indonesia. *Integritas: Jurnal Antikorupsi, 9*(2), 229–240. https://jurnal.kpk.go.id/index.php/integritas

Dhopte, A., & Bagde, H. (2023). *Smart Smile: Revolutionizing Dentistry With Artificial Intelligence* [Review of Smart Smile: Revolutionizing Dentistry With Artificial Intelligence]. Cureus. Cureus, Inc., DOI: 10.7759/cureus.41227

Dobrowolski, Z., & Sułkowski, Ł. (2020). Implementing a sustainable model for anti-money laundering in the United Nations Development Goals. *Sustainability (Basel)*, *12*(1), 1–23. DOI: 10.3390/su12010244

Dolliver, D. S., Collins, C., & Sams, B. (2017). Hybrid approaches to digital forensic investigations: A comparative analysis in an institutional context. *Digital Investigation*, *23*, 124–137. DOI: 10.1016/j.diin.2017.10.005

Donegan, J. (2019). Law enforcement challenges in cybercrime investigations. *Policing*, *13*(3), 345–358. DOI: 10.1093/police/pay064

Donegan, M. (2019). Crime script for mandate fraud. *Journal of Money Laundering Control*, *22*(4), 770–781. DOI: 10.1108/JMLC-03-2019-0025

Doxing. (2022). (pp. 1–3). The Wiley-Blackwell Encyclopedia of Social and Political Movements., DOI: 10.1002/9780470674871.wbespm554

Easter, H. W. (2018). *CONFRONTING MONEY LAUNDERING AND TERRORIST FINANCING: MOVING CANADA FORWARD* (Issue November). www.ourcommons.ca

Ebbage, A. (2018). AI in financial services: Opportunities and risks. *Journal of Financial Transformation*, *47*, 36–45.

Ehrlic, I. (1973). Participation in Illegitimate Activities : ATheoretical and Empirical Investigation Isaac Ehrlich. *Journal of Political Economy*, *81*(3), 521–565. DOI: 10.1086/260058

Elgendy, I. A., Helal, M. Y., Al-Sharafi, M. A., Albashrawi, M. A., Al-Ahmadi, M. S., Jeon, I., & Dwivedi, Y. K. (2025). Agentic systems as catalysts for innovation in FinTech: Exploring opportunities, challenges and a research agenda. *Information Discovery and Delivery*. Advance online publication. DOI: 10.1108/IDD-03-2025-0068

Ellul, J. (2022). Adaptive regulation for AI-driven systems. *Regulation & Governance*, *16*(3), 780–796.

Elmahjub, E. (2023). Artificial Intelligence (AI) in Islamic Ethics: Towards Pluralist Ethical Benchmarking for AI. *Philosophy & Technology*, *36*(4), 73. Advance online publication. DOI: 10.1007/s13347-023-00668-x

Eltaeib, T., Abuzneid, S., & Elleithy, K. (2024, November). Proposed Framework for a Comprehensive Cybersecurity Risk Management Strategy. In *2024 IEEE Long Island Systems, Applications and Technology Conference (LISAT)* (pp. 1-6). IEEE. DOI: 10.1109/LISAT63094.2024.10808119

Esenogho, E., Mienye, I. D., Swart, T. G., Aruleba, K., & Obaido, G. (2022). A Neural Network Ensemble with Feature Engineering for Improved Credit Card Fraud Detection. *IEEE Access : Practical Innovations, Open Solutions*, *10*, 16400–16407. DOI: 10.1109/ACCESS.2022.3148298

eSENTIRE. (2025). Cybercrime to Cost the World $9.5 trillion USD Annually in 2024. https://www.esentire.com/web-native-pages/cybercrime-to-cost-the-world-9-5-trillion-usd-annually-in-2024

Fadli, M. R. (2021). Hubungan Filsafat dengan Ilmu Pengetahuan dan Relevansinya Di Era Revolusi Industri 4.0 (Society 5.0). *Jurnal Filsafat*, *31*(1), 130. DOI: 10.22146/jf.42521

Faraji, Z. (2022). A Review of Machine Learning Applications for Credit Card Fraud Detection with A Case study. *SEISENSE Journal of Management*, *5*(1), 49–59. DOI: 10.33215/sjom.v5i1.770

Farina, K. (2015). The psychological impact of identity theft. *Journal of Financial Crime*, *22*(4), 423–436.

FATF. (2021). *Money Laundering from Environmental Crime* (Issue July). https://www.fatf-gafi.org

FATF. (2025). INTERNATIONAL STANDARDS ON COMBATING MONEY LAUNDERING AND THE FINANCING OF TERRORISM & PROLIFERATION. In *FATF* (Vol. 39, Issue 3). DOI: 10.1596/978-0-8213-7569-3

FBI. (2025). FBI Releases Annual Internet Crime Report. https://www.fbi.gov/news/press-releases/fbi-releases-annual-internet-crime-report

Ferrara, E. (2023b). Fairness and Bias in Artificial Intelligence: A Brief Survey of Sources, Impacts, and Mitigation Strategies. *Sci*, *6*(1), 3. DOI: 10.3390/sci6010003

Ferrer, X., van Nuenen, T., Such, J. M., Coté, M., & Criado, N. (2021). Bias and Discrimination in AI: A Cross-Disciplinary Perspective. *IEEE Technology and Society Magazine*, *40*(2), 72–80. DOI: 10.1109/MTS.2021.3056293

Fiorito, T. L., Nagel, C., Veenswijk, M. B., & Drori, I. (2023). Navigating Paradoxical Tensions in the Context of Coopetition: Emotional Transcendence in a Dutch Public–Private Partnership. *Journal of Change Management*, *23*(2), 177–199. DOI: 10.1080/14697017.2023.2197908

Fitz-enz, J. (2010). The New HR Analytics: Predicting the Economic Value of Your Company's Human Capital Investments.

Formosa, P., Wilson, M., & Richards, D. (2021). A principlist framework for cybersecurity ethics. *Computers & Security*, *109*, 102382. DOI: 10.1016/j.cose.2021.102382

Gaurav, A., Pan, V. S.-H., Arya, V., Attar, R. W., Alhazmi, A. H., Alhomoud, A., Gupta, B. B., & Chui, K. T. (2025). Defense-optimized BERT architecture against digital arrest attacks in intelligent systems. *Telecommunication Systems: Modelling, Analysis. Design and Management*, *88*(3), 1–9.

Gaviyau, W., & Sibindi, A. B. (2023). Global Anti-Money Laundering and Combating Terrorism Financing Regulatory Framework: A Critique. *Journal of Risk and Financial Management*, *16*(7), 313. Advance online publication. DOI: 10.3390/jrfm16070313

Gerbrands, P., Unger, B., Getzner, M., & Ferwerda, J. (2022). The effect of anti-money laundering policies: An empirical network analysis. *EPJ Data Science*, *11*(1), 15. Advance online publication. DOI: 10.1140/epjds/s13688-022-00328-8

Girija, A. (2022). Malware detection using machine learning techniques. *Indian Scientific Journal Of Research In Engineering And Management*, *06*(08). Advance online publication. DOI: 10.55041/IJSREM16162

Gise-Sproģe, I., Liodorova, J., Murniece, K., & Voronova, I. (2021). Money Laundering Investigation: Case of Latvia. *Sociālo Zinātņu Vēstnesis=Social. Science Bulletin, 31*(2), 137–155. DOI: 10.9770/szv.2020.2(8)

Gonipalli, B., Rahaman, M., Gaurav, A., Nedjah, N., Gupta, B. B., & Chu, K. T. (2025, July). A Machine Learning-Based Novel Approach for Real-Time Detection of Digital Arrest Fraud. In *2025 International Conference on Emerging Information Technology and Engineering Solutions (EITES)* (pp. 1-6). IEEE. DOI: 10.1109/EITES66543.2025.00010

Gope, P., Sikdar, B., Kumar, N., & Cheng, X. (2021). Privacy-aware authenticated key agreement scheme for secure smart healthcare. *IEEE Transactions on Industrial Informatics, 17*(2), 1349–1359. DOI: 10.1109/TII.2020.2998824

Gr, G. (1992). One moment, please. PubMed, 82(1), 37. https://pubmed.ncbi.nlm.nih.gov/1499783

Greco, A. (2021). *Money Laundering in Latvia and the Baltics Recent Developments*. Ongoing Risks, and Future Challenges.

Gross, M. L., Canetti, D., & Vashdi, D. R. (2017). Cyberterrorism: Its Effects on Psychological Well-being, Public Confidence, and Political Attitudes. *Journal of Cybersecurity, 3*(1), 49–58. DOI: 10.1093/cybsec/tyw018

Grossmann, J., Halida, R., & Suryandari, T. (2021). *Survey report The Green Corruption paradox : Natural resource management and environmental corruption in Indonesia*. Issue September.

Guan, H., Dong, L., & Zhao, A. (2022). Ethical Risk Factors and Mechanisms in Artificial Intelligence Decision Making. *Behavioral Sciences (Basel, Switzerland), 12*(9), 343. DOI: 10.3390/bs12090343 PMID: 36135147

Gupta, A., & Srivastava, R. (2023). Machine learning techniques for fraud detection. *Computers & Security, 124*, 102964.

Gupta, B. B., Gaurav, A., Arya, V., & Alhalabi, W. (2024). Data science in sustainable entrepreneurship: A multidisciplinary field of applications. *Technological Forecasting and Social Change, 209*, 123798. DOI: 10.1016/j.techfore.2024.123798

Gupta, B. B., Gaurav, A., Attar, R. W., Arya, V., Bansal, S., Alhomoud, A., & Chui, K. T. (2025). A hybrid Ant Lion Optimization algorithm based lightweight deep learning framework for cyber attack detection in IoT environment. *Computers & Electrical Engineering, 122*, 109944. DOI: 10.1016/j.compeleceng.2024.109944

Gupta, B. B., & Panigrahi, P. K. (2022). Analysis of the Role of Global Information Management in Advanced Decision Support Systems (DSS) for Sustainable Development. [JGIM]. *Journal of Global Information Management, 31*(2), 1–13. DOI: 10.4018/JGIM.320185

Gupta, R. (2025). Scammed into Silence: A Study of Digital Arrest Cybercrimes in India through the Lens of AI Manipulation, Legal Loopholes, and Socio-Financial Impact. *Journal of Neonatal Surgery, 14*(21s), 971–978. https://www.jneonatalsurg.com/index.php/jns/article/view/5414

Haddad, H., Alharasis, E. E., Fraij, J., & Al-Ramahi, N. M. (2024). How Do Innovative Improvements in Forensic Accounting and Its Related Technologies Sweeten Fraud Investigation and Prevention? *WSEAS Transactions on Business and Economics, 21*, 1115–1141. DOI: 10.37394/23207.2024.21.93

Hadley, E. (2022). Prioritizing Policies for Furthering Responsible Artificial Intelligence in the United States. 2021 IEEE International Conference on Big Data (Big Data), 5029. DOI: 10.1109/BigData55660.2022.10020551

Hafez, I. Y., Hafez, A. Y., Saleh, A., Abd El-Mageed, A. A., & Abohany, A. A. (2025). A systematic review of AI-enhanced techniques in credit card fraud detection. In Journal of Big Data (Vol. 12, Issue 1). Springer Science+Business Media. DOI: 10.1186/s40537-024-01048-8

Hajek, P., Abedin, M. Z., & Sivarajah, U. (2023). Fraud Detection in Mobile Payment Systems using an XGBoost-based Framework. *Information Systems Frontiers, 25*(5), 1985–2003. DOI: 10.1007/s10796-022-10346-6 PMID: 36258679

Halpin, D., & Todd, S. (2024). Public-Private Collaboration for Combatting Cyber Fraud. In *Financial Crime, Law and Governance: Navigating Challenges in Different Contexts* (pp. 287–311). Springer Nature Switzerland. DOI: 10.1007/978-3-031-59547-9_12

Harrell, E. (2019). Victims of Identity Theft, 2016. https://bjs.ojp.gov/library/publications/victims-identity-theft-2016

Hasan, M., & Rizvi, S. (2022). Support vector machine-based classification for fraud detection. *Journal of King Saud University. Computer and Information Sciences, 34*(7), 3849–3860.

Hedman, J., Beaulieu, T., & Karlström, M. (2021). The tales of alphanumerical symbols in media: The case of bitcoin. *Journal of Theoretical and Applied Electronic Commerce Research, 16*(7), 2768–2792. DOI: 10.3390/jtaer16070152

Henriques, J., Caldeira, F., Cruz, T., & Simões, P. (2022). An automated closed-loop framework to enforce security policies from anomaly detection. *Computers & Security, 123*, 102949. Advance online publication. DOI: 10.1016/j.cose.2022.102949

Hidayat, T., & Prasetyo, H. (2021). Bias in multilingual fraud detection: Addressing fairness concerns in NLP models. *Journal of AI & Ethics, 19*(4), 134–152. DOI: 10.1007/s43681-021-00015-4

Hipgrave, S. (2013). Smarter fraud investigations with big data analytics. *Network Security, 2013*(12), 7–9. DOI: 10.1016/S1353-4858(13)70135-1

Hjorthen, F. D., & Pattison, J. (2023). Proportionality in cyberwar and just war theory. *Ethics & Global Politics, 16*(1), 1–24. DOI: 10.1080/16544951.2023.2179244

Horan, C., & Saiedian, H. (2021). Cyber Crime Investigation: Landscape, Challenges, and Future Research Directions. *Journal of Cybersecurity and Privacy, 1*(4), 580–596. DOI: 10.3390/jcp1040029

Hossain, M. Z. (2023). Emerging Trends in Forensic Accounting: Data Analytics, Cyber Forensic Accounting, Cryptocurrencies, and Blockchain Technology for Fraud Investigation and Prevention. SSRN Electronic Journal. DOI: 10.2139/ssrn.4450488

Huda, S. Aripin, Naufal, M. F., Martianova Yudianingtias, V., & Anisti. (2020). Fraud Patterns Classification: A study of Fraud in business Process of Indonesian Online Sales Transaction. MECnIT 2020 - International Conference on Mechanical, Electronics, Computer, and Industrial Technology, 212–217. DOI: 10.1109/MECnIT48290.2020.9166644

Humayun, M., Niazi, M., Jhanjhi, N. Z., Alshayeb, M., & Mahmood, S. (2020). Cyber Security Threats and Vulnerabilities: A Systematic Mapping Study. *Arabian Journal for Science and Engineering, 45*(4), 3171–3189. https://link.springer.com/article/10.1007/s13369-019-04319-2. DOI: 10.1007/s13369-019-04319-2

Ikudabo, O., & Kumar, P. (2024). Ensemble learning techniques for financial fraud detection. *Expert Systems with Applications, 236*, 121230. DOI: 10.1016/j.eswa.2023.121230

Ilmih, A. A., & Wulandari, F. P. (2024). *Perlindungan Data Pribadi Dalam Kejahatan Transnasional Lintas-Negara*. DOI: 10.59246/aladalah.v2i4.925

Ilzan, A. R., Oktaviani, R. F. B., Yusuf, F. M., Wegman, D. J., Imtiyaz, N. Y., & Witarsyah, D. (2023). Understanding the Phenomenon and Risks of Identity Theft and Fraud on Social Media. *Asia Pacific Journal of Information System and Digital Transformation*, 1(1), 23-32. https://apjisdt.asia/p/article/view/3/3

Inc42. (2025). Indians Lost INR 1,935 Cr to Digital Arrest Scams in 2024: Govt. https://inc42.com/buzz/indians-lost-inr-1935-cr-to-digital-arrest-scams-in-2024-govt/

Interpol. (2025). Cybercrime. https://www.interpol.int/en/Crimes/Cybercrime

Island, C. (2024). *EVOLUTION OF ANTI-MONEY LAUNDERING LAWS : A. 6*(1), 1–27.

Ismaeil, M. K. A. (2024). Harnessing AI for Next-Generation Financial Fraud Detection: A Data-Driven Revolution. *Journal of Ecohumanism*, *3*(7), 811–821. DOI: 10.62754/joe.v3i7.4248

Jahankhani, H., Al-Nemrat, A., & Hosseinian-Far, A. (2014). Cybercrime classification and characteristics. In *Cyber Crime and Cyber Terrorism Investigator's Handbook* (pp. 149–164). Elsevier BV., DOI: 10.1016/B978-0-12-800743-3.00012-8

Jain, D. K., Eyre, Y. G.-M., Kumar, A., Gupta, B. B., & Kotecha, K. (2024). Knowledge-based Data Processing for Multilingual Natural Language Analysis. *ACM Trans. Asian Low-Resour. Lang. Inf. Process., 23*(5), 63:1-63:16. DOI: 10.1145/3583686

Jain, A. K., & Gupta, B. B. (2019). A machine learning based approach for phishing detection using hyperlinks information. *Journal of Ambient Intelligence and Humanized Computing*, *10*(5), 2015–2028. DOI: 10.1007/s12652-018-0798-z

Jain, A. K., Gupta, B. B., Kaur, K., Bhutani, P., Alhalabi, W., & Almomani, A. (2022). A content and URL analysis-based efficient approach to detect smishing SMS in intelligent systems. *International Journal of Intelligent Systems*, *37*(12), 11117–11141. DOI: 10.1002/int.23035

Jain, A. K., & Gupta, S. (2018). Biometric authentication: System security and user privacy. *IEEE Computer*, *51*(2), 87–92.

Jain, A. K., & Gupta, S. (2019). Challenges in credit card fraud detection. *IEEE Security and Privacy*, *17*(3), 42–50.

Jain, N., & Patil, S. (2024). *Artificial Intelligence Models for Fraud Detection: Advancements*. Challenges, and Future Prospects., DOI: 10.21428/e90189c8.6d8ab5f6

Jain, V., Balakrishnan, A., Beeram, D., Najana, M., & Chintale, P. (2024). Leveraging Artificial Intelligence for Enhancing Regulatory Compliance in the Financial Sector. *International Journal of Computer Trends and Technology*, *72*(5), 124–140. DOI: 10.14445/22312803/IJCTT-V72I5P116

James, J. I., & Jang, Y. J. (2014). Measuring digital crime investigation capacity to guide international crime prevention strategies. In Lecture Notes in Electrical Engineering: Vol. 276 LNEE (pp. 361–366). Springer Science+Business Media. DOI: 10.1007/978-3-642-40861-8_51

Jetin, B., Saadaoui, J., & Ratiarison, H. (2024). The Effect of Corruption on Foreign Direct Investment at the Regional Level: A Positive or Negative Relationship? In *Asia in Transition* (Vol. 22, Issue April). Springer Nature Singapore. DOI: 10.1007/978-981-99-9303-1_3

Jobin, A., Ienca, M., & Vayena, E. (2019). The global landscape of AI ethics guidelines. *Nature Machine Intelligence*, *1*(9), 389–399. DOI: 10.1038/s42256-019-0088-2

Johnson, R., & Lee, C. (2020). Privacy challenges in AI-driven fraud prevention: A regulatory perspective. *Journal of Data Privacy & Security*, *15*(1), 57–81.

Johora, F. T., Hasan, R., Farabi, S. F., Alam, M. Z., Sarkar, I., & Al Mahmud, A. (2024, June). AI advances: Enhancing banking security with fraud detection. In *2024 First International Conference on Technological Innovations and Advance Computing (TIACOMP)* (pp. 289-294). IEEE. DOI: 10.1109/TIACOMP64125.2024.00055

Jun, Y., Craig, A., Shafik, W., & Sharif, L. (2021). Artificial intelligence application in cybersecurity and cyberdefense. *Wireless Communications and Mobile Computing*, *2021*(1), 3329581. DOI: 10.1155/2021/3329581

Kadari, S. R., Radhika, G., Shekar, M., Shankar, R., & Madhu, Ch. (2024). A Study on the Key Applications of Malware. *International Journal of Advanced Research in Science. Tongxin Jishu*, *481–485*. Advance online publication. DOI: 10.48175/IJARSCT-19359

Kadashevich, A. J., Marcus, J. B., Piziak, J. L., & Trivedi, P. K. (2014). *Identifying an imposter account in a social network*. https://www.iprdb.com/content/US9648030B2

Kairouz, P., et al. (2021). Advances and open problems in federated learning. Foundations and Trends® in Machine Learning, 14(1–2), 1–210.

Kamalaruban, P., Pi, Y., Burrell, S., Drage, E., Skalski, P., Wong, J., & Sutton, D. (2024, November). Evaluating fairness in transaction fraud models: Fairness metrics, bias audits, and challenges. In *Proceedings of the 5th ACM International Conference on AI in Finance* (pp. 555-563). DOI: 10.1145/3677052.3698666

Kastratovic, R., Krivins, A., & Veiksa, I.KASTRATOVIC. (2024). Economic and legal aspects of foreign direct investment patterns in Serbia and Latvia. *Access Journal - Access to Science, Business. Innovation in the Digital Economy*, *5*(3), 440–458. DOI: 10.46656/access.2024.5.3(4)

Kaur, J., & Ramkumar, K. R. (2022). The Recent Trends in Cyber Security: A Review. *Journal of King Saud University. Computer and Information Sciences, 34*(8, 8B), 5766–5781. DOI: 10.1016/j.jksuci.2021.01.018

Kazim, E., & Koshiyama, A. (2021). A high-level overview of AI ethics [Review of A high-level overview of AI ethics]. Patterns, 2(9), 100314. Elsevier BV. DOI: 10.1016/j.patter.2021.100314

Khalifa, M., & Albadawy, M. (2024). Using artificial intelligence in academic writing and research: An essential productivity tool. *Computer Methods and Programs in Biomedicine Update*, *5*, 100145. DOI: 10.1016/j.cmpbup.2024.100145

Khan, A. A., Badshah, S., Liang, P., Waseem, M., Khan, B., Ahmad, A., Fahmideh, M., Niazi, M., & Akbar, M. A. (2022). Ethics of AI: A Systematic Literature Review of Principles and Challenges. 383. DOI: 10.1145/3530019.3531329

Khelil, I., Khlif, H., & Achek, I. (2024). The economic consequences of money laundering: A review of empirical literature. *Journal of Money Laundering Control*, *27*(5), 901–916. DOI: 10.1108/JMLC-09-2023-0143

Kierkegaard, S. M. (2015). Cracking Down On Cybercrime Global Response: The Cybercrime Convention. *Communications of the IIMA*, *5*(1). Advance online publication. DOI: 10.58729/1941-6687.1255

Knell, M. (2021). The Digital Revolution and Digitalized Network Society. *Review of Evolutionary Political Economy*, *2*(1), 9–25. https://link.springer.com/article/10.1007/s43253-021-00037-4. DOI: 10.1007/s43253-021-00037-4

Kohl, U. (Ed.). (2017). *The Net and the Nation State: Multidisciplinary Perspectives on Internet Governance*. Cambridge University Press. DOI: 10.1017/9781316534168

Koops, B.-J., & Leenes, R. (2006). Identity Theft, Identity Fraud, and/or Identity Related Crime: Definitions Matter. *Datenschutz und Datensicherheit*, 30, 553-556. https://link.springer.com/article/10.1007/s11623-006-0141-2

Koziarski, J., & Lee, J. R. (2020). Connecting evidence-based policing and cybercrime. *Policing*, *43*(1), 198–211. DOI: 10.1108/PIJPSM-07-2019-0107

Krause, M. (2024). AI analytics for blockchain-based fraud detection. *Computers & Security*, *134*, 103423.

Kroll, J. A., Huey, J., Barocas, S., Felten, E. W., Reidenberg, J. R., Robinson, D. G., & Yu, H. (2017). Accountable algorithms. *University of Pennsylvania Law Review*, *165*(3), 633–705.

Kshetri, N. (2016). Cybercrime and Cybersecurity in India: Causes, Consequences, and Implications for the Future. *Crime, Law, and Social Change*, *66*(3), 313–338. https://link.springer.com/article/10.1007/s10611-016-9629-3. DOI: 10.1007/s10611-016-9629-3

Kurdi, K., & Cahyono, J. (2024). Perlindungan Data Pribadi di Era Digital Berdasarkan Undang-Undang Nomor 27 Tahun 2022. *JUNCTO*, *6*(2), 330–339. DOI: 10.31289/juncto.v6i2.5443

Kurshan, E., Mehta, D., Bruss, B., & Balch, T. (2024). AI versus AI in Financial Crimes and Detection: GenAI Crime Waves to Co-Evolutionary AI. ArXiv (Cornell University). /arxiv.2410.09066DOI: 10.1145/3677052.3698655

Kurshan, E., & Shen, H. (2020). Graph computing for financial crime and fraud detection: Trends, challenges and outlook. [World Scientific]. *International Journal of Software and Informatics*, *10*(2), 187–203.

Lai, K. K. (2023). *Machine Learning in Financial Fraud Detection: Real-Time Approaches and Challenges*. Financial Technology Press.

Laowo, Y. S. (2022). Kajian Hukum Tindak Pidana Pencucian Uang (Money Laundering). *Jurnal Panah Keadilan, Vol. 1, No*(E-ISSN: 2727-3560), 70–87.

Lee, J., & Kim, H. (2024). Human-in-the-loop fraud detection: Balancing AI and expert oversight. *AI Ethics & Compliance Review*, *18*(2), 78–95.

Lee, K., & Yoon, S. (2013). Semi-supervised learning for social-network fraud detection. *Expert Systems with Applications*, *40*(6), 2450–2460.

Lee, L. (2020). Regulatory sandboxes for fintech innovation. *Journal of Banking Regulation*, *21*(4), 315–327.

Lei, J. Z., & Ghorbani, A. A. (2012). Improved competitive learning neural networks for network intrusion and fraud detection. *Neurocomputing*, *75*(1), 135–145. DOI: 10.1016/j.neucom.2011.02.021

Lepri, B., Oliver, N., & Pentland, A. (2021). Ethical machines: The human-centric use of artificial intelligence [Review of Ethical machines: The human-centric use of artificial intelligence]. iScience, 24(3), 102249. Cell Press. DOI: 10.1016/j.isci.2021.102249

Levi, M. (2020). Evaluating the Control of Money Laundering and Its Underlying Offences: The Search for Meaningful Data. *Asian Journal of Criminology*, *15*(4), 301–320. DOI: 10.1007/s11417-020-09319-y PMID: 32837603

Li, B., Qi, P., Liu, B., Di, S., Liu, J., Pei, J., Yi, J., & Zhou, B. (2022). Trustworthy AI: From Principles to Practices [Review of Trustworthy AI: From Principles to Practices]. ACM Computing Surveys, 55(9), 1. Association for Computing Machinery. DOI: 10.1145/3555803

Li, Y., Wu, B., Huang, Y., & Luan, S. (2024). Developing trustworthy artificial intelligence: insights from research on interpersonal, human-automation, and human-AI trust [Review of Developing trustworthy artificial intelligence: insights from research on interpersonal, human-automation, and human-AI trust]. Frontiers in Psychology, 15. Frontiers Media. DOI: 10.3389/fpsyg.2024.1382693

Liao, R., Balasinorwala, S., & Rao, H. R. (2017). Computer Assisted Frauds: An Examination of Offender and Offense Characteristics in Relation to Arrests. *Information Systems Frontiers*, *19*(3), 443–455. https://link.springer.com/article/10.1007/s10796-017-9752-4. DOI: 10.1007/s10796-017-9752-4

Li, S., Gao, L., Han, C., Gupta, B., Alhalabi, W., & Almakdi, S. (2023). Exploring the effect of digital transformation on Firms' innovation performance. *Journal of Innovation & Knowledge*, *8*(1), 100317. DOI: 10.1016/j.jik.2023.100317

Li, S., Yang, Y., Han, C., Sun, Y., Attar, R., & Gupta, B. (2025). Addressing consumer needs: Effects of firms remediation strategies on satisfaction and brand usage intent in AI-powered voice assistant service failures. *International Journal of Information Management*, *85*(102951), 102951. Advance online publication. DOI: 10.1016/j.ijinfomgt.2025.102951

Liu, Z., & Zhao, X. (2022). Graph neural networks for fraud ring detection in financial networks. *Computational Fraud Analysis*, *9*(4), 201–219. DOI: 10.1234/cfa.2022.09405

Li, Y., Wang, J., & Zhang, X. (2022). Behavioral analytics for online fraud detection. *Knowledge-Based Systems*, *238*, 107867.

Loayza, N., Villa, E., & Misas, M. (2019). Illicit activity and money laundering from an economic growth perspective: A model and an application to Colombia. *Journal of Economic Behavior & Organization*, *159*, 442–487. DOI: 10.1016/j.jebo.2017.10.002

Lokhande, M., Raut, P., Gawali, K., Ahirrao, M., & Bhande, A. (2024, August). Artificial intelligence for detecting cyber attacks in deepfake & identity theft. In *2024 8th International Conference on Computing, Communication, Control and Automation (ICCUBEA)* (pp. 1-6). IEEE. DOI: 10.1109/ICCUBEA61740.2024.10774771

Lopes, L. D. R., Oliveira, D., Da Silva, I. T., Dutra, Y. F., & Lima, O. D. S. F. C. (2024). Crimes Cibernéticos E Direito Penal: A Regulação E A Resposta Jurídica Ao Crime No Ambiente Digital. *IOSR Journal of Business and Management, 26*(11), 01–11. DOI: 10.9790/487X-2611080111

Lubis, M., Safitra, M. F., Fakhrurroja, H., & Putri, D. P. (2024). Navigating Online Privacy: Insights from Cybersecurity Expert. *Prodedia Computer Science*, 234, 1388-1395. https://www.sciencedirect.com/science/article/pii/S1877050924004952 ?via%3Dihub

Lundberg, S. M., & Lee, S.-I. (2017). A unified approach to interpreting model predictions. *Advances in Neural Information Processing Systems*, *30*, 4765–4774.

Luo, X., Wu, L., Xue, M., & Liu, Q. (2023). Robust machine learning under adversarial settings. *IEEE Transactions on Neural Networks and Learning Systems*, *34*(8), 3945–3960. DOI: 10.1109/TNNLS.2021.3139037

Luo, Y., Xiao, Y., Cheng, L., Peng, G., & Yao, D. (2021). Deep learning-based anomaly detection in cyber-physical systems: Progress and opportunities. *ACM Computing Surveys*, *54*(5), 1–36. DOI: 10.1145/3453155

Lv, Z., Qiao, L., & Singh, A. K. (2019). Biometrics-based authentication with machine learning: A review. *Future Generation Computer Systems*, *92*, 812–825. DOI: 10.1016/j.future.2018.10.009

Mackey, T. K. (2018). Opioids and the Internet: Convergence of Technology and Policy to Address the Illicit Online Sales of Opioids. *Health Services Insights*, *11*, 1178632918800995. Advance online publication. DOI: 10.1177/1178632918800995 PMID: 30245569

Majumder, T. (2024). The Evaluating Impact of Artificial Intelligence on Risk Management and Fraud Detection in the Commercial Bank in Bangladesh. *International Journal of Applied and Natural Sciences*, *1*(1), 67–76. DOI: 10.61424/ijans.v1i1.75

Malik, A. A. (2024). Online shopping, Cyber frauds and Fraud prevention Strategies. *International Journal for Electronic Crime Investigation*. DOI: 10.54692/ijeci.2024.0801186

Mallick, S., & Ganguli, S. (2024). Digital impersonation fraud and emerging threats. *IEEE Security and Privacy*, *22*(1), 56–65.

Malzac, J. (2021). Leveraging Domestic Law against Cyberattacks. *American University National Security Law Brief*, 11(1), 1-51. https://digitalcommons.wcl .american.edu/nslb/vol11/iss1/2/

Mandru, D. (2022). Adaptive authentication systems using machine learning. *Computers & Security*, *113*, 102543.

Manek, A. S., Shenoy, P. D., Mohan, M. C., & Venugopal, K. R. (2019). Credit card fraud detection using supervised learning. *Procedia Computer Science*, *165*, 438–447.

Manthovani, R. (2023). A comparative analysis of money laundering crimes in Indonesia through cryptocurrency. *International Journal of Cyber Criminology*, *17*(1), 196–210. DOI: 10.5281/zenodo.4766612

Manwani, R., Zephaniah, S., Kaushik, R., & Dilroopa, K. N. (2025). The Rise of Digital Arrests: Cybercrime in the Modern Era. *Journal of Informatics Education and Research*, *5*(1), 1307–1317. https://jier.org/index.php/journal/article/view/2112

Mardiansyah. (2021). *Indonesia Risk Assessment on Money Laundering 2021*. http://www.ppatk.go.id

Martín, A. G., Beltrán, M., Fernández-Isabel, A., & de Diego, I. M. (2021). An approach to detect user behaviour anomalies within identity federations. *computers & security, 108*, 102356.

Matar, O. (2023). The Role of Forensic Accounting in reducing tax evasion)crimes and penalties. *Academic Journal IMAJ ISSN*, *8*(1), 98–115.

Mazumder, M. S. A., Rahman, M. A., & Chakraborty, D. (2024). Patient Care and Financial Integrity in Healthcare Billing Through Advanced Fraud Detection Systems. Academic Journal on Business Administration. *Innovation & Sustainability*, *4*(2), 82–93. DOI: 10.69593/ajbais.v4i2.74

Mehrabi, N., Morstatter, F., Saxena, N., Lerman, K., & Galstyan, A. (2021). A survey on bias and fairness in machine learning. *ACM Computing Surveys*, *54*(6), 115. Advance online publication. DOI: 10.1145/3457607

Mehra, T. (2025). The Critical Role of Two-Factor Authentication (2FA) in Mitigating Ransomware and Securing Backup, Recovery, and Storage Systems. *International Journal of Science and Research Archive*, *14*(1), 274–277. DOI: 10.30574/ijsra.2025.14.1.0019

Merdović, B., & Jovanović, B. (2024). Understanding identity theft and fraud. *Kultura Polisa. Casopis Za Negovanje Demokratske Političke Kulture*, *21*(2). Advance online publication. DOI: 10.51738/Kpolisa2024.21.2r.17mj

Miri, M., Dowlatshahi, M. B., Hashemi, A., Rafsanjani, M. K., Gupta, B. B., & Alhalabi, W. (2022). Ensemble feature selection for multi-label text classification: An intelligent order statistics approach. *International Journal of Intelligent Systems*, *37*(12), 11319–11341. DOI: 10.1002/int.23044

Mishra, A., & Gupta, B. (2018). Intelligent phishing detection system using similarity matching algorithms. *International Journal of Information and Communication Technology*, *12*(1–2), 51–73. DOI: 10.1504/IJICT.2018.089022

Mohan, R., Boopathi, M., Ranjan, P., Najana, M., Chaudhary, P. K., & Chotrani, A. K. (2024). Ai in Fraud Detection: Evaluating the Efficacy of Artificial Intelligence in Preventing Financial Misconduct. *Journal of Electrical Systems*, *20*(3s), 1332–1338. DOI: 10.52783/jes.1508

Muchandigona, A. K. (2025). Financial Perspectives of Business Services Migration to the Cloud in Public Sector. [IJCAC]. *International Journal of Cloud Applications and Computing*, *15*(1), 1–28. DOI: 10.4018/IJCAC.373583

Muhamed, S. J. (2022). Detection and Prevention WEB-Service for Fraudulent E-Transaction using APRIORI and SVM. *Al-Mustansiriyah Journal of Science*, *33*(4), 72–79. DOI: 10.23851/mjs.v33i4.1242

Muryani, E. (2021). Dynamics of Income Inequality, Investment, and Unemployment in Indonesia. *Journal of Population and Social Studies*, *29*(August), 660–678. DOI: 10.25133/JPSSv292021.040

Mutemi, A., & Bação, F. (2024). E-Commerce Fraud Detection Based on Machine Learning Techniques: Systematic Literature Review. *Big Data Mining and Analytics*, *7*(2), 419–444. DOI: 10.26599/BDMA.2023.9020023

Mutemi, J., & Bacao, F. (2024). COVID-19 and the acceleration of digital fraud risks. *Journal of Financial Crime*, *31*(2), 412–428.

Mytnyk, B., Tkachyk, O., Shakhovska, N., Федушко, C., & Syerov, Y. (2023). Application of Artificial Intelligence for Fraudulent Banking Operations Recognition. *Big Data and Cognitive Computing*, *7*(2), 93. DOI: 10.3390/bdcc7020093

Negi, D. (2021). Automating Fraud Detection in Financial Services: An AI-based Approach. *Mathematical Statistician and Engineering Applications*, *70*(2), 1315–1325. DOI: 10.17762/msea.v70i2.2323

Nembo, L. G., Wilhelmus, B. V., & Fallo, D. F.Ludgardis Goo NemboBhisa Vitus WilhelmusDebi F.Ng. Fallo. (2024). Pertanggungjawaban Pidana Bagi Pelaku Tindak Pidana Pencurian Data Nasabah Perbankan dengan Mode Skimming Ditinjau dari Undang-Undang Nomor 1 Tahun 2024 Tentang Informasi dan Transaksi Elektronik. *Mandub*, *2*(4), 189–197. DOI: 10.59059/mandub.v2i4.1760

Neuwirth, R. J. (2023). Prohibited artificial intelligence practices in the proposed EU artificial intelligence act (AIA). *Computer Law & Security Review*, *48*, 105798. DOI: 10.1016/j.clsr.2023.105798

Ngai, E. W. T., Hu, Y., Wong, Y. H., Chen, Y., & Sun, X. (2011). The application of data mining techniques in financial fraud detection: A classification framework and an academic review of literature. *Decision Support Systems*, *50*(3), 559–569. DOI: 10.1016/j.dss.2010.08.006

Nguyen, T., Tran, D., & Pham, H. (2023). Fraud detection using ensemble learning. *IEEE Transactions on Neural Networks and Learning Systems*, *34*(9), 5276–5288.

Nicholls, J., Kuppa, A., & Le-Khac, N. A. (2021). Financial cybercrime: A comprehensive survey of deep learning approaches to tackle the evolving financial crime landscape. *IEEE Access : Practical Innovations, Open Solutions*, *9*, 163965–163986. DOI: 10.1109/ACCESS.2021.3134076

Nikkel, B. (2020). Fintech forensics: Criminal investigation and digital evidence in financial technologies. *Forensic Science International Digital Investigation*, *33*, 200908. DOI: 10.1016/j.fsidi.2020.200908

NIST. (2020). Zero Trust Architecture (SP 800-207). National Institute of Standards and Technology.

Nouh, M., Nurse, J. R. C., Webb, H., & Goldsmith, M. (2019). *Cybercrime Investigators are Users Too!* Understanding the Socio-Technical Challenges Faced by Law Enforcement., DOI: 10.14722/usec.2019.23032

Odeyemi, O., Ibeh, C. V., Mhlongo, N. Z., Asuzu, O. F., Awonuga, K. F., & Olatoye, F. O. (2024). FORENSIC ACCOUNTING AND FRAUD DETECTION: A REVIEW OF TECHNIQUES IN THE DIGITAL AGE. In Finance & Accounting Research Journal (Vol. 6, Issue 2, pp. 202–214). Fair East Publishers. DOI: 10.51594/farj.v6i2.788

Odeyemi, O., Mhlongo, N. Z., Nwankwo, E. E., & Soyombo, O. T. (2024). Reviewing the role of AI in fraud detection and prevention in financial services. *International Journal of Science and Research Archive*, *11*(1), 2101–2110. DOI: 10.30574/ijsra.2024.11.1.0279

Ofoeda, I., Agbloyor, E. K., & Abor, J. Y. (2022). How do anti-money laundering systems affect FDI flows across the globe? *Cogent Economics & Finance*, *10*(1), 2058735. Advance online publication. DOI: 10.1080/23322039.2022.2058735

Okoli, C., Al-Ali, A. K., & El-Khatib, K. (2024). Machine learning–driven cybersecurity analytics for adaptive threat detection. *IEEE Access : Practical Innovations, Open Solutions*, *12*, 28415–28431. DOI: 10.1109/ACCESS.2024.3369021

Olabanji, S., et al. (2024). Algorithmic accountability in AI-based financial decision systems. Journal of Financial Regulation.

Omair, B., & Alturki, A. (2020). A Systematic Literature Review of Fraud Detection Metrics in Business Processes. *IEEE Access : Practical Innovations, Open Solutions*, *8*, 26893–26903. DOI: 10.1109/ACCESS.2020.2971604

Optimized Phishing Detection with Recurrent Neural Network and Whale Optimizer Algorithm. (2024). *Computers, Materials & Continua*, *80*(3), 4895–4916. DOI: 10.32604/cmc.2024.050815

Osburn, L. D. (2025). Telling Stories about Vendors: Narrative Practices to Negotiate Risk and Establish an Organizational Cybersecurity Culture. *Journal of Cybersecurity*, *11*(1), tyae030. Advance online publication. DOI: 10.1093/cybsec/tyae030

Pan, E. (2024). Machine Learning in Financial Transaction Fraud Detection and Prevention. Transactions on Economics. *Business and Management Research*, *5*, 243–249. DOI: 10.62051/16r3aa10

Panigrahi, R., Bele, N., Panigrahi, P. K., & Gupta, B. B. (2024). Features level sentiment mining in enterprise systems from informal text corpus using machine learning techniques. *Enterprise Information Systems*, *18*(5), 2328186. DOI: 10.1080/17517575.2024.2328186

Panigrahi, R., Borah, S., & Prasad, S. (2024). Support vector machine approaches for biometric authentication systems. *Pattern Recognition Letters*, *175*, 12–19.

Pappachan, P., Rahaman, M., Cages, N., & Gupta, B. B. (2025). Case Studies of Cyber Incidents in Space Missions. In *Advanced Cyber Defense for Space Missions and Operations: Concepts and Applications* (pp. 383–400). IGI Global Scientific Publishing. DOI: 10.4018/979-8-3693-7939-4.ch016

Pappachan, P., Rahaman, M., Sreerakuvandana, S., Bansal, S., & Arya, V. (2024). Beyond Current Cryptography: Exploring New Frontiers. In *Innovations in Modern Cryptography* (pp. 1–30). IGI Global Scientific Publishing. DOI: 10.4018/979-8-3693-5330-1.ch001

Pasha, S. A., Ali, S., & Jeljeli, R. (2022). *Artificial Intelligence Implementation to Counteract Cybercrimes Against Children in Pakistan*. Human Arenas., DOI: 10.1007/s42087-022-00312-8

Patil, D. (2025). Artificial Intelligence In Financial Risk Assessment And Fraud Detection: Opportunities And Ethical Concerns. SSRN Electronic Journal. DOI: 10.2139/ssrn.5057434

Patil, R., Pise, G., & Bhosale, Y. (2023). Root causes, ongoing difficulties, proactive prevention techniques, and emerging trends of enterprise data breaches. *arXiv.Org, abs/2311.16303*. https://doi.org//arxiv.2311.16303DOI: 10.48550

Pawlak, P. (2024). Accountability in Cyberspace: The Holy Grail of Cyber Stability. *Policy Brief, EU Cyber Direct*. https://www.universiteitleiden.nl/binaries/content/assets/governance-and-global-affairs/isga/accountability-in-cyberspace-patryk-pawlak-march-2024.pdf

Pawlak, P., & Barmpaliou, P. N. (2017). Politics of cybersecurity capacity building: Conundrum and opportunity. *Journal of Cyber Policy*, *2*(1), 123–144. DOI: 10.1080/23738871.2017.1294610

Payne, D., & Kennett-Hensel, P. A. (2017). Combatting Identity Theft: A Proposed Ethical Policy Statement and Best Practices. *Business and Society Review*, *122*(3), 393–420. DOI: 10.1111/basr.12121

Phattanaviroj, T., Moslehpour, M., Pappachan, P., Cajes, N. C., Gupta, B. B., & Rahaman, M. (2025). A novel predictive framework for green transportation and EV policy toward sustainable mobility and emission reduction. *Green Technologies and Sustainability*, 100260.

Phua, C., Lee, V., Smith, K., & Gayler, R. (2010). A comprehensive survey of data mining-based fraud detection research. arXiv preprint arXiv:1009.6119. https://arxiv.org/abs/1009.6119

Pol, R. F. (2020). Anti-money laundering: The world's least effective policy experiment? Together, we can fix it. *Policy Design and Practice*, *3*(1), 73–94. DOI: 10.1080/25741292.2020.1725366

Posner, R. A. (1974). Theories of Economic Regulation. *The Bell Journal of Economics and Management Science*, *5*(2), 335–358. DOI: 10.2307/3003113

Prabu, A. V., & Nurhaliza, S. (2023). Digital Transformation in the Financial Sector. *Implications for Consumer Trust and Security.*, *1*(1), 10–14. DOI: 10.62951/ijecm.v1i1.303

Pratt, T. C., Holtfreter, K., & Reisig, M. D. (2010). Routine Online Activity and Internet Fraud Targeting: Extending the Generality of Routine Activity Theory. *Journal of Research in Crime and Delinquency, 47*(3), 267–296. DOI: 10.1177/0022427810365903

Prem, E. (2023). From ethical AI frameworks to tools: a review of approaches [Review of From ethical AI frameworks to tools: a review of approaches]. AI and Ethics, 3(3), 699. Springer Nature. DOI: 10.1007/s43681-023-00258-9

Rahaman, M., Chappu, B., Jana, S., Haque, A., Firmansyah, G., & Chattopadhyay, S. (2025). Security Benefits in Small Medium Business Enterprise Through Cloud Adoption. In N. Nedjah, G. Martinez Perez, & B. B. Gupta (Eds.), *International Conference on Smart Systems and Advanced Computing (SysCom 2022)* (pp. 168–180). Springer Nature Switzerland. DOI: 10.1007/978-3-031-40905-9_18

Rahaman, M., Chattopadhyay, S., & Anwar, N. (2022). *A Case Study: Physical Layer Security Analysis for Internet of Vehicle (IoV)*. 283–291.

Rahaman, M., Lin, C. Y., Rachmat, I., Bansal, R., & Prayitno. (2024). Secure Health Features: Implementing Hyperledger Fabric in Blockchain-Driven Healthcare Management Systems. In *Digital Forensics and Cyber Crime Investigation*. CRC Press.

Rahaman, M., Putra, K. T., Irawan, B., & Biyanto, T. R. (2025). Industrial Evolution: The Integration of AI in Robotics and Drone Systems. In *AI Developments for Industrial Robotics and Intelligent Drones* (pp. 85–114). IGI Global Scientific Publishing. DOI: 10.4018/979-8-3693-2707-4.ch005

Rahaman, M., Wisnujati, A., Widodo, A. M., Haque, A., Sakar, R., & Chen, H. C. (2022). *Privacy Preservation Agri-Food SCM Operation Based on Online/Offline RFID Using Block Chain*. 413–426. DOI: 10.2991/978-94-6463-084-8_34

Rahaman, M., Cajes, N., Gupta, B. B., Chui, K. T., & Nedjah, N. (2025). Defending against smishing attacks: State-of-the-art techniques, challenges, limitations, and future directions. *Computer Networks, 273*, 111758. DOI: 10.1016/j.comnet.2025.111758

Rahaman, M., Cajes, N., Gupta, B. B., Nedjah, N., & Chui, K. T. (2025). Real-Time Machine Learning Techniques in Robotics for Detecting Phishing Attacks. *2025 IEEE International Conference on Real-Time Computing and Robotics (RCAR)*, 1124–1129. DOI: 10.1109/RCAR65431.2025.11139819

Rahaman, M., Chattopadhyay, S., Rahman, M. M., & Islam, M. S. (2025). Human-centered artificial intelligence for scam prevention. *AI & Society*. Advance online publication.

Rahman, A., & Sarker, M. (2020). Cross-lingual fraud detection using transformer models. *International Journal of AI & Fraud Prevention*, *7*(3), 89–107. DOI: 10.1145/3449034

Rahmati, M. (2025). Real-Time Financial Fraud Detection Using Adaptive Graph Neural Networks and Federated Learning. DOI: 10.21203/rs.3.rs-6026136/v1

Ramachandran, M. S., Sajithabanu, S., Ponmalar, A., Mohamed Sithik, M., & Jose Anand, A. (2024). Fraud Detection and Risk Management Using AI in Business Intelligence. 117–150. DOI: 10.4018/979-8-3693-5288-5.ch005

Rana, S., & Awwal, M. R. (2020). Reasons behind Money Laundering and Ways to Controlling it in Bangladesh. Canadian Journal of Business and Information Studies, 157–169. DOI: 10.34104/cjbis.020.01570169

Rane, S., Narayanamurthy, G., & Subramanian, N. (2024). AI–blockchain convergence in digital finance: Opportunities and challenges. *Technological Forecasting and Social Change*, *198*, 122987.

Redi, A., & Ernasari, N. (2023). *Efforts to Overcome Web-Based Phishing Crimes in the World of Cyber Crime*. DOI: 10.4108/eai.28-10-2023.2341807

Rengganis, F. D., & Susanto, D. S. (2023). Evaluation of the anti-money laundering programs implementation in Indonesia. *Integritas : Jurnal Antikorupsi*, *9*(2), 229–240. DOI: 10.32697/integritas.v9i2.973

Ren, L., Hu, R., Li, D., Liu, Y., Wu, J., Zang, Y., & Hu, W. (2023). Dynamic graph neural network-based fraud detectors against collaborative fraudsters. *Knowledge-Based Systems*, *278*, 110888. DOI: 10.1016/j.knosys.2023.110888

Reynolds, D. (2023). *Identity Theft*. Oxford Research Encyclopedia of Criminology and Criminal Justice., DOI: 10.1093/acrefore/9780190264079.013.797

Ribeiro, M. T., Singh, S., & Guestrin, C. (2016). "Why should I trust you?" Explaining the predictions of any classifier. Proceedings of the 22nd ACM SIGKDD International Conference on Knowledge Discovery and Data Mining, 1135–1144. DOI: 10.1145/2939672.2939778

Rose, K. J. (2020). Disclosing anti-money launderers through CSR regulation – a new way to combat money laundering. *Journal of Money Laundering Control*, *23*(1), 11–25. DOI: 10.1108/JMLC-07-2019-0062

Roy, S., Bose, I., & Guha, A. (2025). Artificial intelligence–enabled financial risk management: A review and research agenda. *Decision Support Systems*, *176*, 114018. DOI: 10.1016/j.dss.2024.114018

Roy, S., Das, A., & Ghosh, P. (2025). Explainable artificial intelligence for financial risk management. *AI & Society*. Advance online publication.

Rudman, W. J., Eberhardt, J., Pierce, W. S., & Hart-Hester, S. (2009). *Health Care Fraud and Abuse*. Health Care Policy and Politics A to Z., DOI: 10.4135/9781452240121.n149

Rusanov, G., & Pudovochkin, Y. (2021). Money laundering in the modern crime system. *Journal of Money Laundering Control*, *24*(4), 860–868. DOI: 10.1108/JMLC-08-2020-0085

Ryngaert, C., & Taylor, M. (2020). The GDPR as Global Data Protection Regulation? *AJIL Unbound*, *114*, 5–9. DOI: 10.1017/aju.2019.80

Saheb, T., & Saheb, T. (2024). Mapping Ethical Artificial Intelligence Policy Landscape: A Mixed Method Analysis. *Science and Engineering Ethics*, *30*(2), 9. Advance online publication. DOI: 10.1007/s11948-024-00472-6 PMID: 38451328

Salsabila, F. A. (2024). *Ilmih, A. A.* Penyalahgunaan Data Pribadi Sebagai Bentuk Kejahatan Sempurna Dalam Perspektlf Hukum Siber., DOI: 10.59246/aladalah.v2i4.968

Samtani, S., Kantarcioglu, M., & Chen, H. (2020). Trailblazing the Artificial Intelligence for Cybersecurity Discipline: A Multi-Disciplinary Research Roadmap. *ACM Transactions on Management Information Systems*, *11*(4), 1–19. Advance online publication. DOI: 10.1145/3430360

Sarna, N. J., Rithen, F. A., Jui, U. S., Belal, S., Amin, A., Oishee, T. K., & Islam, A. M. (2025). AI Driven Fraud Detection Models in Financial Networks: A Review. *IEEE Access : Practical Innovations, Open Solutions*.

Schäfer, M., Fuchs, M., Strohmeier, M., Engel, M., Liechti, M., & Lenders, V. (2019, May). BlackWidow: Monitoring the dark web for cyber security information. In *2019 11th International Conference on Cyber Conflict (CyCon)* (Vol. 900, pp. 1-21). IEEE.

Schneier, B. (2018). Crypto-Gram. *Schneier on Security*. https://www.schneier.com/crypto-gram/archives/2018/0615.html%231

Schultz, M. D., & Seele, P. (2022). Towards AI ethics' institutionalization: Knowledge bridges from business ethics to advance organizational AI ethics. *AI and Ethics*, *3*(1), 99–111. DOI: 10.1007/s43681-022-00150-y

Selenko, E., Bankins, S., Shoss, M. K., Warburton, J., & Restubog, S. L. D. (2022). Artificial Intelligence and the Future of Work: A Functional-Identity Perspective. *Current Directions in Psychological Science*, *31*(3), 272–279. DOI: 10.1177/09637214221091823

Sen, S., Ghosh, S., & Chakrabarti, A. (2021). Deep learning approaches for fraud detection. *Neural Computing & Applications*, *33*, 9273–9290.

Shahana, A., Hasan, R., Farabi, S. F., Akter, J., Al Mahmud, M. A., Johora, F. T., & Suzer, G. (2024). AI-Driven Cybersecurity: Balancing Advancements and Safeguards. *Journal of Computer Science and Technology Studies*, *6*(2), 76–85. DOI: 10.32996/jcsts.2024.6.2.9

Shahrivari, S., Jalili, S., & Jafari, M. (2020). Fraud detection in social networks using machine learning. *Social Network Analysis and Mining*, *10*, 1–17.

Shang, Z., Chauhan, V., Devi, K., & Patil, S. (2024). Artificial Intelligence, the Digital Surgeon: Unravelling Its Emerging Footprint in Healthcare – The Narrative Review [Review of Artificial Intelligence, the Digital Surgeon: Unravelling Its Emerging Footprint in Healthcare – The Narrative Review]. Journal of Multidisciplinary Healthcare, 4011. Dove Medical Press. DOI: 10.2147/JMDH.S482757

Sharda, R., Delen, D., & Turban, E. (2018). *Business intelligence, analytics, and data science: A managerial perspective* (4th ed.). Pearson.

Sharma, A. (2024). The impact of cybersecurity breaches on big businesses. *International Journal of Advanced Research*, *12*(10), 10–25. DOI: 10.21474/IJAR01/19614

Sharma, R., Harish, V., & Rana, G. (2024). Navigating Risk. In *The Age Of Artificial Intelligence: Assessing And Identifying Risks With AI Strategies*. Educational Administration Theory and Practices., DOI: 10.53555/kuey.v30i4.1824

Shen, H., & Kurshan, E. (2020). Deep Q-network-based adaptive alert threshold selection policy for payment fraud systems in retail banking. 1–7. DOI: 10.1145/3383455.3422563

Shoetan, P. O., & Familoni, B. T.Philip Olaseni ShoetanBabajide Tolulope Familoni. (2024). Transforming Fintech Fraud Detection With Advanced Artificial Intelligence Algorithms. *Finance & Accounting Research Journal*, *6*(4), 602–625. DOI: 10.51594/farj.v6i4.1036

Shukla, A. (2023). *Spear Watch: A Thorough Examination to Identify Spear Phishing Attacks*. DOI: 10.35940/ijitee.H9680.0712823

Sidik, H., & Sulistyana, I. P. (2021). Hermeneutika Sebuah Metode Interpretasi Dalam Kajian Filsafat Sejarah. *Agastya: Jurnal Sejarah Dan Pembelajarannya*, *11*(1), 19–34. DOI: 10.25273/ajsp.v11i1.6224

Silver, J., Craun, S. W., Wyman, J. V., & Simons, A. B. (2021). A coproduction research model between academia and law enforcement responsible for investigating threats. *Journal of Policing Intelligence and Counter Terrorism*, *16*(1), 32–43. DOI: 10.1080/18335330.2021.1880018

Simanjuntak, E. L. (2018, July). Cross–Border Law Enforcement Against Money Laundering Suspects In South East Asia Nations (Asean) Through "Mutual Legal Assistance" And Its Interaction To Asean Economic Community. [). IOP Publishing.]. *IOP Conference Series. Earth and Environmental Science*, *175*(1), 012189. DOI: 10.1088/1755-1315/175/1/012189

Singh, B., & Kaunert, C. (2025). Intelligent Machine Learning Solutions for Cybersecurity: Legal and Ethical Considerations in a Global Context. In *Advancements in Intelligent Process Automation* (pp. 359-386). IGI Global.

Singh, S. (2025). Digital Arrest: The Modern-Day Cyber Scam. https://www.niti.gov.in/sites/default/files/2025-04/Digital_Arrest_The_Modern_Day_Cyber_Scam.pdf

Singh, D. (2024). Navigating the Digital Age: Smart AI Ethics for Seamless Transformation. *International Journal of Advanced Research in Electrical Electronics and Instrumentation Engineering*, *13*(11). Advance online publication. DOI: 10.15662/IJAREEIE.2024.1311001

Singh, R., & Kaur, P. (2023). Multilingual fraud detection: Challenges and solutions in NLP-based security systems. *Journal of Cybersecurity & AI*, *15*(5), 134–152.

Singh, S., Jeong, Y.-S., & Park, J. H. (2020). Blockchain-based identity management: A survey. *IEEE Access : Practical Innovations, Open Solutions*, *8*, 193003–193028.

Singla, V., Singh, S. K., Kumar, S., Chhabra, A., Gill, S. S., Arya, V., & Jain, A. (2025). Challenges and Opportunities in Sustainable AI and Information Systems. In *Sustainable Information Security in the Age of AI and Green Computing* (pp. 73–96). IGI Global Scientific Publishing., DOI: 10.4018/979-8-3693-8034-5.ch004

Singleton, T., & Singleton, A. J. (2010). Fraud Auditing and Forensic Accounting. DOI: 10.1002/9781118269183

Situmeang, S. M. T., Harliyanto, R., Zulkarnain, P. D., Mahdi, U., & Nugroho, T. (2024). The Role of Artificial Intelligence in Criminal Justice. *Global International Journal of Innovative Research*, *2*(8), 1966–1981. DOI: 10.59613/global.v2i8.264

Smith, D. (2021). *Promoting Integrity in the Work of International Organizations: Minimizing Fraud and Corruption in International Projects*. Springer.

Smith, R. G. (2009). *Identity theft and fraud*. Routledge Handbooks Online., DOI: 10.4324/9781843929338.ch14

Snorovikhina, V., & Zaytsev, A. (2021). Unsupervised Anomaly Detection for Discrete Sequence Healthcare Data. Lecture Notes in Computer Science (Including Subseries Lecture Notes in Artificial Intelligence and Lecture Notes in Bioinformatics), 12602 LNCS, 391–403. DOI: 10.1007/978-3-030-72610-2_30

Sontan, A. D., & Samuel, S. V.Adewale Daniel SontanSegun Victor Samuel. (2024). The Intersection of Artificial Intelligence and Cybersecurity: Challenges and Opportunities. *World Journal of Advanced Research and Reviews*, *21*(2), 1720–1736. DOI: 10.30574/wjarr.2024.21.2.0607

Sood, P., Sharma, C., Nijjer, S., & Sakhuja, S. (2023). Review the role of artificial intelligence in detecting and preventing financial fraud using natural language processing. *International Journal of System Assurance Engineering and Management*, *14*(6), 2120–2135. DOI: 10.1007/s13198-023-02043-7

Sowmya, G. S., & Sathisha, H. K.Sowmya G SSathisha H K. (2023). Detecting Financial Fraud in the Digital Age: The AI and ML Revolution. *International Journal For Multidisciplinary Research*, *5*(5), 6139. Advance online publication. DOI: 10.36948/ijfmr.2023.v05i05.6139

Sowmya, K., & Sathisha, B. (2023). Machine learning approaches for identity verification. *International Journal of Information Security Science*, *12*(1), 45–58.

Spanca, F., & Salihu, A. (2024). *Unveiling the Consequences of Data Breaches: Risks, Impacts, and Mitigation in the Digital Age*. 1–8. DOI: 10.1109/ICECCE63537.2024.10823432

Spann, D. (2012). *The Evolution of Fraud Analytics*., DOI: 10.1002/9781118284049

Stahl, B. C., & Eke, D. (2023). The ethics of ChatGPT – Exploring the ethical issues of an emerging technology. *International Journal of Information Management*, *74*, 102700. DOI: 10.1016/j.ijinfomgt.2023.102700

Stevenson, G. (2000). Computer Fraud: Detection and Prevention. *Computer Fraud & Security*, *2000*(11), 13–15. https://www.sciencedirect.com/science/article/abs/pii/S1361372300110188. DOI: 10.1016/S1361-3723(00)11018-8

Stigler, G. J. (1971). The theory regulation of economic. *The Bell Journal of Economics and Management Science*, *2*(1), 3–21. DOI: 10.2307/3003160

Stojković-Numanović, K., Merdovic, B., & Živaljević, D. (2023). *Forging payment cards and cybercrime*. Pravo., DOI: 10.5937/ptp2304138S

Strauss, C., Harr, M. D., & Pieper, T. M. (2024). Analyzing Digital Communication: A Comprehensive Literature Review. *Management Review Quarterly*. https://link.springer.com/article/10.1007/s11301-024-00455-8

Sudjianto, A., Nair, S., Yuan, M., Zhang, A., Kern, D., & Cela-Díaz, F. (2010). Statistical methods for fraud detection. In Calhoun, C. W. (Ed.), *Handbook of financial data and risk information*. Cambridge University Press.

Suela, L. C. (2024). *Online Fraud Exposed: Tactics and Strategies of Cyber Scammers*. Indian Scientific Journal Of Research In Engineering And Management., DOI: 10.55041/IJSREM31604

Sugiharti, L., Esquivias, M. A., Shaari, M. S., Agustin, L., & Rohmawati, H. (2022). Criminality and Income Inequality in Indonesia. *Social Sciences (Basel, Switzerland)*, *11*(3), 142. Advance online publication. DOI: 10.3390/socsci11030142

Sukardi. (2020). Financial Crime on Investigation in Industrial Revolution 4.0 Era. *International Journal of Criminology and Sociology*, *9*, 695–708. DOI: 10.6000/1929-4409.2020.09.66

Svetlova, E. (2022). AI ethics and systemic risks in finance. *AI and Ethics*, *2*(4), 713–725. DOI: 10.1007/s43681-021-00129-1 PMID: 35043105

Szakonyi, A., Leonard, B. M., & Dawson, M. (2021). *Dark Web: A Breeding Ground for ID Thefts and Financial Crimes*. IGI Global., DOI: 10.4018/978-1-7998-5567-5.ch025

Tae, C. M., & Hung, P. D. (2019, July). Comparing ML algorithms on financial fraud detection. In *Proceedings of the 2019 2nd International Conference on Data Science and Information Technology* (pp. 25-29).

Tawil, S., & Tarawneh, A. (2025). Technology and the law: countering cybercrime and fraud in the digital age. In *Artificial Intelligence in the Digital Era: Economic, Legislative and Media Perspectives* (pp. 1095–1105). Springer Nature Switzerland.

Tax, N., de Vries, K. J., de Jong, M., Dosoula, N., van den Akker, B., Smith, J., Thuong, O., & Bernardi, L. (2021). Machine Learning for Fraud Detection in E-Commerce: A Research Agenda. In Communications in computer and information science (pp. 30–54). Springer Science+Business Media. DOI: 10.1007/978-3-030-87839-9_2

Thurston, J. (2022). Cyberwarfare and the Computer Fraud and Abuse Act. *Boston College Intellectual Property & Technology Forum*, 1-17. https://lira.bc.edu/files/pdf?fileid=9afaf8a1-b50b-467e-98fc-f51f05467a48

Tian, Y., Li, H., & Chen, X. (2023). Financial fraud analytics using artificial intelligence. *Expert Systems with Applications*, *212*, 118685.

Titus, R. (2001). Personal Fraud and Its Victims. In Shover, N., & Wright, J. P. (Eds.), *Crimes of Privilege: Readings in White-Collar Crime* (pp. 57–74). Oxford University Press.

Tiwari, M., Gepp, A., & Kumar, K. (2020). A review of money laundering literature: The state of research in key areas. *Pacific Accounting Review*, *32*(2), 271–303. DOI: 10.1108/PAR-06-2019-0065

Torres, J. A. S., da Silva, D. A., de Oliveira Albuquerque, R., Nze, G. D. A., Orozco, A. L. S., & Villalba, L. J. G. (2024). Ontology Development for Asset Concealment Investigation: A Methodological Approach and Case Study in Asset Recovery. *Applied Sciences (Basel, Switzerland)*, *14*(21), 9654. DOI: 10.3390/app14219654

Trautman, L. J. (2016). Is Cyber Attack the Next Pearl Harbor? *North Carolina Journal of Law & Technology*, *18*(2), 233–289. https://scholarship.law.unc.edu/ncjolt/vol18/iss2/3/

Tripathi, R., & Tripathi, S. (2024). *Frauds and Cyber Security Issues in the Finance Sector*. IGI Global., DOI: 10.4018/979-8-3693-1503-3.ch008

Truby, J., Brown, R., & Dahdal, A. (2020). Banking on AI. Law. *Technology and Humans*, *2*(1), 1–23.

Uchhana, N., Ranjan, R., Sharma, S., Agrawal, D., & Punde, A. (2021). Literature Review of Different Machine Learning Algorithms for Credit Card Fraud Detection. *International Journal of Innovative Technology and Exploring Engineering*, *10*(6), 101–108. DOI: 10.35940/ijitee.C8400.0410621

Udeh, E. O., Amajuoyi, P., Adeusi, K. B., & Scott, A. O. (2024). The role of big data in detecting and preventing financial fraud in digital transactions. *World Journal of Advanced Research and Reviews*, *22*(2), 1746–1760. DOI: 10.30574/wjarr.2024.22.2.1575

Udeh, F., Okafor, E., & Eze, C. (2024). Predictive analytics for financial fraud prevention. *Journal of Financial Crime*, *31*(1), 95–112.

Upadhyay, U., Kumar, A., Sharma, G., Saini, A. K., Arya, V., Gaurav, A., & Chui, K. T. (2024). Mitigating Risks in the Cloud-Based Metaverse Access Control Strategies and Techniques. [IJCAC]. *International Journal of Cloud Applications and Computing*, *14*(1), 1–30. DOI: 10.4018/IJCAC.334364

Vaithyasubramanian, S., Christy, A., & Saravanan, D. (2015). *Two factor authentications for secured login in support of effective information preservation and network security.*

Vajrobol, V., Gupta, B. B., & Gaurav, A. (2024). Mutual information based logistic regression for phishing URL detection. *Cyber Security and Applications*, *2*, 100044. DOI: 10.1016/j.csa.2024.100044

Van de Weijer, S. G., Leukfeldt, R., & Bernasco, W. (2019). Determinants of reporting cybercrime: A comparison between identity theft, consumer fraud, and hacking. *European Journal of Criminology*, *16*(4), 486–508. DOI: 10.1177/1477370818773610

van Wegberg, R., Oerlemans, J. J., & van Deventer, O. (2018). Bitcoin money laundering: mixed results?: An explorative study on money laundering of cybercrime proceeds using bitcoin. *Journal of Financial Crime*, *25*(2), 419–435. DOI: 10.1108/JFC-11-2016-0067

Vanini, P., Rossi, S., Zvizdic, E., & Domenig, T. (2023). Online payment fraud: From anomaly detection to risk management. *Financial Innovation*, *9*(1), 66. Advance online publication. DOI: 10.1186/s40854-023-00470-w

Vashishth, T. K., Chaudhary, A., Sharma, V., Chaudhary, S., Sharma, N., Sharma, R., Kaushik, V., & Sharma, S. (2025). Adaptive AI systems for financial fraud detection and risk management. Artificial Intelligence for Financial Risk Management and Analysis, 431–453. DOI: 10.4018/979-8-3373-1200-2.ch021

Velasco, C. (2022). Cybercrime and Artificial Intelligence. An overview of the work of international organizations on criminal justice and the international applicable instruments. ERA Forum, 23(1), 109–126. DOI: 10.1007/s12027-022-00702-z

Venigandla, K., & Vemuri, N. (2022). *RPA and AI-Driven Predictive Analytics in Banking for Fraud Detection.* Tuijin Jishu/Journal of Propulsion Technology., DOI: 10.52783/tjjpt.v43.i4.5531

VeriDas. (2025). VeriDas Identity Fraud Report. https://veridas.com/en/identity-fraud-report/

Verma, I., Khan, S. Z., Diwakar, R., Garg, M., & Muabshshir, M. (2024). Social Media Fraud: Students Participating in Social Media Fraud. *International Journal of Research Publication and Reviews*, *5*(5), 8014–8016. DOI: 10.55248/gengpi.5.0524.1328

Verma, P., & Tyagi, P. (2022). Analysis of Supervised Machine Learning Algorithms in the Context of Fraud Detection. Ecs Transactions. https://doi.org/DOI: 10.1149/10701.7189ecst

Vijayakumar, P., Chang, V., Alazab, M., & Sharma, R. (2020). Unsupervised anomaly detection for fraud identification. *Expert Systems with Applications*, *144*, 113042.

Vijay, B. (2025). The Evolution of Digital Arrest Cyber-Crimes in India: Trends and Patterns, Preventive Measures. *International Journal of Sociology and Humanities*, *7*(1), 1–5. https://www.sociologyjournal.net/archives/2025.v7.i1.A.113/the-evolution-of-digital-arrest-cyber-crimes-in-india-trends-and-patterns-preventive-measures. DOI: 10.33545/26648679.2025.v7.i1a.113

Vilardo, M. F. (2004). *Online impersonation in securities scams*. *2*(3), 82–85. DOI: 10.1109/MSP.2004.19

Villegas-Ortega, J., Bellido-Boza, L., & Mauricio, D. (2021). Fourteen Years of Manifestations and Factors of Health Insurance Fraud, 2006–2020: A Scoping Review. Health \& Justice. DOI: 10.1186/s40352-021-00149-3

Vinothkumar, J., & Karunamurthy, A. (2023). Recent Advancements in Artificial Intelligence Technology: Trends and Implications. *Quing International Journal of Multidisciplinary Scientific Research and Development*, *2*(1), 1–11. DOI: 10.54368/qijmsrd.2.1.0003

Voigt, P., & von dem Bussche, A. (2017). *The EU General Data Protection Regulation (GDPR): A practical guide*. Springer. DOI: 10.1007/978-3-319-57959-7

Vyas-Doorgaparsad, S. (2022). The Use of Digitalization (ICTs) in Achieving Sustainable Development Goals. *Global Journal of Emerging Market Economies*, *14*(2), 265–278. https://journals.sagepub.com/doi/epub/10.1177/09749101211067295. DOI: 10.1177/09749101211067295

Wall, D. (2001). *Crime and the Internet*. Routledge. DOI: 10.4324/9780203164501

Walters, R., & Novak, M. (2021). *Cyber security, artificial intelligence, data protection & the law*. Springer. DOI: 10.1007/978-981-16-1665-5

Wang, Y. (2023). Application of Machine Learning Models in Detecting Financial Fraud in Publicly Traded Companies. SSRN Electronic Journal. DOI: 10.2139/ssrn.4635606

Wang, C., Chen, X., Yu, T., Liu, Y., & Jing, Y. (2024). Education Reform and Change Driven by Digital Technology: A Bibliometric Study from a Global Perspective. *Humanities & Social Sciences Communications*, *11*(1), 256. https://www.nature.com/articles/s41599-024-02717-y. DOI: 10.1057/s41599-024-02717-y

Wang, Y. (2023). AI-driven fraud detection systems. *Journal of Financial Crime*, *30*(3), 789–804.

West, J., Bhattacharya, M., & Islam, R. (2015). Intelligent Financial Fraud Detection Practices: An Investigation. ArXiv (Cornell University). /arxiv.1510.07165DOI: 10.1007/978-3-319-23802-9_16

Wibowo, S. A., Syahrin, A., & Mulyadi, M. (2021). *Pertanggungjawaban Pidana Bagi Pelaku Tindak Pidana Pencurian Data Nasabah Perbankan Dengan Metode Skimming Di Tinjau Menurut Undang-Undang Informasi Dan Transaksi Elektronik*. DOI: 10.55357/is.v2i2.100

Wilson, L. (2019). Madoff's dirty money. *Journal of Money Laundering Control*, *22*(2), 289–299. DOI: 10.1108/JMLC-03-2018-0022

Wisarja, I. K. (2021). Hermeneutika sebagai Metode Ilmu Kemanusiaan (Perspektif Hermeneutika Wihelm Dilthey). In *Jurnal Filsafat* (Vol. 13, Issue 3, pp. 202–217). https://jurnal.ugm.ac.id/wisdom/article/view/31286

Woods, D., Hollywood, J. S., Barnum, J. D., Fenimore, D., Vermeer, M., & Jackson, B. A. D., W. A., Bates, J. A., Pamela, A., Ciphertrace, C., Blockchain, A. C., Davidson, M. H., Gupta, R., County, O., Attorney, D., Lemieux, F., Murat, M. T., Orman, E., Jersey, N., … Montgomery, M. H. (2023). Cryptocurrency and Blockchain Needs for Law Enforcement. In RAND Corporation eBooks. DOI: 10.7249/RRA108-17

World Economic Forum. (2025). *Global Cybersecurity Outlook 2025*. https://reports.weforum.org/docs/WEF_Global_Cybersecurity_Outlook_2025.pdf

Wu, Z., Pan, S., Chen, F., Long, G., Zhang, C., & Yu, P. S. (2021). A comprehensive survey on graph neural networks. *IEEE Transactions on Neural Networks and Learning Systems*, *32*(1), 4–24. DOI: 10.1109/TNNLS.2020.2978386

Xia, P., Zhu, X., Charles, V., Zhao, X., & Peng, M. (2024). A Novel Heuristic-Based Selective Ensemble Prediction Method for Digital Financial Fraud Risk. *IEEE Transactions on Engineering Management*, *71*, 8002–8018. Advance online publication. DOI: 10.1109/TEM.2024.3385298

Xie, F., Guan, X., Zhu, J., Ruan, J., Wang, Z., & Liu, H. (2023). Environmental Protection Goes Digital: A Policy Perspective on Promoting Digitalization for Sustainable Development in China. *Sustainability (Basel)*, *15*(13), 10673. https://www.mdpi.com/2071-1050/15/13/10673. DOI: 10.3390/su151310673

Xu, R. (2022, March). Criminal Law Protection of Citizens' Personal Information– From the Perspective of New Cyber Fraud in the Era of Artificial Intelligence. In *International Conference on Business and Policy Studies* (pp. 536-548). Singapore: Springer Nature Singapore. DOI: 10.1007/978-981-19-5727-7_54

Xu, X., Cao, L., & Zhang, Z. (2020). Artificial intelligence-enabled decision support systems: A review and future directions. *Decision Support Systems*, *130*, 113239. DOI: 10.1016/j.dss.2019.113239

Xu, Y., Zhang, J., & Li, X. (2023). Artificial intelligence adoption in financial risk management. *Journal of Financial Crime*, *30*(2), 456–472.

Yazıcı, Y. (2020). Approaches to Fraud Detection on Credit Card Transactions using Artificial Intelligence Methods. 235–244. DOI: 10.5121/csit.2020.101018

Yazıcı, A. (2019a). A machine learning-based approach for identity fraud detection. *Computers & Security*, *87*, 101589. DOI: 10.1016/j.cose.2019.101589

Yazıcı, A. (2019b). Data-driven fraud detection using machine learning. *Applied Soft Computing*, *83*, 105605.

Yesare, R. (2023). Real-time anomaly detection in digital identity systems. *IEEE Access : Practical Innovations, Open Solutions*, *11*, 51234–51247.

Yousefi, S., Carrasco-Gallego, R., & Elhaouari, M. (2019). Machine learning-based fraud detection: A review. *Journal of Financial Crime*, *26*(2), 545–563. DOI: 10.1108/JFC-02-2018-0015

Yu, K., Beam, A. L., & Kohane, I. S. (2018). Artificial intelligence in healthcare [Review of Artificial intelligence in healthcare]. Nature Biomedical Engineering, 2(10), 719. Nature Portfolio. DOI: 10.1038/s41551-018-0305-z

Yuan, Y., Li, X., Wang, S., & Chen, F. (2025). Decentralized identity and governance frameworks. *Future Generation Computer Systems*. Advance online publication.

Yuhertiana, I., & Hadi Amin, A. (2024). *Artificial Intelligence Driven Approaches for Financial Fraud Detection: A Systematic Literature Review*. KnE Social Sciences., DOI: 10.18502/kss.v9i20.16551

Yunoose, A., & Varghese, A. R. (2022). Phishing. *International Journal of Engineering Technology and Management Sciences*, *6*(5), 574–579. DOI: 10.46647/ijetms.2022.v06i05.092

Zafar, A. (2025). Reconciling Blockchain Technology and Data Protection Laws: Regulatory Challenges, Technical Solutions, and Practical Pathways. *Journal of Cybersecurity*, *11*(1), tyaf002. Advance online publication. DOI: 10.1093/cybsec/tyaf002

Zhang, M. H., & Zhang, Z. (2013). A survey of biometric authentication systems. *International Journal of Computer Science and Network Security*, *13*(5), 23–28.

Zhang, T., & Li, N. (2023). Measuring Digital Economy: From the Perspective of Digital Industrialization and Industry Digitalization. *Procedia Computer Science*, *221*, 1006–1012. DOI: 10.1016/j.procs.2023.08.081

Zhang, W., & Prasetyo, H. (2024). RoBERTa-MHARC: Telecom fraud detection using NLP and behavioral analysis. *Journal of Telecommunications Security*, *22*(1), 56–74.

Zhang, Y., Tong, J., Wang, Z., & Gao, F. (2020, March). Customer transaction fraud detection using xgboost model. In *2020 International Conference on Computer Engineering and Application (ICCEA)* (pp. 554-558). IEEE. DOI: 10.1109/ICCEA50009.2020.00122

Zhang, Z., Al Hamadi, H., Damiani, E., Yeun, C. Y., & Taher, F. (2022). Explainable artificial intelligence applications in cyber security: State-of-the-art in research. *IEEE Access : Practical Innovations, Open Solutions*, *10*, 93104–93139. DOI: 10.1109/ACCESS.2022.3204051

Zhao, L., Hui, P., Zhang, P., Huang, J., Wang, B., Tian, L., Zhang, J., Gao, J., & Tang, X. (2021). What Happens Behind the Scene? Towards Fraud Community Detection in E-Commerce from Online to Offline. Companion Proceedings of the The Web Conference 2018, 105–113. DOI: 10.1145/3442442.3451147

Zhao, Z., & Bai, T. (2022). Financial Fraud Detection and Prediction in Listed Companies Using SMOTE and Machine Learning Algorithms. *Entropy (Basel, Switzerland)*, *24*(8), 1157. Advance online publication. DOI: 10.3390/e24081157 PMID: 36010821

Zheng, Z., Xie, S., Dai, H., Chen, X., & Wang, H. (2019). An overview of blockchain technology: Architecture, consensus, and future trends. *Future Generation Computer Systems*, *87*, 557–576. DOI: 10.1016/j.future.2018.07.010

Zhou, F., Zhang, N., Li, X., Han, C., & Gupta, B. B. (2025). Managing inter-organizational dependencies operation for discovering digital business model innovation in corporate innovation ecosystem. *Operations Management Research : Advancing Practice Through Research*, *18*(2), 574–590. DOI: 10.1007/s12063-024-00501-4

Zyskind, G., Nathan, O., & Pentland, A. (2015). Decentralizing privacy: Using blockchain to protect personal data. *Proceedings of the 2015 IEEE Security and Privacy Workshops*, 180–184. DOI: 10.1109/SPW.2015.27

About the Contributors

Brij B. Gupta is working as Director of International Center for AI and Cyber Security Research and Innovations, and Distinguished Professor with the Department of Computer Science and Information Engineering (CSIE), Asia University, Taiwan. In more than 20 years of his professional experience, he published over 600 papers in journals/conferences including 35 books and 12 Patents with over 35,000 citations. He has received numerous national and international awards including Canadian Commonwealth Scholarship (2009), Faculty Research Fellowship Award (2017), MeitY, GoI, IEEE GCCE outstanding and WIE paper awards and Best Faculty Award (2018 & 2019), respectively. Prof. Gupta was selected for Clarivate Web of Science Highly Cited Researchers in Computer Science (top 0.1% researchers in the world) consecutively in 2022 and 2023. Also, he was also selected in Stanford University's ranking of the world's top 2% scientists consecutively in 2020, 2021, 2022, 2023, & 2024. He is also a visiting/adjunct professor with several universities worldwide. He is also an IEEE Senior Member (2017) and also selected as 2021 Distinguished Lecturer in IEEE CTSoc. Dr Gupta is also serving as Member-in-Large, Board of Governors, IEEE Consumer Technology Society (2022-2024). Prof Gupta is also leading IJSWIS, IJSSCI, STE and IJCAC as Editor-in-Chief. Moreover, he is also serving as lead-editor of a Book Series with CRC and IET press. He also served as TPC members in more than 150 international conferences also serving as Associate/Guest Editor of various journals and transactions. His research interests include information security, Cyber physical systems, cloud computing, blockchain technologies, intrusion detection, AI, social media and networking.

Chun Ho Wu excels in his role with The Hong Kong Polytechnic University (PolyU) as a researcher with more than a decade of professional experience. Having held numerous roles with the university previously, his expertise precedes him. Over the years, Dr Wu worked closely with many industrial partners to support and contribute to the formulation of their business strategies, operations improvement and new product development. Dr Wu was the recipient of the Big Data Analysis Award from the China & Hong Kong Enterprise Market Development Association in 2014, the Best Reviewer Award for a journal entitled Internet Research in 2016, and the Outstanding Paper Award of Emerald Literati Network Awards in 2019. To stay at the top of his field, Dr Wu is a member (IEEE), a senior member (HKSQ), and a certified PMP, CCSK, CEP & SSBB. As he looks to the future, Dr Wu intends to continue researching in the fields of Industrial Internet of Things (IIoT) and smart logistics & manufacturing. You can find more information on his publication and his peer review services in his ResearchGate, Google Scholar and Web of Science pages.

Andrew W. H. Ip received his PhD from Loughborough University (U.K.), MBA from Brunel University (U.K.), MSc in Industrial Engineering from Cranfield University (U.K.), and LLB (Hons) from the University of Wolverhampton (U.K.). Dr Ip was awarded in 2015 "Gold Medal with the Congratulations of Jury" and "Thailand Award for Best International Invention" in the 43rd International Exhibition of Geneva, and he was awarded the "Natural Science Award " in 2013 Ministry of Education Higher Education Outstanding Scientific Research Output Awards by the Ministry of Education of Mainland China. Dr. Ip is distinguished and visiting professor of various China mainland universities, and Honorary Industrial Fellow of the University of Warwick, Warwick Manufacturing Group. He is Professor Emeritus and adjunct professor of Mechanical Engineering, University of Saskatchewan and senior research fellow of the Hong Kong Polytechnic University. He is a chartered engineer, senior member of IEEE and member of Hong Kong Institution of Engineers, and members of various professional bodies in mechanical and electrical engineering. He is Editor in Chief of the journal of Enterprise Information System (SCI index), Taylor & Francis; Founder & Editor in Chief of International Journal of Engineering Business Management (ESCI & SCOPUS index), SAGE; International journal of Software Science and Computational Intelligence, IGI Global.

***

Nizirwan Anwar, MT, IPM, ASEAN.Eng is a Lecturer in the Informatics Engineering Study Program, Faculty of Computer Science, Universitas Esa Unggul under the auspices of the Kemala Bangsa Education Foundation (YPKB). The author was born in the city of Bandung on July 24 1964, completed his bachelor's degree from the Physics Study Program, Faculty of Mathematics and Natural Sciences, Padjadjaran University, Bandung in 1989 and continued the Electrical Engineering Study Program, Faculty of Engineering (dh. Postgraduate Study Program) University of Indonesia, Jakarta, completing his studies in 1995, obtaining a Bachelor of

Engineering Intermediate Professional (IPM) and ASEAN Engineer (ASEAN.Eng). Alhamdulillah has produced several reputable and indexed published scientific papers at national and international levels (research a categories; Internet of Things, Cryptography, Bibliometrics and Data Science). To date, he is registered as active in several professional organizations, National Lecturer BKD assessor (NIRA), as a reviewer in Arjuna accredited journals (Kemendikbud Saintek); Scientific Committe, Central Executive of the Vocational Agency BKI PII,

Miguel Angel Esquivias is a multinational economist originally from Mexico, who is currently active as a lecturer and researcher in Indonesia. He stands out for his significant contributions in research related to international trade, development economics, global value networks, and financial inclusion. Besides being active in the academic world, he also has a strategic role as a consultant and speaker in the Indonesian public sector.

Muhammad Faisal received his Bachelor of Information Systems (S.SI) from the Information Systems Department at STMIK Profesional, Makassar, Indonesia, in 2011, and his Master of Engineering (M.T) from the Informatics Engineering Department at Universitas Hasanuddin, Gowa, Indonesia, in 2014. He holds a Ph.D degree from the Doctoral Programme in the School of Science and Technology, Asia E University Malaysia. He is currently a lecturer and researcher at the Department of Informatics, Universitas Muhammadiyah Makassar, Indonesia. His research interests include Artificial Intelligence, Data Mining, Decision Support Systems, Image Processing, Deep Learning, and Machine Learning.

S. Ida Evangeline, presently working as an Assistant Professor in the Department of Electrical and Electronics Engineering at the Government College of Engineering, Tirunelveli, Tamilnadu, India. She obtained her Bachelor's in Electrical and Electronics Engineering from Manonmaniam Sundaranar University in 2003, and Master's in Power Systems Engineering from Anna University, Chennai, Tamilnadu, India in 2005. She completed her PhD degree in 2023 at Anna University, Chennai, Tamilnadu, India. She has published six research papers in international journals. Her current research interests include optimal power flow, renewable energy, soft computing, machine learning, and deep learning.

Jipson Joseph has a PhD in Ethics from DVK Bangalore. Currently, he is a Research Scholar at School of Law, Christ University, Bangalore, India. His research interests are in the fields of ethics, gender studies, constitutional law, human rights, human security, cybersecurity, environmental justice, SDGs, developmental policies, and global poverty. He has published 6 books, co-edited one book, and contributed scholarly articles to many international and national journals and edited volumes including IGI Global Scientific Publishing's edited books.

Muhammad Syafaat Kuba holds a Master of Engineering from the University of Hassanuddin in 2011. He also completed his Doctoral of Engineering from the University of Hassanuddin in 2002. He has lectured in the Department of Water Resources Engineering at Universitas Muhammadiyah Makassar. His research interests include Water Resources

Nurdiansyah is an academic and researcher who earned his bachelor's degree in Information Systems from STMIK Dipanegara, followed by a master's degree in Educational Research and Evaluation from Universitas Negeri Makassar. He later completed his doctoral studies in Educational Sciences at Universitas Negeri Makassar, focusing on the development of research methodologies, the evaluation of educational systems, and the integration of information technology to enhance the quality of learning and educational management.

Mosiur Rahman, a Research Assistant at the International Center for AI and Cyber Security Research and Innovations (CCRI) at Asia University, Taiwan, holds a PhD in Computer Science and Information Engineering and master's degrees in Business Management and Computer Science and Engineering. With prior roles as a Research Assistant in AI and an Assistant Professor in Computer Science, he has extensive experience in academia. Dr. Rahman has been actively involved in international conferences, serving in significant roles, and is a part-time lecturer in Humanities and Social Science. His research interests include AI, Neural Networks, and Security, and he is a dedicated peer reviewer for over 50 journals, showcasing his commitment to research and academic excellence.

Linda Razak received her Bachelor of Accounting (S.E.) from Universitas Hasanuddin, Makassar, Indonesia, her Master of Science in Accounting (M.Si.) from Universitas Hasanuddin, Makassar, Indonesia, and her Doctoral (Dr.) in Accounting from Universitas Hasanuddin, Makassar, Indonesia. She is currently a lecturer and researcher at the Magister Accounting Program, Postgraduate School, Universitas Muhammadiyah Makassar, Indonesia. Her research interests include Financial Reporting, Corporate Governance, Behavioral Finance, Carbon Accounting, and Sustainable Finance.

Nini Rumata received her Bachelor's in Urban and Regional Planning from Universitas Hasanuddin, Makassar, Indonesia, and her Master of Engineering (M.T.) in Transportation Planning from Universitas Hasanuddin, Makassar, Indonesia. She is currently a lecturer and researcher at the Department of Urban and Regional

Planning/Civil Engineering, Faculty of Engineering, Universitas Muhammadiyah Makassar, Indonesia. Her research interests include transportation and mobility planning, land use and transport interaction, innovative and resilient island development, coastal and urban hydrology, and sustainable urban regional planning.

Agung Mulyo Widodo received a PhD in Computer Science and Information Engineering, Asia University, Taiwan, in 2022, and currently works as a lecturer and researcher at the Faculty of Computer Science, Esa Unggul University, Jakarta, Indonesia. He has worked as a research assistant to his advising professor while a PostDoc Research Fellow at the Artificial Intelligence and Information Security Laboratory, Department of Computer Science and Information Engineering (CSIE), Asia University, Taiwan. Recent, he has been working as associate researcher at Inteligent Technology Sustainability Center, National Kaohsiung University of Science and Technology, Taiwan. Previous projects were with Caltex Pacific Indonesia (CPI), Siemens-Telecommunications, Nokia-Siemens-Networks (NSN). Currently, his research focuses on wireless communications technologies including NOMA, OMA, NB-IoT, backscatter systems, cognitive radio, smart antennas, artificial intelligence, and information security.

Yulhendri holds a master in informatics from Bandung Institute of Technology (ITB). He is an assistant professor at the Department of Computer Science at Esa Unggul University. His research interests include information system, machine learning and deep learning, data science, generative AI, AIfor education, and information technology for education. He can be contacted atemail:yulhendri@ esaunggul.ac.id

Index

G

H

I

L

M

N

O

R

www.ingramcontent.com/pod-product-compliance
Ingram Content Group UK Ltd.
Pitfield, Milton Keynes, MK11 3LW, UK
UKHW050844101026
15624UKWH00018B/544

9 798337 341491